W9-BMY-234

The Mystery of the Duchess of Malfi

The Mystery of the Duchess of Malfi

Barbara Banks Amendola

SUTTON PUBLISHING

First published in 2002 by
Sutton Publishing Limited · Phoenix Mill
Thrupp · Stroud · Gloucestershire · GL5 2BU

British Library Cataloguing in Publication Data
A catalogue record for this book is available from the British Library

ISBN 0-7509-2840-9

Typeset in 11/14.5 Sabon.
Typesetting and origination by
Sutton Publishing Limited.
Printed and bound in England by
J.H. Haynes & Co. Ltd, Sparkford.

This book is dedicated to the memory of John Banks and Plinio Amendola

Contents

	Map of Italy	viii
	Principal Characters	ix
	Chronology	xv
Preface	*The Real Duchess*	xvii
1	*The Seeds of Dissension*	1
2	*Duchess of Amalfi*	17
3	*Before a Tempest*	32
4	*Tumult in the Kingdom*	48
5	*Bereavement*	61
6	*Partition*	78
7	*A New Life: Antonio Bologna*	93
8	*The Love Affair*	106
9	*The Ambitious Young Cardinal*	114
10	*The Devil's Quilted Anvil*	123
11	*The Flight of the Duchess*	138
12	*Fugitives*	150
13	*Bologna's Exile*	166
14	*The End of the Cardinal*	178
15	*Epilogue: The Portraits*	194
Appendix	*Synopsis of John Webster's* The Duchess of Malfi	207
	Acknowledgements	209
	Genealogical Tables	210
	Notes	220
	Select Bibliography	237
	Index	243

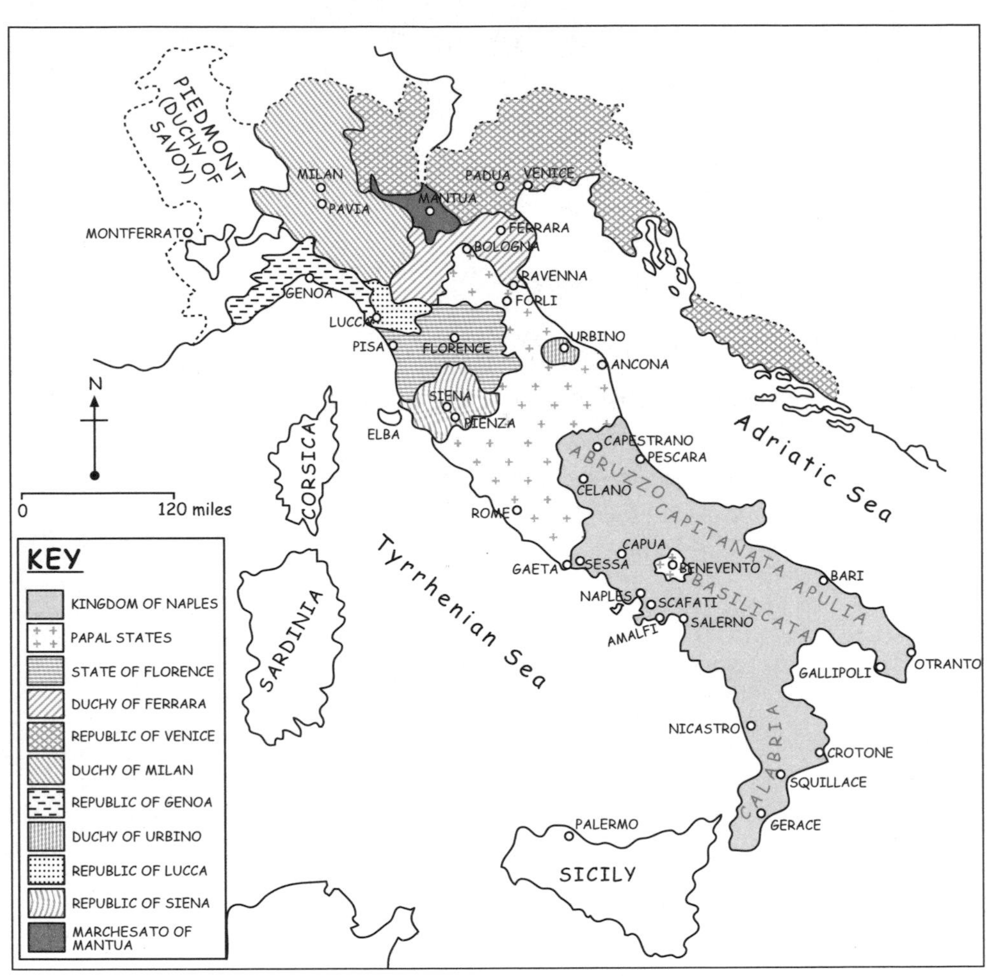

Map of Italy at the end of the fifteenth century

Principal Characters

THE COURT OF NAPLES

GIOVANNA D'ARAGONA of Gerace, Duchess of Amalfi

ENRICO D'ARAGONA:	Marquis of Gerace; son of King Ferrante I of Naples; *Giovanna's father.*
POLISSENA CENTELLES:	*Giovanna's mother.*
CATERINA D'ARAGONA:	*Giovanna's elder sister.*
LUIGI D'ARAGONA:	Marquis of Gerace; later Cardinal; *Giovanna's elder brother.*
CARLO D'ARAGONA:	Marquis of Gerace (once Luigi became Cardinal); *Giovanna's younger (probably twin) brother.*
IPPOLITA D'ARAGONA:	Countess of Venafro; *Giovanna's illegitimate half-sister.*
KING FERRANTE I OF NAPLES:	(reigned 1458–94); *Giovanna's paternal grandfather.*
DIANA GUARDATI:	mistress of King Ferrante I; *Giovanna's paternal grandmother.*
ANTONIO CENTELLES:	Marquis of Crotone; *Giovanna's maternal grandfather.*
KING ALFONSO V OF ARAGON AND I OF NAPLES:	(reigned 1442–58); *Giovanna's paternal great-grandfather.*
ELEONORA D'ARAGONA:	Duchess of Amalfi; half-sister of King Alfonso I; *Giovanna's great-aunt.*
KING ALFONSO II:	(reigned 1494–5); son of Ferrante I and known as Duke of Calabria during his father's reign; *Giovanna's uncle.*
KING FERRANTE II:	(reigned 1495–6); known as Ferrandino, son of Alfonso II, Prince of Capua, then briefly Duke of Calabria; *Giovanna's cousin.*
KING FEDERICO III:	(reigned 1496–1501); brother of Alfonso II and known as Don Federico until he became king; *Giovanna's uncle.*
QUEEN ISABELLA DEL BALZO:	second wife of Federico III; *Giovanna's aunt.*
FERDINANDO D'ARAGONA:	Duke of Calabria, son of above; *Giovanna's cousin.*

QUEEN GIOVANNA III:	known as the old Queen, sister of Ferdinand the Catholic of Spain and second wife of King Ferrante I; *Giovanna's step-grandmother.*
QUEEN GIOVANNA IV:	daughter of King Ferrante I and Queen Giovanna III. Known as the Infanta until her marriage to her nephew King Ferrante II, after which she was known as the young Queen; *Giovanna's aunt.*
BEATRICE D'ARAGONA:	Queen of Hungary, daughter of King Ferrante I; *Giovanna's aunt.*
ISABELLA D'ARAGONA:	legitimate daughter of King Alfonso II, Duchess of Milan and Bari; *Giovanna's cousin.*
SANCIA D'ARAGONA:	Princess of Squillace, illegitimate daughter of King Alfonso II; *Giovanna's cousin.*
CESARE D'ARAGONA:	illegitimate son of Ferrante I; *Giovanna's uncle.*
MARIA D'ARAGONA:	Duchess of Amalfi, illegitimate daughter of King Ferrante I. Married Antonio, the first Piccolomini Duke of Amalfi; *Giovanna's aunt.*
FERRANTE D'ARAGONA:	Count of Arena, disgraced, rehabilitated, then Duke of Montalto; illegitimate son of King Ferrante I; *Giovanna's uncle.*
GIOVANNA D'ARAGONA:	Princess Colonna; daughter of Duke of Montalto and putative subject of Louvre portrait by Raphael; *Giovanna's cousin.*

THE PICCOLOMINI FAMILY

ALFONSO I TODESCHINI PICCOLOMINI D'ARAGONA:	2nd Duke of Amalfi; *Giovanna's first husband.*
ALFONSO II TODESCHINI PICCOLOMINI D'ARAGONA:	3rd Duke of Amalfi; *Giovanna's eldest son.*
CATERINA TODESCHINI PICCOLOMINI D'ARAGONA:	*Giovanna's eldest daughter.*
ANTONIO TODESCHINI PICCOLOMINI D'ARAGONA:	1st Duke of Amalfi; *Giovanna's father-in-law.*
MARIA MARZANO:	Duchess of Amalfi; *Giovanna's mother-in-law.*
ELEONORA TODESCHINI PICCOLOMINI D'ARAGONA:	Princess of Bisignano; *Giovanna's sister-in-law.*
ENEAS SILVIO PICCOLOMINI:	Pope Pius II; *great-uncle of Giovanna's first husband.*

THE BOLOGNA FAMILY

ANTONIO DA BOLOGNA:	*major-domo to Giovanna, subsequently her second husband.*
ANTONINO DA BOLOGNA:	father of above; *Giovanna's second father-in-law.*

FEDERICO BOLOGNA D'ARAGONA:	*Giovanna's eldest son by Antonio Bologna.*
ELEONORA (?) BOLOGNA D'ARAGONA:	*Giovanna's daughter by Antonio Bologna.*
LUIGI (?) BOLOGNA D'ARAGONA:	*Giovanna's youngest son.*
ANTONIO BECCADELLI DA BOLOGNA:	known as Il Panormita; *grandfather to Giovanna's second husband.*

THE ESTE FAMILY OF FERRARA

ERCOLE D'ESTE:	Duke of Ferrara; *Giovanna's uncle.*
ELEONORA D'ARAGONA:	Duchess of Ferrara, daughter of Ferrante I of Naples; *Giovanna's aunt.*
ALFONSO D'ESTE:	Duke of Ferrara; *Giovanna's cousin.*
IPPOLITO D'ESTE:	Cardinal; *Giovanna's cousin.*
ISABELLA D'ESTE:	Marchioness of Mantua (married to Francesco Gonzaga, Marquis of Mantua); *Giovanna's cousin.*
BEATRICE D'ESTE:	Duchess of Milan (married to Ludovico Sforza, Duke of Milan, known as Il Moro); *Giovanna's cousin.*

THE GONZAGA COURT OF MANTUA

FRANCESCO GONZAGA:	Marquis of Mantua; *married Giovanna's cousin Isabella d'Este.*
SIGISMONDO GONZAGA, CARDINAL:	Papal Legate of Ancona in 1510 and brother of Francesco.
FEDERICO GONZAGA:	Lord of Bozzolo; cousin of the Marquis of Mantua; *married to Giovanna Orsini, Giovanna's niece.*
DOROTEA GONZAGA, MARCHIONESS OF BITONTO:	sister of Federico; *married to Giovanna's nephew Gianfrancesco Acquaviva, Marquis of Bitonto.*
ANTONIA GONZAGA:	sister of above; married to Alfonso Visconti, Count of Saliceto.
ELEONORA BROGNA DE' LARDIS:	La Brognina; lady-in-waiting to Isabella d'Este at the Mantuan court.

THE BORGIAS

RODRIGO BORGIA:	Pope Alexander VI.
CESARE BORGIA:	Cardinal, then Duke of Valentinois and Romagna; natural son of Rodrigo.
LUCREZIA BORGIA:	natural daughter of Rodrigo; *married Giovanni Sforza, then Giovanna's cousins Alfonso*

	d'Aragona, Duke of Bisceglie and Alfonso d'Este, Duke of Ferrara.
JOFFRE BORGIA:	Prince of Squillace; *married Giovanna's cousin Sancia d'Aragona.*
JUAN BORGIA:	Duke of Gandia, son of Rodrigo Borgia.

MILAN AND THE SFORZAS

MATTEO MARIA BANDELLO:	author of the first version of Giovanna's story.
LUCIO SCIPIONE ATTELLANO:	friend of Bandello.
LUDOVICO MARIA SFORZA:	Duke of Milan, known as Il Moro; *married to Giovanna's cousin Beatrice d'Este.*
GIAN GALEAZZO SFORZA:	Duke of Milan, nephew of Il Moro; *married Giovanna's cousin Isabella d'Aragona.*
IPPOLITA MARIA SFORZA:	Duchess of Calabria; sister of Il Moro, wife of King Alfonso II of Naples; *Giovanna's aunt.*
IPPOLITA SFORZA:	patron of Matteo Bandello; member of a minor branch of the Sforza family and married to Alessandro Bentivoglio of Milan.
SILVIO SAVELLI:	*condottiere* in the pay of the Sforzas.
ALESSANDRO BENTIVOGLIA:	patron of Bandello.
ALFONSO VISCONTI:	gave hospitality to Antonio Bologna.
CESARE FIERAMOSCA:	*condottiere* in the pay of the Sforzas. Hired to murder Antonio Bologna.
DANIELE DA BOZZOLO:	assassinated Antonio Bologna.

THE DELLA ROVERE FAMILY

GIULIANO DELLA ROVERE:	Pope Julius II.
FRANCESCO MARIA DELLA ROVERE:	nephew of Pope Julius; *married Leonora Gonzaga, daughter of Marquis of Mantua and Giovanna's cousin Isabella d'Este.*

THE MEDICI FAMILY OF FLORENCE

LORENZO DE' MEDICI:	Lord of Florence, known as Il Magnifico.
GIOVANNI DE' MEDICI:	Pope Leo X; son of Lorenzo.
GIULIANO DE' MEDICI:	Duke of Nemours; son of Lorenzo.
PIERO DE' MEDICI:	Lord of Florence; son of Lorenzo.
GIULIO DE' MEDICI:	Cardinal; cousin of the above (illegitimate son of Lorenzo's brother Giuliano). Later Pope Clement VII.
LORENZO DE' MEDICI:	Duke of Urbino; son of Piero.

ROME AND THE PAPAL COURT

GIULIA CAMPANA:	(also known as Giulia Ferrarese); courtesan and putative mistress of Cardinal Luigi d'Aragona.
TULLIA D'ARAGONA:	courtesan, daughter of above and putative daughter of Cardinal Luigi d'Aragona; *Giovanna's niece?*
BERNARDO DOVIZI, CARDINAL:	known as Bibbiena.
JOHANNES BURKHARDT:	papal master of ceremonies under Popes Alexander VI, Pius III and Julius II.
MARCO CORNARO, CARDINAL:	executor of Luigi d'Aragona's will and close friend.
FRANCIOTTO ORSINI, CARDINAL:	cousin of Pope Leo X who succeeded to Luigi d'Aragona's title.
PARIDE DE' GRASSI:	papal master of ceremonies under Popes Julius II and Leo X.
ALFONSO PETRUCCI, CARDINAL:	leader of the plot to assassinate Pope Leo X.
NICOLA ORSINI:	Count of Pitigliano, commander of the papal army; *father-in-law of Giovanna's sister Caterina.*
GENTILE ORSINI:	*brother-in-law of Giovanna (her sister Caterina's husband).*
GIAMBATTISTA CYBO:	Pope Innocent VIII.
TEODORINA CYBO:	daughter of above and mother-in-law of Luigi d'Aragona.
BATTISTINA USODIMARE:	daughter of Teodorina Cybo and wife of Luigi d'Aragona; *Giovanna's sister-in-law.*

Popes 1431–1550

EUGENE IV:	Gabriele Condulmer of Venice, 1431–47.
NICHOLAS V:	Tommaso Parentucelli of Sarzano, 1447–55.
CALLIXTUS III (OR IV):	Alfonso Borgia of Játvia, Valencia, 1455–58.
PIUS II:	Enea Silvio Piccolomini of Corsignano, near Siena, 1458–64.
PAUL II:	Pietro Barbo of Venice, 1464–71.
SIXTUS IV:	Francesco della Rovere of Celle Ligure near Savona, 1471–84.
INNOCENT VIII:	Giovanni Battista Cybo of Genoa, 1484–92.
ALEXANDER VI:	Rodrigo Borgia of Jàtvia, Valencia, 1492–1503.
PIUS III:	Francesco Todeschini Piccolomini of Siena, 1503.
JULIUS II:	Giuliano della Rovere of Albisola near Savona, 1503–13.
LEO X:	Giovanni de' Medici of Florence, 1513–22.
HADRIAN VI:	Adriaan Florensz of Utrecht, 1522–23.
CLEMENT VII:	Giulio de' Medici of Florence, 1523–34.
PAUL III:	Alessandro Farnese of Canino, near Viterbo, 1534–50.

THE KINGDOM OF NAPLES: 1442–1519

ALFONSO I: (Alfonso V of Aragon)	1442–58
FERRANTE I:	1458–94
ALFONSO II:	1494–5
FERRANTE II:	1495–6
FEDERICO III:	1496–1501

1501–3: the Kingdom of Naples divided between Louis XII of France and Ferdinand II of Aragon.
1503: the French expelled. Naples governed by a Spanish viceroy.
1516: the Spanish throne passed to Charles, Duke of Burgundy, who later became the Holy Roman Emperor, Charles V.

THE ARAGONS OF SPAIN

KING FERDINAND II:	reigned 1479–1516; known as The Catholic; *cousin of Giovanna's grandfather, King Ferrante.*
ISABELLA OF CASTILLE:	first wife of King Ferdinand II.
JUANA D'ARAGONA:	daughter of above; married Philip, Duke of Burgundy.
HOLY ROMAN EMPEROR, CHARLES V:	son of Juana and Philip.
RAIMONDO DE CARDONA:	Viceroy of Naples; reputedly the illegitimate son of King Ferdinand II.

KINGS OF FRANCE

CHARLES VIII:	reigned 1483–98
LOUIS XII:	reigned 1498–1515
FRANCIS I:	reigned 1515–47

Chronology

EVENTS IN THE LIVES OF GIOVANNA AND HER FAMILY

1458 Giovanna's grandfather becomes Ferrante I, King of Naples

1465 Marriage of Giovanna's parents, Enrico, Marquis of Gerace and Polissena Centelles

1474 Birth of Giovanna's elder brother, Luigi d'Aragona

1478 Death of Giovanna's father; birth of Giovanna d'Aragona (and her twin brother, Carlo)

1483 Birth of Antonio Bologna

1484 Giovanna flees from the plague in Calabria

1488 Marriage of Giovanna's sister Caterina (to Gentile Orsini) and their cousin Sancia (to Onorato Gaetani)

1490 Marriage of Giovanna to Alfonso Piccolomini, heir to the Duchy of Amalfi

1492 Marriage of Giovanna's brother to granddaughter of Pope Innocent VIII.

1493 Death of Antonio Piccolomini, Duke of Amalfi. Giovanna becomes Duchess of Amalfi.

1494 Giovanna's brother, Luigi, becomes Cardinal; the title, Marquis of Gerace, passes to her younger brother, Carlo

1495 Alfonso, Giovanna's husband, fights on Ferrandino's side against the French

1496 Deaths of Giovanna's cousin, King Ferrante II, and her mother-in-law

ITALY AND THE WIDER WORLD

1442 King Alfonso V of Aragon seizes the throne of Naples and becomes King Alfonso I of Naples

1458 Death of King Alfonso: Alfonso's illegitimate son Ferrante succeeds to the throne as King Ferrante I

1459–62 First baronial rebellion of Ferrante's reign

1485–87 The *Grande Congiura*, the Great Barons' Revolt

1492 The Moors expelled from Spain
Columbus sets sail for the Indies and discovers America
Death of Lorenzo de' Medici
Roderigo Borgia becomes Pope Alexander VI

1494 Death of King Ferrante I. His eldest son, Alfonso, Duke of Calabria becomes King Alfonso II of Naples

1495 King Charles VIII of France invades Italy. Alfonso II abdicates in favour of his son Ferrandino, who becomes King Ferrante II. He is forced to flee

1497 Duke of Amalfi wounded in skirmishes against the French. Giovanna's sister dies from the plague
1498 Death of Giovanna's husband, Duke of Amalfi
1499 Birth of Alfonso, Giovanna's first, and the Duke's posthumous, son
1505 Antonio Bologna returns to Naples and enters the service of Giovanna as her major-domo
1506? Either early this year or late in 1505 Giovanna secretly marries Bologna. Birth of their son Federico
1508 Birth of a daughter; death of Giovanna's aunt, Queen Beatrice of Hungary
1509 Visit of Giovanna's brothers and brothers-in-law to Amalfi
1510 Antonio Bologna fears discovery and takes refuge in Ancona with his children by Giovanna. Giovanna, pregnant again, joins him in Ancona
1511 Giovanna and Antonio flee from Ancona to Siena
1512 Death of Giovanna's brother Carlo. Giovanna and Antonio are intercepted on their way from Siena to Venice. Antonio escapes to Milan but Giovanna is taken back to Amalfi, where she dies towards the end of the year or in 1513
1513 Cardinal Luigi fails to obtain the papal crown, which goes to Giovanni de' Medici. Antonio Bologna murdered in Milan
1517–18 Cardinal Luigi travels through Europe while a plot to kill the Pope causes upheaval in Rome
1519 Death of Giovanna's brother, Cardinal Luigi

to Sicily as the French invade Naples. Charles VIII is crowned King of Naples, but when he leaves to return to France, Ferrandino reconquers the Kingdom and returns as King
1496 Marriage of King Ferrante II to his aunt, the Infanta
Death of King Ferrante II. His uncle, Don Federico, succeeds to the throne of Naples
1497 Coronation of King Federico III
1499 The French invade Italy again: Ludovico Sforza driven from Milan
1500 Secret Treaty of Granada: France and Spain agree to conquer and divide the Kingdom of Naples
1501 The French sack Capua. King Federico abdicates. Amalfi becomes French naval base
1503 War resumes between France and Spain
Death of Pope Alexander VI
Election of Francesco Piccolomini (uncle of Giovanna's late husband) as Pope Pius III.
Death of Pope Pius III: election of Giuliano della Rovere as Pope Julius II
1504 Gonsalvo de Cordova completes Spanish conquest of Naples and becomes first Spanish Viceroy
1506 Pope Julius II sets out to subjugate the Romagna
1512 Battle of Ravenna
1513 Pope Julius II dies. Election of Giovanni de' Medici as Pope Leo X
1515 Battle of Melegnano
1516 Ferdinand the Catholic, King of Aragon and Naples, dies in Spain and is succeeded by his grandson, Charles of Burgundy (the future Holy Roman Emperor, Charles V)

Preface: The Real Duchess

She stains time past: lights the time to come.

John Webster, *The Duchess of Malfi*, 1623, I.i.131

Is it a sinne to marry? Is it a fault to fly, and avoyde the sinne of whoredome? What lawes be these, where the marriage bed, and joyned matrimony is pursued wyth lyke severity, that murder, theft, and advoutry are? And what Christianity in a cardinall, to shed bloud which he ought to defend?

William Painter, *The Palace of Pleasure*, *The unfortunate marriage of a gentleman, called Antonio Bologna, wyth the Duchesse of Malfi, and the pitifull death of them both*, 1567

Your ruined prison belvedere looks down
from its high cliff on a thriving tourist town
in siren land, the sea-front strung with light.
I wonder does your ghost walk here at night
as we like to think, a lantern in one hand,
its grave-clothes rippling in a south wind,
insisting still in your resilient voice
on your right to take the lover of your choice.

from 'A Dirge (Giovanna Duchess of Amalfi)' by Derek Mahon, *Collected Poems*, The Gallery Press, 1999

John Webster's play *The Duchess of Malfi*, about a noblewoman persecuted and murdered by her brothers for falling in love with and marrying a man beneath her social station, has intrigued writers for centuries. His seventeenth-century drama was derived from William Painter's sixteenth-century translation of a contemporary Italian novella and over the years many other versions of the story have been published throughout Europe. The Duchess of Malfi has inspired not only novelists, playwrights and artists but poets too, most recently the Irish poet Derek Mahon. Almost 500 years separate Painter's novella and Mahon's poem and still the Duchess continues to exert her fascination. But who was the real Duchess of Malfi who provided this inspiration?

She was in fact the Duchess of Amalfi, not Malfi (the latter being an antiquated form of the place-name) and though Webster does not refer to his heroine by name – she is merely the Duchess – the protagonist of the real-life Renaissance drama, on which he based his stage play, was Giovanna d'Aragona, Duchess of Amalfi from 1493 until her mysterious disappearance some time after 1511. She was of royal blood, a grand-daughter of the King of Naples, but she fell passionately in love with her steward, Antonio Bologna, and dared to defy convention by marrying him, even though he was her social inferior. It was a crime against the hierarchies of degree that shocked her contemporaries and induced her brothers, Cardinal Luigi and Carlo d'Aragona, to remove the slur on their royal name by a brutal vendetta executed in Amalfi and Milan. Amalfi, once the grand medieval capital of a flourishing mercantile maritime republic, then a prosperous feudal duchy, today is a picturesque southern Italian seaside resort, squeezed into a narrow valley between white limestone mountains which rise precipitously from the sea. High on a cliff above the town is a castle watch tower called the Torre dello Ziro where, according to local legends, the Duchess Giovanna and two of her children were imprisoned by her brothers and strangled to death.

Giovanna's story made such a deep impression on her contemporaries that writers in Italy, France, Spain and England took it up again and again in the years following her disappearance. To what extent the version passed down to us through these literary works is merely the fruit of the authors' vivid imaginations and just how far the life of the real *Duchess of Malfi* differs from Webster's play are questions that this book seeks to answer, but its main theme is the life and times of Giovanna d'Aragona and the mystery which surrounded not only her death but the deaths of other close members of her family.

I lived in Amalfi for many years and wondered, each time I looked up at the tower, what really happened to Giovanna. I was spurred into seeking an answer when I discovered the existence of two Renaissance portraits from Raphael's workshop entitled 'Portrait of Giovanna d'Aragona'. One was in the Louvre in Paris, the other in the Doria Pamphilj Gallery in Rome. The paintings were almost identical: the women wore the same opulent crimson velvet gown and matching jewel-encrusted beret, but the faces were different. The Louvre version showed an exquisite, delicate-faced young woman in her late teens. The Doria Pamphilj subject was older, probably nearing thirty, and instead of the rather vapid naivety of the teenage face in the Louvre portrait, the expression recalled the intensity and style of the *Mona Lisa*. In fact this painting had once been attributed to Leonardo da Vinci. The enigma intrigued me. One was obviously a copy, but for some reason the face had been changed. Which was the original and did either represent the Duchess of Amalfi? Further research into the life of Raphael and his patrons brought a probable explanation for the two portraits and a possible connection with the Duchess.

Another link with Raphael came about when I noticed a similarity between his portrait of an unidentified cardinal and the effigy on the tomb in the church of Santa Maria sopra la Minerva in Rome of the Duchess's elder brother, Cardinal Luigi d'Aragona. Considering this similarity, the date of the painting and Luigi's pre-eminent position in the clerical hierarchy of the time, there was much to indicate that it was in fact his portrait (see Epilogue).

The portraits, however, were merely catalysts in the search for the real Duchess, which proved no easy task. Very few documents from the period have been preserved in the Naples State Archive and those that did survive the various Neapolitan popular uprisings of the seventeenth and eighteenth centuries were for the most part accidentally destroyed during the Second World War. This paucity of original material makes the essence of her character difficult to pinpoint and, as in John Webster's play, she comes into perspective by a process of comparative reflection with her contemporaries.

In the play (there is a brief summary in the Appendix), the main female foils are an elderly courtier, a servant and a whore; in the real story the servant and the whore remain, but the cast is widened to include the Duchess's cousins who were connected with the great influential Italian families of the time: the Gonzagas, the Sforzas, the Medici, the Estensi, the Orsini and the infamous Borgias. The noble courts of these families were rife with intrigue, illicit love affairs and murders, while their progeny made their fortunes as *condottieri* (mercenary soldiers or soldiers of fortune) exploiting the political conflicts and petty rivalries that were the order of the day.

Italy at the time was divided into three political units. In the north was a collection of small city-states forever at odds with one another, and in the south was the extensive feudal Kingdom of Naples ruled over by the Duchess of Amalfi's family. (It is frequently referred to as merely 'The Kingdom', being the only one in Italy at the time; other states were either republican city-states or ruled by noble overlords.) These two areas were separated by the third unit, a central buffer zone of feudal domains loosely united under the papacy. For centuries, the Italian peninsula had been at the mercy of the rivalry between France, Spain and the Holy Roman Empire, all of which struggled for political hegemony by playing off one individualistic petty Italian state against another. The papacy, not wishing to be dominated by any state, adopted a policy of 'divide and rule' and encouraged the mutual antagonisms.

While Italian political individualism led to conflict and disunity, it also fostered a climate of intellectual freedom which facilitated a sudden burgeoning of ideas; and from the revival of ancient classical learning grew an era of intense transformation, subsequently dubbed by historians, 'The Renaissance'. Throughout the fifteenth century and early sixteenth centuries, new frontiers were opening up. Intellectual horizons expanded with the development of humanist philosophy, which emphasised the role of rational systems rather than religious speculation in dealing with human needs. The boundaries of learning were widened with the invention of Gutenberg's printing press, which facilitated the diffusion of new ideas. And commercial and geographical horizons were broadened by the discovery of America, which began to realign the balance of power in Western Europe. These physical and intellectual centrifugal forces eventually led to the breakdown of the feudal commitments of the medieval world and initiated a movement towards the creation of modern autocratic nation states, though paradoxically, Italy, the cradle of the Renaissance, did not follow this trend.

Giovanna d'Aragona grew up during this period of flux in which new ideas were engendering rapid changes in society and ways of thought, while the essential fabric of life was still rooted in the Middle Ages. Her dilemma was a symptom of this paradox. The education of women meant that they became more conscious of their inherent free will, but convention prevented them from exercising it. Giovanna's attempt to seize the right to spend her life with the person of her choice was a precocious stance which constituted a wilful overturning of the established social code. For many of her contemporaries she was merely a deceitful, foolish, wanton woman unable

Matteo Bandello, author of the original story of the Duchess of Amalfi. Engraving by Lapi from a 1791 edition of Bandello's *Novelle*.

to dominate her carnal desires and keep them from overriding her duties to her family and estates. This egocentricity brought pain and destruction to Giovanna herself and to those she loved – her second husband Antonio, two of his children and her faithful maid all reputedly perished with her. And yet the distinctions between good and evil are subtly blurred, for Giovanna placed the noble sentiments of love and respect above the cold dictates of her family's political ambitions and, had she been so wanton, an amorous relationship without the formality of marriage would have sufficed. It is Giovanna's complexity and ambiguity that still fascinate us today.

Mysteriously, much more of Webster's drama corresponds to the real circumstances than his attributed sources can account for. The original source of the story was an Italian novella written in 1514 by a gossipy, socialite, Dominican friar called Matteo Bandello. Bandello became acquainted with Giovanna's second husband, Antonio Bologna, in Milan in 1513 and when he wrote his novella he inserted himself as a character, using the pseudonym Delio. Bandello, then, is the real Delio, who corresponds to Webster's character of that name. But it is still a matter of debate among Webster scholars as to whether Webster used Bandello's original Italian version published in 1554, the subsequent French translation by François de Belleforest (1565), or the English translation of the latter by William Painter

(1566–7). It is possible that he consulted all three. Webster was writing in 1612, some hundred years after the events took place, and there are several anachronisms in the text. For example, although Webster specifies that the Duchess's first child by Bologna was born in 1504, one of the characters mentions the work of Galileo (II.iv.16), who was born fifty-two years after the conclusion of the events. This was deliberate dramatic licence on Webster's part, included for the benefit of his audience, since news of Galileo's telescope and discoveries was arriving in England at the time he was writing. Webster's aim was to create a drama inspired by the story, not to reproduce an exact chronology. But despite the anachronisms, his version bears some remarkable and unaccountable similarities to the real story. The most notable one concerns the Duchess's birth. Webster portrays her and her younger brother as twins, which they probably were, though this is not mentioned by Bandello, or elsewhere in the sources. A coincidence, perhaps, but not the only one to emerge.

This is the dramatic story of the Duchess of Amalfi, her husband Antonio Bologna and her brother Cardinal Luigi d'Aragona, set against the backdrop of their time and narrated as it really happened, not as it has been distorted in subsequent literary works. All three met mysterious deaths: to understand how they died, we need to establish how they lived.

CHAPTER 1

The Seeds of Dissension

ANTONIO . . . a prince's court
Is like a common fountain, whence should flow
Pure silver drops in general, but if't chance
Some curs'd example poison't near the head
Death and diseases through the whole land will spread.

John Webster, *The Duchess of Malfi*, I.i.11–13

In August 1509,[1] Cardinal Luigi d'Aragona and his younger brother Carlo d'Aragona, Marquis of Gerace, paid an official visit to the court of their widowed sister, Giovanna d'Aragona, at Amalfi. Also present were the Duchess's son Alfonso Piccolomini, the ten-year-old Duke of Amalfi, for whom Giovanna ruled the Duchy as regent, and his paternal uncles Giambattista Piccolomini, Marquis of Deliceto and Francesco Piccolomini, Bishop of Bisignano.

Ostensibly the visit was a religious pilgrimage to pay homage to the relics of St Andrew the Apostle preserved in the cathedral of Amalfi. In reality it was a gathering of the Duchess's nearest male relatives to observe her court at first hand and discover how much basis there was in the rumours which abounded in the Kingdom of Naples that she had taken a secret lover and borne him at least one child. These relatives intended to interrogate members of her court and perhaps persuade some to spy upon the activities of their mistress in order to glean the truth.

It was not just a question of protecting the morals of the Duchess and the reputations of the Aragona and Piccolomini families; there were important considerations of state to be safeguarded. The Duchess was an indispensable pawn in the chessboard of political alliances and could not be sacrificed to any man at will. When the moment came to give her away, there had to be adequate rewards in terms of power for her family; if these were not forthcoming, she was destined to remain a widow.

John Webster's play opens with just such a visit to the court of the Duchess in Amalfi. The scene represents the conclusion of a tournament in honour of her brothers' visit; and the victor of the tournament is Giovanna's new steward, Antonio Bologna. For dramatic effect, Webster places the scene some time early in 1504, for he knew from his sources that Antonio returned to Naples after the death of the exiled King in that year. When the Duchess falls in love with her handsome young steward, the wheels of tragedy are set in motion.

The real Duchess's life was coloured by tragedy from its very outset. She came into this world in mournful circumstances. She was a posthumous child, born just a few weeks after her father, Enrico d'Aragona, had died from poisoning. Enrico was the eldest, but illegitimate, son of the King of Naples, Ferrante I d'Aragona. His mother, Diana Guardati, was a noblewoman from Sorrento who had had an affair with Ferrante in the early 1440s.[2] She died giving birth to Enrico and Ferrante soon moved on to other mistresses, but as his first child, Enrico always held a special place in his father's heart.

He was brought up at court and, in 1465, was married to Polissena Centelles as part of Ferrante's peace treaty with Polissena's rebellious father, Antonio Centelles. Centelles, a powerful baron and inveterate adventurer, was dubbed by a contemporary 'the Ulysses of his time'.[3] He had led numerous rebellions and been a long-standing thorn in the flesh of the Neapolitan House of Aragon. Giovanna d'Aragona's grandfathers played cat and mouse with each other for several years – though perhaps 'scorpion and spider' would be a more apt metaphor for the ruthless Ferrante and the conspiratorial Centelles. After numerous swashbuckling escapades, which entailed capture and escape by scaling castle walls, Centelles decided he had more to gain by making his peace with Ferrante and aiding him to repulse the invasion of the French House of Anjou. Ferrante welcomed this help at a crucial moment and rewarded Centelles by returning his wife's confiscated domains and promoting him to Prince of Squillace in Calabria. To seal their alliance Ferrante offered to marry his son, Enrico, to Centelles's younger daughter, Polissena.

The marriage of Giovanna's parents was celebrated in October 1465 and Centelles was lulled into believing that he had obtained all he desired, and more besides from the King. But the wily Ferrante was just biding his time.

Gerace, Calabria, from an old print.

Those who had betrayed once may do so again; they had to be eliminated. And like the sudden flick of a sleepy scorpion's tail, just a few months after the wedding, Ferrante struck.

He arranged that Centelles be invited by the vicar of one of his newly acquired possessions to participate in the celebrations for Palm Sunday. The priest had barely begun to recite the mass when Enrico d'Aragona suddenly strode forward and declared his father-in-law under arrest by order of King Ferrante. The stunned Centelles was taken away to Naples, under armed escort, where he was imprisoned in the dungeons of the King's residence at Castelnuovo. He was not charged or subjected to an official trial; he simply disappeared into the castle, never to be seen or heard of again.[4]

The incident marred the outset of Enrico's marriage but did not prevent him from producing two children with Polissena before Giovanna's birth in 1478. It is not known when her elder sister Caterina was born, but she was probably older than Luigi, who was born in Naples in September 1474.[5] There was also an illegitimate daughter, Ippolita, from an extramarital affair.

Enrico progressed in his father's favour and was given the title of Marquis of Gerace in May 1473. He was also made vice-lieutenant of Calabria, which he governed for his father's legitimate heir, Alfonso Duke of Calabria, and it was in Calabria that Enrico met his death. According to a dedicatory poem written to commemorate him, Enrico was an able governor, loved by the Calabrians.[6] There is no mention in contemporary documents of rivalry with his half-brother, the Duke of Calabria, though the Duke's volatile character would lead us to suspect its existence. In any event, when Enrico died, the Duke was too far away (taking the waters at the spa of Petriolo, near Siena) for there to be any speculation as to his involvement in a plot to assassinate his more popular, elder half-brother.

The news quickly spread in Naples of how Don Enrico had supped at the dour castle of Terranova in Calabria on the night of 22 November 1478.[7] It was the season for fresh mushrooms, which suddenly spring forth at the onset of autumn rains after the torrid summer heat. Enrico, his steward, and other members of his household were served the seasonal fare that evening for dinner. The mushrooms turned out to be poisonous and all who had eaten them died. Everyone, that is, except for Enrico's half-brother, Cesare, to whom there is a cryptic reference in the dedicatory poem. It says: '*Don Cesaro, che stava per morire, poi ca fo morto lo frate baruni*' (Don Cesare, who was about to die, then his brother the baron was killed instead).* The duplicitous Cesare d'Aragona, King Ferrante's second illegitimate son,[8] took Enrico's place as vice-lieutenant in Calabria and some twenty years later he enters the Duchess's story at a crucial moment.

What had led Enrico to be so imprudent? Usually members of the royal family employed food-tasters to avoid the risk of poison. Had he overlooked this wise protocol because the mushrooms had been a gift from someone in whom he had complete trust, or had they been slipped into the food without his knowledge? The poet does not tell us, but he does provide a considerable amount of information about Giovanna's family and gives us an idea of the circumstances of her birth.

The poem, written in the Calabrian dialect, is one of the earliest known compositions of its kind. The author, as he tells us himself, was a certain Ioanne Maurellu (Giovanni Morelli), who had been in the service of Don Enrico for many years. He was probably a court apothecary, for one of that

*'fo morto' translates 'was killed' not 'died'.

name appears in the records of April 1456.[9] It is not impossible that twenty-two years later he was still in Enrico's service. Morelli must certainly have known who the members of Enrico's family were and he gives us an exhaustive list of all the relatives who mourned his passing, but he mentions only two of Enrico's four children by Polissena: Caterina and Luigi. There is no reference to the future Duchess of Amalfi, Giovanna, or to her younger brother, Carlo. Considering the accuracy of Morelli's list, his long service with and knowledge of the family, it seems an inexplicable omission. However, Morelli does inform us that Enrico's widow was heavily pregnant[10] when her husband died, and since he makes no mention of Giovanna and Carlo, it would be justifiable to infer that Polissena gave birth to posthumous twins, a boy and a girl, shortly after her husband's death in the late autumn of 1478.[11]

The main figure in Giovanna's childhood was her grandfather King Ferrante (Plate 17). His grief was immense when the news of her father's death was delivered to him in Naples. He locked himself away in his chamber for two days and nights, refusing to eat or drink or to see or speak to anyone until he had rid himself of his anguish sufficiently to be able to confront his court and Kingdom with due composure. This outpouring of personal sorrow somewhat belies the traditional view that Ferrante was cold and unfeeling. It was, rather, the reaction of a man of deep sentiment, who found himself obliged, in the interests of government, to keep that sentiment well guarded and concealed. Such single-minded detachment was the secret of his statecraft, which maintained him firmly in the seat of power for almost forty years; and it was the lack of it which soon unhinged his descendants.

Whether Giovanna's mother, Polissena, was the grieving widow described in Morelli's poem we do not know, but, in any event, it can have been no easy task to bring up her four children in those unsettled times without the protection of a close male relative. Her father and husband were dead; her only brother, another Antonio Centelles, had fled to Sicily for fear of meeting the same end as his father. The obvious figure to turn to was her father-in-law, King Ferrante, but he was naturally too involved with pressing affairs of state to be able to closely oversee the welfare of Enrico's children. So who was to take the place of Giovanna's father? It is probable that her family had closer links with King Ferrante's second son, Don Federico d'Aragona, than with the heir to the throne, Duke Alfonso of Calabria. Certainly Giovanna's brothers served Federico unflinchingly to the end of his days and it is with him that we next hear of her and her family.

Federico's character contrasted sharply with that of his elder brother, Alfonso. The sixteenth-century Italian historian Camillo Porzio sums up the difference succinctly: Alfonso wished to be feared for his power, but Federico loved for his virtues. The Duke of Calabria was brash and overbearing, where Federico was mild and patient. Sometimes Federico's gentle disposition caused him to be a less effectual politician, but he was generally well liked and certainly more physically attractive than Duke Alfonso. The Duke's tendency to self-indulgence had made him overweight and a wound to his right cheek had left one eye damaged, for which the Neapolitans nicknamed him Il Guercio (The One-eyed). Alfonso did not enjoy much popularity either with his peers or his subjects, for he was unreliable and stingy with his friends and ferocious with his enemies. Politically speaking he was cunning, but he lacked his father's wisdom and self-control. Federico, by contrast, was approachable and benign with even the most humble and always ready to reward those of merit. He was a pious man rather than a religious fanatic like his elder brother, and loved learning.[12]

In the Monteoliveto Church in Naples (Sant' Anna dei Lombardi) there is a tableau of life-sized terracotta figures portraying the family of Christ mourning his death.[13] It almost certainly contains likenesses of the two brothers and of their sister, Beatrice, Queen of Hungary. The Duke of Calabria is portrayed as Joseph of Aramathea, the rich Jew who donated his tomb for Christ's sepulchre (Plate 18). The intense look of anguish on his face is moving and was perhaps inspired by his grief at the death of his younger son Pietro just before the work was commissioned. But the expression also reveals the violence and passionate emotion that governed the Duke's behaviour. From the face of the other mature male figure in the group, meant to represent Nicodemus (who wrote the account of the Harrowing of Hell), there transpires a contrasting air of sad gentleness. This figure is thought to be a portrait of Don Federico (Plate 19), and would have been a fitting likeness, for he was more given to contemplative intellectual pursuits.

Feudal overlords of the fifteenth century habitually visited their estates and often spent considerable time there. Although Giovanna's mother, as a member of the royal family, possessed apartments at the royal residence of Castelcapuano in Naples, she would have spent a good part of the year with

Nicastro, from an old print.

her family in their fiefdom of Gerace. King Ferrante had passed Gerace to Enrico's elder son Luigi six months after his father's death, but since he was only five years old, his mother naturally administrated his domains.

The town of Gerace, on the underside of the Calabrian toe of Italy, perches on the cliffs of a narrow snaking tufa outcrop from which it dominates the surrounding lowlands as far as the coastal town of Locri. In the fifteenth century it was a prosperous city, with the largest cathedral in southern Italy to attest to its importance. The castle of Gerace was safely set apart from the town on an isolated spur of rock, accessible only via the span of an enormous drawbridge, but, nevertheless, Giovanna's mother cannot have felt at ease during the early months of 1484, as the war between Venice and Naples gradually spread southwards along the Kingdom's Adriatic coast. She probably decided that it would be safer to take her children and travel north-west, towards the Tyrrhenian coast, and seek refuge with her late husband's half-brother, Don Federico, in his castle at Nicastro.

Unfortunately, when the family arrived at the relative safety of Nicastro, they were beset by new dangers. A serious outbreak of plague suddenly spread panic in the surrounding area. Federico soon departed to command

The castle of Nicastro today (*photograph courtesy of Marcello Rochira*).

his father's fleet in the Adriatic, and Polissena was left to govern Nicastro on his behalf. At the end of May 1484, she wrote an alarmed letter to her father-in-law, King Ferrante, informing him that the plague, which had broken out at the beginning of the month at Crotone and Francavilla, had now spread to the vicinity of Nicastro. Ferrante wrote back on 7 June exhorting her to take the necessary precautions as governor to prevent its taking hold in Nicastro. It would cause him much anxiety, he said, if this were to happen, since both she and her children were living there. Although he had promised to send a galley to bring her and her children back to the safety of Naples, a sudden development in the war with Venice had made this impossible.

Ferrante had come into conflict with Venice two years earlier, when the Venetians had invaded the adjacent Duchy of Ferrara, ruled by his elder daughter Eleonora and her husband, Ercole d'Este, Duke of Ferrara. Ferrante had sent Alfonso of Calabria to lead a Neapolitan army, to defend Eleonora. Now the Venetians had retaliated by invading the *terra d'Otranto* and occupying Gallipoli in the heel of Italy. All the galleys in the fleet were engaged in the military campaign to drive the Venetians out of the Kingdom. Because of this state of affairs, Ferrante advised Polissena and her children to make their way back to Naples overland.[14]

And so, in the high summer of 1484, fleeing the epidemic in Calabria, Giovanna and her family made the long journey back to Naples. That she,

Caterina, Luigi, and Carlo all survived, we know from subsequent references, but after this time there is no further mention of their mother, so we cannot be certain that she too escaped the contagion.

Spread out along the curving shore of a panoramic bay, at the foot of the volcano Mount Vesuvius, lies the city of Naples. First settled by the ancient Greeks, it became a thriving holiday resort for the patricians of the vast Roman Empire, earning for itself the name *Campania Felix* – the happy or prosperous region of Campania. Despite the political vicissitudes of medieval times, thanks to its mild climate and fertile volcanic soils, its economy continued to prosper. It was the 'happy country' which the poet Jacopo Sannazaro (1458–1530) wrote of in his pastoral idyll, *Arcadia*, a literary work that inspired writers of the English Renaissance such as Sir Philip Sidney and William Shakespeare.

Sannazaro eulogised the area surrounding Naples, its tranquil lakes and islands, its low rolling volcanic hills covered with vines and orchards, and the paradisical pleasures of the thermal baths of the Flegrean Fields, which the ancient Greeks had dubbed the gates of Hades. But he also praised the joys of the city itself. In 1476 a visiting Florentine named Bandini left the following appraisal of Naples:

> . . . physically splendid and in a happy natural position; enriched by grand buildings such as the royal palaces of Castelnuovo and Castelcapuano, which are surrounded by parks and gardens. The whole city is well-paved and always exceptionally clean, full of pleasant gardens and playing fountains everywhere . . . there are a great number of wealthy civilised lords and gentlemen and an infinite number of artisans, the most skilled that I know in all manner of crafts. There is an abundance of primary necessities for all and the cultural level is high. Liberty is enjoyed by all. People can live, dress and come and go as they wish for the city gates are never closed. The people are sociable and there are no civic disturbances.[15]

The decision of Giovanna's great-grandfather, King Alfonso V of Aragon, to settle in Naples in the mid-fifteenth century and make it his capital, had given a notable impetus to the city's growth, and it continued to expand throughout the century. It was a cosmopolitan city with a flourishing mercantile port. Trade was managed by diverse colonies of foreign merchants, but was mainly in the hands of the Catalonians who had financed and encouraged King Alfonso's conquest.

Alfonso of Aragon first set his sights on expanding his empire into peninsular Italy at a time when France was struggling to throw off the yoke of the ineffectual young English monarch Henry VI, and England was moving inexorably towards the chaos of the Wars of the Roses. Alfonso's dominions spanned the Mediterranean from the Iberian Peninsula through the Balearics and Sardinia as far as Sicily. The Kingdom of Naples, the largest political unit of the peninsula, stretched from Gaeta, just south of Rome, to the toe of Italy. It had once been united with Sicily, but, following the War of the Sicilian Vespers in the thirteenth century, the Spanish House of Aragon occupied Sicily, while the peninsular part of the Kingdom remained under the domination of the French House of Anjou. The rivalry between Spain and France for control of the Kingdom of Naples was to colour its politics for the next four hundred years and this rivalry ineluctably influenced the destiny of Giovanna d'Aragona and her family.

In the early fifteenth century, the childless Angevin Queen of Naples found herself in political difficulties and agreed to adopt Alfonso V of Aragon as her son and heir, in place of a rival Anjou claimant to the throne, in exchange for his help. While she later reneged on this, after her death in 1435 Alfonso used the agreement as a pretext for ousting her Anjou successor[16] and seizing the throne of Naples for himself. He then took the title of King Alfonso I of Naples and established his court in the city, declaring it the capital of his empire. The relaxed, pleasure-loving atmosphere of Naples was far more congenial to him than the severity of the Spanish court. He did not return to Spain, nor did he ever again see his barren wife, Queen Maria of Castille.

It was thanks to his patronage that the Renaissance, born in Tuscany, began to take hold in Naples. Alfonso was a cultured, sensitive intellectual and in his newly refurbished residence of Castelnuovo he soon established an after-dinner sodality of talented, educated men. Great contemporary scholars flocked to Naples to consult and augment the King's precious library and to participate in his evening symposia.[17]

Alfonso went to great lengths to have his only son, the illegitimate Ferrante, recognised as his successor in the Kingdom of Naples. The rest of his empire passed to his younger brother, Juan, King of Navarre, but he justified this renewed separation of the crown of Naples from that of Spain by affirming that its acquisition had been due to his personal conquest rather than to dynastic inheritance, and he therefore claimed the right to dispose of it as he saw fit.

The Kingdom of Naples was theoretically a feudal dominion of the papacy and, since it was the pope who invested the King of Naples with his crown, papal approval of the accession was vital. This was assured by a legal loophole – Ferrante's mother was married when he was born, although not to his natural father, and so Ferrante was therefore technically legitimate by birth. It may have been politically convenient enough to satisfy a pope, but did not assuage many of the Neapolitan barons and was to serve as a pretext for their future opposition to Aragonese rule.

It must, however, be borne in mind that the attitude towards illegitimacy in the Italy of this period was fairly tolerant, especially in the higher echelons of society. Illegitimate children born into important families enjoyed virtually the same rights and privileges as the legitimate, and the dynastic policies of these families built the foundations of their power and influence on an extended horizontal network of marriage alliances, which encompassed all offspring, legitimate or otherwise, instead of a vertical system that set aside the illegitimate cadet branches. Very often primogeniture and personal distinction overrode considerations of legitimacy in questions of succession.[18]

Giovanna's grandfather Ferrante succeeded to the throne in 1458. His ferocious character contrasted sharply with the relative mildness of his father, who had been given the sobriquet 'Magnanimous' by the Neapolitans. But his illegitimacy had notably weakened his political position vis-à-vis his feudal barons, for the concessions that King Alfonso had granted them, to secure their acceptance of his accession, had considerably undermined and diminished the power of the crown for the rest of the century. Ferrante was obliged to use much harsher methods than his father to keep himself in the seat of power, but keep himself there he did for thirty-six years.

Though his reign saw Naples torn apart by internecine struggles as the old feudal world struggled to maintain itself in the face of the increasing centralisation of the evolving modern state, it also saw an economic expansion which financed the artistic and intellectual Renaissance that made Naples the largest city and one of the most important cultural centres of Europe at the dawn of the sixteenth century. It was certainly larger than Paris or London and had three times as many inhabitants as Rome.[19] A tempera painting known as the *Tavola Strozzi* (*c.* 1465) gives us a vivid impression of how Naples appeared at the time of the marriage of Enrico and Polissena in 1465 (Plate 7). It must have appeared much the same when their six-year-old daughter Giovanna returned there in the late summer of 1484. Most of the city is clustered within the crenellated walls which enclose it inland from the beach. The low, stone buildings, at most three or four storeys high, are aligned along the old Graeco-Roman grid in a close network of shady narrow streets and alleyways that periodically open into wide, majestic, sunlit piazzas. Clearly visible in the painting are the royal palaces that Giovanna knew well: Castelnuovo and Castelcapuano.

Her grandfather, King Ferrante, lived in Castelnuovo, where he kept one of the most lavish courts of the time, for he had learnt from his father the importance of pomp and splendour as an expression of power. King Alfonso had reduced the former Angevin stronghold, the Maschio Angioino, to a heap of rubble during his siege of Naples in 1442 and the new castle that rose from the ruins was renamed, appropriately, Castelnuovo. The Spanish architect Sagrera was responsible for most of the reconstruction with its low, thick, walls to resist the onslaught of fast-developing firearms. In fact, it was built so sturdily that when the Aragonese were forced temporarily to abandon it to the French invaders in 1495, it was only with great difficulty that they managed to bombard them out again. At the entrance to his palace, lest the people of Naples ever forget his glorious conquest, King Alfonso had placed a magnificent white marble triumphal arch, one of the masterpieces of the Neapolitan Renaissance.

When the young Giovanna returned to Naples, her grandfather was living in Castelnuovo with his second wife, Queen Giovanna III, and their daughter, the Infanta. His first wife had died in 1465 and twelve years later, when he was fifty-four, he had married his 22-year-old cousin, Giovanna, daughter of King Juan d'Aragona of Spain. Their daughter, known as the Infanta Giovanna (another Giovanna d'Aragona!), was born in April 1479 and was just a few months younger than her step-niece and namesake, Giovanna, daughter of Don Enrico of Gerace. However, Enrico's daughter would have had limited contact with these two namesakes during her childhood, for they tended to keep themselves apart from the rest of Ferrante's numerous family housed in Castelcapuano, at the other side of the city.

It was to Castelcapuano that Giovanna returned to live at the end of the summer of 1484. Since a period of intense political instability ensued, it is doubtful that she ever returned to Gerace and more probable that she spent the rest of her childhood at Castelcapuano. What kind of place was it and how did it influence the formation of her character? The doyenne of the castle, Alfonso of Calabria's wife, Ippolita Maria Sforza, set a high intellectual tone: her favourite pastime was the translation of ancient Greek texts into the vernacular.

One of the principal characteristics of the Renaissance period was the extension of education to the daughters of important families. They were expected to be the cultural equals of their male counterparts and sometimes, since they were less distracted by the necessities of military campaigns, they often superseded their menfolk in their knowledge of classical antiquities and their fluency in Latin and Greek. According to a contemporary tract:

> The culture of women must resemble that of men, to whom they are equal. In the various branches of science and the arts she must [*sic*] possess sufficient knowledge to discuss them with wisdom and intelligence even when she is not well versed in them. Women must be well-versed in literature, know something of fine art, be experts in dancing and the art of being well-dressed . . . her morals, honesty and domestic virtues must be in accord with her intellectual qualities. She must be chaste but courteous, shrewd but discreet. . . .[20]

We can presume that Giovanna, as the King's granddaughter, would have had an education of this sort. As far as we can tell from her insistence on marrying Antonio Bologna, her 'morals and domestic virtues' were 'in accord with her intellectual qualities'. She was shrewd and tried to be discreet. Only her honesty can be called into question, although her deliberate deception can be counterbalanced to a certain extent by her noble motivation to preserve her secret husband from harm.

King Ferrante was by inclination pragmatic and had no real taste for the intellectual wrangling that his father had so enjoyed – he took greater pleasure from his pack of hounds at the hunt than from the hair-splitting of ideas in an after-dinner symposium. But he continued to patronise distinguished intellectuals, and encouraged them to frequent his court and participate in the education of his children and grandchildren. The eminent humanist scholar Iuniano De Maio, for example, tutored Giovanna's brother Carlo.[21] Ferrante also ensured that his father's library was expanded and enriched by a team of scribes and illuminators. The introduction of the printing press during his reign began to make books, though still extremely expensive, more quickly and more widely available. Certainly Giovanna would have had access to books and she grew up in a stimulating intellectual environment. Her uncles, the Duke of Calabria and Don Federico, acted as patrons to some of the finest Italian writers, artists and musicians of the day.

By 1484 King Ferrante's family had become numerous. He led a libertine life not unusual for his time and, in addition to his seven legitimate offspring, he fathered some nine illegitimate children. He has often been portrayed as a monster of cruelty and vice and yet he proved to be an indulgent father to all these children. Even when one of his sons openly betrayed him, he was not executed alongside his fellow-conspirators.[22] Ferrante's fine political acumen and successes have tended to be obfuscated by horrifying accounts of his cold-blooded cruelty. While the merits of his contemporaries, such as Lorenzo il Magnifico of Florence, were praised by a long line of direct descendants, Ferrante's memory, not unlike that of his other contemporary, Richard III of England, was subject to a negative interpretation. The rival dynasty of Ferdinand the Catholic of Spain encouraged scandalous stories about Ferrante and his descendants, and these were freely circulated in manuscripts like the Coronas (see Select Bibliography) to undermine any remaining sympathies for his line. The story of his granddaughter the Duchess of Amalfi must be interpreted in this context.

The excessive number of relations rendered Castelcapuano cramped for the Duke of Calabria and his court and so he began to draw up plans to build a new independent residence on adjacent land. This was not completed, however, until the end of 1489, and during the second half of the 1480s, when Giovanna lived there, the Duke was making do with alterations to his existing apartments, building new rooms and decorating the old ones with precious arrases and frescoes.

There are detailed records of the work and the artists called in to decorate the chambers. A new bathroom, for example, was built in March 1487.[23] The very fact that a separate bathroom existed at all at this time is an indication of the civilised standards of personal hygiene at the Neapolitan court. In a period in which the royal courts of northern Europe still spread their dirty stone floors with straw and took baths infrequently, at the courts of Castelnuovo and Castelcapuano and the noble palaces of Naples, the floors were clean and often decorated with precious majolica tiles or luxurious rugs; the walls adorned with priceless tapestries; the bedchambers draped with rich silk brocades and satin; and personal hygiene was commonplace. The French King Charles VIII, after invading Naples in 1495, returned to his meagre palace of Blois, loaded with a booty of treasures and ideas from the magnificent *palazzi* of Naples.

Life for Giovanna at Castelcapuano in the late 1480s was a *dolce vita*. During the summer there were the magnificent banquets that her uncle, Duke Alfonso of Calabria, liked to give outdoors in the larger of the two castle gardens beneath the perfumed pergolas of vines and citrus groves. In winter, grand state banquets were held in the *camera pinctata*, where the walls were decorated with frescoes by Costanzo de Moyses which depicted scenes from the Barons' Revolt of 1459–62. Giovanna, Caterina, Luigi and Carlo must have observed these pictures of the exploits of their maternal grandfather, Antonio Centelles, whom they had never known, and wondered what kind of man he had been and how much of his rebellious character had been passed down to them. Giovanna would prove to have inherited a conspicuous share.

Since the quashing of Centelles's rebellion, there had been almost twenty years of relative peace within the Kingdom, but at the time of Giovanna's return to Naples the storm clouds of civil unrest were gathering anew on the horizon. Just a few months later, in November 1484, from the windows of Castelcapuano, she could have watched her uncle, the Duke of Calabria, make his triumphal return to the city through the adjacent Porta Capuana, after the conclusion of the war against Venice.

Politically it was a critical moment. The Duke was angry that he and his father had been forced, by their alliance with Ferrara, to empty the royal coffers for the war against Venice. It was a war which they had deemed vital to the safety of their Kingdom, but to which most of the Neapolitan barons had refused to contribute because in their eyes it was a personal dynastic matter pertaining to the House of Aragon – the King was merely defending his daughter, the Duchess of Ferrara, rather than Neapolitan interests. Duke Alfonso swore to punish the barons' betrayal of their feudal obligations by sweeping away all those who occupied lands within thirty miles of the city. As a sardonic jest intended to drive the message symbolically home to these recalcitrant feudal vassals, some months later he paraded through the streets of Naples with a black slave sweeping the street

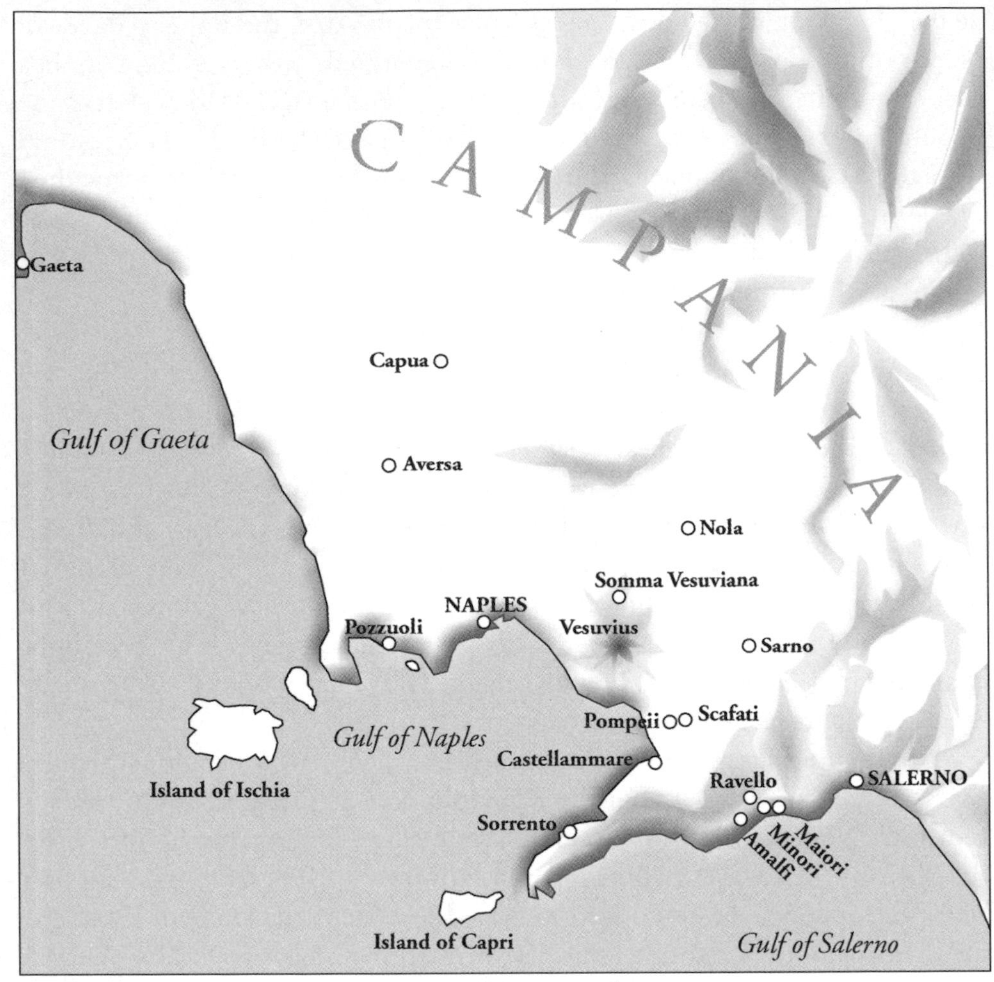

Map of Campania

in front of his horse. Perhaps John Webster had this episode in mind when he wrote of the Duke of Calabria:

> The Duke there? a most perverse and turbulent nature:
> What appears in him mirth, is merely outside;
> If he laughs heartily, it is to laugh
> All honesty out of fashion.[24]

If a member of the Neapolitan House of Aragon was the inspiration for Webster's fictitious Ferdinand, Duke of Calabria, it was Giovanna's uncle, Duke Alfonso.

CHAPTER 2

Duchess of Amalfi

CASTRUCHIO . . . that realm is never
long in quiet where the ruler is a soldier.

John Webster, *The Duchess of Malfi*, I.i.103–4

The fear and anxiety among the nobility provoked by Duke Alfonso's veiled threats propelled the mechanism of a new and more serious baronial revolt than that engineered by Giovanna's grandfather, Centelles, almost thirty years before. It also initiated a chain of events which led to her marriage to the heir to the Duchy of Amalfi.

The alarmed Neapolitan barons decided to appeal to the newly elected Pope Innocent VIII (Giambattista Cybo) for his support in their opposition to King Ferrante and Duke Alfonso. The Duke had stopped off in Rome on his way home from northern Italy and managed to quarrel with the new Pope over the question of the payment of the *census*, the feudal tribute, which the monarchs of Naples owed to the Pope as their feudal overlord. Hearing of this litigation, the barons were sure of the Pope's sympathetic ear.

In the conflict that ensued, even some of those closest to King Ferrante sided with the conspirators – his illegitimate son the Count of Arena, his secretary Antonello Petrucci and his financier, the enormously rich Francesco Coppola, Count of Sarno. The young Count of Arena had been inveigled into the plot by his wife's family, the Sanseverinos; Petrucci sided with the barons, mainly because his elder son had become involved with the conspirators, and Coppola did so because he feared that Duke Alfonso intended to cancel the crown's crippling debts with him by putting an end to his life.

In October 1485, King Ferrante sent his 22-year-old son, Cardinal Giovanni d'Aragona, to negotiate with Pope Innocent, but Giovanni died of a mysterious fever shortly after his arrival in Rome and poison was rumoured.[1] The barons then sequestered Don Federico in the castle of the Prince of Salerno, Antonello Sanseverino, and offered to make him king in place of his father and elder brother. Federico was a docile, more malleable character whom they were convinced they would be able to manipulate. But he refused their offer and managed to escape. It had been an unpardonable affront that King Ferrante would never forget, but for the time being he feigned coming to terms with the rebels.

By the summer of 1486, Ferrante managed to regain control of the situation; then he set his trap. Still pretending to ignore Coppola's betrayal, he made him an irresistible offer – the hand of his granddaughter, Maria Piccolomini, for Coppola's son, Marco. It was a repeat of the tactics Ferrante had used on Antonio Centelles, and Centelles's grandchildren would certainly have been invited to attend their cousin Maria's wedding on 13 August 1486.

The occasion was to prove a crucial turning point and an opportunity for Giovanna, Luigi, Carlo and Caterina to witness at first hand their grandfather's own particular brand of *realpolitik*. Perhaps Giovanna, at eight years of age, was not yet able to comprehend the political subtleties, but for twelve-year-old Luigi it must have been an important lesson which helped to mould his own political acumen. For Giovanna the occasion had more personal connotations: if she had not yet met her future husband Alfonso Piccolomini, she would have seen this eldest son of the Duke of Amalfi mixing with the guests at his half-sister's wedding.[2]

Two days before the ceremony, Ferrante signed a truce with the Pope in which he promised to pardon all the rebellious barons. He then proceeded to ignore this pardon, and Maria's wedding turned out to be merely another of his skilful, cunning dissimulations. Only the Queen, the Duke and Duchess of Calabria and the keeper of Castelnuovo were aware of the King's plan. Even the bride's father had not been informed.

The guests were assembled in the great hall of Castelnuovo and the celebrations were in full swing. The younger guests had taken to the floor to entertain the company with the latest dances, when, suddenly, the low rumbling of the castle drawbridge being hauled up set a discordant tone against the music. Guards began to filter in around the edges of the hall as the keeper of the castle strode into the middle of the dance floor and held up his sword for the festivities to cease. There was a moment of deathly silence; then he began reading out the list of barons present who had conspired against the King. They were all arrested, as were their wives, children and servants (the bridegroom, his parents and his brother were included in this list) and taken off to the castle dungeons.

King Ferrante then made a speech justifying his conduct to the astounded foreign ambassadors who had been invited to his granddaughter's wedding. He accused Petrucci of embezzling crown funds and Coppola of having the effrontery to try to impose this unseemly marriage upon the monarch's granddaughter. Not the exact truth, but a manipulated version destined to assuage the discomfort felt by the foreign diplomats at having been unwilling parties to Ferrante's trickery. For Giovanna it should have been a lesson on the dire consequences of 'unseemly' royal marriages.

In the days that followed, Ferrante's deliberate flouting of his accord with the Pope came to light, but he continued undeterred, arresting barons and their families until the city prisons were overflowing. Many had their possessions confiscated and some of the most recalcitrant were eventually murdered in their prison cells on Christmas Eve 1491, when a terrible storm allowed the victim's bodies to be thrown into the sea and washed away without trace.[3]

Meanwhile, after breaking his truce with the Pope, Ferrante had to search for allies in the brewing conflict with the papacy. The support of the powerful Gaetani family was sealed with the betrothal of the Duke of Calabria's nine-year-old illegitimate daughter, Sancia, to Onorato Gaetani, Count of Traietta. Then diplomatic preparations began for the marriage of his legitimate daughter, Isabella, to her cousin Gian Galeazzo Sforza, Duke of Milan.[4]

The King then turned to the Orsini, a powerful family who held sway in Rome and whose extensive network of *condottieri* spread throughout Italy. Maria Piccolomini, whose marriage to Marco Coppola had never been finalised, found a proper bridegroom when she was given in marriage to the Orsini Duke of Gravina. But it was necessary to ensure the benevolence of even more powerful members of the Orsini clan. At the beginning of the Barons' Revolt, the loyalty of Nicola Orsini, Count of Pitigliano, had been bought with the gift of the fiefdom of Nola; now, since it looked as if he was about to become commander of the papal forces, Ferrante sought to tie him to the Neapolitan House of Aragon by marriage.

On a stormy night in mid-September 1488, Nicola Orsini's wife, Elena, Countess of Pitigliano, arrived in Naples and was given hospitality at Castelnuovo. The following morning she had an audience with King Ferrante and then went to dine with the Duke of Calabria at the monastery of Monteoliveto.[5] The motive for these discreet meetings was presumably to discuss the terms of a marriage alliance, for the Countess returned a few days later with her son, Gentile, while Giovanna's sister Caterina was called to her uncle's apartments in Castelcapuano to meet her future husband and mother-in-law. Gentile seems to have been aptly named for he was a timid youth, who stood shyly aside, cap in hand, while his mother embraced Caterina and welcomed her into her new family. Gentile was then allowed to accompany Caterina back to her own apartments so that they could get to know one another.[6] Whether or not they liked each other was superfluous, for their families had decided that they were to be united. The King wanted the heir of the future commander of the papal forces to father children of Aragonese blood and Pitigliano welcomed the rich dowry of Aragonese gold to fill his war coffers. The chronicler makes no mention of Caterina's mother being present during the negotiations for her daughter's marriage, so it would be legitimate to presume that Polissena was definitely dead by this time.

On 22 October 1488, ten-year-old Giovanna must have watched her elder sister marry Gentile Orsini with a mixture of joy and melancholy. The wedding was a very subdued affair, for not only was the court still in mourning for the death of the Duchess of Calabria in August, but Caterina's new mother-in-law, the Countess of Pitigliano, had also died suddenly at the beginning of the month. For Caterina it was an inauspicious beginning to her married life and after the quiet ceremony she departed immediately for her father-in-law's fiefdom of Nola,[7] leaving Giovanna alone in their Castelcapuano apartments, with only her personal maid and the members of her own tiny court for companionship. She would miss the daily contact with Caterina, but fortunately Nola was no great distance from Naples and there would be opportunities to be reunited on court occasions.

Such an occasion soon materialised when, in February the following year, their cousin Isabella married the Duke of Milan at Castelnuovo. Since Giovanna and Caterina were part of the royal entourage, it is to be presumed they were not among the crowds on the steps leading up to the *Gran Sala* when the stone balustrade gave way. The pressure of people pushing to enter the hall in order to participate in the splendid celebrations caused it to collapse and many were injured, though not too severely, as they toppled from the steps into the stone courtyard.

Throughout her life Giovanna's closest and most constant companion was her personal maid, Lucina Bonito, but her principal compeers at the royal court of Castelcapuano were her elder sister, Caterina, and their cousins, Isabella and Sancia. By 1489 they had all left the castle for their husbands' households. Once they had gone, the Duke of Calabria transferred his court to the adjacent, newly built palace of the Duchesca. If Giovanna had begun to feel lonely in the rapidly emptying royal residence, this would not be the case for long; plans were already afoot to find a husband for her too.

In 1490 the old Duke of Amalfi, Antonio Piccolomini, was ailing and this troubled King Ferrante. Ever since he transferred himself to the Kingdom from his native Tuscany, Piccolomini had demonstrated fierce loyalty to the Aragons of Naples. The King had rewarded him with the Duchy of Amalfi and the hand of his illegitimate daughter, Maria d'Aragona, and when Maria died at the age of twenty, after bearing him three daughters (though no male heir), Ferrante, eager to keep Piccolomini loyal to the Aragon cause, gave him another Aragonese bride. The new bride, Maria Marzano, provided him with three healthy sons and two more daughters, but was less politically satisfactory. Maria was the daughter of the francophile rebel baron, Marino Marzano, who, together with Antonio Centelles, had led the first baronial revolt of 1459–62. Like Giovanna's grandfather Centelles, Marino Marzano had met a mysterious end in the dungeons of Castelnuovo – perhaps deservedly so, since he had treacherously attempted to assassinate Ferrante in 1460, despite the fact that he had married Ferrante's half-sister, Eleonora.

It was thanks to her mother Eleonora that Maria Marzano bore royal Aragonese blood in her veins. Eleonora had once been Duchess of Amalfi herself, but Ferrante confiscated this title in 1461 because of her support for her husband's defection. He then proceeded to marry off Eleonora's daughters to suit his own political purposes. Maria's marriage was probably intended to appease Eleonora for the confiscation, since her offspring would now inherit the Duchy she had lost.

But as time went by, the King began to suspect, not without foundation, that Maria Marzano had never fully renounced the francophile leanings she had imbibed from her family. As her husband's health declined, Ferrante decided that it would be politic to give her eldest son, Alfonso Piccolomini, an Aragonese bride too, to eschew the risk of his mother persuading him to contract a marriage alliance with the supporters of the Angevin cause, with which she sympathised. The choice fell on his granddaughter Giovanna, who was by now twelve years old. Ironically, this union of the

The Palatine Chapel of Castelnuovo, Naples, where Giovanna d'Aragona married Alfonso Piccolomini, eldest son of the Duke of Amalfi, on 25 July 1490.

grandchildren of Marzano and Centelles was made to shore up the throne of the very King these barons had tried to unseat.

The extent of Giovanna's dowry is not known, but since her cousin Sancia's was 12,000 ducats and her illegitimate sister Ippolita's, a year later, was 7,000 ducats,[8] it is reasonable to assume, considering her dynastic position, that it was somewhere between the two; perhaps about 10,000 ducats. It was an honourable and respectable sum and certainly provided by her grandfather, whose interests the marriage was intended to protect.

To modern eyes it seems scandalous that a girl of twelve should be married, but it was not unusual for the period. Sancia and Maria d'Aragona had only been nine when they were betrothed. Giovanna may even have welcomed the marriage; she was, after all, being given to a young man of almost her own age, for Alfonso Piccolomini was probably about sixteen or seventeen at the time.[9] Not all brides were so fortunate. Her sister-in-law Eleonora Piccolomini, for example, was unhappily married to a man more than twenty years her senior.

A brief account of Giovanna's wedding is given by the governor of the Duke of Calabria's pages, Giampiero Leostello, in his *Effemeridi*[10] and it is one of the few direct references to Giovanna in contemporary records. At nine o'clock on the morning of 25 July 1490 the Duke of Calabria rode to

Castelnuovo to confer with his father. Later that morning, Giovanna too rode to Castelnuovo for the most important event of her young life. At one p.m., after the King and Duke had dealt with the state affairs of the day, they accompanied the Queen and the Infanta across the patio (courtyard) of the castle to the Palatine Chapel, to join the other members of the royal family already assembled there for the marriage of Giovanna d'Aragona of Gerace to Alfonso Piccolomini, heir to the Dukedom of Amalfi. Leostello does not tell us whether Giovanna was shy and nervous or proud and confident, but she must have been emotionally charged, wondering what lay in store. She was doubtless relieved to be entering a household where at least there were two young girls of her age and rank to act as her companions: Alfonso had two sisters, the above-mentioned Eleonora and another Giovanna.

Of Giovanna Piccolomini, probably the younger, very little is known. She grew up, married a member of the Caracciolo family and lived and died without incurring any notoriety. Not so Eleonora, who was the object of much scandalous gossip. Her story is as colourful and tragic as that of her sister-in-law Giovanna d'Aragona and one cannot help but wonder how much a shared adolescence influenced the similarly wilful behaviour of these two strong-minded young women.

Giovanna d'Aragona was certainly escorted to the Palatine Chapel by the head of her family, her elder brother, Luigi. Her younger brother, Carlo, would have been present and probably Caterina and Sancia too. Her cousin Isabella was now far away in Milan, but her uncle Federico, if affairs of state had permitted him to be in Naples, would have attended his niece's wedding.

Music was one of her grandfather's great passions and grand occasions provided an opportunity for him to indulge it. The mass was sung by the chapel choir, whose members were drawn from all over Europe. There was even a female member, an Englishwoman called Madama Anna. They were accompanied by the monumental chapel organ that Ferrante had acquired from Bologna some twenty years earlier. Carved, frescoed and gilded, it was a magnificent work of art as well as a superb musical instrument.

But the beautiful music did little to alleviate the tediousness of the intense summer heat as the midday sun streamed implacably through the high Gothic windows, illuminating the narrow coloured friezes that were the meagre remnants of Giotto's great frescoes destroyed by the great earthquake of 1456.

Eneas Silvio Piccolomini. Copy of an original bust in the basilica of San Benedetto Po (*Palazzo Ducale, Mantua, © Ministero per I Beni e le Attività Culturali; photograph by Finaffer*).

Giovanna's wedding was a much grander affair than her sister Caterina's had been and after the religious ceremony in the Palatine Chapel, the bride and groom were paraded triumphantly through the streets of Naples to the Piccolomini palace near the church of San Domenico Maggiore. Here the celebrations continued with a sumptuous reception given by the Duke of Amalfi. The festivities continued well on into the night, with farces, music and dancing following the wedding banquet. Leostello tells us it was four o'clock in the morning when the Duke of Calabria finally returned to the Duchesca.

Giovanna spent her first night in her new home, Palazzo Piccolomini, as a married woman. Although she had probably reached puberty, given her young age it is unlikely that the marriage was consummated immediately. The precariousness of pregnancies at too early an age were well known, and since royal marriages were made for reasons of state, with the primary aim of siring heirs, the ruining of a valuable heiress by obliging her to bear children when she was too young, could have important political consequences. Margaret Beaufort bore the future King Henry VII of England at the age of thirteen and was thought to have been 'spoiled' by this premature childbearing, for she produced no more children.[11] The survival of a single heir, while ruling out rivalry, left the family inheritance in a position of insecurity.

Palazzo Piccolomini, Pienza, built by Pope Pius II. The Duchess of Amalfi may have taken refuge here when she fled from Ancona with Antonio Bologna and their children.

However, Giovanna did have a daughter, named Caterina, who died at the age of eight. The child probably predeceased her father, for there was a moment of confusion in the succession to the Duchy of Amalfi that is probably attributable to the lack of direct heirs. If the age of Caterina was reported correctly, it is thus possible that Giovanna did lie with her husband almost immediately and conceived her first child at this early age. In Giovanna's case the 'spoiling' was perhaps that this precocious marital experience heightened her sexual appetites and rendered her widowhood an insufferable burden.

The Piccolomini family into which Giovanna married had had a chequered history. They originated in Siena, where, during the twelfth and thirteenth centuries, they emerged as one of the richest and most influential families. They had begun in the wool trade (for which they travelled abroad as far as England), before expanding their business interests into banking. With the rise of a newly affluent artisan class in fourteenth-century Siena, the power of the established noble families was challenged and eventually overthrown by a revolt that brought to power a popular oligarchy, the *Dodici*, in 1335. The Piccolomini found themselves forced into exile at their fief of Corsignano in the Val d'Orcia. Their fortunes declined, but on a clear day from the hill of Corsignano the ochre walls of Siena could still be seen in the distance and the Piccolomini never forgot their Sienese roots.

Eneas Silvio Piccolomini, who became Pope Pius II in 1458, was born at Corsignano in 1405. He attended university in Siena and in his youth led the life of a profligate, siring at least one illegitimate child. He wrote and studied profusely, immersing himself in humanist studies, as his *Commentaries* reveal. (The work includes a tract on the brutal crimes committed by his contemporary Count Vlad Dracula.) But when, later in life, he decided to enter the Church, he considered it opportune to disclaim some of his more lascivious, youthful tracts, such as the *Tale of Two Lovers*.[12]

Eneas became an accomplished poet and received the poet's crown from Emperor Frederick III of Germany, to whom he eventually became secretary. In 1450 Frederick dispatched him to Naples to negotiate a marriage with the niece of King Alfonso I and Eneas returned there on other subsequent diplomatic missions. He soon became a close friend of King Alfonso and found himself thoroughly at ease in the cultivated society of scholars and artists at the Neapolitan court. Among the chief literary lights there at the time was Antonio Beccadelli da Bologna, better known as Il Panormita, whom Eneas had known in Siena. Eneas spent his leisure time in Naples compiling four books of anecdotes and epigrams to add to Il Panormita's work on the life and reign of Alfonso.[13] He also visited places of interest in the area such as the site of the Greek Sibyl at Cumae, and Amalfi, where the relics of St Andrew the Apostle were preserved. True to his humanist canons, he sought out both classical remains and saintly relics with equal fervour.

Eneas entered the Church in 1446 at the mature age of forty-one, and, rising rapidly in the Vatican hierarchy, was nominated cardinal in 1456. On the death of Pope Callixtus III (Alfonso Borgia) two years later, after a long and stormy conclave, of which Eneas gives an amusing description in his *Commentaries*, he emerged as Pope Pius II.[14] Immediately, he set his sights on rebuilding his family's former wealth. His first project was to transform his birthplace of Corsignano into an ideal city, which he renamed Pienza after himself. He intended the city to become the focal point of the papacy and obliged his cardinals to build palaces there. But his reign was brief and, following his death, Pienza returned to being a provincial backwater, albeit an embellished one.

Since Pius himself had no surviving offspring or brothers, his two sisters, Laudonia and Caterina, both of whom had made respectable but by no means brilliant marriages, assumed for themselves and their children the surname of Piccolomini. Laudonia was married to Nanni Todeschini of Siena and had four sons – Antonio, Francesco, Giacomo and Andrea.[15]

Francesco Todeschini Piccolomini followed in his uncle's footsteps by becoming first Archbishop, then Cardinal, of Siena and finally, very briefly in 1503, Pope Pius III. But his brother Antonio demonstrated little inclination for study or for intellectual pursuits of any kind. Eneas had occasion to lament this fact to Antonio's father Nanni Todeschini in September 1453: 'We understand that Antonio is no scholar and is doing little good. We gathered as much from his letters, which are execrably written. We trust that he will mend his ways, and at least learn to express himself better. . . .'[16]

Fortunately, his uncle's election as Pope in 1458 enabled Antonio Piccolomini to cast aside his books and take up a military career. He soon showed that his real talents lay more on the battlefield than in his uncle's magnificent library. He was immediately nominated keeper of Castel Sant' Angelo in Rome, and when Pius set himself to rebuild the decayed Piccolomini fortunes and create new domains for his family, he found Antonio a ready and able instrument.

Shortly after his elevation to the papacy, Pius II sent Antonio to aid King Ferrante of Naples in the baronial revolt of 1459–62, which was headed by Centelles and Marzano. Pius was of a nervous temperament and wholly without military experience. Sometimes he wavered in his support for Ferrante, who was then obliged to reassure him with gifts to members of his family. Antonio Piccolomini won the lion's share of these gifts: the hand of Ferrante's illegitimate daughter Maria; the Duchy of Amalfi; the fiefdom of Scafati;[17] and those of Celano and Capestrano, together with other minor fiefdoms in Abruzzo. After a failed attempt to appropriate some of the domains of the Malatesta in the Papal Marches, Antonio withdrew to the Kingdom of Naples and spent the rest of his life faithfully serving Ferrante's cause there.

Giovanna's marriage to Antonio Piccolomini's eldest son and heir, Alfonso, seems to have been a happy and successful union. He was a young man of courage and spirit and, like his father, favoured the martial arts rather than philosophy. As a member of the cultured Aragon court he would not have been illiterate, but no mention is made of his pursuing intellectual achievements.

After her marriage, Giovanna moved from Castelcapuano to her husband's household at the Palazzo Piccolomini in Naples. Its exact location is uncertain; there are merely references to its being in the vicinity of the church and adjacent monastery of San Domenico Maggiore, which during the thirteenth century had been the home of St Thomas Aquinas. The only remaining physical evidence of the presence of the Piccolomini family in the city is the magnificent tomb that Antonio built for his first wife, Maria d'Aragona, in the church of Monteoliveto.

There is no trace either of the Palazzo Piccolomini in Amalfi. According to the nineteenth-century Amalfitan historian, Matteo Camera, the palace was sited on the seafront between the Porta della Marina, the ancient arsenal, and the Vicoletto delle Piscine, but any remains which survived have, over the centuries, been gradually incorporated into successive buildings and are no longer visible.[18]

During the period in which the Piccolomini governed Amalfi, the town was still important and prosperous, but its fortunes had begun to decline from the rich splendour of the independent medieval maritime republic. The number of religious institutions that the city was able to support in proportion to the number of inhabitants attests to this. Its agriculture flourished, producing citrus and other fruits in abundance, despite the ruggedness of the steep terrain. But Amalfi's most important resource in this period was timber from the forest-covered mountains. Amalfitan ships transported timber to North Africa and with the gold acquired in exchange, they sailed on to the coasts of Syria, Palestine and Byzantium, where they purchased spices, silks, precious stones, gold artefacts and jewellery, which they then sold in the third phase to various Italian cities. This 'commercial triangle' had greatly enriched the city in medieval times and although by the fifteenth century it had begun to wane, the mercantile tradition was still strong and a source of wealth to the Duchy.[19]

A vivid description of a visit paid by a young English gentleman, Thomas Hoby[20] in the spring of 1550 serves to give an idea of what life must have been like in sixteenth-century Amalfi. When the nineteen-year-old Hoby was shipwrecked at Minori, on the Amalfi coast, he and his companions sought hospitality with Giovanna's grandson, Inigo Piccolomini, Marquis of Capestrano, whom they had already had occasion to meet in Siena. He was greatly impressed by the luxurious tenor of the Piccolomini's lifestyle and the hospitality he received. He writes in his journal on 26 March 1550 that Don Inigo had sent one of his men to invite some of them

> . . . up into the castle to him, the rest of our company remaining beneath in the town, where we supped all together, every man served his mess severally at the table to himself in silver very honourably. And there had with him at supper the Captain of the town the better to entertain us all.
>
> When supper was done every man was brought to his rest: Whitehorn and I were had into a chamber hanged with cloth of gold and velvet, wherein were two beds, the one of silver work and the other of velvet, with pillows, bolsters and sheets curiously wrought with needlework. In another chamber hardby lay Stradlinge and Grinwaye . . . Handfort and Frauns Williams were led to the Captain's house of the town, where they lay sumptuously, and were greatly feasted.

The following morning was dark, rainy and misty, and despite Inigo's entreaties to stay longer, Hoby and his companions insisted that they had to leave for Naples. They had decided to go overland 'the better to see the country', without fully realising the dangers and difficulties this would entail. The mountains were rife with outlaws and the Spanish garrison, which was stationed in Amalfi,

> . . . issued out abroad many times to take such banished men called forusciti [outlaws] as lying upon the hills did great damage to the inhabitants of the country.

Inigo offered them an armed escort of a dozen Spanish soldiers to conduct them 'through the jeopardous places thereabout, where those kind of banished men were more likely to be', but they refused his solicitous offer, thanked him and set off. The Marquis, seeing the soldiers return, sent two or three to follow Hoby and his companions with 'their pieces charged'. They were to see the party over the mountain and make sure they had everything they needed. The trek was harder than expected:

> To pass to the top of this hill of Amalfi it is steep, hard stony, narrow, wearisome and troublesome way, for we ascend always upon degrees and stairs of stone set there by the men of the country to pass to and fro. When we came to the top of the hill there we found ready provision made for us against our coming, both fruits of all sorts to present us, and also horses to ride onwards upon our journey. Which horses we refused saying that we could better go down on foot than come up. From Amalfi

> to the top of the hill it is reckoned eight miles, and hitherto did the Spaniards conduct us.
>
> At the bottom of the hill we passed over the river Sarno, commonly called Scafaro [Scafati], which passage belongeth to the Duke of Amalfi. . . .[21]

The Piccolomini held many other fiefs besides Amalfi, and Giovanna's life as Duchess was spent moving in progression from one to another with her husband, while an annually nominated vice-duke carried out the day-to-day government of the Duchy. (They were nominated annually to prevent them from usurping the Duke's powers.) Hoby mentions the Piccolomini fiefdom of Scafati, which bordered the Duchy of Amalfi. It was a flourishing market town, adjacent to the long-forgotten site of Pompeii, whose ancient commercial function it had taken on. However, by the time Giovanna entered the Piccolomini household, the area surrounding Scafati was becoming extremely unhealthy. Antonio Piccolomini had unwisely dammed sections of the River Sarno to drive his water mills and the resulting stagnation of the water had caused malarial marshes to develop.[22]

Much healthier was the air of the Abruzzo mountains where the Piccolomini held several fiefs, the most important of which was the massive castle of Celano, overlooking the shallow Lake Fùcino (page 60). Celano held an important strategic position, near the border between the Kingdom of Naples and the Papal States; it was imperative for Ferrante that it should be in the hands of those loyal to him. Duke Antonio Piccolomini had also received the title of Count of Celano.

One of Duke Antonio's favourite residences in Abruzzo was at his fief of Capestrano, where he had built a new castle perched high on a crag that dominated the panoramic Tirino valley. Huddled around the castle, clinging to the steep narrow streets, was a tiny medieval town. Where the present town square is situated was once the Duke's *giardino all' italiana*, which must have resembled the garden still to be seen today at the home of his uncle, Pope Pius II, in Pienza. It was here at Capestrano that Antonio Piccolomini, Duke of Amalfi, died in January 1493, and his body was laid to rest in the tiny church of Santa Maria della Concezione,[23] at the foot of the steep slope that leads up to the gates of the castle.

The Duke's death inevitably brought into focus new political players and new anxieties. The command of the Duchy passed to his eldest son, Alfonso, and Giovanna, at little more than fourteen years of age, became the new Duchess of Amalfi. When King Ferrante learnt that his son-in-law and loyal friend was gravely ill he sent his best doctors to his bedside to treat him; but to no avail. On hearing of the Duke's death, he exclaimed, 'a true model of fidelity has passed away'.[24] But the extent of Ferrante's concern and anxiety is evident from a series of letters he wrote from his hunting lodge of Tripergola, just after the news had reached him there.[25] They were sent to Antonio Piccolomini's three brothers: Giacomo, Andrea and Cardinal Francesco. After conveying his condolences in a manner reminiscent of the poem written after the death of Enrico d'Aragona – that death was a natural thing and to be accepted as such – Ferrante expresses his apprehension that a Duchy as strategically important as Amalfi should fall into the hands of an heir too immature to hold the reins of government firmly and wisely. He even goes so far as to suggest that Giacomo Piccolomini should temporarily take over the government of his brother Antonio's possessions. The impending threat of a French invasion of Naples had become very real. Any defection of the border fiefs under the sway of the Duke of Amalfi, or of the Duchy of Amalfi itself, could have been critical. Ferrante was certainly anxious about the influence that the new Duke Alfonso's mother, Maria Marzano, might exert over her youthful son's political inclinations. His Aragonese wife, Giovanna, was as yet too young for her opinions to count.

CHAPTER 3

Before a Tempest

DUCHESS . . . like to calm weather
At sea before a tempest, false hearts speak fair
To those they intend most mischief.

John Webster, *The Duchess of Malfi*, III.v.24–6

The death of the old Duke of Amalfi in January 1493 brought about a sudden change in Giovanna's life, obliging her to take on the onerous adult responsibilities appropriate to her new role as the Duchess of Amalfi. But as this transformation came about in her private world, so the external world around her began to tremble and tilt out of kilter. Momentous changes had occurred during the preceding year, changes which were to abruptly overturn life as she had hitherto known it. The conquest of Granada by Ferdinand, King of Aragon, and the consequent expulsion of the Moors from Spain; the death of the great mediator Lorenzo de' Medici in Florence; and the death of Pope Innocent VIII in Rome, which led to the rise of the perfidious Borgia family – all these factors suddenly converged to transform the tenuous equilibrium of Italian politics and radically disturb the balance of the political status quo in Western Europe.

The year 1492 was one of far-reaching changes, and especially for Spain. On 2 January Granada fell to the Spanish monarchs Ferdinand of Aragon and his wife, Isabella of Castille, who were then able to expel the Moors from their kingdom. It was hailed as a victory for Christendom and they became known as 'The Catholic Monarchs' in recognition of their achievement.

In March Ferdinand and Isabella compounded their victory for Christianity by also expelling from Spain all Jews who refused to embrace the Catholic faith. By August of that year, Giovanna would have noticed the shiploads of exiled Jews docking at the port of Naples and establishing themselves in the city, where they were tolerantly received by her less punctilious grandfather, King Ferrante. But while the Spanish Jews were still journeying towards Naples, her attention, and that of the city, had been occupied by the great festivities organised at court to honour Ferdinand and Isabella as the saviours of Christianity.

The news of the fall of Granada took a month to arrive in Naples and when it did, three days of solemn processions through the city streets celebrated the event.[1] The festivities at court continued into the carnival season, culminating in two grand banquets given by Alfonso of Calabria and his brother Federico at Castelcapuano to honour their father and stepmother, respectively cousin and sister of the saviour of Christendom, Ferdinand of Aragon. Masques to entertain the guests at these banquets were hurriedly composed by the court poet Jacopo Sannazaro, and members of the royal family participated personally as actors – the Duke of Calabria's son Ferrante (Ferrandino), Prince of Capua, at his father's apartments and Don Federico at his own.[2] If the young Antonio Bologna were already in Don Federico's household at this time, Giovanna might have seen him; though if his epitaph is correct, he must have been only about ten years old to her thirteen or fourteen.

When, at the close of the festivities, Queen Giovanna III thanked her two stepsons for the entertainment they had provided and expressed her pleasure and satisfaction at all the tributes offered to both her brother and her husband, she was perhaps unaware that this same wily husband had been secretly inciting the Moors against her brother for some years! King Ferrante put a good face on it and smiled throughout the celebrations, but in reality he was extremely disquieted by the events. His claim to the Kingdom of Naples was derived from an illegitimate title, while Ferdinand's represented the legitimate line of the House of Aragon. Ferrante's fears were justified: as long as the Spanish king had been preoccupied with driving out the Moors, he had little opportunity to occupy himself with Naples; but with the problem of the Moors resolved, Ferdinand soon began to turn his attentions to Italy.

On 9 April 1492, shortly after the festivities for the fall of Granada, Lorenzo de' Medici, Lord of Florence, died at the age of forty-three. With his death, Italy lost an important intermediary and buffer in the conflict between the papacy and the Kingdom of Naples. As the feudal overlord of the Kingdom, the Pope could refuse to grant the right of succession to Ferrante's descendants, transferring it instead to the French King, who had taken over the Anjou claim to the Neapolitan throne. A letter written to Lorenzo by the Florentine ambassador in Naples summed up the anxieties of the time regarding the papacy and the balance of power in Italy.

> King Ferrante's minister, Pontano, knows that the demise of his master would be a great loss in Italy; if the pope dies before him he could be followed by another more foolish or more intelligent pope; if he were more foolish he could be bowled over by a few stones thrown at his breast; if he were more intelligent he would wish to maintain the church's reputation and the consequence would be a serious war between two intelligent men. If, on the other hand, his majesty were the first to go, everyone could, if they wished, please themselves as the occasion suited them and such a confused political situation must be avoided at all costs.[3]

Unfortunately it was Lorenzo, the vital mediating element in the political equilibrium of the peninsula, who unexpectedly died before either King Ferrante or the Pope. His successor, his son Piero, was unfortunately not of the same calibre as his father, and he proved incapable of steering either Florence or Italy away from the disaster course on which they were set.

Lorenzo had been well aware of the importance of holding sway over the papacy and, for this reason, in 1487 he married off his fifteen-year-old daughter Maddalena to Franceschetto Cybo, the rough, uncouth son of Pope Innocent VIII. In exchange for this sacrifice, Lorenzo's fourteen-year-old son, Giovanni de' Medici, was precociously given a cardinal's hat. The wedding ceremony of Maddalena scandalised contemporaries because the banquet took place in the Vatican Palace, thus giving the Pope's offspring a sort of recognised legitimacy. The papal master of ceremonies, Johannes Burkhardt,[4] noted with regret that it was the first time a successor of Saint Peter had sat down and entertained a woman at his table, contravening the norm *mulieres esse in convivio cum pontifice*, which forbade it. But Pope Innocent had set a precedent, and a year later the situation was repeated when his granddaughter Peretta was also married in the Vatican Palace.

King Ferrante, urged by Lorenzo to follow his example and seek a matrimonial alliance with the Pope's family, attempted to secure Peretta as a bride for one of his own offspring, but she was already betrothed and the Pope was unwilling or unable to annul the betrothal in order to favour

Ferrante. However, the idea of a marriage alliance was not definitively shelved, and by the summer of 1491, Lorenzo was making new overtures to both the King and the Pope on the subject. In November, Ferrante sent his minister Pontano on a secret mission to Rome to seek a negotiated solution favourable to both parties. This was achieved in January 1492.

In May Ferrante sent his grandson Ferrandino to Rome to ratify the agreement. He also ordered his other grandson, Giovanna's elder brother, Luigi d'Aragona, Marquis of Gerace, to accompany his cousin. It was the beginning of eighteen-year-old Luigi's diplomatic career and a mission in which his role was to be crucial. By this time it had become imperative for Ferrante to pacify the Pope and seal a close bond with his family, if he were to staunch the growing sympathy between France and the papacy that threatened to prejudice the succession of his heirs to the throne of Naples. Luigi was to be the kingpin of this bond.

It was unfortunate that Lorenzo de' Medici died before he could see the accord between King Ferrante and the Pope, which he had so carefully helped to engineer, come to fruition in June of that year. But he must have died comforted by the conviction that the political situation of Italy had been saved from disaster. The contemporary historian Guicciardini looked back nostalgically on this period of apparent concord, when it seemed Italy had reached a new pinnacle of well-being and prosperity and 'such were the foundations of balanced tranquillity in Italy, that not only did no one fear its present alteration, but neither could they conceive of what army could disturb so much peace'.[5] It was merely the calm before the storm. The crisis in relations between France and the Italian states was rapidly coming to a head and soon the loss of Lorenzo's tempered sagacity was to be sadly regretted. 'Once Lorenzo was dead,' Machiavelli's *Florentine Histories* concludes, 'those evil seeds began to be born that . . . ruined and still ruin Italy.'

Although this was his first active involvement, Giovanna's brother, Luigi d'Aragona had been present on previous diplomatic occasions. At the age of twelve, in October 1486, at the height of the crisis of the Great Barons' Revolt, he and two other dignitaries greeted the Spanish ambassador on his arrival in Naples from Rome. In October 1489 he figured more actively when he became the hero of a tournament, held by his grandfather King Ferrante in the tiltyard of Castelnuovo, to entertain the ambassadors of France, Castille, Venice, Florence and Milan. Ferrante was increasingly isolated diplomatically in this period and was at pains to entertain and impress the ambassadors with his family's prestige.

In medieval and early Renaissance society tournaments were not merely sporting events, equivalent to modern football games; rather, they were both military training grounds for the art of war and affirmations of political power, status and wealth. The aim of the tilt was not to kill one's opponent but merely to break his unarmed wooden lance and/or unseat him from his horse. Contests, however, were still fraught with risks. As the knights charged towards one another, separated by a stout wooden fence, swift blows could cause considerable damage. In 1524, for example, Henry VIII of England was almost killed, while in 1559 Henry II of France met his death during a contest.

Luigi was only fifteen and this was probably his first official tournament, but he carried himself off magnificently against older, stronger and more experienced knights. His finely tooled suit of armour, made heavier on the left side to bear the brunt of the wooden lances, barely compensated for his light physique and wiry constitution. Giovanna and the rest of the court would have watched his skill and audacity with a mixture of admiration and apprehension as he broke three of his opponents' lances and even knocked an opponent's horse to the ground, unseating its rider.

We know little of the relationship between Giovanna and Luigi as children, but, in later life, Luigi was a strong, proud, authoritarian man and Giovanna grew into an equally strong-willed but passionate woman. If we presume that these characteristics were forming as they grew up, one wonders if their personalities had already begun to clash. They would have been thrown together during the sojourns of their early childhood at Gerace, but at the royal palace in Naples their paths would have divided, Luigi pursuing masculine activities in the company of male cousins and courtiers. He was almost sixteen when Giovanna finally left Castelcapuano for her husband's household and after that, the emotional separation would have become definitive, for Giovanna then fell under the protection of the Piccolomini family and was no longer legally subject to Luigi as head of the family. Only in widowhood did she revert to the latter.

Renaissance women were subject to the wills of their male relatives, first their fathers, then their husbands and finally their sons. Matteo Bandello, with exceptional modernity, laments this situation of affairs in his introduction to the story of the Duchess of Amalfi. He wonders how men would receive their just deserts if the situation were reversed, and asks if women would be as merciless with men as men are with their womenfolk.

The point is hypothetical, but helps to focus on the similarities and divergences in character between Giovanna and her elder brother. They shared the same qualities of determination and courage and, when necessary, both were cunning and devious, but where Luigi was cold and calculating, Giovanna was governed by passion. However, in the absence of adequate written sources, we cannot know for certain whether they were linked by fraternal love in this early period, or merely tied by family bonds.

Luigi was certainly loved by his grandfather King Ferrante, who was swelled with paternal pride at the tournament of 1489 and immensely gratified that the foreign ambassadors had been suitably impressed by the prowess of this up-and-coming member of the Neapolitan royal family.[6] Luigi had begun to reveal those fearless and warlike traits of character, which in later life were to make him an able and respected soldier.

The following year he appears to have taken in hand the reins of government at his fiefdom of Gerace, but he was as yet still an inexperienced youth and encountered difficulty obtaining due respect from his subjects. In June 1490 he was forced to invoke his grandfather's aid to obtain payment of the *adoha* land tax owing to him. Ferrante seriously reprimanded the inhabitants of Gerace and warned them that any offence or annoyance given to his beloved grandson would be deemed a slight to the King himself.[7]

Ferrante's affection for the late Enrico would in any event have ensured an important position at his grandfather's court for Luigi, but the death of the Duke of Calabria's younger son, Pietro, in 1491, meant that Luigi stepped into his place as the closest collaborator of the Duke's heir, Ferrandino (second in line to the throne). Thus it was that when Ferrandino arrived in Rome on 27 May 1492 to sign the peace agreement between Naples and the papacy, Luigi was chosen to accompany him and seal the peace treaty by marrying the Pope's granddaughter.

The two royal princes travelled to Rome attended by some of King Ferrante's longest-serving and faithful courtiers, among whom was Alfonso D'Avalos, Marquis of Pescara. When Webster introduces the character of 'the old Marquis of Pescara' into *The Duchess of Malfi*, he confuses Alfonso D'Avalos with his son, Francesco Ferrante D'Avalos (born 1490). Alfonso D'Avalos was always a staunch supporter of the Aragon cause and died fighting heroically for them in 1495; but this was some ten years before the love affair between Giovanna d'Aragona and Antonio Bologna.

Another faithful servant of King Ferrante who accompanied Ferrandino and Luigi to Rome in May 1492 was Giovanna's father-in-law, Antonio Piccolomini, Duke of Amalfi. Considering that the projected outcome of the peace negotiations was to be the marriage of Luigi d'Aragona to the Pope's granddaughter, it is reasonable to presume that Luigi's sister Giovanna and her husband Alfonso Piccolomini also accompanied the old Duke, so that they could be present for the celebration of the marriage.

The main object of Ferrandino's visit to Rome was to obtain from Pope Innocent VIII the investiture of the throne of Naples for his father, in order to secure the Aragonese succession. During the spring of 1492, French envoys had been trying unsuccessfully to obtain this for the King of France, Charles VIII, but on 4 June the Pope decided in favour of the Aragonese. The red-faced French envoy, Perron de Baschi, stormed and protested outside the door of the secret consistory to no avail. While the Pope read the Bull, he was barred entry. Only the previous day, the Pope's goodwill towards the House of Aragon had been assured by the marriage of his granddaughter, Battistina Usodimare, to King Ferrante's grandson, Luigi d'Aragona.[8]

The wedding ceremony took place in the Vatican before the Pope, Ferrandino, the Duke of Amalfi, the Marquis of Pescara and other barons and cardinals. Giovanna and her sister Caterina were almost certainly among the eight women present.[9] Caterina's family were by now closely connected to the papacy, for her father-in-law, the Count of Pitigliano, had become Commander-in-Chief of the papal army. Temporarily reunited, the two sisters watched the Archbishop of Ragusa enter the hall and kneel the prescribed two paces from the Pope to deliver his homily on the sacrament of marriage. The sermon, long and tedious, tried everyone's patience. Perhaps it was this that overwhelmed the young Battistina, or maybe there were deeper motives for her anxiety: when the Archbishop finally rose and turned to bless the marriage, it was only after a long moment of silence that she pronounced the fateful 'si' (I do).[10]

The celebrations for both his granddaughter's marriage to Luigi d'Aragona and the definitive cessation of the papacy's hostilities towards King Ferrante furnished a fresh occasion for the Pope to make a display of magnificence in the Vatican Palace. Giovanna and her relations were seated at a long banqueting table covered with all manner of delicacies such as cooked storks, cranes, pheasants, sturgeons and eels. Between courses was a masque: Orpheus appeared plucking his lyre, while Ceres's triumphal float, pulled by tigers, made its way up and down the hall and Perseus released an Andromeda. At each interval this classical cast recited flowery verses in honour of the newly-weds. Notably, all the symbolism of the wedding banquet was pagan – a symptom of an increasingly secular papacy and of the revival of classical learning. The presence of women at the banquet again caused the papal master of ceremonies, Burkhardt, to protest.

How much Luigi was able to enjoy his young wife is uncertain. Battistina was probably in her very early teens, about the same age as her childhood playmate, Lucrezia Borgia, and Luigi's sister Giovanna. It seems unlikely therefore that she was old enough to consummate the marriage. In fact certain sources[11] maintain that the marriage was never consummated. But despite her youth, Battistina was already gaining a reputation for beauty and extravagance. When, just a year later in June 1493, she was bridesmaid at Lucrezia Borgia's marriage to Giovanni Sforza, she almost stole the attention from the bride with her stunning aquamarine gown. Beautiful as she might be, by this time Battistina's situation had changed completely. Her important role had been taken over by Lucrezia Borgia and her marriage to Luigi d'Aragona was now politically obsolete.

A temporary improvement in the health of the ailing Pope Innocent enabled him to take part in the celebrations for Battistina's wedding, but after this he declined rapidly and died on 25 July 1492. So, little more than a month after her marriage, the death of her grandfather annulled Battistina's political usefulness as far as the Neapolitan House of Aragon was concerned. Royal marriages at this date were primarily intended as political alliances. Emotional attachment was an advantage but by no means a necessity. If Luigi had developed any sort of conjugal relationship with Battistina, which is doubtful, he had no choice but to renounce it when it became evident that his grandfather had greater plans for him.

By December 1493 Ferrante was already making overtures to the new Pope, Alexander VI (Rodrigo Borgia), to have Luigi appointed a cardinal, and the marriage with Battistina was simply annulled.[12] Battistina was still alive at the end of 1495, when we hear of Lucrezia Borgia setting off to visit her and being forced to turn back because the Tiber had flooded.[13] Thereafter, no more mention is made of her. The previous year her ex-husband, Luigi d'Aragona, had received his cardinal's hat from Rome, and of him we hear a great deal.

Pope Pius II had inaugurated a tradition of nepotism in the papacy by trying to carve out a state for his Piccolomini nephews. His example was then followed by the Della Rovere Pope, Sixtus IV (1471–84), builder of the Sistine Chapel, who set about increasing the fortunes of his fairly modest family by procuring lands and wealth for his numerous nephews, one of whom at least was reputed to be his illegitimate son. But with Giambattista Cybo, who took the name Innocent VIII (1484–92), nepotism assumed an even more blatant form, whereby children of the Pope were openly recognised and entered the Vatican Palace as such. Such relaxation of moral canons paved the way for the nadir of uninhibited decadence under Innocent's successor, Rodrigo Borgia, who took the name Alexander VI when he was elected Pope in August 1492 (see page 43).

At the outset of Rodrigo Borgia's papacy, however, there was a certain public indignation, not so much for the doubtful moral standards of the new Pope, as for the simoniacal way he obtained the papal crown. The Italian cardinals were determined not to elect a foreign pope, but in the end it was the wealth of this Spanish cardinal which had tipped the balance. Simony had for long been an integral feature of papal elections, but it is said that the wheeling and dealing of Rodrigo Borgia took the practice to new heights.

The general feeling at the time, however, was not unfavourable to Borgia's election.[14] He was regarded as one of the most capable of the cardinals. Contemporaries considered him ambitious, fairly well informed, of ready and incisive speech, but secretive and singularly expert in the conduct of affairs. He was majestic in stature and dignified in manner. His contemporary, Sigismondo de' Conti, says he was 'tall and powerfully built and though he had somewhat twitching eyes, they were penetrating and lively. In conversation he was extremely affable and he understood money matters thoroughly.' The Bishop of Modena described Rodrigo as 'Il più carnale homo' (the most carnal of men) and this was a very accurate assessment.[15]

Born in Spain in 1432, he followed his uncle, Alfonso Borgia, to Italy in 1444, and when this uncle became Pope Callixtus III in 1455, Rodrigo was soon nominated cardinal. In 1460 Pope Pius II, who was by no means narrow-minded and had in his youth lived a life of sensual indulgence, found himself forced to reprimand Cardinal Borgia for an incident that brought the Church into grave disrepute. Rodrigo Borgia had been invited, together with other clerics, to the celebration of a baptism. During the party which followed, Rodrigo and his companions barred the door to the fathers, brothers and husbands of the young women present, and spent the rest of the day in their company, drinking, dancing and 'taking all the liberties they desired'. Someone commented after the affair: 'By God, if all the children born a year hence in this place came into the world in their father's clothes, they'd all be dressed as cardinals and priests!'[16]

When the families of the women complained to the Pope, he reproved Rodrigo, but his complaint fell on deaf ears and Rodrigo continued his libertine lifestyle. He is thought to have fathered at least six illegitimate children, although only the four he had by Vanozza Cattanei – Cesare, Juan, Lucrezia and Joffre – took on political importance. Lucrezia Borgia was little more than a pawn to be shifted strategically through a chess game of marriage alliances, but it was her ambitious elder brother Cesare who was the main piece on the chessboard (Plate 25). In character Cesare was his father's son, but he lacked Rodrigo's saving grace of humanity. Rodrigo's sincere love for his children gave a patina of justification to his policies. In Cesare's heart there was room only for his own ambitions.

On becoming Pope, Rodrigo continued the policy inaugurated by Pius II of carving out a state in Italy for his family. He soon made Cesare a cardinal and set about seeking lands for his other son, Juan. But Cesare, unwilling to take what he perceived as a secondary role in the Church, and jealous of his father's preference for Juan, is thought to have instigated his brother's murder in order to throw off his clerical vestments and set his sights on a temporal throne. Although initially he had been guided by his father, towards the end of Alexander's life their roles reversed and, rather like Frankenstein, Alexander was no longer able to control the monster he had created.

Rodrigo and Cesare Borgia eventually brought the papacy to its lowest moral point and yet, arguably, to its political apogee. Cesare subjugated the undisciplined fiefs of the Papal Marches and re-established effective political control over the petty overlords who nominally bowed to papal authority while effectively ignoring it. At the same time, however, he and his father brought the Church into the greatest disrepute. Certainly the old-fashioned papal master of ceremonies, Burkhardt, a rigid cleric transferred from the chilly climes of his native Strasbourg, never came to terms with the laxity and propensity for joie de vivre that characterised the behaviour of his warmer-blooded Mediterranean counterparts. And by 1501 he must have been despairing of the essential Christian morals of the papacy, let alone the traditional etiquette.

Rodrigo Borgia's papacy opened as it meant to continue. At the wedding of the new Pope's thirteen-year-old daughter, Lucrezia, to Giovanni Sforza on 12 June 1493, Burkhardt was scandalised that many of the guests, in their enthusiasm to participate in the festivities, forgot to bow to his holiness on entering into his presence. He considered this a grave sign of moral anarchy. It was – but there was far worse to come.

After the wedding, at a more intimate dinner held in the papal apartments for a restricted number of guests, the Pope, in a moment of euphoria, began to throw sugar confetti *in sinu multarum mulierum*, as the contemporary Roman diarist, Stefano Infessura, puts it. Whether Pope Alexander actually meant to aim at the women's cleavage is open to speculation, but the hilarity it aroused brought forth the suggestion that the women should bare their breasts and hold a competition to see who could gather up the largest number of confetti without touching them with their hands . . . which meant using their breasts! The Pope's young mistress, Giulia Farnese, won.

Giovanna d'Aragona may not have been present at the wedding, for her husband's family may still have been in mourning for the death of her father-in-law earlier that year. But her new sister-in-law, Battistina, was a maid of honour for Lucrezia, and Caterina was probably present, since her father-in-law, the Count of Pitigliano, was one of the chief functionaries at the ceremony and her sister-in-law, Lella Orsini, was also a maid of honour. Whether or not any of these women took part in the salacious games that titillated the wedding guests is not known, for only Giulia Farnese is named in Infessura's account.[17]

In any event, the occasion set the moral tone for the rest of the papacy. The abyss came on 31 October 1501, paradoxically the eve of All Saints' Day, for the ensuing pagan bacchanal was anything but saintly. Cesare Borgia had invited his father, Pope Alexander, and his sister Lucrezia, to a banquet in his apartments at the Vatican Palace. The event was afterwards nicknamed 'Il ballo delle castagne' (The Dance of the Chestnuts). The punctilious Latin that Burkhardt uses to describe what happened at the end of the banquet denotes a sort of ultramontane resignation that by now must have quelled his northern indignation. Cesare had invited fifty 'honest courtesans' to dance and entertain his father and sister. As they danced they took off all their clothes. It could be argued, rightly, that there is nothing sinful in the beauty of the human form, but matters did not stop there. Thoroughly excited by the naked women, Cesare ordered the lighted

Rodrigo Borgia, Pope Alexander VI: detail of fresco by Pinturicchio (*the Borgia Apartments, the Vatican, Rome,* © *Alinari*).

candelabra to be taken from the tables and placed on the ground. Then he and his father began throwing chestnuts onto the floor amid the burning candles and the women were ordered to pick them up by crawling around on their hands and knees. Not satisfied with this, Cesare had a selection of fine silk capes, stockings and hats brought in, which he offered as prizes to those menservants present who could copulate publicly with the greatest number of women. Burkhardt says tritely 'in aula publice carnaliter tractae arbitrio presentium'.[18] A Florentine emissary, Francesco Pepi, noted that Pope Alexander did not participate in the traditional Remembrance Day mass for the dead in St Peter's the following day, owing to a slight indisposition which had not, however, prevented him from enjoying the revelry of the previous night.

This, then, was the moral climate in which the young Duchess of Amalfi lived and in which those closest to her participated. Her cousin Sancia, her sister Caterina and her sister-in-law Battistina were all closely involved with the Borgia family and cannot have avoided (always assuming they wished to) contact with its now habitual debauchery. Giovanna's behaviour suggests that she strove to set herself apart, on a higher and more noble plane, but, ironically, when she placed love above ambition, many of her contemporaries judged her as harshly as they had judged the Borgias for ceding to the temptations of carnality.

Let us now turn back to the early years of the Borgia papacy and examine the crisis that was brewing around the Duchess of Amalfi in her native Naples. After the death of Pope Innocent VIII, the truce between the papacy and the Kingdom of Naples was destined to be short-lived, and relations between the new Pope Alexander VI and King Ferrante soon became strained. Ferrante was alarmed by the sympathy Alexander immediately manifested towards the francophile Sforzas in Milan.

Ludovico Sforza, better known as Ludovico il Moro (a nickname he gained in his youth because of his dark skin and hair),[19] had long been usurping the powers which rightly belonged to his ineffectual nephew, Gian Galeazzo Sforza, Duke of Milan. Gian Galeazzo had married Giovanna's cousin Isabella d'Aragona in 1489. Isabella's life in Milan was fraught with tensions from the very outset. During the initial scandal of her marriage not being consummated because of her husband's ill-health, she was obliged to fend off the approaches of Il Moro, who, rather than return her conspicuous dowry, was prepared to perform his nephew's duty for him. It would have been no great sacrifice, since Isabella was certainly attractive, as can be seen from the beautiful sketch of her by Leonardo da Vinci's pupil, Giovanni Antonio Boltraffio (Plate 30). Isabella was celebrated as Duchess of Milan by masques and operas directed by Leonardo himself. One, performed in her honour in January 1490, was an allegory of Paradise. But Isabella's life in Milan was far from idyllic. She wrote numerous bitter letters to her father and grandfather in Naples, complaining that Il Moro was behaving as though he were Duke and his new young wife, Beatrice d'Este (also Ferrante's granddaughter, since she was the daughter of Eleonora d'Aragona, Duchess of Ferrara), took precedence at court over herself.

The slights and humiliations in the rivalry between the two young women did not move their grandfather to action, however, until certain political implications came to the fore, namely Il Moro's sympathy towards the French and the sway his brother, Cardinal Ascanio Sforza, held over the new Borgia Pope. In a dispatch sent to his envoy in Spain on 7 March

1493, Ferrante indulged in a bitter invective against Pope Alexander. He complained that Rome was becoming a Borgia tyranny and a Milanese camp with all its sympathies drawn towards France. The outburst was really directed at his brother-in-law, Ferdinand the Catholic, whom he hoped to induce into an alliance in the event of a conflict. Ferdinand had no more desire than Ferrante to see French hegemony in Italy.[20]

The marriage of Lucrezia Borgia to Il Moro's cousin Giovanni Sforza in June 1493 soon confirmed Ferrante's accusations. Ferrante feared that Il Moro's brother was mediating with the new Pope to obtain the crown of Naples for the King of France. In this way Il Moro hoped to secure French support for his own nomination as Duke of Milan in place of his nephew Gian Galeazzo. But, by the end of June, Ferrante and Ferdinand had won Pope Alexander over by offering lucrative marriage alliances for his sons Juan and Joffre Borgia.[21] The agreement was ratified on 1 August and when the French ambassador, Perron de Baschi, arrived in Rome a few days later to demand the investiture of Naples for Charles VIII, he found that he had again been pre-empted.

However, Alexander was by no means reconciled with King Ferrante. This became evident when he nominated a series of new cardinals in September 1493 and Ferrante's family was not represented among the nominations. True, the fifteen-year-old Ippolito d'Este was Ferrante's grandson, but he was chiefly bound to the policies of his father's Duchy of Ferrara. Since the death of Ferrante's son Giovanni in 1485, there had been no Cardinal of Aragon to represent the interests of Naples at the Vatican court. If it was not to be dependent upon the vacillating loyalties of cardinals like Giuliano Della Rovere or Oliviero Carafa, it was essential that Ferrante's family be as powerfully represented in Rome as those of other important Italian ruling families.

It is in the light of this situation that Ferrante began to seek the nomination of Giovanna's elder brother. Luigi was bold and intelligent enough to aspire to the papacy. With a member of the Neapolitan House of Aragon seated on the papal throne, there would be no more need to fear French intrusion in the Kingdom and the future succession of Ferrante's dynasty would be assured. This is what Ferrante had in mind when the first overtures were made to the Pope in December 1493. A letter, dated 20 December 1493, states that, according to the Florentine ambassador, King Ferrante of Naples had asked Pope Alexander to nominate Luigi d'Aragona as cardinal. At first the Pope seemed disposed to promote him, as early as

Christmas, but then he declared he could not make a layman a cardinal: the King must wait for Luigi to become first a *protonotario* or bishop of the Church and then wait a few months for the promotion to come to pass.[22]

Alexander was playing for time, but time for Ferrante was running out. Just a few weeks later a chill forced him to renounce a hunting expedition and return to Castelnuovo. Two days later complications set in. He died on 25 January 1494. Giovanna joined the other members of her family on 27 January to pay her respects to her grandfather's body, embalmed and laid in state in the *Gran Sala* of Castelnuovo. The pivotal force that had shaped her destiny had suddenly been removed. Beyond any personal sorrow at the passing of this monarch, who had been the only kind of father she had known, she must have shared in the general feeling of bewilderment, dismay and fear of future instability that accompanied Ferrante's death. A pall of anxiety spread itself over the Kingdom. Everyone was aware that an era had come to an end.

With the danger of a French invasion fast becoming imminent, Ferrante could not have chosen a worse moment to make his exit from the stage of Italian politics. He had been in his early seventies when he died, and had reigned for almost forty years. For the lower orders of Naples, if not for all the baronage, he had become a point of reference, a long-standing *punto fisso*. Though Alfonso of Calabria had for some time been his father's military arm and political executor, it was Ferrante who, in the last resort, had decided the policies to be adopted. He was no man's fool and even his enemies respected his intelligence. It was a degree of respect that his less stoical son Alfonso was never able to command.

On the evening of 31 January, over a thousand mourners accompanied the dead King by torchlight procession from Castelnuovo to his last resting-place in the church of San Domenico Maggiore. The continuous dragging of the nobles' rich, black velvet trains swept along the streets until they shone. The journey was replete with melancholy splendour. A chronicler describes the bishops in jewelled mitres and capes walking beneath a precious silk canopy estimated to be worth 1,000 ducats; the coffin itself was covered by a cloth of brocade worth 6,000 ducats; at its head lay a crimson cushion bearing a crown inlaid with diamonds and rubies as large as walnuts, worth at least 20,000 ducats. . . . And so the writer continues, informing us of the cost of Ferrante's death and reminding us that the value of a man is measured by the ostentation of his wealth. A finer touch was the funeral oration given by Francesco Pucci, one of the most respected intellectuals of the Aragonese court, who eventually became secretary to Giovanna's brother Luigi.[23]

Ferrante's remains, contained in a lead coffin encased in a more elaborate one made of wood, were left on view beneath a richly draped canopy in the apse of San Domenico Maggiore, as a reminder that Ferrante's eternal spirit still lived on in Naples. Giovanna's palace was adjacent to this church and from now on, when she attended mass, she would render homage to her grandfather's body and perhaps pray for guidance from his spirit. Ferrante had been no saint, but he had certainly been wise.

A month after the funeral, on 1 March, Giovanna's husband was called to the *Gran Sala* of Castelnuovo with other barons of the realm for the ceremony of swearing loyalty to the new King, Alfonso of Calabria, who assumed the title King Alfonso II. It was a sombre moment and the Duke of Amalfi and most of his peers put little faith in Alfonso's ability to take his father's place. The petty ambitions of the multitude of Italian states began to come to the fore in an anarchy of self-interest that Ferrante and Lorenzo de' Medici had tried to eschew, and no one gave a thought to the words of Petrarch, uttered 150 years before in his ode '*Italia mia, benché 'l parlar sia indarno a le piaghe mortali* . . . (My Italy, although it is futile to discuss your great woes . . .),[24] when he had appealed to the lords of the Italian states to put aside their rivalry and desist from inviting foreign mercenaries to fight on Italian soil.

In the autumn of 1494 when Ludovico il Moro opened the gates of Milan to welcome the French in support of their claims to the newly vacated throne of Naples, he set Italy on a course of self-destruction. What Giovanna's grandfather and Lorenzo il Magnifico had worked so hard to avoid had come to pass and she and her family would be caught up, inescapably, in the maelstrom.

CHAPTER 4

Tumult in the Kingdom

BOSOLA So:
What follows? never rain'd such showers as these
Without thunderbolts i' the tail of them.

John Webster, *The Duchess of Malfi*, I.i.248–50

Preparations began for the coronation of the new King. His nickname in Naples, Alfonso 'the Abominable', was in stark contrast to that of his grandfather Alfonso, 'the Magnanimous'. But his grandfather could afford to be magnanimous; the political situation that Alfonso II inherited left little leeway for magnanimity. Quite unexpectedly, Alfonso, the harsh man who had dominated King Ferrante during his last years, when deprived of his father's firm guiding hand, seemed suddenly to lose his grasp of reality in the face of the complex convergence of political circumstances which greeted his accession. He had inherited his father's power but not his political subtlety.

In February 1494 Bernardo Dovizi da Bibbiena, who had travelled to Naples on behalf of Piero de' Medici to negotiate Florence's position with the new King, was astounded by the false sense of security manifested by Alfonso II and his minister, Pontano. When Bibbiena raised the problem of the claims of Charles VIII of France to the throne of Naples, Alfonso shot to his feet and shouted arrogantly: 'Even if all France came, they'd do us no harm; they'd just go back where they came from like they did last time when there were seventeen thousand of them!'[1]

As soon as the news of Ferrante's death reached France, Charles VIII dispatched an emissary to Rome to inform Pope Alexander that if he showed himself favourable to Alfonso's succession in Naples, he would be threatened with a General Council for the reform of the Church –

something from which Alexander had much to fear. In mid-March, King Alfonso sent Giovanna's brother Luigi to Rome as part of a Neapolitan delegation to negotiate with Pope Alexander. A few days later, a consistory was held at which a Bull was read containing the Pope's formal decision in favour of the House of Aragon for the Neapolitan succession. Pope Alexander affirmed that the late Pope Innocent VIII had already granted the investiture of Naples to Alfonso when he was Duke of Calabria and now this could not be revoked. And just as Luigi d'Aragona's marriage was part of the first agreement, now his nomination as cardinal became part of the second.

Luigi returned to Naples and on 5 May resigned his fiefdom of Gerace in favour of his younger brother Carlo. The following day he was made *protonotario* and tonsured by the Bishop of Naples. This ceremonial shaving of the crown of the head symbolised the layman's renunciation of worldly things on his entrance into the priesthood. For nineteen-year-old Luigi it was an empty token. He had no intention of renouncing the temporal for the spiritual. After all, the essential purpose of his nomination had been secular rather than religious.[2]

Two days after he was tonsured, his uncle was crowned King in Naples Cathedral. Luigi was naturally one of the principal figures at the ceremony, as was Giovanna's husband, who held the bridle of King Alfonso's horse during the cavalcade. It was Ascension Day, an auspicious day for Alfonso's apotheosis, but the weather that morning boded ill; the sky was overcast and, as the procession entered the cathedral, it narrowly missed a torrential downpour.[3]

After the ceremony, the newly crowned King rode through the city streets, followed by a retinue of barons and nobles of the realm so splendidly attired that the spectators wondered where all the precious jewels had come from. The reins and saddlecloth of Alfonso's white horse were of silver brocade studded with pearls and diamonds and on the horse's forehead was an enormous ruby valued at 60,000 ducats. Alfonso's crown was richer still, adorned with huge precious gems estimated to be worth the incredible sum of 1,300,000 ducats. To the richness of the King's pageant, the owners of the *palazzi* along its route responded in kind, hanging from their balconies their most valuable arrases, brocades and velvets in an orgy of magnificence.

That evening, Giovanna accompanied her husband to the grand ball in the great hall of Castelnuovo. All the principal court events in her family,

The Duchess of Amalfi's cousin, Sancia d'Aragona, with her father, King Alfonso II (the large figure just behind her) and her new husband, Joffre Borgia, 16 May 1494 (*from the Codice Ferraiolo, Pierpont Morgan Library, New York, MS M. 801, f. 107*).

whether mournful funerals or joyful banquets, had taken place in this hall and by now Giovanna had seen it many times. To one side was the royal throne on an elevated tribune, where her uncle King Alfonso sat, not with his wife, for she had died, but with his stepmother, who could have passed for his wife, being seven years his junior.

In the wall facing the sea was the great monumental fireplace and from the platform above minstrels played festive compositions. Instead of echoing emptily in the high octagonal dome of the ceiling, the music was gently muffled by the huge tapestries that hung from each wall. The scenes portrayed in these priceless works of art were biblical, and while the visit of the Queen of Sheba to King Solomon was not discordant with the evening's mood, Roger van der Weyden's *Passion of Christ* was, for Giovanna, a sobering reminder of its veiled anxiety. But as she glided with her husband through the long slow steps of the *bassadanze*, she must have felt a certain serenity, for her family seemed at the pinnacle of success, now that the Pope had ratified her uncle's succession and nominated her brother a cardinal. Her own life too was set happily on course, for she and her husband had a young daughter, named Caterina after Giovanna's elder sister, who was almost certainly present too that evening, as was their illegitimate half-sister Ippolita (Ippolita had been brought to court and married in 1491).[4] It was a moment of contentment and reunion behind which lurked a recondite uneasiness.

Giovanna's cousin Sancia, the King's illegitimate daughter, was also present at the ball. She arrived on the arm of her new, important but unimpressively adolescent husband, Joffre Borgia. Their marriage had been decided upon and secretly ratified by King Ferrante before he died and formed part of the agreement by which the Pope had appointed Luigi Cardinal. The chief aim of the accord was to forge a new alliance with the papacy, since the marriage of Luigi and Battistina had ceased to fulfil this political role. Sancia was to be the new link. When the news reached her in the autumn of 1493, she was sixteen years old and had already been married for seven years (she was married at the age of nine). She was happily settled with her husband and they had consummated their union. Nevertheless, Pope Alexander annulled the marriage, her husband was given a new bride[5] and Sancia was obliged to marry the Pope's youngest son, Joffre. The whole arrangement was typical of contemporary attitudes towards women, who were little more than chattels to be moved from pillar to post as the necessity arose. The sanctity of marriage vows was a mere hypocrisy and Sancia soon began to manifest a lack of respect for them. The coronation ball was a painful evening for her, as she was obliged to watch the man she had learnt to love from childhood in the arms of another woman, while she was committed to a mere boy two years her junior. The pain added to the humiliation of her wedding night, which was witnessed by numerous officials to ensure that the union was consummated. Little wonder then that Sancia began to think that if she had to make love on command, and in public, she would command, herself.

Giovanna can only have been thankful that her own life was spared the tribulation of Sancia's. And yet, as she danced at this magnificent ball, which to all appearances was ushering in a new era of prosperity, the shadows of chaos were already falling over the new reign. The ball and all the other coronation ceremonies had been impeccably orchestrated by the punctilious papal master of ceremonies, Johannes Burkhardt, invited from Rome by King Alfonso for this specific task. Burkhardt was doubtless more at ease in the refined court of Naples than he had been in the increasingly ill-disciplined and licentious papal court of Rome. But the slick ceremonial did not reflect a similar smoothness in relations with the papacy, despite Sancia's wedding to Joffre Borgia.

The triumphal procession of the newly nominated Cardinal Luigi d'Aragona, 17 July 1494 (*from the Codice Ferraiolo, Pierpont Morgan Library, New York, MS M. 801, f. 104*).

The reign of Alfonso II, which had begun so splendidly, was destined to be short-lived. That squally shower at the doors of the cathedral was just the beginning of the 'tempest'. Only a month after his coronation, moved perhaps by his daughter Isabella's complaints, as well as political considerations, King Alfonso left the Kingdom to make war on Ludovico il Moro and return Milan to its rightful ruler, his son-in-law, Gian Galeazzo, who could more easily be won over to the cause of the Aragons of Naples.

Alfonso's stepmother was left to rule the Kingdom in his absence. But the forces of his army were slow to gather and on 3 July 1494 he wrote to the Queen requesting her to solicit latecomers who were still lingering in Naples. The Duke of Amalfi was one of these.[6] Giovanna's husband was obviously not in a hurry to follow the new King into what might prove a disastrous and futile military campaign. He was deliberately procrastinating, waiting to see how events would evolve and meanwhile he took the opportunity of participating in a family celebration – the triumphal parade of his brother-in-law, Cardinal Luigi d'Aragona.

While the King was away, on 17 July Luigi celebrated his elevation to the cardinalate. Dressed in a magnificent red cape and his newly acquired wide-brimmed red hat, he paraded through the streets of Naples seated on a white mule, preceded by a bevy of heralds and musicians and followed by archbishops, bishops, attendants and numerous other dignitaries.[7] There was pride and ostentation in his parade, but this was not its primary motivation. It was the usual practice at this time for new nominations to be communicated to the population by means of heralds proclaiming the news at the head of a solemn procession. Luigi was now officially a cardinal deacon, which meant that though he was a member of the Church hierarchy, he was unable to celebrate the mass.[8]

As Giovanna's husband had suspected, Alfonso's campaign against Ludovico il Moro was a fiasco. It served only to hasten Italy's descent into chaos, pushing Ludovico more firmly into the arms of the invading French. Alfonso found himself isolated and, without allies, his expedition got no further than Tuscany. He returned to Naples a changed man, as can be seen from the difference in his portraits in the contemporary Ferraiolo's chronicle where his usual self-confident hauteur is replaced by tight-lipped, resigned dejection.

On 9 September 1494 Charles VIII crossed the frontier into Italy, accompanied by the Neapolitan Sanseverino Princes of Salerno and Bisignano, who had been urging him to invade Naples since they had fled from King Ferrante in the wake of the Great Barons' Revolt of 1485–7. He was met at Asti by Ludovico il Moro, on behalf of the Duchy of Milan, and by Ludovico's father-in-law, Duke Ercole d'Este, on behalf of the Duchy of Ferrara. Ercole was also King Alfonso's brother-in-law, for his wife was Alfonso's elder sister, Eleonora d'Aragona. But Eleonora had died in October of the previous year and after her death Ercole, who already sympathised with the French cause, was drawn ever more closely into their camp. It was rumoured that he had had Eleonora poisoned both to stop her communicating his francophile intentions to her father and brother, and for fear that she might have him poisoned at her brother's behest.[9]

Having lost Ferrara as an ally, it was imperative for Alfonso to try to retain some control over his daughter's Duchy of Milan. But on 11 September 1494 it was not the Duchess of Milan who went with her ladies-in-waiting to welcome the young French King to Italian soil; it was her rival, Il Moro's wife, Beatrice d'Este. She was, however, most disagreeably impressed by Charles's unsightly appearance. He had an oversized head set on a tiny malformed body; his face was ugly and flabby and he spoke hesitatingly through thick slavering lips (Plate 26).

Il Moro and Beatrice had now taken over as Duke and Duchess of Milan in all but name, but the official Duke and Duchess were still Gian Galeazzo and Isabella. Accordingly, the King was escorted in gorgeous progress to the castle of Pavia where Gian Galeazzo lay dying. It was rumoured that Ludovico had ordered him to be slowly poisoned and there may have been some foundation in this accusation, although rumours of this sort always seemed to abound when the cause of death was in doubt. After he had recovered from his illness at the beginning of his marriage, Gian Galeazzo had proved to be an ardent husband (excessively so at times, Isabella complained) and had sired three children, two girls and a boy. But he also took to excesses in other respects, eating and drinking too much, and this contributed to his premature decline, which was watched over and encouraged by his uncle.

Isabella, compelled by Il Moro to receive the French King, was justifiably reluctant to do so, since Charles had sworn to destroy her dynasty. Once she was alone with him in her husband's sickroom, she fell at his feet and pleaded abjectly, begging him not to dethrone her father and persecute her family. The essentially good-natured King seemed moved by her pleas, but said that it was now too late for him to turn back. Gian Galeazzo died a few weeks later on 20 October and Ludovico il Moro, ignoring the rightful heir, Isabella's son Francesco, had himself proclaimed Duke of Milan.

King Alfonso hastened to reinforce the defences of the frontiers of his realm, leaving his stepmother in Naples as *Luogotenente* (Chief Lieutenant) of the Kingdom. But his defence plan was hampered by numerous difficulties and was not executed quickly or resolutely enough to be effective. Charles VIII swept down the peninsula virtually unhindered. The mere sight of his formidable artillery mounted on wheels was enough to frighten city after city into submission without a shot being fired. The whole of Italy fell like a row of dominoes before the French invasion. Since the greatest exertion it cost the invaders was for the quartermasters to chalk a mark on the doors of the houses that were requisitioned for the accommodation of the troops, it was nicknamed 'La Guerra di Gesso' (The Chalk War).

The terrified Piero de' Medici surrendered immediately to the French and fled from Florence, leaving the city to Charles and the fanatical priest,

Savonarola. Soon Pope Alexander found the French marching towards the gates of Rome and had no choice but to let them through. As they entered the city by the gate of Santa Maria del Popolo, King Alfonso's son, Ferrandino, left by the gate of San Sebastiano and retreated with his troops towards Naples. Alexander feigned welcoming the French but was in fact their prisoner. There was nothing he could do to stop them marching on to the city of Naples. He did, however, refuse to confer the investiture of the Kingdom of Naples on Charles VIII, despite the fact that the latter had made a formal act of submission to the papacy.

On 28 January 1495, without bothering to obtain the permission of the Pope, Charles left Rome and headed for Naples. Aquila and much of Abruzzo, alienated from the Aragonese by the brutal repression of 1485–6, declared for the French as soon as they appeared in the vicinity. At this point King Alfonso seems to have suffered a nervous collapse. The overconfident outburst to the Florentine emissary had been the first sign of his weakening. This once pitiless soldier suddenly found himself isolated, surrounded by hatred and tormented by remorse for the barbaric atrocities he had perpetrated.[10] Doubting both himself and those about him, he was overtaken by a religious crisis. He began to spend his days among priests and monks, continually reciting holy offices, serving the poor and washing their feet by way of penance for his sins. As the enemy advanced, he was paralysed into inaction and, on 23 January 1495, could think of no better solution than abdication.

It is to be wondered how much the removal of his father's coolly astute guiding hand had left Alfonso like a ship without a rudder, and how much the influence of his ambivalent minister, Pontano, contributed to Alfonso's decline. In a letter written to the new King, Ferrandino on 9 February, Pontano attributes the French invasion to heavenly designs, manifested by particular movements of stars and comets and to the avaricious and violent behaviour of his father and grandfather in their political policies. He did, however, urge Ferrandino to hold firm and resist because the French were 'impetuous and generally disorderly'. He considered they would not last long in the field, especially if Ferrandino managed to discredit them by defeating them in a minor skirmish.[11] This is, in effect, what was to come to pass, but not before Pontano had delivered both a speech of welcome and the keys of the city to Charles VIII when he arrived before the gates of Naples.

King Alfonso retired to Mazara in Sicily, a fiefdom belonging to his stepmother. There, it is said, after a period of meditation, he decided to take holy orders. His religious fervour continued and he spent his days reciting prayers and psalms. Eventually, owing to repeated mortification of the flesh, he caught an infection in a sore on his hand and either died from this or from kidney or gallstones at Messina on 18 December 1495 at the age of forty-seven.

What happened to the Duchess of Amalfi in all this turmoil? We cannot be sure where she was exactly, for only her husband is mentioned in the chronicles. She had probably taken refuge with her mother-in-law, Maria Marzano, and her sister-in-law, Eleonora Piccolomini, at the Piccolomini castle of Scafati, which was held directly as a fief of the papacy, independent of royal patronage. It is unlikely that she went to Amalfi for on 26 September 1494, knowing that Alfonso Piccolomini, Duke of Amalfi, was inclined to be sympathetic to the Aragonese cause, Charles VIII had issued a decree from Vercelli, near Milan, depriving him of his title. The Duchy of Amalfi was given instead to Giovanna's cousin Ferrante d'Este, a younger son of Duke Ercole d'Este of Ferrara, who had joined with the French forces. If Giovanna's husband had had any doubts as to which side to take in the coming conflict, the decision had been made for him in this decree. His interests lay with his wife's family, the House of Aragon, and he came down forcefully on the side of the new King, Alfonso II's son Ferrandino, who took the title Ferrante II.

When the 28-year-old King convoked the chief citizens of Naples to the church of Santa Chiara, the Duke of Amalfi dutifully left his *palazzo* a few yards away and went to listen to his moving speech. Calling them *padri e fratelli* (fathers and brothers) Ferrandino reminded them that he had been born and raised among them and admitted that, in the painful situation in which he found himself, he did not know where to turn or whom to trust. He appealed to them to hold faith with him for a few days, until the arrival of reinforcements. If these did not materialise, he left them free to act as they saw fit. Supplies were becoming scarce in the city, but there were sufficient in Castelnuovo to keep the city for a year and he offered to put the keys of the castle at their disposal. The citizens were moved, but not persuaded or resolved to support him.

Aware of the precarious situation, the Duke of Amalfi would doubtless have made preparations to send his wife and young daughter to the safety of Scafati when he returned to his palace. It is most unlikely, given the edict of Vercelli, that he and Giovanna would have remained in Naples to welcome the King of France as he entered the city claiming to be its new King. A large number of nobles defected from Ferrandino and began preparing to receive the French King when they realised that his arrival was imminent, but the Duke of Amalfi was not among them.

As the month of February progressed, events accelerated and Ferrandino's general, Trivulzio, passed to the French side, ceding Capua to them. When this last bulwark fell, the French proceeded rapidly towards Naples itself. On 20 February a French herald presented himself before the Porta Capuana, demanding that it be opened to the French King. Ferrandino, the old Queen and the Infanta were forced to retreat into Castelnuovo. For two days he was overcome by apathy, refusing to eat or to act despite the entreaties of the two women. He complained bitterly that he was about to lose his Kingdom without even breaking a lance, but was finally moved to action again when he heard that the populace was ransacking the royal stables. With a handful of courtiers and Swiss guards, he wounded a few of the rabble, sent them packing, and recovered some of the stolen horses.

The following day Alfonso D'Avalos, Marquis of Pescara, offered to defend Castelnuovo while Ferrandino retired to the safe haven of the impregnable island of Ischia, off the northern headland of the Bay of Naples. Pescara set about demolishing the arsenal and all the houses in the area contiguous with Castelnuovo, of which the enemy could have made use. As soon as he heard that the King of France's heralds were at the Porta Capuana, he set about bombarding the city from the bastions of Castelnuovo, sowing panic the among the inhabitants and sending them fleeing for safety.

On 21 February 1495, the women of the Aragon royal family and Ferrandino abandoned Castelnuovo and sailed to Ischia. The following day, Charles VIII took up residence in Giovanna's old home of Castelcapuano and gave orders to lay siege to the Marquis of Pescara in Castelnuovo with thirty pieces of artillery. The chronicler Passaro remarks wryly: 'I don't think even a fly would dare stick its nose outside Castelnuovo!'[12] The French began bombarding the castle and by 26 February a rebellion of Pescara's Swiss mercenaries forced him to abandon its defence and embark on a brigantine to join Ferrandino on Ischia. It is more than likely that the Duke of Amalfi also accompanied him, for later we hear of them fighting side by side for Ferrandino.

Ferrandino's arrival at Ischia had not been without incident. The Catalonian on guard there, who was in collusion with the French, at first refused him entry, but then said he could enter alone, which he did. Once inside, Ferrandino fell on the traitor and killed him. This induced enough fright and respect in the other guards to make them open the gates to Ferrandino's followers.

While Ferrandino was fighting his way onto Ischia, Charles had made his triumphal entry into Naples. The population was greatly dismayed at the sight of his big beret and enormous ugly head on a tiny body, which made him look like a hat on a horse! But the Neapolitans became even more disaffected with the uncouth behaviour of the French soldiers. The Arcadia, so praised by the poet Sannazaro, was torn apart as tumult reigned in Naples. Castelcapuano and King Alfonso II's Palace of the Duchesca were ransacked, as were the houses of Jews and *marrano* Christians (converted Jews) and womenfolk took refuge in the churches to escape the debauchery of the marauding French soldiers. The Neapolitans attributed to these invading Frenchmen the *mal franzese* (syphilis) which began to spread through the Kingdom at this time. The infection was, however, probably primarily diffused later by Ferrandino's Spanish soldiers, who had reputedly contracted it in the New World. But the Spaniards became the heroes of the day and eventually the conquerors, so it was more convenient to blame the French. Giovanna's brother Luigi had obviously not adhered to his vows of chastity, for he too became infected. He subsequently received a sympathetic letter of commiseration from his uncle Federico, with advice as to how to treat it.[13]

By mid-April, the whole Kingdom, save for the odd castle and island, was in French hands. Ferrandino, together with Don Federico, the old Queen and her daughter, set sail for Sicily, where they hoped to gain aid from their Spanish relations. The fiefdom of Gerace had fallen to the French commander, Eberhard Stewart d'Aubigny, and Cardinal Luigi d'Aragona certainly followed Ferrandino and his company to Sicily in order to retrieve it, as well as to aid his cousin the King.

It was common for noblewomen of this period to suffer conflicting loyalties, to be torn between the family into which they had been born and nurtured and the family into which they married and to which their children belonged. Giovanna's mother, Polissena Centelles, had suffered in this way and so did her mother-in-law, Maria Marzano, the dowager Duchess of Amalfi.

Maria Marzano may well have thought her son was backing a lost cause by supporting the Aragonese in the spring of 1495. The new French King had already confiscated his title to the Duchy of Amalfi, and the Piccolomini fief-holders in Abruzzo had thrown in their lot with the French invaders. By the time of his arrival in Naples, Charles VIII had decided to confiscate Celano as well as Amalfi from the Piccolomini. Maria set about saving her son's possessions in her own way.

As the daughter of a traditionally francophile family, she had no qualms about presenting herself to the new French King to swear her loyalty to him. Dressed in her finest gold brocade, on 5 March 1495 she arrived by carriage at the palace of Poggioreale in Naples to demand an audience with him. She had had the foresight to bring her spirited young daughter, Eleonora, to delight the King's eyes.[14] Encouraged by her mother to attract the King's attention, Eleonora offered to demonstrate her skills as a horsewoman for, she claimed, the women of Naples were as able as the men when it came to managing a horse. A large Apulian colt was produced and, in the magnificent grounds of the villa that stretched down towards the sea, she amazed the King and his court by riding with such skill that one of the courtiers likened her to an Amazon or a virago. She gave the horse his head and had him galloping, turning, jumping and rearing with such grace and mastery as to put even a man to envy.[15] The episode was repeated on 23 March and by this time Eleonora had really wheedled herself into the King's graces. For a few weeks Charles was quite taken with her and she was invited to return to his court every day. The people of Naples began to murmur that she had become the French King's favourite.[16]

But her moment of glory was short-lived. During Easter Week a woman of the Gonzaga family, who had taken the King's fancy while he had been at Lucca in Tuscany, arrived in Naples and rekindled the King's passion. Eleonora continued to frequent his court but ceased to be considered his favourite. Her flirtation had, however, achieved its objective. Thanks to Eleonora's charms, the fief of Celano was saved. How much Alfonso Piccolomini knew or approved of his mother's and his sister's flirting with the enemy is not known, but it was always wise in those uncertain times to keep a foot in more than one camp. The edict of Vercelli, depriving Alfonso Piccolomini of the Duchy of Amalfi, had never actually taken effect. This may or may not be attributable to Eleonora's ploy. In any event, King Charles did not stay in Italy long enough to enforce the edict.

In mid-May 1495 Charles VIII had himself crowned King of Naples. Since January 1494 Naples had seen four Kings sitting on its throne – Ferrante I, Alfonso II, Ferrante II, and this new King, who took the title

The castle of Celano, Abruzzo, which belonged to the Piccolomini Dukes of Amalfi.

Charles III. But Charles was destined to sit for the briefest time. The rest of Europe suddenly awoke to the dangers of French hegemony over the whole of Italy and, under the auspices of Pope Alexander, the League of Cambrai was formed to combat it. Even Ludovico il Moro decided to join the League, for he was anxious that the French, once firmly established in Italy, might lay claim to their right (via the Visconti family) to the Duchy of Milan. With Il Moro vacillating, Charles knew there was a risk of seeing his return route to France cut off. Before this could come to pass, immediately after his coronation, he decided to retreat in all haste, leaving a viceroy to govern Naples.

CHAPTER 5

Bereavement

DUCHESS ... Charon's boat serves to convey all o'er
The dismal lake, but brings none back again.

John Webster, *The Duchess of Malfi*, III.v.105–6

Once the French King had left Naples, Giovanna's cousin Ferrandino began making his way back towards the city at the head of a Spanish army. The end of the conflict was perhaps in sight and Giovanna's husband, Alfonso, might soon be returned safely to her. But what promised to be a temporary lull in the political turmoil was marred for Giovanna by a series of bereavements.

Her relief at the forthcoming return of Ferrandino was shared by most of the population of Naples, for he was definitely more aesthetically presentable as a king than the Frenchman. Despite a nervous tic when he spoke,[1] he was a handsome young man in his mid-twenties, with lively eyes and head held proudly high. Though slimly built, he was strong and athletic and altogether more inspiring than King Charles.[2] The people were tired of French abuses and were hankering for the old dynasty of Aragon. And yet, although secret negotiations had already taken place with leading citizens before the departure of Ferrandino's fleet from Messina, when it arrived before the city on 7 July 1495, there was no immediate popular movement. Women climbed onto house roofs to watch the fleet's arrival; in the streets rival bands of children fought playful mock battles in the names of the French and the House of Aragon; but those same streets were patrolled by armed French guards, who were still making their presence felt.

Ferrandino, disappointed that there was no spontaneous uprising in his favour, was already directing the bows of his ship towards Ischia when suddenly the precarious balance tipped in his favour. About fifty men hoisted the Aragonese standard over the city and started shouting '*Aragona! Aragona!*' The population began to answer their call. A boat

The triumphal return to Naples of the Giovanna's cousin King Ferrante II (Ferrandino), 7 July 1495 (*from the Codice Ferraiolo, Pierpont Morgan Library, New York, MS M. 801, f. 117*).

rowed out to advise the King of what was happening and Ferrandino went ashore himself.

He entered the city flanked by Alfonso D'Avalos, Marquis of Pescara, and by his chief minister, Benedetto Gareth (known as Il Chariteo), who was also court poet. As well as being an impetuous and valorous soldier, Ferrandino was also a man of culture; he had been nurtured among the poets of the sophisticated Neapolitan court and wrote verse himself. The chorus of '*Ferro, Ferro*' which greeted his entry and echoed through the city reminded him of a quotation from Juvenal and, turning to Gareth with a smile, he murmured: 'Ferrum est quod amant!'[3]

Giovanna's brother Cardinal Luigi had stayed on in Calabria to fight beside the great Spanish commander Gonsalvo de Cordova, from whom he was able to learn much of the art of warfare. He recovered his brother's fief of Gerace, and then he and de Cordova gradually fought their way back up the peninsula towards Naples.[4] On 31 May 1496 a boatload of illustrious pro-French prisoners that they had taken in Calabria docked at Naples harbour. Luigi himself, however, did not return until mid-August,[5] when he arrived just in time for the marriage celebrations of his cousin, the King.

Ferrandino had announced in February his intention to marry his aunt, the Infanta Giovanna. He was twenty-eight and she sixteen. He hoped from this marriage to ensure the aid of her uncle, Ferdinand the Catholic, for he desperately lacked funds and had had to resort to private loans. In January 1496 he had been obliged to cede Trani, Brindisi and Otranto to Venice as collateral for an army of foot soldiers and *stradiotti* (Venetian light cavalry) under the Venetian Captain General, Francesco Gonzaga, Marquis of Mantua.[6]

Throughout the turmoil of the French invasion, the Duke of Amalfi had never wavered in his loyalty to Ferrandino, even though his mother and sister had been openly dallying with the French King and his court in Naples. He probably spent much of 1495 fighting alongside the valiant Marquis of Pescara, with whom we find him in August of that year putting down a pro-French revolt at Venafro (just south of the abbey of Montecassino, between Naples and Rome), which belonged to the husband of Giovanna's half-sister, Ippolita. The mission was a success and the young Duke of Amalfi fought courageously, severely wounding the rebel leader.

Shortly after this the Duke returned to Naples with the Marquis of Pescara, but Pescara was killed in a traitorous ambush on 7 September 1495. The French were barricaded in the monastery of Santa Croce on the hill of Pizzofalcone overlooking and controlling Castelnuovo, which Ferrandino's forces were trying to recapture. Pescara tried to negotiate their surrender. A Moor, who was with the French but had previously been in the service of the Marquis, offered to let him in by night via a wooden ladder placed against the monastery wall. But it turned out to be a trap and the Marquis was mortally wounded by an arrow from a crossbow, which pierced his throat as he tried to scale the wall.[7]

The Duke continued to fight beside Ferrandino to expel the last vestiges of French resistance from the city. Eventually they recaptured the gardens of Castelnuovo and set up a camp there from which to attack the citadel of the castle itself and expel the French garrison. On 14 November he was beside Ferrandino and Don Federico watching Ferrandino's troops unsuccessfully attempting to scale the castle walls.[8] Finally they decided to dig a tunnel in the soft tufa rock beneath the castle and mine it. In the terrible explosion on 27 November, the front wall of the citadel was blown apart and the French expelled. The celebrations for this were soon doused,

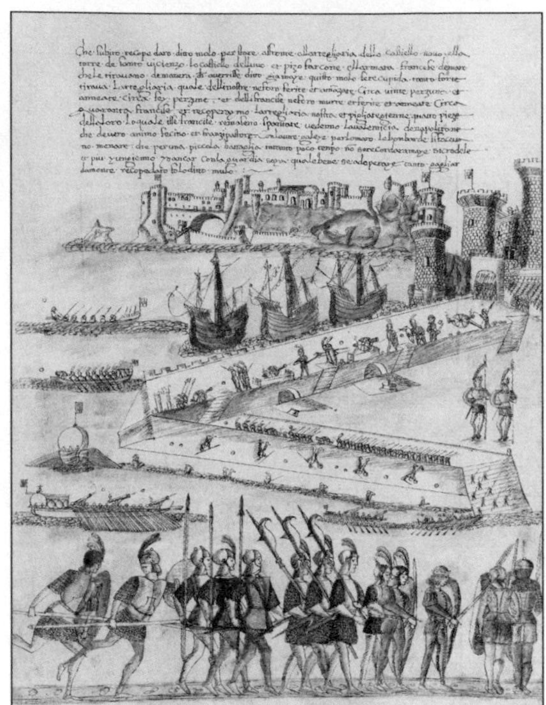

Ferrandino, Alfonso Piccolomini (Giovanna's husband) and her uncle Don Federico watch Ferrandino's troops attempting to expel the French garrison from Castelnuovo, September 1495 (*from the Codice Ferraiolo, Pierpont Morgan Library, New York, MS M. 801, f. 124*).

however, by the news that Ferrandino's father, former King Alfonso, had died in Sicily.

By Christmas Eve enough repairs had been made for the old Queen and her daughter to return to Castelnuovo from Castel dell' Ovo where they had taken refuge. The Duchess of Amalfi may also have returned to Naples at this point, since it had been retaken and her husband was there. But the Duke was not able to stay long in the city, for the war soon spread to Abruzzo, Apulia and Basilicata, where the two sides vied for the levy of the *dogana delle pecore*, the sheep duty, which would have financed and fed the occupying armies. The duty was levied on the transhumance of flocks of sheep from the pastures of the Abruzzo mountains in the summer to those further south in Apulia in the winter – and it was extremely lucrative. Alfonso Piccolomini had to try to gain control of this and defend his possessions in Abruzzo from the French and the francophile barons who were their allies.

He was involved in numerous skirmishes in which Giovanna's younger brother, Carlo d'Aragona, accompanied him. Carlo appears to have been an indifferent soldier, certainly not of the calibre of his elder brother Luigi or Alfonso Piccolomini. The sources make no mention of brave exploits on his part. Nevertheless, it was Carlo who sent the news to Naples at the end of May of how the Duke of Amalfi had attacked a French contingent that was making its way to bring reinforcements to the rebel city of Sulmona. After a fierce battle lasting more than two hours, the French camp was destroyed. Most of the French soldiers were slaughtered and the Duke personally killed their leader.[9]

It seems that about the same time Giovanna's husband was able to settle a personal score too. Because of his defection during the first Barons' Revolt, Ferrante I had deprived Ruggerone Accrociamuro of his fiefdom of Celano and given it to Antonio Piccolomini. Accrociamuro joined the invading French army in 1494 in the hope of regaining his lands. He did not achieve this, thanks to the manoeuvres of Maria Marzano and her daughter at the court of King Charles. But to ensure such claims were not raised again, Alfonso Piccolomini barred his way near the River Pratola, on the plain of Sulmona, and challenged him to a combat to resolve the question. Accrociamuro's imposing stature and superior strength (which earned him the name Ruggerone, meaning big Roger) did not deter the young impetuous Piccolomini. After a long vigorous hand-to-hand fight, he wounded his adversary in the forehead and chest and was about to finish him off. But at this point, perhaps because Alfonso was wounded himself or too fatigued, one of his pikemen, Martino di Siena, stepped in to do the job. Although Alfonso eliminated his rival, it is thought that during the duel he received wounds from which he never fully recovered.[10]

By the beginning of August, Alfonso had probably returned to Scafati and been reunited with his wife and daughter and at this time Giovanna received an official visit from her two namesakes, her stepgrandmother and aunt. Ferrandino was besieging the last remnants of the French army at Atella and he invited his new wife and the old Queen to visit him there to watch the final expulsion of the enemy. On their way back to Naples, the two women stayed at the Piccolomini castle in Scafati.[11]

Ferrandino was attempting to reconcile the divergent parties in his Kingdom by negotiating agreements with the principal francophile barons of the realm. The two chief Neapolitan commanders in the invading French army had been the exiled Antonello Sanseverino, Prince of Salerno, and Berardino Sanseverino, Prince of Bisignano; Ferrandino managed to negotiate a peace settlement with both of them.[12] The Duke of Amalfi doubtless participated in these negotiations and it was probably at Scafati,

The return to Naples of the Infanta Giovanna. She is flanked by the Spanish General Gonsalvo de Cordova and Cardinal Juan Borgia (*from the Codice Ferraiolo, Pierpont Morgan Library, New York MS M. 801, f. 127*).

in this period, that the first discussions took place regarding the marriage of the Duke's sister, Eleonora, to the Prince of Bisignano.

Before this could come about, though, the royal wedding festivities had to take place. There had been an official marriage ceremony in March, but Ferrandino's urgent military campaigns prevented full celebrations. In mid-August the King and his court retired to Somma on the flanks of Mount Vesuvius, where the air was cooler and healthier, for he, the Queen and the Infanta had all contracted a severe malarial fever. Since the fluvial plain of the River Sarno surrounding Scafati had degenerated into malarial marshes, the health of Giovanna's husband may have been further weakened by a bout of malaria too. The malady killed the French commander and eventually crippled the remaining French forces still holding out in the Kingdom.

Giovanna and her husband travelled to Somma for the festivities at the bizarre marriage of her cousin, Ferrandino, to their aunt, the Infanta. Giovanna's elder brother Luigi, the conquering hero from the Calabrian campaign, was also present. It was a moment of respite from the upheaval of the preceding months and the guests were entertained by *gliuommari napolitaneschi*, written by the court poets Sannazaro and Chariteo. These poems in Neapolitan dialect, recited in a catchy 'see-saw' rhythm, made everyone laugh with their tangle of nonsensical rhymes, amusing recipes and ribald jokes about contemporaries, legends and superstitions.[13] After two years of war, tumult and tribulation there was a heartfelt need for a little light comic relief. This was another occasion on which Giovanna might have noticed Antonio Bologna participating in a court festivity. Antonio was now about thirteen, and still a page at one of the royal courts. He may also have come to the notice of another visitor to Somma at this time – the commander of Ferrandino's Venetian allies, Francesco Gonzaga, Marquis of Mantua, in whose service he was later to be found.

After her marriage the Infanta assumed the title Queen Giovanna IV, although she is usually referred to as 'the young Queen Giovanna' to distinguish her from her mother, 'the old Queen Giovanna'. It is fortunate, given their consanguinity, that there were no offspring from the union of Ferrandino and his aunt, although according to some contemporaries, this was not due to Ferrandino's lack of ardour: many attributed his precipitate decline in health after his marriage to his excesses in the marriage bed. This was not the case, however; his health was undermined by a severe form of malaria, which caused internal haemorrhaging.

Once the royal wedding festivities were over, Giovanna and her husband proceeded to Amalfi to oversee the arrangements for the coming wedding in their own family. Eleonora Piccolomini's marriage was to cost the Duke of Amalfi dear, for her dowry was fixed at the considerable sum of 15,000 ducats. With the expenses incurred during the recent conflict and the interruption in the supply of funds because of confiscations, the wedding weighed heavily on the Duke's finances and he became deeply indebted.

According to the Venetian diarist Marin Sanudo, the bridegroom, Berardino Sanseverino, Prince of Bisignano, was of pleasing appearance; but he was a short, rather stout, man of forty, while his bride, Eleonora, was about twenty years his junior and, according to contemporary chronicles like those of Sanudo and the French *Vergier d'Honneur*, very beautiful. Certainly her spirited brio can be assumed from the way she handled a horse better than a man. It was a union destined to cause problems.[14]

Berardino was distantly related to Giovanna on her mother's side. His father had perished in the Great Barons' Revolt of the 1480s and his mother had fled, hiding Berardino and his brother in a convent's laundry basket to smuggle them out of Naples. He then spent six or seven years at the court of the French King with the other Neapolitan exiles. Since Berardino was one of Charles VIII's chief commanders during his invasion of Italy, Ferrandino was now at pains to win him over. Whether because Maria Marzano had made overtures to Bisignano on the subject, or because Eleonora had already caught his eye at the court of King Charles in Naples, it was decided that the marriage should seal the peace agreement.

Giovanna hosted the wedding festivities in Amalfi, together with her now ailing mother-in-law. It was a grand occasion in the town and the Duke left nothing to chance in the organisation of this marriage, which promised to earn much prestige for his family. The halls of the seafront Ducal Palace were adorned with precious tapestries and drapery of the finest damask silks and brocades, as was the palace chapel. At the religious ceremony held on 14 September, the local patrician families vied to outshine one another in the magnificence of their jewels and apparel. Beneath an ornate canopy, specially erected in the chapel, the Archbishop of Amalfi blessed Eleonora and her husband, and then followed four days of celebrations, with banquets, dancing and entertainment.[15]

The Sanseverino Palace in Naples was close by the Piccolomini seat in which Eleonora had grown up. Since Eleonora and Giovanna were approximately the same age, we can presume that when the latter entered her husband's household at the age of twelve, some sort of friendship developed between them and that, living close by, they continued to enjoy each other's company. They may have imbibed the same romantic liberal ideas with which the Renaissance had begun to transform women's lives, for it was ideas of this sort that eventually brought them both to tragedy. In their male-oriented society, women were invited to distribute or prostitute their 'favours' not as they saw fit but merely as family interest dictated. For many women of the period, marriage was effectively a legalised and sanctified whoredom. Some, like Giovanna, were fortunate enough to have husbands with whom they found happiness, but others were less fortunate, as was the case with Eleonora. This loveless marriage with a ruthless middle-aged man was tolerated by the vivacious Eleonora only under sufferance.

Bisignano's truce with the House of Aragon did not last long and the newly achieved political equilibrium was soon upset again, but his mother-in-law, the dowager Duchess of Amalfi, Maria Marzano, did not live long enough to see the new catastrophe. Shortly after Eleonora's wedding, Maria fell gravely ill and died in Amalfi. Her body was not taken to the Piccolomini family tomb in the church of Monteoliveto in Naples; she was interred instead in the vault of the traditionally pro-French Brancia family in the cathedral of Amalfi.[16] For Giovanna, her mother-in-law's death initiated a period of repeated bereavement which severely undermined her spirits.

By the beginning of September 1496 her cousin Ferrandino was also gravely ill; he was certainly not well enough to attend Eleonora Piccolomini's wedding. Two weeks after this, his situation became desperate. The population of Naples began to rise in alarm at the danger of the King's demise. In order to pacify them and to officially recognise his wife as Queen Giovanna IV, she and Ferrandino were carried through the streets in procession, each lying on separate litters (the Queen was also ill, with malarial fever). It is said that during this procession Ferrandino murmured Petrarch's verse:

> Oh cechi, il tanto affaticar che giova?
> Tutti tornate alla gran matre antica
> e il nome vostra appena si ritrova
> (O ye blind, to what avail is so much labour?
> We all return to the ancient mother
> and your name they will barely remember)[17]

The King's appearance in public was followed by two days of prayers and processions through the city, in which all levels of society participated. Despite the fact that the usual 'miraculous' liquefaction of the blood of the city's patron saint (Saint Januarius) had taken place and induced everyone to hope that the Lord intended to be clement, in the early morning of 7 October Ferrandino died.

He was laid to rest beside his grandfather, Ferrante I, in the church of San Domenico Maggiore and was sincerely mourned by pro-Aragonese and francophile alike. Ferrandino had managed in his brief reign to attain what neither his father nor his grandfather had been able to achieve, a modicum of unity and respect in Naples. It was unfortunate for the whole Kingdom that this promising young monarch's life had been prematurely cut short.

The old Queen had hoped that the crown would pass from the late King to his widow, her daughter Giovanna IV, so that she herself would then have been assured of maintaining the power she previously wielded as Lieutenant of the Realm during the absences of the three previous Aragon monarchs. But this was not to be. The nobles of the realm preferred to set her and her daughter aside and choose Ferrante II's uncle, Don Federico, as the successor. The old Queen never forgave Federico and eventually set herself to engineer his destruction. In doing so she would also destroy the independence of the Kingdom of Naples and help to place it in the hands of her brother, Ferdinand the Catholic, who would reward her for her efforts by setting her aside too.

Federico's reign was dogged by trouble from the beginning. Following the defection of the Prince of Salerno after Ferrandino's death, new risings in favour of the French began and, with an almost empty treasury, suppressing these rebellions became a severe problem. Ferrandino had debased the currency and Federico found himself obliged to repeat this expedient in January 1497. Owing to the unstable political situation, it was almost a year after Ferrandino's death before Federico's coronation could take place.

The ceremony was held on 10 August 1497, at Capua. Federico was crowned by the papal legate, the Pope's son Cardinal Cesare Borgia. Cesare, his hands recently marked with the blood of his younger brother, Juan, Duke of Gandia, who was found murdered on 15 June 1497, was considerably relieved at having an excuse to distance himself from his grieving father in Rome. But for Federico to have his crown blessed by such an unworthy cleric, tainted with the blood of fratricide, was an inauspicious opening to his reign. 10 August was also Saint Lawrence's day, traditionally the day of falling stars; and the stars of the House of Aragon of Naples, despite the pomp and circumstance of the occasion, were already in rapid descent.

Sanudo gives a detailed description of Federico's coronation, which was a much less sumptuous affair than that of his brother Alfonso II three years earlier. His crown was more modest and precious jewels much less in evidence; the French invasion had taken its toll on both royal and noble coffers. But the new King's robes of crimson satin and his cape of gold brocade trimmed with ermine gave him the required aura of regality. Since the periods spent in France during his youth,[18] Federico had always favoured French fashions and for the ceremony he was dressed *a la francese* and so were his court. But if he expected this to lie well with francophile barons like the Princes of Salerno and Bisignano, he was mistaken, for although they were invited and expected for the coronation, they did not present themselves.

Just two weeks after Ferrandino's death, Bisignano had been waiting in an ante-room at Castelcapuano for an interview with the new King

Federico, when he was attacked and stabbed three times by a Neapolitan who accused the Prince of dishonouring his wife and mother. Though Federico refused to claim responsibility for the attack and subsequently ordered the assailant to be hanged, drawn and quartered, Bisignano was not convinced. Ferrandino's tenuous truce began to crack.[19]

The Duke of Amalfi, as the King's *Maestro Giustiziere* (Chief Crown Magistrate), was present at the coronation ceremony, where he again had the honour of holding the bridle of the King's horse. Among the other nobles present were his younger brother, the Marquis of Deliceto, and Giovanna's brother-in-law, the Count of Venafro, but notable for their absences were King Federico's closest nephews, Cardinal Luigi and Carlo d'Aragona.

The coronation was held in Capua because of an outbreak of the plague, which, after severely hitting Florence and Rome, had spread to Naples and the surrounding area. Giovanna's sister, Caterina, and her husband, Gentile, contracted the infection at their castle in Nola, where they both died at the beginning of August, just before the coronation took place. Obviously Giovanna and her brothers were in mourning for their sister and not able to attend.[20] We do not know how much affection had developed between Giovanna and her mother-in-law, or how much she mourned her passing, but her sister's sudden premature death doubtless caused her much grief.

In October 1497, however, she was called from her mourning to attend the official welcome to Naples of the new Queen. King Federico's wife, Isabella del Balzo, was thirty-two years old and her family, of French origin (del Balzo being an Italian corruption of des Baux), claimed to be descended from Balthazar, one of the three wise men who rendered homage to Christ.[21] When Federico became King, their eldest son, Ferrante (or Ferdinand), took the title of Duke of Calabria. However, this Ferdinand, Duke of Calabria no more resembled Webster's character of that name than did his late namesake, Ferrandino.

Isabella arrived at the Porta Capuana accompanied by her two young sons, Francesco and Ferdinand, and took up residence at the adjacent Castelcapuano. In the days that followed, the gentlewomen of Naples lined up like long rows of ants (as a contemporary poem puts it) to pay their respects to their new Queen.[22] As Isabella's niece, Giovanna returned to her former home and was one of the first to be presented. She would have been part of the entourage of principal noblewomen of the royal court who eventually accompanied Queen Isabella in triumphal procession from

Castelcapuano to Castelnuovo, to be received by the two widowed Queens in their apartments there.

At Castelnuovo Isabella knelt before the old Queen and kissed her hand, after which they embraced 'like mother and daughter' and went together to the chamber of Ferrandino's widow. This act of homage and submission by Isabella was doubtless intended to placate the hostility of the old Queen, but it did so only superficially. Like the rest of the court, the Duchess of Amalfi knew how much the old Queen resented having to step down from being the prima donna of the realm and, as she observed the scene, she was well aware of the underlying tensions. At twenty years of age, Giovanna was now mature enough to perceive political subtleties.

King Federico was still away fighting the Prince of Salerno and it was February before the King and Queen were officially reunited. However, since Isabella gave birth to a son in May 1498, presumably they must have met somewhere about the time of Federico's coronation. Despite the difference in their ages (Federico was thirteen years older than his wife), perhaps of all the marriages of the royal House of Aragon this seems to have been one of the happiest and most loving. Isabella was waiting at Castelnuovo with the Spanish general, Gonsalvo de Cordova, and the Spanish ambassador, when Federico finally returned. She curtseyed and kissed his hand, but he lifted her up and to the delight of all those present, they embraced and kissed each other on the mouth.

For Giovanna it finally seemed that a period of tranquillity was in sight. She and her husband made their usual progression through their estates during 1497 and spent some time in Abruzzo, to which a document issued by Alfonso from the castle of Celano testifies. It was a communication to the accountant of his tax office in Maiori on the Amalfi coast and concerned debts owed to his creditors.[23] His debts were obviously becoming pressing and his financial situation had still not recovered. But in general the political situation had become calmer. King Federico was now fixed fairly securely on his throne, or so it appeared, and the future seemed brighter and more reassuring in all respects. There were still brief outbreaks of disorder in Abruzzo: in May 1498 Federico sent the Duke of Amalfi to help resolve a quarrel between the Ascolani and the inhabitants of Fermo.[24] But in the absence of serious tensions in that summer of 1498, Alfonso and Giovanna conceived another child. Their joy at this coming event was tempered, however, by the death of their eight-year-old daughter, Caterina, during this same period.

In the space of little more than a year Giovanna had lost her mother-in-law, her cousin Ferrandino, her sister and her precious daughter. The only balm for her sorrow was looking towards the future and the birth of the child she was carrying. Then another affliction was thrust upon her: her husband became gravely ill. Some sources affirm that he had been mortally wounded in an ambush near Sulmona (not far from Capestrano),[25] others that he never fully recovered from wounds received during the preceding war. In any event, Giovanna was three or four months' pregnant when, in the early autumn of 1498, she wrote a desperate letter to her uncle, King Federico, urging him to send a doctor to treat Alfonso as soon as possible. Federico replied on 9 October saying that he would send Messer Jacopo de Varavalle, one of the best doctors in Naples.[26] But Varavalle's treatment failed and Alfonso Piccolomini died on 23 October at his castle of Capestrano. Giovanna had him buried beside his father, Antonio, in the small church of Santa Maria della Concezione adjacent to the castle.

At the time of his death, the late Duke of Amalfi was without issue and his pregnant widow, so prostrated by the loss in such a short space of time of her sister, her only daughter and her husband, was either not considered to be in a fit state to govern the strategically important Piccolomini possessions, or she had forfeited her right to do so as long as she was without offspring. From a series of letters preserved in the Aragonese *Curia Sommaria*, it appears that for a brief period the King's illegitimate half-brother, Don Cesare d'Aragona, took over the title of Duke of Amalfi.[27] It is clear from these same letters that the old Queen was trying to draw Don Cesare into her schemes to cause the downfall of King Federico. Cesare d'Aragona, it will be remembered, was the illegitimate son of King Ferrante I cryptically mentioned in Morelli's poem, who became vice-lieutenant of Calabria after Enrico d'Aragona's death in 1478.

The first mysterious missive was a letter written by the old Queen, Giovanna III, on 28 October 1498, just five days after the death of Alfonso Piccolomini. It was a letter of presentation to 'the Duke of Amalfi' for a man who had been ordered to refer certain 'things' to this 'Duke of Amalfi' on her behalf, concerning she says, '*lo servicio nostro*' (our service). These 'things' were to be communicated only by word of mouth and not committed to paper. The news of the Duke of Amalfi's death would certainly have reached Naples by the time the letter was written and it is to be presumed that it was addressed to the newly nominated Duke of Amalfi,

Cesare d'Aragona, who is specifically referred to by this title in later missives from the same Queen.

Again, on 13 December, Queen Giovanna sends another person to 'the Duke of Amalfi', who introduces himself with a letter of presentation which says '*havemo comisso ve habea da dire ad bocca, da nostra parte*', that is he had, like the messenger in October, to convey a message which could be relayed only by word of mouth. The old Queen was probably trying to communicate to Cesare her wish for him to accompany her to Spain. She intended to seek asylum with her brother, Ferdinand the Catholic, whom she hoped would procure a suitable marriage for her widowed daughter, since King Federico had refused to marry his eleven-year-old son, Ferdinand, Duke of Calabria, to her. Relations between Federico and his stepmother (who was actually three years his junior) broke down over the question of this marriage. Unfortunately, it was the refusal of this and another match (that of his daughter Carlotta with Cesare Borgia) that sealed Federico's fate. Had he agreed to this unnatural marriage, as Ferrandino had, there was a good chance that Ferdinand the Catholic might have left him his Kingdom, since it would have been destined to pass via his niece to the legitimate line of Aragon.

When Federico refused her proposal, the old Queen requested permission to visit her brother in Spain, accompanied by Don Cesare. Federico, suspecting her intentions, replied that Cesare was too valiant and too valuable a soldier to be spared from the Kingdom. As for her permission to leave the country, he procrastinated for as long as he was able. When he finally had to let her go, he made sure she was accompanied by someone in whom he had complete faith – his nephew, Cardinal Luigi d'Aragona.

Luigi was by now one of his uncle's chief ministers and in this period his diplomatic career began to develop alongside his military one. Since his orphaned childhood, Luigi had been linked by esteem and affection to his uncle Federico and once Federico was established on the throne, he turned to this able young nephew as one of his most trusted aides. By 1499 Luigi was president of the *S. regio consiglio* (the Council of State) and he was also nominated *Luogotenente Generale del Regno* (Chief Lieutenant of the Realm), that is the person who acted for the King in his absence. This was the position that had been held by the old Queen, and her renunciation of the role suggested that her relations with Federico had passed breaking point.[28]

Federico repeatedly refused her permission to visit her brother in Spain, but after the deaths of King Ferdinand's daughter and his only son and heir,[29] the

1 Portrait known as 'Giovanna d'Aragona', from the workshop of Raphael. Date unknown (*Galleria Doria Pamphilj, Rome*).

2 View of Amalfi, with the Torre dello Ziro, the tower in which, according to popular legend, Giovanna died, visible on the cliff above the town.

3 Castelcapuano, Naples. Giovanna's childhood home.

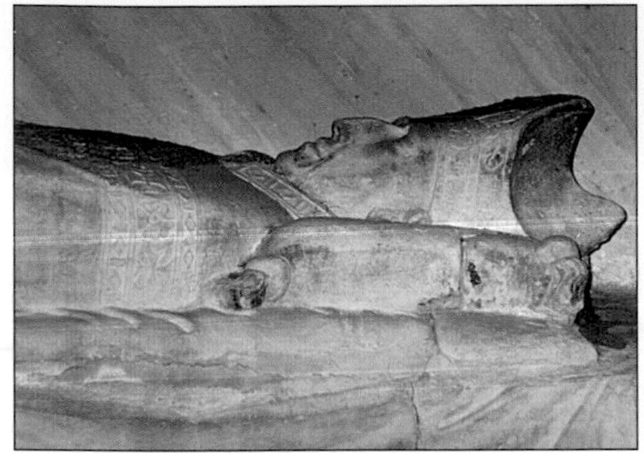

4 Effigy of Cardinal Luigi d'Aragona.

5 Portrait of an unknown cardinal by Raphael, possibly Luigi d'Aragona, Giovanna's brother, *c.* 1511 (*Museo Nacional del Prado, Madrid*).

6 Detail from the *Coronation of Pope Pius III* (see Plate 28): the central figure may represent Giovanna.

7 Naples in 1465, from the painting known as the *Tavola Strozzi*. From left to right: Castel dell' Ovo; the lighthouse tower of San Vincenzo; Castelnuovo; above, on the hill, Castel Sant' Elmo; directly below, slightly to the right and set apart from the city, the church

8 Detail from above: Castelnuovo, the official residence of the Aragon Kings of Naples.

of Monteoliveto, with the cupola of the Piccolomini chapel already visible. Far right: Castelcapuano (*The Museum of Capodimonte, Naples. Photograph: Luciano Pedicini.*).

9 Detail from above: Castelcapuano. The royal standard can be seen flying from the towers.

10 Giovanni de' Medici, Pope Leo X. Portrait by Raphael, *c.* 1518 (*Galleria degli Uffizi, Florence,* © *Alinari*).

11 Giuliano della Rovere, Pope Julius II. Contemporary copy of the original Raphael portrait (*Galleria degli Uffizi, Florence,* © *Alinari*).

12 Lorenzo de' Medici, known as Lorenzo il Magnifico. Portrait by Giorgio Vasari, 1530 (*Galleria degli Uffizi, Florence, © Alinari*).

13 The Viceroy of Naples, Raimondo de Cardona. Copy of an original contemporary portrait by an unknown artist (*by courtesy of Dr Roberto de Cardona*).

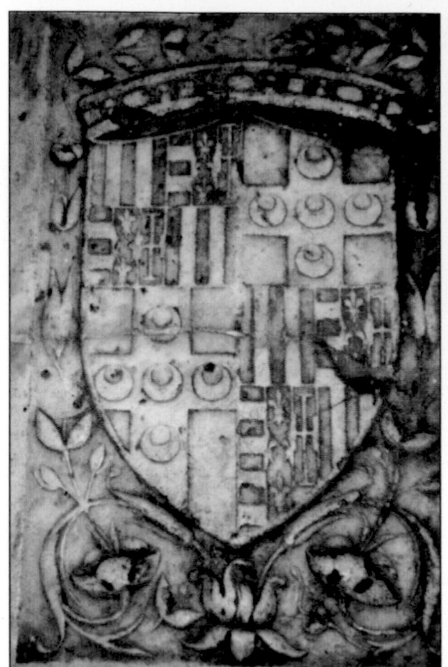

14 Coats of arms: above, left: the Todeschini Piccolomini d'Aragona Dukes of Amalfi, from the Piccolomini Chapel, church of Sant' Anna dei Lombardi (Monteoliveto), Naples; above, right: the Beccadelli da Bologna (the Cathedral Museum, Amalfi); below: the Royal House of Aragon, Giovanna d'Aragona's family.

old Queen became more insistent. She wished, she said, to go to Spain to comfort her brother and sister-in-law in their grave loss. Federico relented, but more out of political necessity than mere sentiment. At the beginning of September 1499, the French seized Milan from Ludovico il Moro. Federico feared (rightly as it turned out) that they would soon set their sights on the reconquest of Naples, in which case an alliance with Ferdinand of Spain would be expedient. However, instead of sending his brother Cesare to accompany the Queen, as she had requested, he sent his nephew Luigi, whose loyalty towards the throne had never been called into question.

As expected, the French began to advance down the Italian peninsula and the consequences of Federico's refusal to seal the marriage alliance with Pope Alexander's son, Cardinal Cesare Borgia, began to be felt. The Orsini family had been officially accused of the murder of Juan Borgia, but many contemporaries laid the blame at Cesare's door. After a period of painful heart-searching, Pope Alexander decided that it was in his family's political interest to drop accusations against his son. Cesare was allowed to renounce his clerical robes and step into Juan's political shoes.

He immediately set about seeking a politically suitable wife and his aspirations fell on Carlotta, the King of Naples's daughter by his first wife. Carlotta had been brought up at the court of France and was related through her mother to the French crown. But she had a mind of her own and, unusually for the times, refused Cesare Borgia's overtures of marriage. Federico, who suspected the Borgias were aiming to gain a claim to the throne of Naples, said he would do nothing to compel his daughter.

This did not sit well with either the Pope or his ambitious son, who were both offended by the refusal. Cesare Borgia's life of debauchery was well known and he was by this time suffering from acute syphilis. He often went about with his face covered by a black velvet mask to hide the terrible festering sores and the layers of white mercury cream with which he treated them. Carlotta's revulsion is understandable, but Federico's countenancing of her refusal was a grave political error, for it set the papacy against him where it might have supported him.

In April 1498, Charles VIII of France died suddenly and was succeeded by Louis XII. The latter needed the Pope's permission to divorce his wife and marry Charles's widow, and to ingratiate himself with Pope Alexander, Louis found another French wife for Cesare and gave him the Duchy of Valence.[30] (Cesare Borgia is often referred to as Il Valentino.) To try to redress the balance of this new situation, the King of Naples attempted to placate the Pope by offering Sancia's brother, Alfonso d'Aragona, Duke of Bisceglie to 'feed to the hungry Borgia lions', in place of Carlotta. In July 1498 Federico sent his reluctant nephew to Rome to marry the Pope's daughter, Lucrezia Borgia.

Sancia was already in Rome. After her marriage to Joffre, she and her husband had been given a *palazzo* near Castelnuovo and set up their court there. When gossip began to reach the Pope of the libertine habits of his daughter-in-law, who often entertained young men of her court in her bedchamber, he sent serious admonitions to her and her family. Not that Alexander could have had many moral qualms, considering his own lascivious behaviour; it was more a question of the political consequences of Sancia falling into disrepute and procreating a bastard who would be passed off as a Borgia. The irony is that Alexander always nurtured serious doubts as to whether he or his mistress's husband was Joffre's father.

A curious letter in defence of Sancia's behaviour and the morality of her court, written by her major-domo Antonio Gurrea, is still preserved in the Vatican archives. The Pope, however, was not to be convinced by Gurrea's pleadings and Sancia and her husband were commanded to transfer themselves to Rome.[31] Here the situation grew more complex. The vivacious and undisciplined Sancia needed a man, not a boy like Joffre. She soon found two rivals for her attentions: her brothers-in-law Juan Borgia, Duke of Gandia, and Cardinal Cesare Borgia. It is thought that Cesare's jealousy of Sancia added to his motives for eliminating his brother Juan.

Sancia had made friends with her sister-in-law, Lucrezia Borgia, who was soon following the wayward Sancia, giggling with her during solemn ceremonies and flouting the stiff Vatican protocol to an extent that shocked many of the clergy. At the solemn feast of Pentecost in St Peter's in 1495, Sancia, bored by the dull sermon of the Bishop of Segovia, nudged Lucrezia and suggested that it would be more fun to see everything from the choirstalls. They raced there with their ladies-in-waiting struggling to keep up with them. Newly seated in this area traditionally reserved for the clergy, they continued to giggle and disturb the ceremony, much to the indulgent amusement of the Pope, who was also bored, but to the angry disapproval of Burkhardt, the papal master of ceremonies.[32]

Since the Duchess of Amalfi had been brought up with Sancia at the court of Castelcapuano, contemporaries tended to consider the behaviour of both women in similar fashion. Sancia's bad reputation tainted her cousin's.

However, during the early period of her widowhood, Giovanna's behaviour was exemplary, and the comparisons drawn with Sancia were unjust. On 10 March 1499, just five months after the death of her husband, for whom she was still grieving, Giovanna gave birth to a son and heir to the Duchy of Amalfi. She named the child Alfonso, in memory of his father, and the young boy soon began to fill the emptiness in her life that the many recent bereavements had left. Her whole existence now became focused on the boy's well-being and she vowed that in future her sole aim would be to nurture him and administer his domains, which probably came into her possession almost immediately after his birth. Giovanna was nominated regent until Alfonso reached his maturity. In the presence of a Piccolomini heir, King Federico had presumably been obliged to revoke the concession of the Duchy to Cesare d'Aragona. Giovanna certainly held the Duchy by February 1500 and was living in Amalfi.[33]

The governing of the vast Piccolomini domains was an onerous task. As well as Amalfi and Scafati near Naples, there were extensive fiefs in the Abruzzo mountains to the north. Giovanna was only twenty-one, but she set herself resolutely to the reordering of her infant son's patrimony and the righting of the Piccolomini's disastrous financial situation. She was determined to consign her son's inheritance in a more prosperous state than she had found it and she showed her ability and intelligence by achieving this in a comparatively brief space of time.

If she needed aid or advice in the administration of her domains in Abruzzo, she could have turned to her brother, Carlo, who had already been managing affairs there with their uncle Cesare d'Aragona during the period that the latter appears to have taken the title of Duke of Amalfi. Cesare had also been governing the old Queen's territories in Abruzzo as special lieutenant since November 1498, but he renounced the office in April 1499 in favour of Carlo, Giovanna's brother. This renunciation appears to be a symptom of the shifting balance of power between King Federico and the old Queen, and of Cesare's decision to stand firmly beside his brother, the King.[34]

Preparations were being made for Carlo's marriage. Federico had decided to reward the D'Avalos family for their unerring loyalty to the House of Aragon by marrying Giovanna's younger brother to Ippolita D'Avalos, sister of the late heroic Marquis of Pescara, Alfonso D'Avalos.[35] The marriage took place some time after September 1499.[36] Giovanna attended the wedding, but their elder brother Luigi did not: he, by this time, had departed for Spain.

CHAPTER 6

Partition

BOSOLA You have bloodily approv'd the ancient truth,
That kindred commonly do worse agree
Than remote strangers.

John Webster, *The Duchess of Malfi*, IV.ii.264–6

On the evening of 7 September 1499, King Federico and his half-sister, Ferrandino's widow, dined with her mother and Cardinal Luigi d'Aragona on board a Genoese ship riding at anchor in Naples harbour. At midnight, the King and his sister disembarked and Luigi and the old Queen set sail for Spain.[1]

They spent the months of October and November at Granada with the Queen's brother King Ferdinand. Tentative negotiations were probably already taking place between Ferdinand and the King of France for a pact to partition the Kingdom of Naples. Since these negotiations took place in the greatest secrecy, it is difficult to assess to what extent this former Queen of Naples participated, or was even aware of them. According to a report made by the Venetian ambassador in Spain, both Queen Giovanna and Cardinal Luigi had expressed their displeasure with the 'Catholic Sovereigns' Ferdinand and Isabella for the little concern they demonstrated at the news that King Louis of France was intending to reattempt the conquest of Naples.[2] Nevertheless, the court poet Sannazaro, in letters written to Luigi in later years, expressed his conviction that Queen Giovanna III played an important role in the downfall of King Federico and the passing of the Kingdom of Naples into her brother's hands. However, if the old Queen was a party to the secret talks, she would hardly have expressed anything which would have revealed their aims to the King of Naples's nephew, Luigi d'Aragona. Luigi had been given the task of closely surveying her dealings with her brother, but he probably knew nothing of the pact until it was too late.

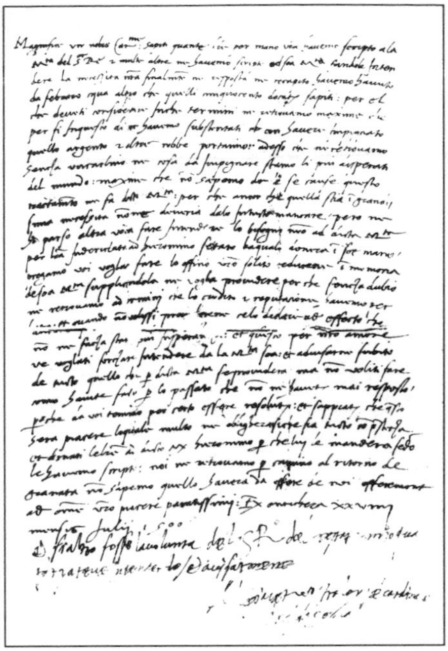

Letter from Cardinal Luigi d'Aragona to Giacomo Milano, 29 July 1500. Luigi's signature uses the Latin form of his name, Aloysius (*MS XXX, B, 12, Biblioteca Storia Patria, Naples, photograph, Luciano s.a.s.*).

By the summer of the following year, Luigi was still in Spain and running seriously short of funds. He had travelled extensively around the Iberian Peninsula, reaching even Portugal,[3] combining his diplomatic mission with a pleasure trip which enriched his perceptions but notably depleted his finances. He was an intelligent young man, whose insatiable thirst for knowledge remained with him throughout his life; unfortunately he spent beyond his means both in his travels and in his patronage of Italian intellectuals at the Spanish court. One of these, Pietro Martire d'Anghieri, dedicated the first part of his *Decades de orbe novo* (an account of the voyages of Columbus to the New World) to Luigi in a letter from Granada on 23 April 1500, saying it was the Cardinal's encouragement that had eventually persuaded him to seek publication. Several weeks later, in another letter to the Cardinal, Martire says 'probably tomorrow you will re-accompany your grandmother to Naples'.[4] But this did not come to pass. It was several years before either Queen Giovanna or Luigi were to see Naples again.

On 29 July 1500 Luigi wrote a desperate letter from Antiquera to an acquaintance in Naples, a certain Giacomo Milano, informing him that, despite the numerous letters he had written since the month of February to his uncle the King requesting funds, there had been no reply and no sign of the much-needed 500 ducats. His state of necessity was such that he had

had to pawn his silverware and other possessions. He was now without any funds, or means of procuring them, and was reduced to the circumstances of '*i più disperati del mondo*' (the most desperate in the world). He could not understand why his uncle should abandon him to such an ignominious fate, for although the crown was also in need, it was certainly not bankrupt. In order to make his uncle aware that he and his party had lost both their credit and their reputation in Spain, Luigi implored Milano to plead his case with the King, as he had done on previous occasions. He concluded by saying that he was making his way back to Granada.[5]

In Granada an unpleasant surprise was awaiting Luigi: the news of the secret pact between the Kings of France and Spain to conquer the Kingdom of Naples. It is obvious from the tone of his letter that Luigi was unaware of what was really happening back home. It was probably difficult for him to keep up with the rapid evolution of events, since he laments the fact that his letters are unanswered. Possibly his mail was being intercepted by order of Ferdinand the Catholic, who wished to keep his agreement with the French secret for as long as possible to prevent King Federico from raising opposition forces.

However, while Luigi was enjoying himself in Spain, spending prodigally and rapidly exhausting his limited funds, in Naples his dynasty was on the point of collapse. Louis XII had established himself in Milan and for Ludovico il Moro time was running out. Having opened the floodgates to the French invaders in 1494, now he was engulfed by the tidal wave which followed. After Il Moro had been forced to flee from the Duchy of Milan, Gian Giacomo Trivulzio (the *condottiere* who had abandoned Ferrandino at a crucial moment of the French invasion and who was now a French general) entered the Sforza castle of the city and, together with the keeper, proceeded to divide up the rich spoils of pictures, gems and tapestries. Il Moro was still not finished; he rallied and raised a Swiss army with the aid of the Emperor Maximilian. But on 10 April 1500 he was captured by the French and spent the last eight years of his life mouldering in a French prison, while Milan became a French province.

On 7 March 1500, Isabella d'Aragona, Duchess of Milan and widow of Gian Galeazzo Sforza, returned to Naples with her two small daughters to take refuge from the invading French. Her nine-year-old son Francesco, the true heir to the Duchy of Milan, had been taken hostage by King Louis and sent off to France. There he was forced to adopt an ecclesiastical career, so that he would not marry and produce heirs to challenge the French claim to Milan. Isabella would not see him again. Her escape from Milan was engineered by Prospero Colonna (a *condottiere* in King Federico's service), and she is reputed to have formed an amorous relationship with him which lasted until his death.[6] Neither of them considered the possibility of marriage. They were well aware that royal marriages were a matter of politics rather than passion; a view that her cousin, the Duchess of Amalfi, chose to ignore.

Ferrante I's dynasty was gradually being abandoned to its fate. In August it was the turn of Federico's nephew, Alfonso, Duke of Bisceglie. Once King Federico was excommunicated in December, members of his family ceased to be of political value, and Cesare Borgia decided to eliminate Alfonso in order to marry off his sister Lucrezia more profitably elsewhere. A first attempt on Alfonso's life was made on 15 July 1500. He went to visit his father-in-law the Pope, who was recovering after lightning had struck part of the Vatican Palace, causing a ceiling to collapse on him. Alexander survived, but many saw the accident as a prophetic sign of God's discontent with the evils of the Borgia papacy. Alfonso was attacked on the steps of the Vatican Palace as he came away. He courageously defended himself, but was wounded in the head, shoulder and leg. While one of his attendants beat off his attackers, another dragged him back towards the palace and hammered on the doors. They were opened and he was carried to the papal chambers. Pope Alexander was said to have been horrified by the sight of Alfonso's wounds, while his wife, Lucrezia, fainted when she saw him. However, by this time Alexander was dominated by his ambitious son, Cesare, and was incapable of opposing his will.

For a month Alfonso was carefully tended day and night in a chamber of the Borgia apartments by his wife and his sister Sancia. He seemed to be recovering when, on the morning of 18 August, Cesare Borgia came to visit him. As he was leaving, Cesare was heard to murmur 'that which isn't consumed at luncheon can be dealt with at supper-time'.[7] In the late afternoon of the same day, Cesare's bloodthirsty henchmen burst into Alfonso's chamber, saying that the two Neapolitan doctors who were treating him were accused of plotting against the Borgias and were under arrest. When Lucrezia and Sancia protested, they were lured from the room on the pretext of presenting a plea to the Pope on the doctors' behalf. While they were gone, Alfonso was left helpless and alone and Cesare's men were able to throttle him undisturbed.

King Federico's sister, Beatrice, Queen of Hungary, also fell foul of the Borgias and, like her niece Isabella, Duchess of Milan, was forced to return to Naples in exile. She had been married to Mattia Corvino, King of Hungary, in 1476, but their union was without issue. After his death, Ladislao, King of Bohemia, married her as a means of gaining the throne of Hungary. Once he had achieved this end, he repudiated her on the grounds of her sterility and asked the Pope for an annulment. Beatrice first opposed this but then requested the return of her dowry from the Kingdom of Hungary. During his first years as Cardinal, Luigi d'Aragona had tried to promote his aunt's cause with the Pope. The case dragged on throughout the 1490s until Pope Alexander, seeing no more need to uphold the Aragonese dynasty of Naples, decided in favour of Ladislao, and Beatrice was compelled to return to her native city in exile, without her dowry. Giovanna's brother, Carlo, headed the group of nobles sent to greet their aunt at the frontier of the Kingdom and escort her back to Naples, where she arrived on 16 March 1501, just a year after the return of Isabella. But Isabella and Beatrice returned to Naples only to take flight again in July 1501, as the French army again invaded the city.[8]

Federico failed to secure an alliance with either the Emperor Maximilian or the Turks and found himself both isolated militarily and without financial resources. The Secret Treaty of Granada had been signed between Louis XII of France and Ferdinand of Spain on 11 November 1500. Federico, unaware of this fact, put his faith in the dissimulated but reassuring demonstrations of alliance made by the two Spanish ambassadors at his court. Nevertheless, news of the secret pact began to filter into Naples and on 18 June the King wrote a letter to Giovanna to inform her that gossip was circulating regarding an accord between France and Spain to divide up the Kingdom. Federico could not (or did not want to) believe it possible; it was inconceivable, he said, that these traditional rivals should have come to terms, and such dishonourable terms at that. He had great respect for King Louis, to whom he was linked by deep bonds of friendship since the time he spent in France during his youth. Nor was he capable of believing that his Aragonese relations in Spain, who in the past had always come to the aid of their Neapolitan cousins, could now forget their blood ties and turn against him. He was convinced that the rumours were without foundation and had been put about by the French to undermine confidence in his throne and prevent him from obtaining credit to finance his opposition to an eventual French invasion. Hence he urged

Giovanna to pay no heed to the rumours and to hold firm, for he was sure that if the majority of barons of the realm remain united behind him, the French could be repulsed.[9]

Despite her affection for her uncle, Giovanna did not allow herself to be convinced by his entreaties. She doubtless realised, or had been informed, that by now the onslaught was inevitable, for the day before this letter was written, the French invaders had reached Rome. When the French and Spanish ambassadors appeared together at a papal consistory, Federico could no longer doubt the reality of their pact. He was condemned by the Pope for turning to the Turks for aid and attempting to call them into Christendom, and a papal Bull of 25 June 1501 officially deprived him of his throne. From Sicily, Gonsalvo de Cordova reassured Federico that the Bull was a misunderstanding and that he was ready to land in Calabria to come to his aid against the French, by order of his master, Ferdinand the Catholic.

These assurances would never have convinced Federico's more astute father, Ferrante I, and although Federico turned to fight the French, who attacked him with the sincerity of an enemy, he was unable to defend himself from the false friendship of his Spanish cousins, whom he hoped were his allies. For this reason, against the advice of his generals, on 27 June 1501 he allowed six Spanish galleys to enter the Bay of Naples to take on board Ferrandino's widow, who was to be transported to Spain, to be reunited with her mother.

The French, joined by Cesare Borgia, began marching from Rome towards Naples and by 12 July were only a few miles from Capua. The city was defended by Fabrizio Colonna, while Fabrizio's cousin, Prospero Colonna, held Naples. Federico moved to Aversa with his troops. On the morning of 24 July, while negotiations were still taking place for the surrender of Capua, French troops suddenly breached one of the city gates. Mayhem ensued. The soldiers broke down doors with axes and dragged the people from houses, convents and churches. The old and the men were killed first, the women and children were raped and then they too were slaughtered. The French continued their savage rampage through the streets, raping, murdering and pillaging, until the pavements flowed red with blood and about 8,000 of the civilian population had perished. In the midst of this carnage was Cesare Borgia, and it is said that the only lives spared in Capua that day were those of forty beautiful women, who were to be used for his enjoyment.[10]

The general revulsion at the sack of Capua led to the collapse of any remaining support for Federico and, to avoid further bloodshed, he decided to seek a truce. The day after the sack, he ceded to the French all the castles and provinces they had requested, reserving for himself only Taranto and the island of Ischia. According to the terms of the truce, hostilities were to cease for the next six months. Frederico hoped against hope that during this time either his Spanish cousins would come to his aid or, failing this, that they would fall out with the French over the spoils of conquest. It was the latter that eventually came to pass, but long after it could have served any purpose for him.

As a guarantee for the truce, Federico consigned six hostages to the French, among whom were Giovanna's brother, Carlo, and their uncle the Count of Arena.[11] Carlo, like Luigi, remained faithful to his uncle Federico to very last. Not so Giovanna. Though she had turned to him in her moment of need, when her husband had been desperately ill, she does not seem to have held faith with him at his moment of need. Had her brother Carlo, who was with the King at Aversa, advised her that the situation was so desperate that any further resistance was pointless and likely to bring murder and pillage to the Duchy of Amalfi? Was she unconvinced by her uncle's ingenuous letter and, despite her personal sentiments towards him, anxious to save her subjects from unnecessary suffering? Or did these subjects autonomously declare for the French to save themselves, and Giovanna merely acquiesce in the fait accompli, knowing resistance was impossible and futile? Whatever the reason, on 18 July 1501,[12] before the sack of Capua had taken place, the standard of King Louis XII of France had already been raised in Amalfi. Once the city had declared in their favour, the French take-over was destined to be less painful.

After the truce was signed, the women of the House of Aragon – Beatrice, former Queen of Hungary, Isabella, former Duchess of Milan, Queen Isabella and four of her children – left Naples to take refuge in the castle of Ischia. The stronghold was kept by the D'Avalos family, so it is likely that Carlo d'Aragona's wife, Ippolita D'Avalos, would have accompanied the party, while Carlo himself was a hostage of the French. There is no proof that the Duchess of Amalfi also fled to Ischia with the other members of the royal family. She may have thought it safer to remain in Amalfi, since the Duchy had declared in favour of the French, or she may have taken refuge again at Scafati. Wherever she was, it must have been a moment of renewed stress and anxiety, and uppermost in her mind had to be the desire to preserve her only remaining child from harm.

Federico called a parliament in front of the arsenal of Naples, thanked his faithful subjects and absolved them of their oath of fidelity. Then, on the night of 2 August, he embarked for Ischia with members of his household and a few remaining friends. During the month he spent there he tried to reach a personal agreement with King Louis, for he was still receiving assurances from Gonsalvo de Cordova that Spanish help would be forthcoming. Gonsalvo must have been aware of his deliberate and dishonourable betrayal of Federico as he invaded the peninsula to conquer the Kingdom not to aid its monarch; but he was merely executing the orders of his ruthless master, Ferdinand the Catholic.

The abject ignominy of the humble letter Federico wrote to the French King illustrates his sense of loyalty and humility as a human being, but added only the dishonour to his dynasty. He offered to be a mere puppet king if Louis would only allow him to keep his title. Louis refused and offered him instead a duchy in France and a pension of 30,000 ducats a year, more or less equal to his depleted income as King of Naples. Federico accepted.[13]

On 6 September 1501, Federico set sail for exile in France with members of his household and some 500 gentlemen of his court. According to Bandello's account of the Duchess of Amalfi, it was also on this occasion that Antonio Bologna travelled to France. Webster's play opens with Delio's words:

> You are welcome to your country, dear Antonio;
> You have been long in France, and you return
> A very formal Frenchman, in your habit.[14]

Presumably Carlo d'Aragona was still a hostage at this time and did not join his uncle. As for the Duchess of Amalfi's other brother, Cardinal Luigi, it seems that he did not return to Naples at all during this period, but travelled instead directly from Spain to France to join his uncle's exiled court.[15]

When the French marched into Naples on 25 July 1501, the people greeted them with the usual popular effusions and offered 60,000 ducats to save the city from plunder. The Kingdom of Naples was now temporarily divided between France and Spain: France had secured the capital city and the northern provinces, while Spain had taken the south. His present task accomplished, Cesare Borgia returned to Rome to celebrate All Saints' Day with his father and sister, entertaining them with the naked courtesans' infamous 'Dance of the Chestnuts'. Carlo d'Aragona's fief of Gerace was conquered by the Spanish commander, Gonsalvo de Cordova, to whom it was given by Ferdinand the Catholic. Carlo was thus deprived of his chief source of income and reduced to straitened financial circumstances. He was now at the mercy of the charity of his brother and sister.

But very soon after their conquest the victors began to fall out over the spoils, and in August 1502 a new conflict arose. The Duchy of Amalfi was firmly in French hands by this time and the Duke of Nemours had concentrated his forces there, while Gonsalvo de Cordova, together with Prospero and Fabrizio Colonna (who had joined the Spaniards after Federico's departure), moved to Barletta in Apulia. The Spaniards remained cooped up on the southern Adriatic coast throughout the winter of 1502/3, held at bay by a superior French force. There was no open conflict as yet, just a series of skirmishes and exchanges of insults which culminated on 13 February 1503 in a historic dual known as the 'Disfida di Barletta'. Thirteen French knights matched their skills against thirteen Italian knights in a tournament to avenge insults made to the French commander, La Motte. In reality the tournament did more to alleviate the boredom of the long siege than to assuage any real offence. The Italian knights won and the hero of the day was Ettore Fieramosca, seconded by Prospero Colonna. In 1513 the Fieramosca family came to play an important part in the story of the Duchess of Amalfi.

Following the 'Disfida di Barletta', Spanish reinforcements arrived and de Cordova resoundingly defeated the French at Cerignola in April 1503. The French never recovered and de Cordova marched up the peninsula, driving them before him. On 16 May 1503 he triumphantly entered the city of Naples and declared the former independent Kingdom a Spanish province. It was destined to remain as such for the next two hundred years.

For Giovanna there may have been little to celebrate in the Spanish takeover, save the restoration of a modicum of peace and order, but, unlike her brother Carlo, she had managed to weather the storm and preserve intact all the estates she governed in her son's name. That she did so, however, was probably due more to the sudden transformation of Vatican politics in August 1503 than to diplomatic ability on her part.

Pope Alexander had been vacillating between the two rivals: France and Spain. He offered to support the French if they would cede the crown of Naples to his son, Cesare, in exchange for the Duchy of Romagna, and to aid the Spaniards if they would help Cesare to conquer Tuscany. But in August 1503 the political situation suddenly changed.

Rome at this time was a notoriously unhealthy city. Its extensive surrounding marshes had made malarial fever endemic, and in the torrid August heat the danger reached its peak. Pope Alexander had a remarkably strong constitution for his seventy-one years and he had not seen fit to remove himself from the city that summer; the farthest he had gone was to a vineyard on the outskirts of Rome. It belonged to the ex-papal secretary, Adriano Castellesi da Corneto, an extremely wealthy, recently nominated cardinal. On the evening of San Lorenzo, 10 August, 'the day of falling stars', Castellesi invited the Pope and his son Cesare to a banquet at his vineyard. Just as Federico's coronation on this day had sealed the fall of the Aragon dynasty of Naples, now, six years later to the day, this fatal banquet sealed the destiny of the Borgia family. The following morning Cesare and his father fell ill. Many contemporaries believed that Castellesi had poisoned his guests because he feared they had set their sights on his immense riches;[16] others, such as the papal master of ceremonies, Burkhardt, speak only of a severe attack of malarial fever. The true cause will never be known, but a week later the Pope was dead and Cesare still gravely ill.

Alexander VI's funeral was as dramatic as his papacy had been. While the redoubtable Burkhardt tried to ensure that protocol was respected, the papal apartments were being ransacked by a hoard of servants, who even carried away the papal throne. The Pope's body was washed, dressed in a white robe and velvet slippers, and placed on a catafalque of crimson satin. That evening it was transported to St Peter's and left behind an iron grille so that the population could pay its respects. But as the hours passed, the torrid heat engendered a rapid decomposition of the corpse, which became livid, swollen and malodorous, giving credence to the rumours of Rodrigo Borgia's pact with the devil. The population fled in terror from the horrific sight and eventually, to stem the panic, the body was covered with a rug. The nightmare did not end there. In the middle of the night the Pope's body was transferred to the church of Santa Maria delle Febbri to be interred. The fetid corpse was now so swollen that it was only with great difficulty that the undertakers were able to squeeze it into the coffin. It was as though Alexander VI, right to the very last, were refusing to renounce the worldly life that had given him so much iniquitous pleasure.

That he himself should be incapacitated at the very moment of his father's death was a circumstance Cesare Borgia had not foreseen. He was now so ill that he was unable to exert much influence over the election of the new pope, although he tried his best to promote the cause of the French Cardinal, George d'Amboise.

The Cardinal of Aragon returned from his uncle Federico's court in France for the conclave in Rome. He arrived on the evening of 10 September, having travelled from Rouen with the influential Cardinal of Rouen, d'Amboise, and Il Moro's brother, Cardinal Ascanio Sforza. They were met on the Ponte Milvio by four other cardinals. Here they dismounted and changed out of their riding apparel into the rochets, scarlet capes, purple hoods and cardinal's hats that protocol demanded. At the conclave, Luigi navigated ably through the corridors of Vatican politics. He let it be thought that he would support the Cardinal of Rouen, but in fact he had no intention of sealing the ruin of his house by forwarding the election of one of the French King's chief ministers.[17] The cardinals were deeply divided but eventually, on 22 September, compromised by choosing a transitional pope, Francesco Todeschini Piccolomini, Cardinal of Siena, brother of Giovanna's late father-in-law. Piccolomini's ill-health had made him prematurely old and he was not expected to live long. As it happened, he died even sooner than expected, his papacy lasting barely two months.

Two months was long enough, however, to serve the cause of the Duchess of Amalfi. At the crucial moment when Gonsalvo de Cordova was conquering the Kingdom of Naples on behalf of Ferdinand of Spain, her right to her title and estates were fortuitously defended by Piccolomini's promotion.

Francesco Piccolomini's election was greeted with great rejoicing in Rome, for the high moral calibre of his reputation was in such stark contrast to his predecessor's debauchery. He was a peace-loving, gentle man and a week after his election he remarked to the Venetian ambassador: 'I do not intend to be a warlike pope, I intend to be one of peace.'[18]

Giovanna would almost certainly have travelled to Rome in this period with her young son, Alfonso, to pay homage to their kinsman, the new Pope, who took on the name Pius III in memory of his illustrious uncle, Pope Pius II. She may even have been portrayed in the fresco that commemorates his coronation on the walls of the Piccolomini library in Siena Cathedral. Vasari, in his *Lives of the Artists*, asserts that some of the people portrayed in the fresco by Pinturicchio (completed February 1504) were members of the Piccolomini family (Plates 6 and 28).[19] Giovanna could be the female figure on the back row, who stands beneath the coat of arms of her husband's family. Her husband's uncle, Andrea Piccolomini, who commissioned the fresco, is known to have been portrayed in the library frescos and the two youths in the far right-hand corner are thought to be Andrea's sons. In all likelihood, the child on a man's shoulders just behind them represents the five-year-old Duke of Amalfi, great-grandson of King Ferrante I of Naples and great-nephew of two Piccolomini popes.

In the vast concourse of people who gathered in Rome on 8 October for Piccolomini's coronation, Giovanna would have finally been reunited with her elder brother, whom she had not seen for over four years. They had been sorrowful years and she was lonely and unhappy. Did she complain of this to him? Did she plead with him to allow her to remarry to alleviate her solitude and the burden of administering her vast domains? Luigi's reply would have been evasive, but he was not unmoved by her plight.

The elaborate coronation ceremony was a great drain on Pope Pius's strength, for he was suffering from gout and had recently undergone a painful operation on his leg. Because he was so weak, his formal entry to the Lateran Church had to be postponed to a later date and he was obliged to remain seated while conducting the mass in St Peter's. He lived for only ten days after his coronation, dying on 18 October 1503.

The brief duration of his papacy had been sufficient, however, for the formidable Giuliano della Rovere to reorganise his tactics and, even before the new conclave had begun, to gather most of the Italian cardinals behind him. The conclave lasted only a few hours and was one of the briefest on record. On 1 November 1503, della Rovere was declared Pope Julius II, a name well suited to his *cesareus animus*.[20] In character this new Pope was very different from his predecessor. Although he shared with Pius the *male del tempo* (gout), Julius was full of exuberant energy, which belied his sixty years. He worked incessantly from dawn to dusk in a neurotic mental and physical *moto perpetuo*. He was so impatient and irascible that ambassadors complained that he would not listen long enough for them to explain their missions. And where Pius had been calm and peace-loving, Julius II was bellicose.

When the new Pope set his sights on freeing the temporal power of the Church from the crushing vice of Franco-Spanish rivalry, Cardinal Luigi d'Aragona, who was no novice to military campaigns, soon entered into Julius's favour. Julius immediately took up the policy of Alexander VI regarding the Papal Marches. The petty feudal lords, whom Cesare Borgia had temporarily vanquished for his own ends in order to create the Duchy of Romagna for himself, were now to be subjugated for the glory and profit of the Church.

One of Julius's first policy decisions after his election was to send reinforcements to the Spanish general Gonsalvo de Cordova, to enable him to definitively expel the French from the Kingdom of Naples, where they were still lingering on the northern border. This Gonsalvo achieved in December 1503. The French army disintegrated and soon the road to Rome was covered with miserable bands of armed French fugitives, on whom the local peasants wreaked their revenge at every opportunity. The massacre at Capua had not been forgotten.

Once removed from Naples, the French were, for the time being, confined to the northern part of Italy, while the Spaniards were contained in the south. Julius's long-term aim, however, was to expel both from Italian soil. Cardinal Luigi d'Aragona was destined to become the cornerstone in the implementation of this policy; and the behaviour of the Cardinal's sister at this critical moment took on crucial political significance for him.

Pope Julius's support for the Spanish conquest of Naples put paid to Federico's hopes of returning to his throne in the immediate future and he settled down to the life of an exile. Although he was not content, he had at least been spared the harsh imprisonment and indignity reserved for Ludovico il Moro. Federico and the members of his court (among whom would have been Antonio Bologna, if Bandello's account is accepted as accurate) had landed at Marseilles on 10 October 1501. At Louis's palace of Blois in March 1502, he received the news that his last stronghold on the Italian peninsula, Taranto, had surrendered to Gonsalvo de Cordova, who imprisoned its governor, Federico's twelve-year-old son, Ferdinand, Duke of Calabria, and eventually sent him off to Spain.[21] The fallen King was obliged to admit that Louis and Ferdinand the Catholic had politically outmanoeuvred him and rather than sign over all his rights to the Kingdom of Naples to his treacherous Spanish cousins, he decided to renounce them in favour of the French King. In return he was given the county of Maine in France (formally bequeathed to him in May 1502) and an annual pension of 30,000 ducats. The French parliament contested the alienation of royal domains by King Louis, but he overrode them, replying that half the Kingdom of Naples was cheap at the price.[22]

The Neapolitan nobles who followed Federico to France were not much taken with the tenor of life there, though Federico's court, if no longer that of a king, was still a pleasant one. He lived, however, like a bird in a golden cage; a virtual prisoner, obliged to follow King Louis wherever he went. When Louis crossed the Alps to visit his newly conquered Duchy of Milan in May 1502, Federico went with him, and many Neapolitan noblemen, disillusioned with life in France, took this opportunity to return home to Naples.

A series of letters, written from Jacopo d'Atri in France to Isabella d'Este, trace the last events in Federico's life. By January 1503 his court had been halved and reduced to 250 men. At this time his nephew Cardinal Luigi d'Aragona can certainly be included in this number. He arrived from Spain and did not leave his uncle's court until late August of that year, when he was called to the conclave in Rome caused by the death of Pope Alexander VI. By the time of Luigi's departure, Federico's health and his finances had deteriorated considerably. He was suffering badly from attacks of gout, and Louis's payments to him were so irregular that he was forced to borrow considerable sums of money.[23]

In September 1503 Federico followed Louis to Macon where he offered himself as mediator in the Franco-Spanish struggle for Naples, believing that he might be reinstated in the Kingdom as a compromise solution to the conflict, since neither Louis nor Ferdinand the Catholic would admit defeat. But at this point (November/December 1503) the new Pope, Julius II, stepped in and settled the dispute, and Federico was forced to resign himself to the idea of never returning to his Kingdom. His health began to deteriorate rapidly. From August 1504 onwards he suffered from an ear infection and a persistent quartan fever, which caused respiratory complications.

Shortly before his death, his house caught fire during the night, with considerable loss of life and property, though Federico was carried to safety.[24] We do not know whether it was an accident or whether the King of France or his advisers attempted to eliminate Federico, who had become an onerous and unjustifiable burden now that the French half of the Kingdom of Naples was effectively lost to Spain. Whatever the case, after the fire Federico was transferred to the Château of Montils at Plessis-lès-Tours, where his condition steadily worsened. He died there on 8 October 1504, surrounded by a small circle of family and friends.[25]

A few weeks later, on 2 December, Federico's half-brother, Cesare d'Aragona, who had followed him into exile in France, also died in the

Above: the Spanish general Gonsalvo de Cordova enters Naples after defeating the French at Ostia. He is flanked by the Archbishop of Tarragona and Don Alfonso d'Aragona (brother of Sancia), who later married Lucrezia Borgia. Below: Alfonso accompanies Giovanna's brother Carlo d'Aragona and their uncle Cesare d'Aragona as they enter Naples, May 1497 (*Codice Ferraiolo*, Pierpont Morgan Library, New York MS M. 801, f. 146v).

same province of Tours.[26] The passing of the two brothers must have proved convenient for King Louis's purse, since by this time he had lost the hoped-for half of the Neapolitan Kingdom which had justified the pension he was paying to the exiled members of the Aragonese House of Naples. After Federico's death, Louis certainly lost no time in informing his widow, Isabella del Balzo, that there was no place or sustenance for her in France. She was forced to return with her children to Italy and rely on the charity of her husband's nephew, Alfonso d'Este, Duke of Ferrara.[27]

The dynasty of Ferrante I was now at its nadir. Of his children there remained in Naples only two illegitimate sons, Don Ferrante, Count of Arena and his dissolute half-brother, Don Alfonso; and two daughters, the former Queen of Hungary, Beatrice, and Ferrandino's widow, Queen Giovanna IV (who returned in 1507). They all came to terms with the conquering Spaniards, and most of Ferrante's grandchildren followed suit, the Duchess of Amalfi included. Only Cardinal Luigi d'Aragona remained aloof from both the Spaniards and the French, never forgiving either for the disaster they had wrought upon his House. He set himself to the restoration of the family fortunes, and in Pope Julius II he found a perfect foil.

CHAPTER 7

A New Life: Antonio Bologna

FERDINAND . . . observe the Duchess;
To note all the particulars of her haviour:
What suitors do solicit her for marriage,
And whom she best affects. She's a young widow:
I would not have her marry again.

John Webster, *The Duchess of Malfi*, I.i.254–9

These, or similar words were probably communicated to Antonio Bologna by Cardinal Luigi d'Aragona some time late in 1504 or early 1505, when his sister's lamentations eventually moved him to enlist someone to help her with her duties as Duchess of Amalfi. By 1504, Naples was restored to normality and Giovanna had returned to her Neopolitan palace, as had her cousin Sancia, who had been accompanied back to Naples from Rome by Prospero Colonna in the autumn of 1503. Colonna's purpose was to confer with the new Viceroy, Gonsalvo de Cordova and the Viceroy generously permitted Sancia to take up residence in her old *palazzo* near Castelnuovo. She lived there with her husband Joffre Borgia but refused to have any contact with him. Sancia had had her fill of Borgias: they had murdered her brother, tormented and then imprisoned her in the Castel Sant' Angelo. But the Borgia star was now in decline, while that of Gonsalvo de Cordova was rising high; and it was to Gonsalvo that she turned her attentions. Gonsalvo was not insensible to Sancia's charms. One day he found her at mass in the church of San Sebastiano and gallantly accompanied her through the streets of Naples back to her palace. From their political discussions (Sancia was privy to many secrets of the Borgias) developed a mutual attraction. Ambassadors noted that the Viceroy visited Sancia and stayed till late at night, and when Gonsalvo fell ill it was Sancia who stayed by his bedside to minister to him.

Prospero Colonna's name became linked with that of Sancia's half-sister, Isabella, formerly Duchess of Milan and now Duchess of Bari. They too reputedly had an amorous relationship. When Isabella returned to Naples from Bari on 7 March 1504, Prospero went to greet her and accompanied her to her old home of Castelcapuano, where Sanudo pointedly mentions, he '. . . accompanied her right to her room'. Giovanna was drawn into her cousins' romantic quartet. She and Sancia were present to welcome Isabella home and two days after her return they went together to pay her a visit at Castelcapuano. Had it not been for the absence of Giovanna's dead sister Caterina, it was almost like old childhood times. But the joy of reunion was short-lived; soon bereavement was thrust upon Giovanna again. Later that year Sancia died, at the age of twenty-seven. She was given a magnificent funeral by her grieving lover, Gonsalvo de Cordova.[1]

In October, ex-king Federico also died, in exile in France, and a pall of sadness must have again cast its shadow over Giovanna's life. It was probably this sadness which rendered the burden of her duties intolerable and drove her either to appeal to her brother Luigi for help or, as Bandello would have it, induced her to take matters into her own hands, when it came to her attention that one of King Federico's servants, a handsome, gallant and cultured young man called Antonio Bologna, had returned to Naples. Perhaps she already knew Bologna and noticed him strolling along the street beneath her palace window on his way to and from his family home at the nearby Palazzo Panormita. Or she may have been informed that Bologna, a man educated at the Aragon courts of Naples, had returned to the city and was seeking employment. In any event, Bandello (and most of the sources that follow his version) has Giovanna writing to Antonio Bologna herself, inviting him to become her major-domo.

But in those times when the actions of women were so subject to the scrutiny of their menfolk, it seems hardly credible that Giovanna would have written a letter on her own initiative to a little-known person. 'She was lonely,' says Bandello by way of justification for his account, 'and seeking a handsome, accomplished young man to aid her with the government of her domains, keep her company and perhaps fill her bed.' The latter assumption might have been true, but his direct mention of it is a presumption on his part.

An early transcript of the Corona manuscripts[2] gives a differing version. It affirms that Bologna was sent to the Duchess by the Cardinal himself, like the character Bosola in Webster's drama, primarily to keep an eye on her. This seems a more plausible hypothesis. Giovanna would have been more likely to trust the recommendation of her elder brother than to write to Bologna of her own initiative. According to the manuscript, the Duchess had mentioned to her brothers that she would like to remarry, in order to alleviate the burden of governing her vast domains and the loneliness which that entailed. The Cardinal replied vehemently that she should put the thought aside since the political situation would not permit it. For the moment, as long as her son was a minor, there was no question of her abandoning her powerful position as Duchess of Amalfi or of her sharing it with anyone. However, as a palliative, he decided to send a Neapolitan gentleman in his trust to aid her in her administrative duties. The gentleman of his choice was Antonio Bologna.

Bologna was an ideal candidate. He was an able knight, 'whom few could equal at wielding a sword or breaking in a horse',[3] and an accomplished courtier, who wrote poetry, sang well and composed music for the lute, which he played excellently. But above all he had been educated at the royal Aragonese courts of Naples and had been employed by members of Giovanna's family in the past. Bologna, says Bandello, had been major-domo to King Federico for 'many years' and after his master's death in France, he had been left without employment and decided to return to Naples.[4] The veracity of this 'many years' is doubtful. He was certainly not Federico's major-domo in 1499, nor is he mentioned in Federico's court, in any capacity.[5] It must be presumed, therefore, that this was artistic licence on Bandello's part, in what was essentially a literary rather than a biographical work. But who, then, was this Antonio Bologna and where did he come from?

He was not of royal blood, but neither was he of low descent, socially or intellectually. His surname was in fact Beccadelli. His family took their name from the castle of Beccadello, not far from Bologna. Some sources affirm that the family may even have originated in England[6] and, according to the writings of Antonio's eminent grandfather, Antonio Beccadelli da Bologna (better known as Il Panormita), a legend had been passed down in the family that they were descended from a twelfth-century English ambassador to the Vatican, who subsequently established his family in Italy. This ambassador to Pope Alexander III was reputedly a kinsman of Saint Thomas à Becket, the surname 'Beccadelli' being an Italian corruption of the English 'Becket'. Certainly there is evidence that the Beccadelli family, after its transfer to Naples, had connections with a church dedicated to Saint Thomas à Becket there and a later ancestor, Galeazzo Beccadelli, was knighted by the English King, Edward I (1272–1307), at Forlì.[7] Ironically, the city of Forlì played a decisive part in Bologna's love story with Giovanna d'Aragona.

Internecine factional conflicts led to the expulsion of Antonio's forebear Vannino Beccadelli from Bologna in 1335, in much the same way as the Piccolomini had been forced to flee from their native Siena. Vannino moved to Sicily and there, in remembrance of his Bolognese origins, added 'da Bologna' to his surname. (Some sources carry 'di', others 'da' or 'de' Bologna.) In time, the 'Beccadelli' was dropped and their surname became da Bologna and then just Bologna.[8]

Though Vannino Beccadelli had fallen on bad times, during the course of the fourteenth century the family's fortunes began to recuperate in Palermo and by the last decade of that century Vannino's son Enrico was first magistrate in the city (from 1395–9). The Neapolitan branch of the family was founded by Enrico's son, Antonio Beccadelli da Bologna (1394–1471), who became one of the most respected literary figures of fifteenth-century Italy and was known as Il Panormita (from Panormum, the Latin name for his birthplace, Palermo).

In 1419 Antonio Beccadelli da Bologna left his native Palermo to enrol at the University of Siena, where he came into contact with the young Eneas Silvio Piccolomini, who later became Pope Pius II. He studied history, rhetoric, poetry, and other forms of literature, took a degree in law, and became one of the chief orators and poets of his time. He soon realised, however, that writing poetry at the court of some prince or powerful overlord would be more profitable and less stressful than practising as a lawyer scurrying between cases. Eventually he found a suitable position at the court of Duke Filippo Maria Visconti in Milan. Visconti nominated him *poeta aulico* and this led to the Holy Roman Emperor, Sigismund, crowning him poet laureate at Parma.

For the academic year 1430/1 he was given a teaching post at the University of Pavia, but after a disagreement over his salary in 1434 he left Pavia and returned to Palermo, where he joined the court of King Alfonso V of Aragon. When Alfonso set out to conquer Naples the next year, Antonio Beccadelli da Bologna followed him and remained an important member of the Neapolitan court once Alfonso had become

Elevation of the Palazzo Panormita, Antonio Bologna's home in Naples.

established there. He eventually rose to become the King's secretary and adviser.

While in the service of King Alfonso (from 1435 onwards), Antonio Beccadelli da Bologna contributed much to bringing Renaissance learning to Naples. He enriched the precious library that King Alfonso was establishing at Castelnuovo with his own writings and his transcriptions of ancient manuscripts. He was a great humanist scholar and the leading light of King Alfonso's post-prandial symposia. He also tutored the King's son, Ferrante.

King Alfonso used Il Panormita as his ambassador on several delicate diplomatic missions and paid him well for his services. He was soon wealthy enough to begin building himself a fine palace in Naples. It was situated in the very heart of the city, in the narrow Vico de' Bisi, opposite the *Seggio del Nido*, of which he was soon co-opted a member. The *seggi* were prestigious administrative institutions, whose members (with the exception of the *Seggio del Popolo*) were all nobles and patricians.

Il Panormita wrote profusely, sometimes scurrilously, and is mainly remembered in the history of Italian literature for his *L'Hermaphroditus*, a collection of ribald epigrams, reminiscent of the works of Ovid and

Photograph of the *palazzo* today. The building just visible to the left was the *Seggio del Nido*, to which both Bologna and the Duke of Amalfi belonged.

Martial. (Perhaps something of Panormita's excessive sensuality was passed down to his grandson Antonio Bologna.) But Panormita is better remembered for more sober compositions, such as his highly praised memorial of the reign of King Alfonso I of Naples.

After the death of King Alfonso in the summer of 1458, the post-prandial symposia, which the old King had so enjoyed but for which his successor showed no inclination, were transferred to the luxuriant shady gardens of Panormita's newly built *palazzo*. Here he founded the Academy for Philosophical Studies, which eventually became known as the Accademia Pontaniana after the name of his acolyte, Giovanni Pontano. Panormita's influence lent a poetic bent to this renowned Neapolitan school of humanist studies. Until his death, the Academy met at his home in Naples or, when the summer heat was excessive, at his other residence on the flanks of Vesuvius, at Resina (Herculaneum).[9]

On 7 January 1471, at the venerable age of seventy-eight, Il Panormita died in Naples and was buried in the church of San Domenico Maggiore. After King Alfonso's death, the fortunes of the ageing Panormita had begun to decline and those of his son Antonino continued to do so after Panormita's death – to such an extent that by 1484, work to complete the family *palazzo* in Naples had to be suspended. By this time Antonino had married a noblewoman of the distinguished and wealthy De Sangro family. Her rich dowry failed to relieve the Beccadelli's ailing finances, but before her premature death, she bequeathed a son to Antonino, who was named Antonio after his illustrious grandfather. Since the Milan necrology gives Antonio Bologna's age as thirty at the time of his death in October 1513, he was presumably born in 1483.

The young Antonio grew up in Naples in his grandfather's partially completed *palazzo*, which was situated in the vicinity of the Palazzo Piccolomini, and he inherited his grandfather's position as a respected member of the *Seggio del Nido*. This was the same *seggio* to which the Duchess of Amalfi's late husband, Alfonso Piccolomini, belonged, and this fact, together with the proximity of their homes, could be seen to suggest that Antonio Bologna and the Duchess of Amalfi had come into contact before she took him into her service.

After his mother's death, Antonio's father remarried and had two more sons, plus an illegitimate son; in addition to his three sisters, Antonio had three half-brothers (Federico, Giovanni and Jacopo). Bandello states that during his youth Antonio spent time at the courts of Alfonso II, Ferrandino and Federico and this is quite probable; the children of the nobility often became pages at the royal courts in order to learn courtly skills. As we have seen, it is possible that Antonio had first come to the Duchess's notice at some court function or festivity.

Bandello and the old Corona manuscript agree that Antonio was considered worthy of his position of trust in the Duchess's household mainly because of his faithful service to her uncle, King Federico. But since there is no sign of him in the records of Federico's court, where was he during the years which immediately preceded his entering the Duchess's service? A major-domo called Antonio da Bologna was to be found at the court of Francesco Gonzaga, Marquis of Mantua, from about 1499 until the end of 1504. This may be a homonym (so frequent in the period), but as the last mention of this Antonio da Bologna at Mantua is in 1505, the dates coincide precisely with the Duchess's story.

Francesco Gonzaga was married to the Duchess of Amalfi's cousin, Isabella d'Este (Plate 29), who was considered *la dama per eccellenza* of the Italian Renaissance. She was a great patron of the arts and cultivated her image as 'the first woman of her time' with great care. Her magnificent gowns were embroidered with enigmatic symbols and

Francesco Gonzaga, Marquis of Mantua. Bust by Gian Cristoforo Romano (*Palazzo Ducale, Mantua, © Ministero per I Beni e le Attività Culturali; photograph by Finaffer*).

classical mottoes, which other noblewomen hastened to imitate. Her Mantuan castle on the River Mincio was full of ancient statuary and artefacts, precious paintings and books and augmenting her collections became the principal aim of her life. Her paintings were eventually bought in the seventeenth century by Charles I, King of England.[10] Like her peers, Isabella was fluent in Latin, and had studied Greek. She made herself a celebrity among the humanists of the day by corresponding with artists, poets and other literary figures, whom she importuned for examples of their works (preferably dedicated to her). However, as one perspicacious biographer, Maria Bellonci,[11] puts it: although she liked to present herself as a 'most ardently free spirit in the inventions of life', her tastes were circumscribed and anchored to fashion, and she was more informed than illuminated.

Isabella was, in fact, the antithesis of the Duchess of Amalfi. Where Giovanna was willing to renounce her position and worldly goods to pursue the higher spirituality of her love for her husband and children, Isabella spent her life filling an emotional void with adulation and material possessions. She was petty in her sentiments and paranoiacally jealous both of her younger sister, Beatrice (who married Ludovico il Moro), and of her own daughter, Eleonora, when the latter's beauty began to outshine her own. But if her intellectual pretensions were not all she would have wished them to be, Isabella's artistry in intrigue was exceptional. She held a complex network of correspondence with all the courts of Italy (and many European ones too), which enabled her to gauge the political situation very accurately. She was certainly more able than her husband in this: as her biographer says, she was, 'informed'. And her cousin, Cardinal Luigi d'Aragona, was among her correspondents.

The first mention of Antonio da Bologna at the Gonzaga court is a letter written to him by Isabella on 9 August 1499 regarding his mission to her brother, Alfonso d'Este, in Ferrara, to obtain an urgently needed loan on her behalf.[12] By January of the following year Antonio is named as the *salvarobbe* (a sort of chamberlain) to Isabella's husband, Francesco Gonzaga, in an edict by Francesco granting him the privilege of tax exemption.

Soon Bologna seems to have occupied a position of absolute trust in the Gonzaga household and, in a letter dated 23 July 1502, we find Isabella imploring her impetuous but erring husband to place his personal safety in Antonio's hands. Isabella was concerned that Francesco might be poisoned by order of Cesare Borgia: Gonzaga had outspokenly condemned and insulted Borgia at the French court in Milan, calling him (according to Sanudo) 'the bastard of a priest' and threatening to annihilate him. Isabella was alarmed at her husband's undiplomatic and dangerous arrogance and in her letter she urges him to be more prudent:

> . . . Your Excellency has spoken angry words against Valentino [Cesare Borgia] before the Most Christian King [Louis XII of France] and the Pope's servants, and whether this is true or not, they will doubtless reach the ears of Valentino, who, having already shown that he does not scruple to conspire against those of his own blood [the murder of Cesare's brother Juan], will, I am certain, not hesitate to plot against your person. And being jealous for your life, which I count dearer than my own, and knowing how your natural goodness leads you to take no precautions for your safety, I have made enquiries of Antonio da Bologna and others, and hear from them that you allow all manner of persons to serve you at table, and that Alessandro da Baesso eats with you, leaving grooms and pages to do the offices of carvers and cupbearers. So that I see it would be perfectly easy for anyone to poison

> Your Excellency, since you have neither guards nor proper servants. I pray and implore you therefore, if you will not take care for your own sake, to be more careful for my sake and that of our little son, and I hope that you will in future order Alessandro to discharge his office of carver with the greatest caution. If he cannot do this, I will send Antonio or some other trustworthy servant, because I had rather run the risk of making you angry than that both I and our little one should be left to weep for you.

In the postscript she adds, with a humbleness that was far from her real character:

> My dearest lord, do not laugh at my fears and say that women are cowards and always afraid, because their malignity is far greater than my fears and your own courage.[13]

What Isabella was really doing was reproving Francesco Gonzaga for his reckless bravado, which might have put the tiny enclave of Mantua in danger of being engulfed by Cesare's Borgia's voracious army, as Urbino and other small Italian states had been. But Isabella could not make her political astuteness too obvious, for fear of alienating her husband. The fact that she had asked Antonio Bologna how her husband was behaving at the French court could indicate that he had spent some time there with his master. Antonio may, therefore, have been at the French court, as Bandello asserts, but in Milan rather than in France.

At the beginning of August 1502, Cesare Borgia appeared in person at the French court in Milan and, according to Sanudo, had a violent argument with Gonzaga regarding his insults. Borgia was not one to pardon easily any lack of respect and he challenged Gonzaga to a duel. This was avoided only by the mediation of the French King, who required the services of both men. He needed the support of Borgia and his father, Pope Alexander, against Spain, and he wanted Gonzaga to lead the French troops against the Spaniards in Naples.

In October Louis took Gonzaga off to France to plan their strategy. He stayed there until after Christmas and a letter, written by Antonio Bologna from Mantua in December to his master in France, has survived in the Mantuan archives. It announces the death of one of the Marquis's seneschals.

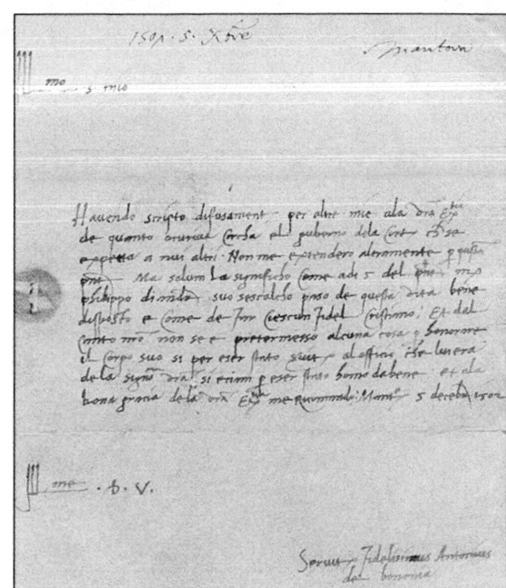

Letter written by Antonio Bologna to his master the Marquis of Mantua, Francesco Gonzaga (*Archivo Gonzaga, Busta 2459, c. 630. State Archive of Mantua*).

1502 5 December Mantua

My illustrious Lord

Having written to your Excellency at length about other affairs regarding what was needed for the government of the court that is expected from us, I will not enlarge further on that here. I will mention only that on the fifth of this month Master Schipo of Modena, your seneschal, passed out of this life as resigned as any true, faithful Christian. And for our part, no honours to his body were omitted, considering the dignity of the office he held at your Lordship's court and for the fact that he had always been an honourable man: I commend myself to your Excellency's good grace: Mantua 5 December 1502.

Your very faithful servant
Antonio da Bologna[14]

From his position of trust, Antonio began to acquire financial gain and in March 1503 he purchased a property from the convent of San Ruffino in Mantua.[15] However, it seems that either Bologna had excited jealousies at court, which caused him to be the victim of a plot, or he was not the respectable man of principles Bandello would have us believe, for by the end of the following year the 'very faithful servant Antonio da Bologna' had fallen into disgrace and been imprisoned as a traitor.

It appears he had been pocketing funds which rightfully belonged to his master, Gonzaga. According to a letter written by Gonzaga to Antonio Tebaldeo at the Este court of Ferrara in December of 1504, Bologna had ordered clothes for himself and his household, pretending that they were for the Marquis and his family.[16] Bologna had by this time been promoted to the position of major-domo at Gonzaga's court and had profited from his position of trust to become a petty embezzler – at least this is what his master had been led to believe.

But there was a more serious charge of political intrigue against the Marquis to which Bologna had to answer. He may have become involved in plots at the instigation of the Este family, perhaps even with the tacit encouragement of Gonzaga's wife, Isabella. Relations between the bordering states of Mantua and Ferrara were always in tenuous equilibrium and Isabella was perennially torn between her loyalties to both. Between 1504 and 1505, her brothers Alfonso and Cardinal Ippolito plotted to eliminate Gonzaga's favourite, known as 'the Milanese', because his excessive influence over the Marquis threatened to undermine their sister's power. Bologna may have been drawn into this conspiracy, though it is not certain from the surviving documentation whether or not this was the case. It appears, however, that the Este brothers did have some connection with Bologna's plight, for in answer to a plea for mercy, made on his behalf by Lucrezia Borgia, Gonzaga says he will suspend all action against the offender until he has had a personal consultation on the matter with his Este brothers-in-law.

Why had Lucrezia Borgia written to Gonzaga in November 1504, pleading with him not to sentence Antonio da Bologna to death?[17] Lucrezia was by this time Gonzaga's sister-in-law, for in 1502 she had married Isabella's brother, Alfonso d'Este, heir to the Duchy of Ferrara. She may have made this emphatic plea for mercy on behalf of Antonio Bologna because he had once been in her service, or in the service of her second husband, Alfonso d'Aragona, Duke of Bisceglie, and something of this sort is implied in her letter to Gonzaga. Or, more simply, Lucrezia could have developed a particular affection for him after meeting him at the court of Ferrara, when Isabella had sent him there on an errand.

At the time of Lucrezia's letter to Gonzaga, her new husband, Alfonso d'Este, was away visiting England and she was just beginning to feel the first stirrings of attraction for her swarthy, swashbuckling brother-in-law, the Marquis of Mantua. In Gonzaga's reply there is a hint of jealousy in the petulant protest that Lucrezia seems more concerned for Bologna's welfare than for his own, a reproof which indicates that her passion was already being reciprocated. Eventually their clandestine affair threatened to become an affair of state, but, unlike the Duchess of Amalfi, neither Francesco Gonzaga nor Lucrezia Borgia was willing to throw off the political chains which bound them to their dynastic positions. Once the liaison was discovered by the Este family, Francesco abandoned it altogether, much to Lucrezia's chagrin.

Although Bologna had initially been condemned to death by the Marquis in the autumn of 1504, there is no mention in the Mantuan necrology of an Antonio da Bologna being executed or dying in 1504 or 1505. There is a record of a payment made to him on 5 September 1505,[18] and then no further mention of him at Mantua. It seems likely, therefore, that during 1505 the Este family persuaded Gonzaga not to execute him but merely to expel him from the Gonzaga domains.

In Lucrezia Borgia's letter to Gonzaga, Antonio da Bologna is specifically defined as major-domo. It could be a coincidence that at this time there were two attractive young major-domos at Italian courts by the name of Antonio da Bologna, and that both changed their employers around 1504/5; but this is unlikely. While the documentation is incomplete and the evidence inconclusive, it is highly probable that these two were one and the same person. Since the dates match so closely the Antonio da Bologna from the Gonzaga court who returned to Naples was almost certainly the same man who entered the Duchess of Amalfi's service shortly after the death of her uncle, King Federico, in France in October 1504. If Bologna had been scheming on behalf of the Este brothers, it is possible that they recommended him to their cousin, the Cardinal of Aragon, as a suitable agent to spy on his sister. If this was so, the plan went terribly awry.

CHAPTER 8

The Love Affair

CARDINAL The marriage night
Is the entrance into some prison.

John Webster, *The Duchess of Malfi*, I.i.324–5

According to the old Corona manuscript, when her brothers announced the arrival of the new administrator, Giovanna had expected a rather solemn old man, but she was pleasantly surprised to see a handsome, young gentleman dismount in the courtyard of her castle. Bologna was immediately admitted to her presence, where he introduced himself elegantly, paying her flowery compliments, the like of which she had not heard for a considerable time. She was pleased and flattered and already the pall of melancholy began to lift from her.

Within a week of his arrival, the Duchess had eyes and ears only for her handsome, new steward. Once the business of the day was concluded, they rode together up and down the panoramic mountain tracks of the Amalfi coast, discoursing on all manner of subjects. The evenings, too, passed sweetly in his company, as he chivalrously wooed her with his poems, songs and lute-playing. Soon she had fallen irretrievably in love. If Antonio read the desire in her eyes and reciprocated her love, he could not reveal his sentiments. Any such presumption towards his mistress would have been disrespectful and could even have been considered traitorous.

It had to be Giovanna herself who broached the subject. The torment of being beside him daily without making her feelings known became intolerable and, no longer able to contain herself, one day she confessed to him her love. Once he had overcome his initial fears, Bologna took her gently in his arms and, while he assured her that he loved her above all others in the world, he explained that he could not bring himself to take their relationship further and betray the position of trust in which her brothers had placed him.[1] Apart from considerations of honour, they both knew his life would be at risk if such an affair were to come to light. The matter rested for a while, but Giovanna felt herself ever more unbearably attracted to Bologna. She had to find a solution that would reassure him. Finally, one day she called him to the room in which they habitually dealt with the government of her domains. She bade him sit beside her in the window seat and began with a guise of discussing some administrative business:

> I would be wary of speaking on this matter with anyone but you, Antonio. But I know you for a discreet and perceptive gentleman, nurtured at the royal courts of my relatives, the Kings Alfonso, Ferrante and Federico and I am sure that once you have understood my motives, you will agree with me, for if you do not I shall be obliged to revise my opinion of your merits.
>
> As you know, since the death of my dear husband the Duke left me widowed very young, I have conducted my life so irreproachably that not even the point of a needle could stain my honesty. With the same rigour I have ruled my son's estates, so that when he comes of age he will find them more florid than when his father left them. As well as paying off 15,000 ducats in debts accumulated during the preceding wars, I have bought more lands in Calabria,[2] which supply a good income, and I find myself without a tornese [Neapolitan coin] of debt and my house well-provided for.
>
> I had intended to remain a widow, and continue to conduct my life as I have until now, spending my time governing my son's domains, moving day by day to this estate and that, from one castle to another, or to my palace in Naples for a little diversion. But now I feel I must change my intentions and take up a new lifestyle. I believe it would be much better to procure myself a husband, rather than do as some women, who with offence to God and the eternal condemnation of the world, give themselves up to the arms of lovers. I know well what is said about a certain Duchess of this kingdom, that she still loves and is loved by one of the chief barons of the realm, and I know you understand whom I mean. [She is referring to her cousin Isabella d'Aragona, ex-Duchess of Milan, and Prospero Colonna.]
>
> But returning to my own situation, you can see that I am young; I am not cross-eyed or lame, neither do I have the face of a Baronzi [a noble Florentine family famous for their ugliness] that is unfit to appear in

public. I live as you see each day and I cannot stop myself from being drawn towards thoughts of love.

I would not know how to go about seeking a husband of my own rank, for unless I take some youth, who, once he was tired of me would kick me out of the marriage bed to replace me with some young whore, there are no barons of a suitable age who are marriageable. So after pondering long upon the problem I have decided to seek out a well-qualified gentleman and take him for my husband. But to avoid popular gossip and the wrath of my relations, especially my brother the Cardinal, I wish to keep the matter a secret until it can be revealed without danger.

The person I intend to marry has an income of about a thousand ducats. I, with my dowry and the increase in income that I have created since my husband's death, have over two thousand ducats, plus the moveable articles in my homes which are my own property. And if I cannot keep my rank as Duchess, I shall be happy to live as a gentlewoman.

I would like you to tell me what you advise me to do.[3]

Antonio was at a loss for words. He loved her as she loved him and had no wish to see her married to someone else. He sat mutely, his expression revealing all his sentiments. Then, instead of answering, he merely sighed deeply. This was more eloquent than any reply and Giovanna ceased her teasing and smiled; she told him to take heart for he was the person she intended to marry.[4]

If she took him for her husband instead of her lover, she argued, Antonio would neither betray his oath of honour to her family nor ignore the commandments of the Church. The matter would be kept secret until the time was appropriate to place before her brothers the fait accompli. They were men like him and had felt the sentiments of passion; they would understand and eventually respect her decision to become a wife rather than a concubine. They would appreciate the fact that she might have brought shame on her name by merely giving free rein to her desire, but that she had preferred to make her peace with God and her own conscience.

Her arguments convinced Antonio up to a point, but in his heart he was not persuaded and could not bring himself to share the rosy hopes that Giovanna nurtured of the Cardinal's pacific reaction once he had been informed that the marriage had taken place without his involvement or consent. But Antonio loved her and for him also it was torment to live beside her every day in denial of this love. God only knew what it cost him to fend off her approaches; what desperation induced him to gallop away along the steep mountain tracks to an isolated peak where he could seek solace, alone, watching the galleys plying slowly up and down the Amalfi coast.[5] And so, probably against his better judgement, he agreed to the secret marriage, which took place some time during 1505.

Bandello and the old Corona manuscript differ quite considerably on the nature of the marriage. Bandello affirms that they were only married by the *per verba de praesenti* rite, which was a betrothal with immediate present effect, as opposed to a betrothal *per verba de futura*, which specified some future date. If a betrothal *per verba de praesenti* were consummated, it had the status in Church law of a marriage and, in exceptional cases, where an ordained member of the Church was not available to witness the betrothal, a third person (agreed upon by the parties involved) could act as witness. In Giovanna's case the witness was her personal maid. Though Bandello does not name her, saying merely that she was the daughter of the Duchess's childhood wet-nurse, some of the Corona manuscripts give her name as Lucina Bonito.[6]

The Bonitos were a family of minor nobility from Amalfi. Lucina had probably served Giovanna for much of her life and there was doubtless a deep affection between the two women. Nevertheless, it was a dire predicament for Lucina. If she were to betray Giovanna, she would incur both her mistress's enmity and a dishonourable dismissal. But, by keeping faith with her mistress, she was putting her own life at risk and would receive no mercy should the deception come to light. Without Lucina's discreet collaboration, however, Giovanna would have been unable to engage in an intimate relationship with Antonio Bologna, let alone marry him. One of the ambiguities of Giovanna's dilemma is that she can perhaps be accused of blind egoism for exposing Lucina and Antonio to such mortal danger merely for her own satisfaction and fulfilment.

According to the early Corona manuscript, the marriage was not merely *per verba de praesenti*; it was also celebrated by a cleric. One evening, some time in 1505, Giovanna and Antonio rode up to a small hamlet in the mountains above Amalfi where they begged a Capuchin friar to unite them in matrimony. Two rough uncouth fishermen from the hamlet were called to witness the marriage. Neither they nor the friar were aware of the identity of the young couple. Only the Duchess's faithful maid was informed that her mistress had officially married her steward; only she knew why the woman who once considered herself the saddest in the Kingdom was now the happiest.[7]

Who are we to believe, the Corona manuscript, Bandello, or both? Since Giovanna wished her union to be sanctified before God and men, it is likely that, after the *verba praesenti* ceremony, she would have had her union blessed by a priest, even though the full sacraments of the marriage ceremony could not be celebrated. If the priest had dared to officiate at a proper wedding, he would certainly have fallen foul of the Cardinal's vendetta when the marriage was revealed.

Bologna and the Duchess found themselves confronted by a moral and a social dilemma. Giovanna did not wish to become his mistress, which, if the affair had been kept secret, would have been the most sensible way of conducting their relationship. She did not want a sordid casual affair of the sort enjoyed by ladies of the court and members of her family, such as her cousin Sancia. Paradoxically, the downfall of the Duchess of Amalfi, offspring of two generations of illegitimate fathers, was to be her marriage. She wanted to be Bologna's wife, to belong to him indissolubly for the rest of her life and enjoy the children she would bear him. She insisted on marrying him so that their union would be sanctified in the eyes of God and, thus, she hoped in the eyes of her brothers. It was a naïve and foolish hope, but she clung to it, affirming an independence of action unusual for a woman of her rank and time.

As a member of the royal family, Giovanna was not free to contract a marriage of her own volition; royal marriages were affairs of state with complex political implications. But, as she had affirmed to Bologna, Giovanna feared the unhappiness and frustration that a dynastic marriage might bring. For men in unhappy marriages there were always the consolations of concubines, an arrangement that was tolerated, and even encouraged. For women the situation was more difficult, and though unhappily married women did take lovers, the consequences could be dire if they were discovered, as the story of Giovanna's sister-in-law, Eleonora Piccolomini, demonstrates.

Eleonora and her husband had retired to France after the Spaniards had taken Naples, and they returned from exile in 1507. During her travels Eleonora had made the acquaintance of Cardinal Pedro Luis Borgia, a charming and handsome nephew of the late Pope Alexander. When Borgia came to live in Naples, he and Eleonora had an affair. On discovering Eleonora's betrayal the fury of the Prince of Bisignano was cold and calculating. On 4 October 1511 he invited Cardinal Borgia to a banquet at his newly acquired palace, opposite the church of Santa Chiara in Naples, feigning to know nothing of the illicit relationship between the Cardinal and his wife. During the banquet it is thought that he had them both poisoned, using, presumably, one of the so-called *veleni a termine* – slow-acting poisons which took effect over a certain number of days so there could be no way of connecting him directly with the deed.[8]

The day after the banquet, Cardinal Borgia suddenly left Naples to return to Rome. His excuse was that rumours were circulating in the city of Pope Julius's imminent death, but it is possible that at the banquet he had realised, or been warned, that the Prince of Bisignano had discovered his liaison with Eleonora and had consequently thought it more prudent to flee. It was already too late. On the road between Naples and Rome the poison began to take effect: collapsing, the Cardinal fell from his horse and died.[9] Two days after his death, Eleonora died too. She had been ill for three days – since the evening of the banquet. Her husband gave her a magnificent funeral, worthy of a Princess of the House of Sanseverino; a meagre consolation for the vivacious Eleonora Piccolomini.[10]

In the introduction to his novella about the Duchess of Amalfi, Bandello makes an interesting reflection on the injustices of the plight of women in his time. 'It is a great cruelty, he complains,

> that we men always want to satisfy every whim that comes to our mind, and we do not want poor women to satisfy theirs. . . . It seems to me a great stupidity that men consider that their honour and that of their house be vested in the appetite of a woman. If a man makes a mistake, however great, his relations do not lose their noble status. If a young man strays from the ancient virtuous path of his ancestors, who were valiant men, the latter do not lose their dignity. . . . There was, for example, that count (I will refrain from giving his name) who took a baker's daughter for his wife, and why? Because she had a great deal of property, and no one reprimanded him. Another count, noble and rich, took for his wife the daughter of a mule driver without even a dowry, for no more reason than it pleased him to do so, and now she has the place and rank of a countess and he is still a count as before. . . .[11]

It would be appropriate to pause here and discuss two other episodes contemporary with and very similar to the case of the Duchess of Amalfi, for they give a useful insight into the attitudes of the time. In *The Courtier*, Baldassarre Castiglione paints an idealised picture of the refined life at the court of the gentle Duke of Urbino, Guidobaldo di Montefeltro. But during the year (1507) in which Castiglione set his work, not only was the tragic love affair of Giovanna and Antonio Bologna maturing in Amalfi, but another, with a similarly tragic end, was coming to fruition in Urbino. Castiglione, however, discreetly refrains from making any reference to this in his serene dialogues at the Urbino court.

Duke Guidobaldo was childless and his heir was Francesco Maria della Rovere. Francesco's elder sister, left a young widow by her husband's death at the hands of Cesare Borgia, retired to her uncle Guidobaldo's court at Urbino with her infant son. In 1507 Francesco Maria was seventeen and she twenty-six. She soon fell in love with and began a relationship with Francesco Maria's handsome favourite, Giovanni Andrea Bravo da Verona.

When Francesco Maria discovered that Giovanni Andrea had, by the canons of the time, so abused his position of honour and trust, he was almost crazed with fury and set up a cowardly trap. He invited Giovanni Andrea to dine with him and after dinner suggested they amuse themselves by pitting their skills in a fencing match. Once the duel had begun, at a given signal, some of Francesco Maria's men entered the room, seized Giovanni Andrea and held him firm while their master ran him through repeatedly with his sword until he had killed him.

Francesco Maria was the Pope's nephew and thus untouchable; no reprisals were taken against him. His sister, it was rumoured, later gave birth to a child and was quietly married off to a very minor member of the Sforza family. Her sad face is thought to have been immortalised by Raphael in his portrait of *The Mute Woman*.[12]

Ten years earlier, in 1497, a lonely, young, divorced Lucrezia Borgia had taken one of her father's servants, Pedro (Perotto) Calderón, into her bed, and they too had been discovered, by her brother (Cesare Borgia). After surprising Calderón red-handed, Cesare pursued him to the papal throne-room, where he slaughtered him while he was begging Cesare's father, Pope Alexander, for mercy. Burkhardt, the papal master of ceremonies, notes a few days later that Calderón's body and that of Lucrezia's personal maid, Pantasilea, had been fished out of the Tiber. No punishment was meted out to Lucrezia and, when she gave birth to a son a few months later, a duplicitous confusion of papal Bulls declared the child to be son of both Pope Alexander and Cesare Borgia.[13] Speculation about incest, it seems, was preferable to the dilution of noble blood with that of social inferiors. Certain parallels can be drawn with the Duchess of Amalfi's story, and it will be noted that no harm was done to either of the erring sisters.

Giovanna was not an adulteress like her sister-in-law, Eleonora, who had sinned against the laws of the Church. The only sin Giovanna had committed by her secret marriage was one against society – a society that kept women abjectly subjugated. Though contemporaries like the chronicler Filonico Alicarnasseo accused her of '*concupiscenza con vergogna*' (shameful lust) for ceding to her carnal desires and betraying the honour of her family and her royal blood, she was, in fact, rebutting the condoned whoredom of arranged marriages and affirming a superior type of union based on the sincerity of love and esteem rather than material interests.

Soon after her marriage, Giovanna gave birth, in secrecy, to her first child by Antonio Bologna. John Webster gives 19 December 1504 as the child's birth date, but this was a fictional invention and probably varies by about a year from the real date.[14] If we presume that Bologna returned to Naples in early 1505, it seems likely that their first child would have been born late that year or early in 1506. That a son by Bologna was secretly born to the Duchess in this period is certain. He was baptised Federico, after Giovanna's uncle and after Bologna's younger half-brother.[15] There was no question of Giovanna keeping the child with her. Antonio took the baby away and gave him to a trusted wet-nurse, who was presumably not told the mother's identity.

They managed to conceal this first pregnancy effectively and, miraculously, no one in Giovanna's court had been aware of it, save Lucina. With Lucina's connivance, Antonio and Giovanna continued to sleep secretly together at night as man and wife, and to behave as steward and Duchess by day, for another two years[16] without suspicions of any sort being aroused. But when Giovanna became pregnant with another child, state events in Naples made this second pregnancy more difficult to conceal. And at the forefront of these events was her brother, Cardinal Luigi d'Aragona, whose political ambitions were soon to cross her path.

CHAPTER 9

The Ambitious Young Cardinal

DELIO Now, sir, your promise: what's that cardinal?
I mean his temper? they say he's a brave fellow,
Will play his five thousand crowns at tennis, dance,
Court ladies, and one that hath fought single combats.

John Webster, *The Duchess of Malfi*, I.i.156–9

While the Duchess of Amalfi lived with the fear that her brother, the Cardinal, might discover her relationship with Antonio, this brother was by no means leading the life of an ascetic churchman in Rome. Since he had not entered the Church in pursuit of a religious calling, but merely to further his family's political designs and interests, he continued to live as normal a life as possible in the circumstances. When called upon to take up arms, he did so, and when the pleasures of the flesh enticed him, he did not turn away.

By the time Giovanna had fallen in love with Antonio Bologna, Luigi had begun a liaison with a beautiful Roman courtesan called Giulia Campana (also known as Giulia Ferrarese since her family came originally from Ferrara). Here is another mysterious interweaving between reality and Webster's play. Giulia was not mentioned in any of the main sources ascribed to Webster (see Appendix), and yet Webster gives the Cardinal's mistress this name (written Julia). Is it just another coincidence, on a par with his reference to the Duchess as a twin? The name and the accuracy of the portrayal of Giulia's/Julia's character would lead us to infer that it was not. The real Cardinal, however, did not poison his mistress. She survived into old age, dying only in 1549.

Giulia Campana was born in Rome and probably began her relationship with Luigi in 1503 when he returned to Rome for the conclave which followed the death of Pope Alexander VI. She lived in a house belonging to the Augustinian Order, in the parish of San Trifone, situated in the bustling *rione* of Campo Marzio. In 1505, or thereabouts, she gave birth to a daughter by the Cardinal. She was named Tullia.

Tullia does not seem to have been officially recognised by Luigi in contemporary documents, but she repeatedly claimed to be his daughter and carried the surname d'Aragona. It appears that Giulia's husband, Costanzo Palmieri, added 'd'Aragona' to his surname thanks to Giulia's relationship with the Cardinal, for there is no record of a noble family by the name of Palmieri d'Aragona at this time.[1] Presumably Tullia's birth had been legitimised by a marriage of convenience similar to that which had legitimised her great-grandfather, King Ferrante I. If she were to be of any usefulness to the Cardinal in the dynastic marriage game, her legitimacy was an important factor.

What kind of woman was the real Cardinal of Aragon's mistress? As a *cortigiana*, or courtesan, she could be classed as a woman of 'loose morals', a type of woman with which Rome in this period was overflowing. The *cortigianeria* had begun to develop during the fourteenth century, but it received a notable impetus from the licentious climate of the court of the Borgia Pope, Alexander VI, who openly had an amorous relationship with Giulia Farnese, a young noblewoman little older than his daughter. By the early sixteenth century courtesans had been officially recognised as a social category in the city and contemporary papal documents complain that their numbers were excessive.[2] They were categorised into various types. There were 'honest' courtesans (*cortesane honeste*), women of a certain standing who mixed in the highest social circles; 'prostitute' courtesans (*cortesane putane*) with fewer intellectual and social pretensions; and the common prostitutes, who attracted their clients by placing a candle or lamp on their windowsills (*cortesane da candela, da lume e de la minor sorte*).

Outside papal Rome, the *cortigianeria* evolved in places like Venice, Siena, Ferrara and Medicean Florence, where it mirrored the widening cultural boundaries of the new learning. Some Renaissance scholars maintained the idea of *amor libero tra liberi* (free love between free individuals), as did the writer Speron di Speroni in his *Dialogo d'Amore*, in which he speaks of Tullia d'Aragona and her lover, the writer Bernardo Tasso.[3] Similar sentiments were expressed by Pietro Aretino, who was in favour of *l'amore assolutamente libero* (absolute free love) and who wrote about the Cardinal of Aragon's relationship with Giulia in his *Ragionamenti*.[4] Other writers, such as Pietro Bembo and Baldassarre Castiglione, praised a higher, more spiritual, form of platonic love.

Renewed interest in classical learning had led to a transformation of the medieval concept of femininity, and brought it to two diverse, but not necessarily conflicting, extremes: on the one hand, was a serious cultural development in the education of women, and on the other, a licentiousness born of a wide interpretation of their new-found liberty. It was a liberty which educated women like the Duchess of Amalfi and Eleonora Piccolomini sought but were denied.

Paradoxically, Tullia d'Aragona, the daughter of the man who had so restricted his sister's freedom while indulging his own libertine tastes, achieved a semblance of independence in the modern sense. She moved freely wherever she wished, without seeking the permission of a male relative, and she had amorous affairs with whomsoever took her fancy. Like her mother, she became a courtesan, was able to earn her own living, albeit immorally, and managed her own finances. But her life as a courtesan subsidised her real career as a writer. Tullia became one of the most respected poets of her day and is best remembered for her *Dialogo sull'infintà dell' amore* (Dialogue on the infinity of love).

During a visit Tullia made to Ferrara in June 1537, a courtier wrote the following letter to Isabella d'Este, giving a vivid description of the Cardinal's daughter:

> Your Excellency will have heard that a noble Roman lady, called Signora Tullia, is spending some months here. She is very gentle, discreet and clever, and endowed with the rarest gifts of body and mind. She sings all manner of songs, reads music at sight, and her conversation is altogether unique, while her manners are so charming, that there is neither man nor woman here can hold a candle to her, not even the Most Illustrious Marchioness of Pescara [Vittoria Colonna]. This lady knows everything, and is ready to talk with others on any subject they may choose. Her house is full of the most learned men, and the doors are open to all, but she is abundantly supplied with money and jewels, and has in fact everything she requires.

Tullia had obviously inherited her father's love of music and his talent for singing (he was reputed to have a good singing voice) and his highly educated, intelligent daughter was able to hold her own in any, even the most elevated, company. She was an ideal Renaissance woman despite, or notwithstanding, her dubious morals, which seemingly brought her so much wealth. A fellow writer, Giambattista Giraldi, however, gives a less glowing description of Tullia than Stabellino, when he describes her as no great beauty, with her wide thin-lipped mouth and prominent, hooked nose. Giraldi continues in an unflattering and sometimes vituperative tone, which reads like that of a resentful spurned suitor, but his description does suggest that Tullia resembled Luigi physically and had inherited his famous Aragon nose (if we can presume that he is the cardinal of Raphael's portrait and that of the tomb effigy in the Minerva).[5]

'Honest' courtesans like Giulia Campana and her daughter Tullia lived as luxuriously as their more respectable contemporaries who belonged to the grandest noble families. Bandello describes the home of one in his *Novelle*. The walls of her rooms were decorated with precious drapes of velvet and brocade and the floors covered by the finest rugs. A visiting Spanish ambassador found himself so overawed by the décor that when he was possessed by an irresistible need to spit, he was at a loss where to do so without desecrating something precious. In the end he relieved himself by spitting on his servant![6]

The 'honest' courtesans were often talented, well-educated, attractive young women, and many of them, like Tullia, became important literary figures. They were almost reincarnations of the hetaerae, the refined, cultured courtesans of ancient Greece. Not only were they admitted into the exclusive circles of humanist writers to discuss Platonic philosophy and the nature of love and the soul, they also presided over conversations at noble banquets where, as well as lending decoration to the occasions with their physical beauty, they entertained the guests with social accomplishments such as singing, lute-playing and dancing. The 'honest' courtesans were an elite minority who sold both their bodies and their literary talents to the highest bidders. A banker would pay in cash; an attractive poet could have his way in exchange for a dedication in one of his sonnets; and an artist would offer a painting as payment for the courtesan's favours.

There is no evidence that Giulia Campana had literary talent, but, whatever her education, she possessed a sharp enough wit to be charming and entertaining to men of discernment like Luigi d'Aragona. A story goes that while walking along a street in Rome, the brand new paving of which Pope Leo X had paid for with money collected in taxes from the city's prostitutes, she and a gentlewoman accidentally bumped into one another. The woman was angry and began hurling insults at Giulia, who calmly turned to her, saying: 'Madonna perdonatemi, ch'io so bene che voi avete più ragione in questa via che non io' (Do excuse me ma'am, I know you have a much greater right to be on this street than me!).[7]

Strangely enough, while Tullia made claims to be Luigi's daughter, she does not appear to have made much mention of him in her writing. He was probably a distant figure whom she barely knew, a man whose life was taken up with military exploits, politics and pleasure. He was certainly not the dour reactionary that the old Corona manuscript would have us believe. He was a *bon viveur*, like most of the other young cardinals of his time. He had certainly embraced wholeheartedly the teachings of Lorenzo Valla, the abrasive Roman humanist who had been secretary to his great-grandfather, King Alfonso I. Valla's tract of 1433, *De Vero bono* (On Pleasure), had asserted that a life dedicated to pleasure is not intrinsically sinful; a certain joie de vivre was an essential motivating factor in all human activity, and a springboard towards true, divine bliss. His tract greatly influenced Renaissance society's liberal attitude towards pleasure and sin.[8]

The portrait which emerges of the Cardinal of Aragon from contemporary reports is that of a handsome, affluent young man, always ready to enliven a social gathering with his rich (usually non-clerical) apparel, carnival disguises and his pungent sense of humour. He was at the centre of a coterie of similar young men who had entered the Church not by vocation but merely to satisfy and further the ambitions of their families. There was Alessandro Farnese, who had received his cardinal's hat thanks to his sister Giulia Farnese's sharing the bed of Pope Alexander VI. In later life, however, Farnese managed to rise above this rather ignominious beginning and proved to be a very competent pope (Paul III 1534–50).

Destined to play an important role in Giovanna's story was the brother of the Marquis of Mantua, Cardinal Sigismondo Gonzaga. Fat and gouty, he was in the habit of gorging himself on oysters and patronising the courtesans of Rome.[9] Like Luigi, he too suffered from syphilis. Another assiduous patron of the courtesans was Luigi's devious and cunning cousin, Cardinal Ippolito d'Este, who, according to Sanudo, was more concerned with weapons than anything else.[10] He had many amorous affairs, including one with his cousin Sancia d'Aragona. A violent fit of jealousy at his rejection by one of Lucrezia Borgia's maids of honour in favour of his more handsome, illegitimate half-brother, led him to order his henchmen to gouge out his brother's eyes! (Significantly, the woman in question, Anna

Bernardo Dovizi da Bibbiena. Portrait by Raphael (*Galleria Palatina, Palazzo Pitti, Florence,* © *Alinari*).

Borgia, was the sister of Eleonora Piccolomini's lover, Cardinal Borgia.) Of a more tranquil nature was Luigi's good friend, the handsome, cultured, Venetian cardinal, Marco Cornaro.

Together with one or two others, these young men formed a restricted circle of worldly, pleasure-loving clerics. When they were not called by duty to participate in the Pope's wars, as often as not they threw off or disguised their cardinals' robes and flung themselves into a life of indulgence and vice. An example of the sort of antics they got up to is given by Baldassarre Castiglione in *The Courtier*.

Castiglione (Plate 24) was a close friend of Bernardo Dovizi da Bibbiena (later Cardinal Bibbiena) and he included Bibbiena as a character in his book. At the time in which the work is set (four successive evenings during March 1507), Bernardo Bibbiena was secretary to Cardinal Giovanni de' Medici. Giovanni, almost the same age as Luigi d'Aragona, led a more discreet life than most of his fellow young cardinals, if not necessarily a more virtuous one. He wished to appear to be following the admonitions his father Lorenzo had made to him when he became a cardinal at the age of fourteen. Bibbiena, on the other hand, was not above participating in the ribald high life of the clique of young cardinals in all its forms. In *The Courtier*, Castiglione has the character Bibbiena narrate an amusing episode in which he was the butt of a joke played on him by Cardinal Luigi d'Aragona. It is used to illustrate how men intending to deceive can themselves be deceived. This was very apt, for Luigi himself was being deceived by his sister at this time.

One day during the carnival period of the winter of 1507, the Cardinal of Aragon and a merry band of revellers decided to take a trip along the Via dei Banchi in Rome to the house of one of their acquaintances, and they invited Bibbiena to accompany them. They knew he loved to tease and torment unfortunate priests who crossed his path at carnival time, so they arranged one for him to find. When they arrived at the house, Bibbiena immediately spied a humble-looking priest hovering by the door. He made straight for his poor victim and the others left him to it, entering the house and climbing up to the top floor so they could get a better view of what was going on in the street below.

Bibbiena approached the priest and asked his name. The priest replied and Bibbiena, solemnly shaking his head, said: 'Ah I knew it. You're the one that the prefect of the city has issued a warrant of arrest for.'

The priest, alarmed by the news, protested that he had done nothing wrong and was an honourable law-abiding person.

Bibbiena smirked: 'Yes, you look like a decent sort of man. I have connections in high places; perhaps I could help you out. Come with me and we'll go and talk to someone I know who will fix everything, I'm sure.'

The priest, still frightened out of his wits, was hesitant, so Bibbiena reassured him: 'Come on get up behind me in the saddle of my horse and I'll take you.'

Trembling with terror, the priest climbed up and Bibbiena spurred his horse off at a gallop along the street, nearly unseating the poor man. He clung on for dear life, but once Bibbiena had reached the end of the street, he just turned the horse about and galloped back again. Back and forth he went, up and down the Via dei Banchi with the terrified priest clinging to him, pleading to be set down. The Cardinal of Aragon and his companions were watching all this from the upstairs windows of the house, jeering and cheering every time Bibbiena galloped past.

Not content with this amusement, they started pelting Bibbiena and the priest with eggs each time they passed beneath the window. Bibbiena wasn't much bothered by this because his good clothes were protected by his *domino*, the long black cloak used for disguising one's identity at carnival time. The poor priest was almost in tears. His habit was dripping with raw eggs and he was pleading with Bibbiena to leave him to his fate.

Finally tiring of the jest, Bibbiena reined in his horse in front of the house to set down the unfortunate priest. As he did so, behind his back, some grooms waiting by the door gave the priest a handful of eggs. Casting an eye up at the cardinals hanging out of the windows, he squashed the eggs all over Bibbiena's head and shoulders. When everyone had finished laughing and throwing more eggs, the priest dismounted and, making a deep bow, he said: 'Messir, I believe the joke is on you. Allow me to present myself. I am a humble stable groom, I am no priest.'

From the Cardinal of Aragon and his companions at the upstairs window, there were hoots of laughter. Bibbiena did not know whether he was suffering more from shame or anger, but the next day he dared not show his face and even the mere thought of the ridicule to which he had been subjected continued to pain him.[11]

The episode Castiglione describes is not the sort of behaviour one would associate with a solemn cardinal of the Holy Catholic Church, but it is typical of the young cardinals of the period. Luigi d'Aragona's main passions in life were those of his grandfather, King Ferrante I: hunting, music and women, probably in that order of preference. He is frequently named in the Venetian Sanudo's diary as a member of the hunting parties of Popes Julius II and Leo X at Ostia and Magliano. In his funeral oration, Cardinal Cornaro cites Luigi's excessive dedication to this sport as one of his only possible vices. He goes on, however, to justify it as a noble activity, indulged in by many great men through the ages, from Cyrus to Caesar, the better to refresh both their bodies and souls.[12]

Luigi's love of music was a passion he shared with Giovanni de' Medici (Pope Leo X) to whom he once presented a magnificent organ, and on his journey through Europe in 1517–18, he sought out church organs, purchased many musical instruments, and enlisted the services of numerous minstrels to take back to Italy.[13]

But in addition to his more frivolous activities, Luigi also dedicated himself to serious intellectual pursuits. He had received a thorough education at the cultured Aragonese court of Naples and continued to enjoy the company of men of learning when he moved to Rome. During the first decade of the sixteenth century his personal secretary was Francesco Pucci, the Florentine humanist scholar who had been a pupil of Poliziano and a distinguished member of the Aragonese court of Naples of Luigi's youth. Pucci had taught rhetoric in Naples and had been court librarian. He was left without employment when King Federico was exiled and Luigi took him into his service.[14]

Luigi was a patron of the arts and letters and furthered the careers of writers such as Trissino[15] and Pietro Martire d'Anghieri.[16] But perhaps his greatest literary connection was his friendship with the author of *Arcadia*, Jacopo Sannazaro. His correspondence with Sannazaro continued to the end of his life. Sannazaro, who had no love for the Spanish viceroys, whom he felt exploited Naples solely to enrich themselves and their native Spain, clung to his friendship with Cardinal Luigi d'Aragona because he represented one of the last remnants of the Aragonese dynasty of Naples. In Sannazaro's eyes this dynasty had made the Kingdom a great independent power and he regarded with intolerance its diminished status as a mere colony of Spain. Luigi had been nurtured on the works of Sannazaro and seen many court festivities featuring Sannazaro's masques as the focal point. For him, too, Sannazaro represented nostalgia for his dynasty's lost Kingdom, a vanished 'Arcadia'. To commemorate the work and honour the loyalty of his old friend, during his official visit to Naples in May 1507, Luigi commissioned the sculptor Gian Cristoforo Romano to strike a medal of Sannazaro.[17]

Luigi was also an enthusiastic art collector. One of the artists he patronised was the Renaissance master, Sebastiano del Piombo. Vasari tells us that the Cardinal of Aragon commissioned a fine painting from del Piombo. It was not a serene, pure Madonna and child, but a magnificent naked woman of rare beauty.[18] The subject, supposedly Saint Agatha, was portrayed at the moment of her martyrdom, when her breasts were amputated. Torment and sensuality were an appropriate theme for Luigi and his family.

CHAPTER 10

The Devil's Quilted Anvil

BOSOLA A politician is the devil's quilted anvil;
He fashions all sins on him, and the blows
Are never heard.

John Webster, *The Duchess of Malfi*, III.ii.321–3

It was Luigi's political ambition that eventually determined the tragic end of his sister's secret family. The incompatibility between the two was like a 'devil's quilted anvil'. During the period 1507–10 the Cardinal's political career developed apace and he began to play an active role in papal diplomacy. In early January 1507 he visited his cousin Alfonso d'Este, Duke of Ferrara. For many years an intermediary in the conflict between the Duke of Ferrara and the papacy, Luigi walked a fine tightrope between the two, always following, however, the path most profitable to his own interests. Though the Este family's ducal title had been bestowed by the Holy Roman Emperor, Ferrara was nominally a fief of the papacy and Pope Julius II was determined to enforce this subordination. Fearing that Julius would at best limit his freedom of action and at worst confiscate Ferrara, Alfonso d'Este continued to ally with the King of France throughout Julius's papacy, as a counterbalance to his policies.

From Ferrara Luigi visited Venice, travelling there at the Duke of Ferrara's expense, on one of his boats. He arrived incognito on 15 January, accompanied by a party of thirteen people. The following day he visited the city arsenal and that evening dined with the father of his friend Cardinal Marco Cornaro. In his account of Luigi's visit, the Venetian diarist Marin Sanudo comments that the Cardinal resembled his grandfather King Ferrante and that his annual income had now risen from 2,000 to 8,000 ducats and that he could expect another 5,000 from Ferdinand the Catholic of Naples.[1]

When he was received by the Doge of Venice, Luigi was heard to say that he had merely come on a pleasure trip to admire the famous city. Nonetheless, he had a private discussion with the Doge, in which he probably outlined the Pope's plans regarding Perugia, Bologna and other cities of the Papal Marches, and intimated the Pope's desire that Venice should remain neutral and not intervene in the conflict in Romagna. He probably also discussed the position of his cousin the Duke of Ferrara, who lived uncomfortably close to the expanding Venetian border.

Julius II had begun his reign determined to re-establish papal authority in the Papal States. He first called upon Venice to push back her encroachment in the province of Romagna, after the duchy established there by Cesare Borgia collapsed. In the face of an opposing international alliance headed by the papacy, the Venetians were forced to back down. Julius then turned his attentions to the over-mighty feudal lords, like the Baglioni of Perugia and the Bentivoglio of Bologna, who openly flouted all papal authority.

A symbol of the Church's new power under Julius was the rebuilding of St Peter's Basilica in Rome. Julius has been much criticised for the destruction of the precious antiquities of the ancient Roman basilica, but the work was not undertaken solely out of a mania for grandeur. The building had become unsafe and was in need of extensive repairs. Julius called the architect Bramante to begin the project and, in April 1506, he ceremoniously laid the foundation stone of the first pier of the new basilica. Immediately afterwards he set off with an army of cardinals and their followers to subjugate the Papal States in Romagna. Luigi d'Aragona was among these cardinals.

By August 1506 Julius had driven the Baglioni from Perugia and moved on to deal with the Bentivoglio of Bologna. They, too, quickly succumbed and were forced to flee. Putting aside his *triregno* (papal tiara) for a helmet and his pastoral staff for a sword, Pope Julius was initiating a new development in the papacy in an Italy which thought it had already seen, with the Borgias, every deformation of the institution. He was sixty-four years old when he became Pope, but during his papacy he endured all the discomforts of military campaigns – sleeping outdoors in tents, marching though rain, thunderstorms and blizzards – with the energy and determination, even the alacrity, of a man half his age. He travelled over mountains so rugged that he had to get down from his horse and proceed on foot, supported by two helpers because of the gout which tormented him, but he never faltered.

Julius received significant help from the King of France in his campaign to reconquer Perugia and Bologna, and paid an equally significant price. Once the full sum had been exacted, relations began to deteriorate. After a dispute over the liberty of Genoa, Julius feared that the French might try to reinstate the Bentivoglio in Bologna and hence, at the time of Luigi d'Aragona's visit, the necessity of negotiating the neutrality of Venice and Ferrara, so they would not ally with France in such an enterprise.

When Luigi returned to Ferrara from Venice in February 1507, the carnival season had begun and he found a group of his fellow young cardinals waiting to celebrate with him. They were all guests of the Duke of Ferrara's brother, Cardinal Ippolito d'Este. Laying aside their cardinals' robes, they donned fancy dress and, incognito, made their way to the Palazzo Schifanoia to taste the rich Ferrarese dishes, the plates of sugar confetti and other sweet pleasures the beautiful women of Ferrara had to offer. In the Sala dei Mesi, decorated with the colourful and sensual allegorical frescoes of de Roberti, Tura and del Cossa, they whirled and danced and tried to forget that in a few hours they would return to their clerical habits and march off to fight again for the Pope.

The star of the evening was the Duchess of Ferrara, Lucrezia Borgia, who had risen from her sickbed to host this coterie of charming, brilliant young men – such a contrast to her rather dour and brusque husband, Alfonso d'Este. As she danced, the cardinals whispered and sniggered among themselves. She had recently fatigued herself to such an extent, by dancing over and over again with her debonair brother-in-law, Francesco Gonzaga, commander of the papal forces, that she had miscarried Alfonso's child, a son. It was even rumoured that she and Gonzaga were having an affair and wasn't it obvious to everyone that they were in love with each other? How would the Este brother and sister, Alfonso and Isabella, react to such a betrayal? It was said that Ippolito, too, was infatuated with his sensuous sister-in-law. As the gossip passed back and forth between them, Luigi laughed, never imagining that in Naples a similar sort of embarrassment was awaiting him.

The cardinals were loath to drag themselves away from the festivities in Ferrara, but duty called and they were bound to join Pope Julius in Bologna and report on their various missions. Cardinal Cornaro commented bitterly before they left that he wished the Pope had stayed in Ferrara instead of Bologna. Duke Alfonso and Cardinal Ippolito were doubtless relieved that he had not.

The Pope departed from Bologna on 22 February and began wending his way slowly back southwards towards Rome. Luigi d'Aragona returned to Rome more rapidly, before the carnival season had come to an end, and, still in high spirits from his escapades in Ferrara, he and his companions organised the hoax on Bibbiena described by Castiglione. But with the coming of the solemn Lent season in March, there was a change of mood and of fortune for Luigi and his master. Pope Julius received the welcome of a conquering hero, worthy of those of ancient Rome, when he returned to the city on Palm Sunday. He was at the peak of his glory; but Spain, France and Venice were already beginning to move against him to undermine his new conquests.

Back in Naples, Giovanna and the rest of the Kingdom had come to terms with the Spanish take-over. Ferdinand the Catholic's general, Gonsalvo de Cordova, had established himself as Viceroy but the Neapolitans anxiously awaited the arrival of the new King himself.

The Viceroy's first policies had not been implemented smoothly. In 1504 Ferdinand the Catholic ordered Gonsalvo to introduce the Spanish Inquisition to Naples, as had already been done in Sicily. This would have furnished an effective weapon to counter any remaining hostility among the barons and the population in general. But it would also have weakened the influence of the existing Papal Inquisition; consequently, Pope Julius opposed the Viceroy's policies and took every opportunity to encourage the population of Naples to do likewise. The death of Isabella of Castille in November of that year induced King Ferdinand to let the matter drop. With the delicate political situation created by his wife's death, he could not afford to provoke a reaction in Naples which might destabilise his tenuous hold there.[2]

On her death, Queen Isabella left her possessions not to her husband Ferdinand, but to her eldest surviving child, her daughter Giovanna (Juana). At this point, another Giovanna d'Aragona enters the story of the Duchess of Amalfi. She will be referred to by her Spanish name, Juana, to differentiate her from the other Giovannas. As well as bearing the same name, she was also the same age as both the Duchess of Amalfi and the young former Queen, Giovanna IV of Naples. Although Juana never actually visited the Kingdom, she was her father's official heir to the throne of Naples, to which she nominally succeeded on his death in 1516.

Juana was married to Philip, Duke of Burgundy, son of the Emperor Maximilian, in 1495 when she was sixteen. She fell passionately, almost obsessively, in love with her handsome, charming husband. He had long, blond hair and twinkling, blue eyes, and his missing teeth cannot have excessively marred his impudent smile. He astonished her by embracing her in public at their first meeting. Then, after a brief blessing by a priest, he hurried her off to a hunting lodge to bed her before the official marriage ceremony took place. Unfortunately for Juana, Philip's passion soon palled and he turned elsewhere for his pleasures. She had been brought up in the strict morality of the Spanish court, where her mother, Queen Isabella, slept with her daughters when their father was absent so there could be no gossip regarding her fidelity. The splendour and licentiousness of her husband's court overwhelmed Juana, and soon the strain of living with his continuous amorous betrayals began to unbalance her mind. She became mentally unstable, which only served to drive her beloved Philip further away from her.[3]

Unfortunately for King Ferdinand's political designs, after the death of Queen Isabella, his son-in-law Philip, on Juana's behalf, began to make claims to her Spanish dominions, which had remained under the governorship of her father in her absence. With the stability of both Aragon and Castille in jeopardy, Ferdinand dared not risk any distracting disorders in his newly acquired Kingdom of Naples.

Disorders, however, there were during the winter of 1504/5; not because of the Inquisition, but because Gonsalvo de Cordova had not been able to impose law and order as he would have wished and had allowed himself to become involved in a financial swindle regarding the provision of food supplies to the city. A rich Catalonian merchant, Paolo Tolosa, failed to supply the contracted amount, thus provoking great hardship among the population. The *seggi* decided that Tolosa should be fined, but Cordova intervened to annul the fine and public opinion accused the Viceroy of exploiting the supplies and lining his own pockets to the tune of 40,000 ducats.[4] The Neapolitans did not forgive him and lost no time in avenging themselves the following year, when Ferdinand the Catholic visited the city to take official possession of the Kingdom.

Giovanna waited anxiously for the moment she would be called to Naples to greet the new King. News was brought that he had arrived at Gaeta, the northernmost port of the Kingdom, but he remained there some time, having been informed of the death of his son-in-law, Philip of Burgundy, at Burgos. A man accused of poisoning Philip was rapidly and mysteriously exonerated and Neapolitan gossip said King Ferdinand had had a hand in the affair.[5] Ferdinand's daughter Juana, already politically and emotionally cast aside

Porta Capuana, Naples. One of the finest Italian Renaissance city gates, it was built in 1484 by Giovanna's grandfather, King Ferrante I, to a design by Guiliano da Maiano.

and imprisoned by her husband, now received exactly the same treatment from her father. She passed the rest of her life in prison.

As Naples waited impatiently and optimistically for the new King to make his appearance, there were squabbles among its most important citizens over protocol and whether or not full mourning should be observed for the death of the King's little-loved son-in-law. Finally, on All Saints' Day (1 November) 1506, Ferdinand arrived in Naples harbour. Giovanna, as his relative and representative of one of the chief barons of the realm, watched him disembark onto the specially built wooden platform in front of Castelnuovo to a joyful chorus of canon salutes from the other castles and ships in the bay. Alongside the barons, she was obliged to pay homage to the new liege lord, but her heart must have been heavy and she had to disguise the resentment she felt towards this man who had brought ruin to her dynasty.

In the decade or so since her grandfather Ferrante's death, she had seen six kings sit on his throne in rapid succession – Alfonso II, Charles VIII (III), Ferrante II, Federico III, Louis XII and now Ferdinand the Catholic; for the next decade there was to be only one. Did she share the general hope in Naples that Ferdinand would, like his uncle, Alfonso the Magnanimous, establish the capital of his empire in Naples? If she did, it was a vain hope, for the gravitational centre of economic and political affairs was shifting westwards towards the New World. Ferdinand spent little over seven months in his new dominion. He left in June 1507, never to return.

During these seven months, however, Giovanna would have been obliged by her rank and her family links with the new King to make numerous appearances at court on state occasions. If she fell pregnant by Antonio Bologna for a second time during this period, the pregnancy would have proved far more difficult to hide.

The first state occasion would have been her presentation to the new Queen, Ferdinand's second wife, Germaine de Foix. Aged seventeen, she was two years younger than Ferdinand's youngest daughter, Catherine, but youth was the only attraction Germaine possessed; she was fat, lazy, greedy and of a 'rare ugliness'.[6] She bore little resemblance to her heroic, handsome brother, Gaston de Foix, the victor of the battle of Ravenna in 1512. Her main attraction for Ferdinand, however, had been a political one. She was a niece of the King of France and by the marriage Ferdinand had intended to detach Louis XII from his alliance with Juana's husband, Philip of Burgundy.

Ferdinand's sister, the dowager Queen of Naples, and her daughter had been present at his wedding to Germaine at Valladolid in March 1506 and they too accompanied him to Naples. Giovanna would perforce have been beside her half-sister, Ippolita, Countess of Venafro, to welcome their kinswomen back. Ippolita was appointed maid of honour at the court of the young Queen. According to the Filonico manuscript, this choice was not looked on favourably by the old Queen, who disapproved of Ippolita's 'undisciplined desires, licentious habits and impertinent tongue'. In Filonico's opinion, Ippolita had been corrupted by her half-brother, the Cardinal of Aragon.[7]

While living in Spain, the old Queen had sought in vain a suitable husband for her daughter; but after negotiations with the widowed King of England, Henry VII, came to nothing, the young Queen found herself in a similar situation to that of the Duchess of Amalfi: there were few suitable candidates of her age and rank. Unlike the Duchess, though, this Giovanna was destined to remain a widow for the rest of her life.

The two Queen Giovannas had returned to stay. The elder Queen hoped that her brother would nominate her as vicereine in place of Gonsalvo de Cordova. This he did, if only for a very brief period, for as soon as

Ferdinand arrived, the Neapolitans lost no time in complaining of Gonsalvo de Cordova's misrule, implying very strongly that the Viceroy was accruing power and wealth in order to acquire the Kingdom of Naples for himself. Ferdinand took the bait and when he sailed from Naples in June 1507, Gonsalvo went back to Spain with him.

Towards the end of Ferdinand's sojourn, Giovanna must have been thrown into panic by the sudden arrival of her brother, Luigi. He had been sent by Pope Julius to negotiate with, and, if possible, placate King Ferdinand, whom Julius was keeping hanging on a string, waiting for the investiture of the crown of Naples, which, like Ferrara, was a feudal dominion of the papacy. Luigi had not forgotten the Spanish King's treachery towards his dynasty and must have revelled in his discomfort. Considering his personal resentment towards Ferdinand, he was probably not the most suitable ambassador for a diplomatic mission that aimed to mollify him and neutralise his opposition to the Pope's policies. Nevertheless, Julius sent him, and he arrived in Naples on 27 May 1507.

Not surprisingly, he was unsuccessful in his mission. Two weeks later the King set sail for Spain and though Julius travelled to Ostia to await him there for a personal colloquy, Ferdinand snubbed the Pope and sailed straight past. He headed instead for Savona, ironically, the Pope's native city. There he awaited a meeting with the King of France, Louis XII. The reconciliation achieved at Savona posed a serious threat to Julius and his plans. Luigi d'Aragona and his fellow cardinals pursued Ferdinand by ship from Naples to Savona, but they were unable to disturb the new Franco-Spanish accord. Luigi was back again in Naples in the autumn and we hear of him departing for Rome on 24 October, taking with him the sculptor Gian Cristoforo Romano.[8]

If Giovanna was expecting a child during this period, Luigi's visits to Naples would have increased the risk of his discovering for himself, or of his being informed of, her pregnancy. Her second child by Antonio was a daughter. Bandello and the Corona manuscripts do not give her name, but the Spanish playwright Lope de Vega in his drama *El mayordomo de la Duquesa de Amalfi*, calls her Eleonora. This corresponds to the name of the Duchess's daughter in a family tree in the sixteenth-century Filonico manuscript. Caterina, the Duchess's daughter who died in infancy, is not mentioned in the family tree, but Eleonora, it appears, grew up to marry Paolo Antonio Poderico. If this is correct, Eleonora cannot have been murdered at the same time as her mother died. The Filonico manuscript may not be completely reliable, but the work was probably transcribed when Eleonora was still alive, or had not been long dead, when her origins would have been known.[9]

In any event, if Luigi's suspicions had not been aroused in May 1507, they most certainly were by September of the following year, when a sudden death in the family brought about a reunion of the fallen dynasty.

During the period of Luigi's visit to Naples, the author Matteo Bandello was also in the city. Throughout the spring and early summer of 1506 he was travelling through southern Italy with his uncle, Vincenzo Bandello, head of the Dominican order. They visited Naples, then proceeded to Cosenza, where his uncle fell ill and died. Matteo brought the body back to Naples to be buried in the church of San Domenico Maggiore, only to fall ill himself. He was nursed back to health by Giovanna's aunt, the former Queen Beatrice of Hungary, who, at her own expense, administered to him extremely costly remedies, which included crushed emeralds.

Once he had recovered, Bandello spent some time at Beatrice's court, where he met at least one of the Aragon brothers, as we can glean from the introduction to his thirty-second novella, dedicated to Cardinal Luigi d'Aragona. (Bandello's novella, number XXXII, dedicated to Luigi, follows that of the Duchess of Amalfi, number XXVI, but must have been composed earlier.) Speaking of the circumstances at Queen Beatrice's court in which he first heard the story he is about to recount, Bandello says, addressing Luigi, 'You, who were beside her at the time too, must remember what she said.'[10]

Though Bandello was no ascetic, his tone in describing the hedonistic Cardinal is subtly sarcastic. Clerics, he says, more than others, wish to be considered pure, which means they are at greater pains to hide their vices. But these, like grass beneath the snow, inevitably come to light and turn their hosts into objects of ridicule. Not that Luigi was making any great effort to conceal his vices, but Bandello, by linking his discourse to Luigi's name, subtly implies that he should curb them. He concludes, however, with a reverent act of homage to Luigi to avoid offence.

Since her Neapolitan palace was close to the Dominican monastery of San Domenico Maggiore, where Bandello first stayed, did he have the opportunity of meeting the Duchess of Amalfi as well as her aunt and brother? He says nothing of this, so we must presume that he did not. But he remained ever grateful to her Aunt Beatrice for her kind ministering to

The Castello Aragonese, Ischia. The fortification was virtually impregnable and enclosed a small, self-sufficient village.

him during his illness and he composed a series of sonnets which he dedicated to her before her death in 1508.

After a period of exile of about two and a half years on the island of Ischia, during the French domination of Naples, Queen Beatrice went to live at Castelcapuano with her niece Isabella, Duchess of Milan and the two ex-Queen Giovannas. These courts of four unmarried women gave rise to all manner of scurrilous rumours, most of which were doubtless false or exaggerated. But the many stories which freely circulated during the period of the viceroy's office were aimed primarily at denigrating the reputations of these remnants of the fallen dynasty of Ferrante I.

Beatrice came to terms with the authors of her family's ruin, and she was treated with the respect due to a queen during her last years in Naples. These years, though, were characterised by financial problems and marred by the frustration of being unable to retrieve her dowry from Hungary, which should have been repaid, since her union with the King had been without issue. When she died, she left 40,000 ducats of this dowry to Giovanna's brother Luigi, plus a donation of 15,000 ducats towards the rebuilding of St Peter's as an inducement to Pope Julius II, in the hope that these two beneficiaries of her will would continue to pursue the question after her death. It worked in part, for Julius tried to exact her dowry from the King of Hungary in order to obtain his share. But it seems the money was never paid, and it is therefore doubtful whether Luigi ever obtained his 40,000 ducats either.

After her death, the memory lived on in Naples of Beatrice's charity and generosity to those poorer and less fortunate than herself, as Matteo Bandello had had occasion to experience personally. But her generosity was such that in the end it bankrupted her. The efficient management of her finances had never been Beatrice's strong point; even as a teenager she got herself frequently into debt by gambling at cards. Perhaps her favourite nephew, Cardinal Ippolito d'Este (her sister Eleonora's son), tired of subsidising her continuous acts of charity.

While Queen of Hungary she treated Ippolito as the son she had never had and donated numerous benefices to him; but she was badly repaid. After she returned to Naples, he did not visit her once, and when she died he did not even bother to attend her funeral. His first preoccupation when he received news of her death was to ascertain the contents of her will.[11] The largest bequests had been made to himself and to her other nephew, Ferdinand, Duke of Calabria (Federico's son), still a prisoner in Spain. These bequests were also presumably to be paid from her dowry, for a letter written on 31 August 1508 states that she was completely bereft of funds. It begs Ippolito for money to pay for treating the severe fever which had afflicted her for four days. On 13 September she succumbed to the fever and died.[12]

The Duchess of Amalfi was living at the castle of Scafati at the time, where the news must have reached her almost immediately. If she was pregnant, the thought of having to meet her brothers and other members of the court must have alarmed her. It would have been impossible to avoid attending such an important occasion as a queen's funeral, the Queen who was her aunt to boot, without drawing untoward attention to herself. She could have feigned illness, but then her brothers might have visited her, which would have been equally undesirable. She had no choice but to travel to Naples.

Perhaps to invoke divine protection from the gossip and suspicions of which she would be the object at the funeral service, that very same day Giovanna donated a parcel of land in her fiefdom of Scafati to the nuns of the convent of Sant' Elena,[13] just outside the walls of Amalfi. In exchange for the donation she asked the nuns to pray night and day for her ancestors, her dearest and eldest son the Duke, and herself.[14] It is interesting to note that she refers to the young Duke as her 'eldest' son. Officially she only had one son, but in the eyes of God she had two.

She knew that in the coming months she would have great need of divine intercession as her situation became ever more fraught with danger. As Antonio Bologna had suspected, they had not reached that suitable moment when they could freely reveal their marriage to her brothers; and the funeral of Queen Beatrice was certainly not the appropriate time.

On the evening of 13 September, the members of the old royal family paid their last respects to the corpse, laid out in state in the chapel of Castelcapuano, and the following day the funeral took place at the church of San Pietro Martire. It is not known for certain whether Giovanna was present, but it is known that during the family reunion at Beatrice's funeral, the gossip circulating at the royal courts of Naples about the Duchess of Amalfi's secret amorous 'affair' reached the ears of her nearest relations. A family 'summit' was called and it was decided that her chief male relatives – her brothers, the Cardinal and Carlo, and her two brothers-in-law, Giambattista Piccolomini, Marquis of Deliceto and Francesco Piccolomini, Bishop of Bisignano – would pay an official visit to the Duchy of Amalfi to survey the situation at firsthand. Meantime, the Aragon brothers set their spies to work.

The period between the declaration of subservience to Ferdinand the Catholic in September 1503 and the visit of the Cardinal of Aragon in 1509, had been anything but serene for Amalfi. First there was the anarchy brought on by war, then nature intervened to further upset the balance of life. From 1503 to 1505 the Duchy was scourged by plague, and violent squabbles arose between the inhabitants of the various towns and villages as those infected and expelled from one place crossed into the borders of another.[15] Then, as the plague began to recede, in March 1505 the area was shaken by an earthquake. Fortunately, it did not do too much damage, but that same year adverse weather conditions caused the harvest to fail all over Italy and a widespread famine ensued.

In the midst of this general misery of the poor was a system of moral and political corruption in the higher echelons of society, including the clergy. Bands of brigands infested the mountainous areas and even within the towns the precarious authority of the vice-dukes was often ignored.

The population, illicitly armed, divided itself into jealous rival factions to exert political influence and pursue petty vendettas. Murder was the order of the day. Gambling was rampant in the taverns, cellars and warehouses, despite the prohibition, bringing ruin to rich and poor families alike and adding to the state of civil disorder.

Giovanna had put her family's finances to rights, but in the arduous task of re-establishing a disciplined, orderly government in her domains, she had made few inroads. She was doubtless preoccupied by her own private problems, which came to a head in August 1509 with the visit to Amalfi of her brothers and brothers-in-law.[16] We can only hypothesise on what was discussed during this visit. There is no evidence to indicate that Carlo d'Aragona behaved in any way like Webster's character, Ferdinand. He may have railed at and accused his sister, but the image that emerges from the few historical references to be found is not one of a man of choleric nature.

Unlike his brother, Luigi, Carlo did not enjoy a reputation as a man of arms, though he had participated in several wars. He was staunchly loyal to his uncle King Federico and for this he forfeited his lands under his uncle's successor, Ferdinand the Catholic. His wealth necessarily declined when he lost his fiefdom of Gerace, but, since he had married a rich wife, Ippolita D'Avalos, and as his brother and sister continued to augment their wealth during the period of foreign domination, so he was borne up on their wings, as an image in a Spanish poem composed in this year suggests.[17]

The poem, 'Dechado de amor hecho por Vazquez a peticion del Cardenal de Valencia, endereçado a la Reyna de Napoles' was commissioned by the same Cardinal of Valencia, Pedro Luis Borgia, who perished as Eleonora Piccolomini's lover. The voice is supposedly that of Borgia, who invites the ladies of the courts of the two Queen Giovannas to embroider a coloured coverlet to illustrate the sufferings of their 'lovers' (or, more correctly, their champions). He tells each what images she must portray and what motto must be written beneath.

The partnerships are strangely mixed up,[18] but the poem was an expression of the contemporary concept that marriage was a political and commercial transaction, and that chivalrous courtly love of the medieval *romain courtois* type, with its rigidly prescribed limits and resolute innocence, was its tamed complement. Antonio Bologna was nurtured in this troubadour tradition, whose courtly conventions required the 'lady' and her 'lover' to keep their distance. As her champion he could compose *chansons* to woo her, but at most he could aspire to her grace and favour;

he should never even contemplate possessing her physically. He and Giovanna began their relationship in this key, but gradually allowed their passions to overtake them and carry them to their fatal contravention of the rules.

In the poem, Cardinal Borgia tells Eleonora Piccolomini to embroider the prophetic motto:

La vida que bive escura
y en peligro poco dura.
(A life lived in obscurity
Runs the danger of being short.)

Eleonora's life was in fact cut tragically short by her infringement of the rules when she indulged in an amorous relationship with Cardinal Borgia. But in the poem he is not her champion.

The drab brown and dark ochre wings that Cardinal Borgia tells a certain Donna Isabella to embroider for Carlo d'Aragona smack of depression, but these wings, says the motto beside them, should uplift him from the suffering inflicted by his love.[19]

Are we meant to interpret this as Carlo living on his laurels after the misfortune of losing his lands has rendered his life less onerous? It is probable that at the time this poem was written, his wife, Ippolita, had died and he was freely amusing himself with the ladies of the courts of Castelcapuano, happily frittering away his reduced resources. His only child by Ippolita, Eleonora, was later forced to contract a very inferior marriage with a certain Berardino Caracciolo, Lord of Piciotta, who accepted her meagre dowry merely because it enabled him to use the royal 'd'Aragona' after his surname.[20]

The Duchess of Amalfi is conspicuously absent from this poem that contains the names of so many of her relatives, both Aragon and Piccolomini. Since her relationship with Antonio Bologna had developed beyond the prescribed limits, she probably felt little need to be entertained by frivolous events at court. She kept herself apart and participated only when ceremonial required, for she felt sufficiently fulfilled, spending her time in her remote castles at Amalfi or Capestrano, in Bologna's stimulating and amorous company. She was not, however, in his company when her brothers visited Amalfi in August 1509. She had sent him to check on the harvests in some of her distant estates. It was more prudent for him not to be present lest the exchange of some casually affectionate glance betray them to her brothers.[21]

According to the old Corona manuscript, it was the Cardinal, not Carlo d'Aragona, who harangued the Duchess regarding the rumours of her secret lover. He interrogated and threatened his sister to make her confess, but she denied all knowledge of the gossip. This was Giovanna's real 'Magnanima mensogna' (noble lie) alluded to by Webster in his play.[22] In order to keep Antonio from harm she deliberately deceived her brothers when they challenged her about her secret love affair. Luigi searched in vain for her steward, not because he suspected him of seducing his sister, but in order to obtain his collaboration in discovering the truth of the matter. He left instructions that as soon as Bologna returned from his commission, he should report to him in Naples.[23]

It is doubtful whether Antonio did in fact report to the Cardinal in Naples; but his failure to do so would equally have aroused suspicions. Soon even the remote haven at Capestrano was no longer safe. The Duchess's brothers had planted spies everywhere, and messengers were constantly arriving at her court on every sort of pretext in search of clues and information.

CHAPTER 11

The Flight of the Duchess

CARIOLA . . . I do not like this jesting with religion,
This feignèd pilgrimage.
DUCHESS Thou art a superstitious fool.

John Webster, *The Duchess of Malfi*, III.ii.316–18

Antonio Bologna did not feel at ease. After several months of coping with anxiety, he confessed to Giovanna his apprehension that her brothers would soon discover everything. He was concerned that her personal maid, Lucina, might be intimidated into betraying her mistress to save her own skin, or that one of the ladies-in-waiting at her court would be induced to spy on them. He knew the Cardinal's violent character[1] and felt sure he would not hesitate to avenge himself upon the culprit once he had been identified. It was pointless to think of informing the Duchess's brothers of the marriage; Bologna was sure that they would not harm Giovanna herself, but equally sure that he himself would be assassinated as soon as they discovered he had contracted the marriage without their permission and had fathered her children. He decided, therefore, to go to Naples to settle his financial affairs, and then to flee beyond the Kingdom, to Ancona.

Ancona at this time held the status of a republic, under the overall protection of the papacy. It was a flourishing Adriatic port that vied with Venice for control of trade routes to the Bosphorus, but why did Antonio choose it? He may have had friends there who would be willing to help him, or he may have been attracted by the fact that, as a port, it would have made for an easy escape route by sea if the necessity arose. Or perhaps Giovanna, in order to be reunited with her exiled husband, had already decided to use the subterfuge of a pilgrimage to Loreto, not far from Ancona, as a way of leaving the Kingdom of Naples without drawing undesirable attention to herself.

Although Bologna had been accused of fraud at the Gonzaga court, Giovanna did not use the excuse of sacking him for embezzlement, the 'Magnanima mensogna' that Webster has her adopt, to explain his sudden dismissal from her service.[2] As far as her court was concerned, Bologna had merely moved on elsewhere. In the late spring or early summer of 1510, he travelled to Naples to put his affairs in order there. Bandello says he entrusted them to his cousin, but it seems more likely he would have turned to one of his half-brothers, Federico, Giovanni or Jacopo (the last being illegitimate), to see that his income was forwarded to Ancona.[3]

He took his children, Federico and Eleonora, with him to Ancona, where they were soon established in a comfortable *palazzo*, equipped with the number of servants appropriate to their rank. The intention was probably to wait in Ancona and see how the situation evolved with the Duchess's brothers. If Antonio was discovered, then the Duchess would try to pacify them and negotiate his safe return; otherwise, he would seek a passage on an outgoing boat and escape abroad.

Antonio's flight to Ancona must have taken place in the late summer of 1510, for by the early autumn of that year the Duchess discovered that she was pregnant again, a fact that accelerated the train of events. The prospect of trying to secrete this third pregnancy without Antonio's love and support proved intolerable for her and, in desperation, she decided to have done with all the subterfuges and join him in Ancona. There she would live with him openly as his wife and they would take their chances with her brothers' anger. But by exposing her marriage publicly, Giovanna was in effect signing Antonio Bologna's death warrant, for he would be condemned to her brothers' vendetta. She might have nurtured hopes of placating Luigi and Carlo, but she must have known how difficult a task this would prove, given the circumstances. Antonio had no great fortune with which to buy their approval, and although he was a gentleman, he was not of royal blood, or even of the feudal aristocracy. Their only real chance of survival together would be to keep themselves out of the Cardinal's reach.

Luigi d'Aragona was once again marching with the armies of Pope Julius towards Bologna, which was being badly governed by the latter's favourite, Cardinal Alidosi. Many defamatory rumours circulated about Julius's relationship with this attractive but corrupt young cardinal. Julius, so acid and severe with the inefficiency of others, inexplicably continued to support Alidosi when everyone else condemned him. His affection for Alidosi was so strong that Julius's enemies began murmuring that he was the Pope's lover. (Members of the Orsini family wrote a scurrilous tract suggesting this.) Other critics merely affirm that Alidosi was adept at handling Julius's awkward character.[4]

Julius suspected that the French had serious designs to expand their sphere of influence in Italy and he was even more suspicious of their close alliance with Alfonso d'Este, Duke of Ferrara, who continued to act independently and defy papal authority. He decided to move against Ferrara in the summer of 1510. The Ferrarese ambassador to Rome did not initially realise how seriously his master was compromised. Only when the Cardinal of Aragon warned him that Julius was planning an assault on Ferrara, as the first stage of his campaign against the French, and that the war was to be waged with the alliance of Venice and the King of Spain, did the ambassador recognise how precarious the Duke's situation was.[5] The Pope had managed to win Ferdinand the Catholic to his cause by waving at him the reward of the crown of Naples and fanning his fears that the King of France planned to make a new attempt to seize the Neapolitan throne.

The campaign against Ferrara began in early July 1510, with Cardinal Alidosi directing operations. By the end of the month, substantial inroads had been made on Duke Alfonso's lands east of Bologna towards Ravenna. On 9 August, Julius issued a Bull excommunicating Alfonso as a rebel against the Church, and declaring all his titles and fiefs confiscate. Julius threatened to excommunicate the French, too, if they helped Alfonso. They continued to do so, nonetheless; but, despite their support, things progressed badly for the Duke of Ferrara and his second city, Modena, fell to papal forces.

The campaign was so important that Julius could not bear to stay in Rome, far away from the field of action, and suddenly, with his habitual restlessness, on 1 September he decided to go to Bologna to supervise the operations personally. He left that very same day. According to documents in the Vatican archives it appears that most of the Bologna campaign was masterminded by Luigi d'Aragona, and that he advised and collaborated with the Pope throughout.[6]

All the cardinals, except the aged and by now senile Carafa, were ordered to meet in Bologna. The Pope travelled quickly with a small entourage. Passing through Orvieto and Assisi, on 8 September he arrived at Loreto, where he celebrated the Mass of the Nativity. The following day he reached Ancona and boarded a ship for Rimini. He disembarked there and, despite the terrible weather conditions, continued his journey along the Via Emilia towards Bologna. The new papal master of ceremonies, Paride de Grassis (he had succeeded Burkhardt in 1506) notes that, instead of applauding the Pope and his entourage as they passed on their way, battling with the elements, people burst out laughing at their miserable condition.[7] Julius stayed overnight at Forlì and the following day, despite the torrential rain, he proceeded towards Bologna, where he arrived on 22 September.

Was it the news of the Pope's hurried journey which gave Antonio and Giovanna their idea of using Loreto and Ancona? It seems very likely, for her brother, Cardinal Luigi, was among the sodden bedraggled train of cardinals.

The Bolognese were heartily sick of the abuses of their papal governor, Cardinal Alidosi, and made their discontent felt. But their complaints were momentarily put aside when the ageing Pope fell ill with a fever after the arduous journey. The fever rendered Julius immobile but not inactive: from his sickbed, on 14 October he excommunicated all the French generals. In reply, the French King began threatening to call a General Council of the Church to dethrone Julius. Six cardinals passed over to the French side and refused to obey Julius's order to appear in Bologna, which added the threat of schism to that of a General Council.

One of his recent biographers, Christine Shaw,[8] affirms that Julius was not so much unfortunate in his commanders as incapable of choosing the right ones. Francesco Gonzaga, Marquis of Mantua, was not the best choice for commander of the papal troops in the campaign against Ferrara, since he was married to the Duke of Ferrara's sister, Isabella d'Este. Julius had negotiated Gonzaga's release from a Venetian prison and in exchange for this he expected Gonzaga to fight for him. To ensure his loyalty, he had Gonzaga's young son Federico sent to Rome as a hostage. But Gonzaga was physically unfit to command, as his health was being undermined by gout and ravaged by syphilis. Julius's other two commanders, his nephew, Francesco Maria della Rovere, Duke of Urbino, and Cardinal Alidosi, were bitterly jealous enemies, so it was not a recipe for success.

When Francesco Maria arrested the Francophile Alidosi, accusing him of conspiring with the enemy, Julius ordered the Cardinal to be released and rehabilitated, even bequeathing on him (much to the disgust of the Bolognese) the bishopric of Bologna that fell vacant in mid-October. The day after this appointment, the French army, under the now excommunicated general Chaumont, arrived under the walls of Bologna, with the Bentivoglio family in tow, ready to step back into governing their old city.

Bologna was defended by a meagre squadron of 900 men, and Chaumont fully expected Julius to withdraw from the city immediately, which he might well have done had he not been ill in bed. Perhaps the secret of Julius's success was that he never accepted defeat.[9] That night, delirious from his high temperature, he raged and moaned that he would prefer instant death to life in a French prison. The fever receded the following day and he recovered amazingly quickly. He ordered the Venetians to intervene immediately on his behalf, threatening that if they did not he would come to terms with the French. But no sooner had negotiations with the French begun than they broke down again over Ferrara, to which Julius adamantly refused to renounce his claim. As his vexation rose, so his resistance stiffened, and, as an inducement to win over the Bolognese people, he offered tax cuts and other concessions and urged them to take up arms and defend their city from the invading foreigners. His ploy worked and they rallied to the pontiff.

Cardinals Pietro Isvaglies and Luigi d'Aragona were appointed to lead the Bolognese resistance and they paraded through the streets of the city wearing their armour under their cardinals' robes.[10] The Pope's choice was a sign that Luigi was a rising star in the Vatican hierarchy. Alidosi, on the other hand, rehabilitated but still slipping from his position of pre-eminence in the Pope's favour, was resentful that he had not been nominated to lead the resistance and joined the procession uninvited. But the Bolognese would never have followed Alidosi. He would have had more reason to arm himself against them than the French.

Outside the house where Julius was staying, people were enthusiastically calling out the Pope's name and so, still weak from his illness, he staggered out onto the balcony to bless the crowds. Then he crossed his arms over his chest in a theatrical gesture meant to imply that he was laying his person and his honour in the people's hands. It was greeted by an uproarious acclamation. As he returned to his bed smirking, he was heard to murmur complacently: 'Now we have beaten the French!'[11]

During the period of his illness, Julius grew a long grey beard. This was received with a certain consternation because for several centuries popes had not worn beards. But Julius vowed that he did not intend to shave off his beard until he had expelled King Louis of France from Italian soil.

Raphael's famous portrait of the bearded Julius can thus be dated pretty accurately to between November 1510 and the eve of the Lateran Council in May 1512, when, as a sign that he, as well as the Church, was to be reformed, he shaved it off.[12]

Chaumont, instead of acting swiftly, wasted time negotiating with Julius. The French army was forced to retire from the walls of Bologna, mainly because of lack of supplies and the rain, which had turned their camp into a quagmire. The immediate danger had passed, but the French army continued to menace Julius's plans. Remaining in Bologna, over the next two months he had periodic relapses of tertian fever and haemorrhoids. He was an uncooperative patient, eating forbidden foods and threatening to hang his servants if they informed his doctors. He had little faith in medical men anyway, except for one Jewish doctor, whose wise policy of minimum intervention allowed the Pope's own sturdy constitution to defeat his maladies.[13]

The Venetians, eager to keep the pontiff's goodwill and perhaps gain something from the dismemberment of the adjacent Duchy of Ferrara, very soon came to his aid. Ferdinand the Catholic did likewise, as soon as Julius agreed to invest him with the crown of Naples if he promised to provide military aid to the Holy See. Was this to mean the end of all Luigi d'Aragona's hopes of regaining his family's throne in Naples? At the carnival earlier in the year, he and his companions appeared masked as Mamelukes – the military body of Caucasian slaves who seized the throne of Egypt in 1254. The ambition remained and the last word had still not been said.

With Luigi (and very likely Carlo too) stuck in Bologna in October 1510, surrounded by the French army, Giovanna wasted no time in taking advantage of the circumstances which promised to isolate and detain her brothers for a considerable period. She saw to it that her ten-year-old son, Duke Alfonso Piccolomini, was delivered safely into the hands of his tutor, Pirro del Pezzo.[14] Then she repaired to the Neapolitan bank of Paolo Tolosa,[15] that same rather dubious Tolosa who, with Gonsalvo de Cordova, had been involved in the embezzlement scandal of 1504/5.

Tolosa was extremely rich. During the reigns of the last Aragonese kings, he lent large sums to the crown and probably also to the Piccolomini. He possessed a magnificent chapel in the church of Monteoliveto, whose ceiling incorporated four ceramic *tondi* by della Robbia, which are thought to have belonged originally to the Piccolomini chapel in the same church. Tolosa's chapel was built about 1492/5 and the *tondi* were probably either sold to Tolosa or given to him as a guarantee for a loan by Giovanna's first husband and never recovered. It may even have been Giovanna who sold them in an attempt to pay off the family debts. Unfortunately, no relevant documentation has survived.

During the serious famine that hit Italy in 1507/8, the starving population of Naples blamed Tolosa and his business associates, who narrowly missed being lynched.[16] It was only with great difficulty that the Spanish Viceroy was able to place him in safety and restore order. But Tolosa went on to accrue even greater riches and, just as he had financed the Aragonese kings, so he continued to finance the viceroys.

It was to the Neapolitan offices of this long-standing financier of her family that Giovanna went in the early autumn of 1510 to settle the necessary pecuniary matters before her departure to Loreto. First, provision had to be made for the maintenance of her eldest son, the Duke of Amalfi, whom she knew she might not see again for a long time. Secondly, she left directions for the maintenance of members of her court and provisions for the dowries of her ladies-in-waiting. It was usual for the dowries of women who served members of the royal family to be provided for by their mistresses. Giovanna did not wish to be accused of causing unnecessary suffering, or of depriving anyone of their due on account of the course of action she was about to take.

Her essential private papers were deposited in the safe keeping of the Mother Superior of the convent of San Sebastiano.[17] It is possible that this was the small convent of San Sebastiano on the hill of Pogerola above Amalfi that was still in existence in the early 1500s but which later disappeared.[18] However, this was a very minor convent, for women of lower social rank, and so it seems more likely that in his account Bandello was referring to the more important convent of San Sebastiano in Naples. This was situated on the eponymous Via San Sebastiano that separated the two Sanseverino palaces of the Princes of Salerno and Bisignano. As Giovanna passed the Bisignano Palace, on her way to her meeting with the Mother Superior of San Sebastiano, did she pause a moment to bid farewell to her sister-in-law, Eleonora? Did she take Eleonora into her confidence and reveal her plan? Perhaps. In any event, they were never to see one another again. Giovanna did not return to Naples and just a year later, Eleonora was poisoned by her husband.

As Giovanna made her way through the streets of Naples to Tolosa's bank and to the convent of San Sebastiano, she would have had to avoid the disorders and processions that were much in evidence in the city at that time. These were demonstrations organised in protest against the attempts of the new Viceroy, Raimondo Cardona, to reintroduce the Spanish Inquisition. Eventually, with pressure from Pope Julius, Ferdinand the Catholic was again obliged to step down on the question. But with all this upheaval in Naples, no one really paid much heed to the Duchess of Amalfi and her entourage when they departed from the Palazzo Piccolomini with a great retinue of litters and baggage trains.

Her departure coincided with her brother Luigi's nomination by the Pope to lead the defence of Bologna against the French. Giovanna knew that he would be too preoccupied to be able to react swiftly when the astounding news reached him of what had come to pass and, with luck, this news might even be delayed by interruptions in communications attributable to the French siege. She and Antonio would have time to organise their affairs and their defensive strategy.

Giovanna let it be known that she was making a pilgrimage to the sanctuary of the Madonna at Loreto to fulfil a vow. It was an excuse that would arouse no suspicions. It was the most popular place of pilgrimage in Italy outside Rome and many people aimed to go there to pray at the 'house of the Virgin Mary' at least once in their lives. This house had reputedly been miraculously transported first to a forest near Loreto and then, in 1294, to the hill where the sanctuary building was begun in 1468. The cross of the transept and the dome of the church were built over the house. Interest in the sanctuary was intense in Giovanna's time and it would have seemed a normal event for the Duchess to go with her entire court to pay homage to such an important holy place. Had not the Pope himself seen fit to go there just a few weeks earlier and order his architect, Bramante, to begin work on the embellishment of its buildings because of its importance for the Catholic faith?

Giovanna has been criticised for feigning an act of religious piety to cover an amorous elopement. Even Webster, who is generally sympathetic to his heroine, has her behave with Machiavellian cynicism at this point, so desperate is she to be reunited with her husband. But this does not tally with her desire to marry Antonio Bologna. Had she been such a sceptic, she would have been satisfied with having him as her lover. She cannot be accused of merely 'jesting with religion'[19] if the vow she wished to beg of the Madonna was a sincere one: to be allowed to live simply, but peacefully, with her children and the man she loved. In order to do so, she was willing to set aside her material comforts and her elevated station in life. This seems neither immoral nor dishonourable to modern eyes, but to her contemporaries it was a traitorous betrayal of her family's prestige; and when she informed her entourage of her intentions they were struck with terror, for they feared that they would be considered accessories in her betrayal.

It was early November when Giovanna reached the sanctuary of Loreto. Webster has the Duchess, Antonio and their children arrive at the shrine at the same time as her brother Cardinal Luigi ceremoniously renounces his cardinal's robes to put on the armour of a soldier. This done, the Cardinal snatches the wedding ring from his sister's finger and declares her and her family officially expelled from the province of Ancona.

The historical events did not take place exactly in this order. Luigi did pass through Loreto with Pope Julius, but several weeks before Giovanna arrived, and he had no need to doff his cardinal's robes in order to don his armour: in the procession that October through the streets of Bologna, he was wearing both. Moreover, the Duchess reached Loreto alone. Her son, the Duke, had been left behind at Amalfi, and Antonio was still in Ancona with the two other children.

Giovanna's first act in Loreto was to participate in a solemn mass in the Basilica; then she offered rich gifts to the Sanctuary as part of the fulfilment of her vow. As soon as this was concluded, her court and household fully expected to return to the Kingdom of Naples, but, she informed them, as though it were a casual idea that had just come to mind: 'We are only fifteen miles from Ancona and since I have been told that it is a beautiful historical city, I intend to visit it for a day or so.' Everyone bowed to the Duchess's wishes and the baggage train was sent on ahead of the main party.[20]

Antonio Bologna had already been secretly informed that Giovanna would be coming to Ancona and he set himself to prepare accommodation and a banquet worthy of her and her court. His *palazzo* was situated on the main road along which Giovanna and her retinue would be obliged to pass as they entered the city. When, early in the morning of her arrival, one of her servants passed beneath it, Antonio stepped outside and spoke to him. The servant recognised Antonio; he knew that he had left their mistress's service, but not for what reason. There was no motive to doubt Antonio's honour, for he was much liked in the household. He told Antonio that he had been sent ahead to organise accommodation and food for the Duchess and her entourage. Antonio replied that there would be no need, for she would be an honoured guest at his home, and he sent the servant back to his mistress to inform her of these arrangements.

When the time was due, Antonio set off on horseback with a group of notable gentlemen of Ancona, and rode three miles outside the city walls to greet the Duchess. As he approached, the members of her court expressed their pleasure at seeing the charming Bologna again. He dismounted and greeted Giovanna by kissing her hand; then he officially invited her and her company to be his guests. Giovanna acquiesced as would a mistress (in the administrative, not amorous, sense) to her loyal servant, not as a wife to her husband.

They all followed Antonio to his home. There must have been a frenetic secret exchange between Giovanna and Antonio before the banquet began. Giovanna could no longer bear the strain of being parted from him and she could not face the impending stress of secreting a third pregnancy without his moral and physical support. Antonio would have known that if their relationship were brought out into the open, he would be condemned to death. If he had not loved her, he might have abandoned her now, saved himself and left her to her fate. But he, too, was tired of all the falseness and subterfuge; he suffered as much as she did from their separation. Resignedly, he agreed. At the conclusion of the banquet, they would, as Bandello says, '*cavarsi la maschera*' (remove their masks) and show themselves to the world as they were and as they were proud to be.

Whether or not this had already been planned by Antonio and Giovanna when he first left for Ancona, or whether the contingency of her third pregnancy had precipitated the decision when they were reunited, we do not know. All the preliminary measures taken by the Duchess to set her affairs in order before her departure from Naples would probably have been executed in any case, as a matter of course, since journeys were hazardous enterprises at this time. But the stress of this third pregnancy during the long and arduous journey undoubtedly exhausted Giovanna's nerves and the joy at being able to greet her husband and children again must have fired her determination to have done with the farce of pretension, and to gamble for all or nothing.

She could have carried on the dissimulation, said nothing and returned again to her son in Amalfi, thus keeping Bologna out of danger. But her will failed and at the end of the banquet, she called all her followers before her in the hall of Antonio's *palazzo* and explained the situation to them, saying:

> It is time for me to manifest before you, gentlemen and servants, what has already been manifested before God. Being a widow, I decided to remarry, but to the husband of my choice. Some years ago, before my chambermaid, present at the moment in this room, I married Signor Antonio Bologna, whom you now see here, and he is my legitimate husband. I am therefore his and intend to remain so.
>
> Until now I have been your Duchess and your 'padrona' [mistress] and you my faithful vassals and servants. In future I expect you to have good care of my son, the Duke, to whom you will be faithful and loyal. You will accompany these ladies-in-waiting back to Amalfi. Before leaving the Kingdom, I deposited their dowries with the bank of Paolo Tolosa and all the relevant documents are at the Convent of Santo Sebastiano in the hands of the Mother Superior. I shall have no further need of any women save my faithful maid [called Lucina in the Corona manuscript]. Signora Beatrice [Beatrice Macedonia, according to the Corona manuscript], who has until now been my chief lady-in-waiting, is, as she well knows, completely satisfied. In the documents that I have mentioned she will find sufficient provision with which to marry the daughter that she still has at home.
>
> If any of my servants desire to stay in my employment, they will be well treated by me. As for the rest of you, when you return to Amalfi, the major-domo will take care of you as he has been instructed. Finally I wish it to be known that I would prefer to live privately as the wife of Signor Antonio Bologna rather than continue to hold the rank of duchess.[21]

For a moment her household remained silent, stupefied by what she had said. But when Bologna brought his children, Federico and Eleonora, into the room, and the Duchess embraced and kissed them, the import of her speech was brought home to everyone. After a brief discussion, all the members of the Duchess's entourage, except for her personal maid and two grooms, decided to return post-haste to Amalfi. They left Bologna's house immediately, not wishing to tarry a moment longer than necessary, and went to a nearby hostelry to spend the night. A further discussion took place there as to what would be the wisest course of action to prevent the predicted vendetta of the Cardinal of Aragon falling upon their heads too.

It was decided that the best thing was to inform the Cardinal of what had come to pass as soon as possible, in order to absolve themselves of all guilt in the matter. One of the gentlemen of their number was chosen to ride to Rome, instead of returning to Amalfi, to inform the Cardinal and his brother.

Here Bandello falls into error again, for the Cardinal was with the Pope in Bologna, not in Rome. His brother Carlo may have been in Rome, but Luigi certainly was not when the news of the scandal broke. This moment can be precisely dated, for Notar Giacomo, the contemporary Neapolitan chronicler, refers to it in his diary:

> On Sunday November 17th 1510, it was common talk throughout the city of Naples, that the illustrious Signora Giovanna d'Aragona, daughter of the late illustrious Don Enrico d'Aragona, and sister of the most Reverend Monsignor Cardinal of Aragon, having let it be known that she wished to make a pilgrimage to Santa Maria of Loreto, had gone thither with a retinue of many carriages and thence departed with Antonio da Bologna, son of Messer Antonino da Bologna, and gone with the aforesaid, saying that he was her husband, to Ragusa, leaving behind her one male child of ten, who was Duke of Amalfi, *scopis ornatus*.[22]

The '*scopis ornatus*' may refer to the fact that the Duchy was in effect governed by the regent, the Duke's mother, and Alfonso merely the titular ruler.

Notar Giacomo was under the impression that Antonio and the Duchess had fled to Ragusa, on the Dalmatian coast, which was then under the influence of Venice. This may have been their original intention or, according to another suggestion, it may have been that her brothers had set this rumour about so that when they managed to capture the pair there would be few questions asked if they suddenly disappeared. Certainly to seize Giovanna and bring Antonio to book for daring to marry her without their consent was now first and foremost in her brothers' minds.

CHAPTER 12

Fugitives

DUCHESS Love mix'd with fear is sweetest.

John Webster, *The Duchess of Malfi*, III.ii.66

The idyll of being together as a normal family was to last just over a year, and during this time Antonio and Giovanna lived on what they knew was borrowed time. For six or seven months they stayed in Ancona, where Giovanna gave birth to their third child, another son. Bandello says he was named Alfonso, but this seems unlikely since Giovanna's eldest child, the Duke of Amalfi, was also named Alfonso. Perhaps this third child is the Luigi with which some sources confuse Antonio's eldest son, Federico.[1] It would have been credible for Antonio and Giovanna to try to win the sympathy of the Cardinal by naming the child after him.

As Christmas approached, so the war against Ferrara intensified and the Cardinal of Aragon was in no position to be able to take decisive action against his erring sister, for he was obliged to remain beside the Pope. Julius had decided that the best way to attack Ferrara was to first take the two small fortified towns of Mirandola and Concordia to the west. Concordia fell on 18 December, but the papal commanders, discouraged by the unusually harsh winter conditions, sent word to the Pope in Bologna that it would be impossible to take Mirandola until the spring. Julius was furious and decided to take command of the campaign himself.

With the most unpapal ejaculation 'Let's see if I've got as much balls as the King of France!',[2] on 2 January 1511 he set off from Bologna for Mirandola, taking with him Luigi d'Aragona, the Cardinals Isvaglies and Cornaro, and the architect Bramante. At San Felice, not far from Mirandola, they met the Venetian army. The Venetian ambassador, Lipomano, reported how Julius seemed recovered from his fever and, with the stamina of a giant, was ready to defy the elements. Despite the icy cold which had frozen the rivers and the raging blizzard that had brought snow drifts to the height of the horses' knees, Julius still went out daily to inspect his troops. Although Luigi and the rest of the Pope's entourage would willingly have abandoned the campaign and retired to the warmer climes of Rome, Julius was immovable. He spoke only of Mirandola, singing it over and over again like a mantra, until everyone began to snigger at him.[3]

When it stopped snowing on 6 January, he set off, to a fanfare of trumpets, to lay siege to Mirandola. At first he established himself in a peasant's house not far from his artillery emplacement; but, not satisfied with this position, he moved nearer still to the scene of action and took up residence in the kitchen of the convent of San Giustina. As the icy blizzards continued, conditions for Julius's entourage became dire. Desperately seeking refuge from the bitter cold, Luigi and his companion, Cardinal Cornaro, pestered the Venetian ambassador to make over to them the open stable that he was occupying. In normal times it would have been considered unfit even for servants to inhabit.[4]

On 17 January, the Pope's room took a direct hit from an arquebus and two of his entourage were injured. He transferred to Cardinal Isvaglies's room, but that was hit too, so he went back to his own, saying that he would rather be shot in the head than withdraw a pace! The Venetians suspected that some of the Pope's own men were signalling his position to the artillery in Mirandola so that he would be driven away.

Certainly, Julius's nephew, Francesco Maria della Rovere, was not showing as much zeal for the campaign as his uncle and, being related by marriage to the Este family (his mother-in-law was Isabella d'Este), it is thought that he was being wooed over to the Este camp. But despite the general lack of enthusiasm from his commanders, Julius managed to conquer Mirandola. It surrendered on 20 January and the ever-restless 67-year-old Pope could not contain his impatience to enter the city. Without waiting for the defensive earthbanks in front of the gates to be removed, he insisted on climbing up a ladder and passing over a breach in the wall. Later, inside the walls, he berated Francesco Maria and Cardinal Alidosi in front of their men for allowing them to pillage the town after he had given explicit orders to forbid it. He had, he grumbled, always to see to everything himself![5]

Having conquered Mirandola, Julius was ready to move immediately against Ferrara, but funds began to run short and, from Ravenna on 10 March 1511, he decided to resort to the nomination of nine new cardinals to replenish his coffers. Among those who paid substantial sums for their nomination were Bandinello Sauli of Genoa and Alfonso Petrucci of Siena. Julius hoped these new cardinals would cancel out the effect of the schismatic cardinals in the consistory.[6] Luigi's freedom of action was already hampered by his involvement in the Pope's military campaign, but his efforts to have Antonio Bologna expelled from his refuge were further impeded by the fact that the papal legate of Ancona, the Cardinal of Mantua, Sigismondo Gonzaga (brother-in-law of Isabella d'Este), had sided with the schismatics against Julius.

The pendulum began to swing against the Pope. The lethargic French commander, Chaumont, died in February. He was replaced by the energetic, experienced Giangiacomo Trivulzio, who had once fought for the Aragon kings of Naples. After a brief return to Bologna, Julius was again forced to retire to Ravenna to avoid being taken prisoner by the French. He left the bickering Francesco Maria della Rovere and Alidosi defending the walls of Bologna. When Bentivoglio supporters organised an uprising, Alidosi, fearing, not without foundation, that della Rovere would abandon him to the mob, took flight, forcing della Rovere to do likewise. On 23 May 1511, Trivulzio took Bologna and re-established the Bentivoglio there.

Bolognese hatred of Alidosi was vented on Michelangelo's masterpiece, the bronze statue of Pope Julius, which had been erected over the door of the Cathedral of San Petronio in 1508. Michelangelo had portrayed Julius with a bunch of keys in one hand and the other raised ('In the act of benediction or malediction?' Julius had asked wryly when he saw it). Now Julius had good reason to condemn the Bolognese. At the end of that year, the statue was smashed and the pieces melted down by the Duke of Ferrara to make a huge cannon that he named, disdainfully, *La Giulia* (The Julia).

The loss of Bologna, the richest city in the Papal States, was a grave blow for Julius. He laid the blame mostly at della Rovere's feet, when probably both he and Alidosi were equally responsible. When his nephew appeared before him at Ravenna to justify himself, Julius treated him to a tirade of recriminations. As he was riding away, della Rovere met Cardinal Alidosi, who merely smiled courteously. Still burning from his uncle's reproof and blinded by his anger, della Rovere pulled his sword from its scabbard and ran Alidosi through, killing him instantly. He was mourned only by Julius. A measure of Alidosi's low standing with his peers is that, despite the grave offence to the dignity of his office that his murder represented, none of his fellow cardinals saw fit to protest, and although della Rovere was subjected to a summary trial, he received no real punishment for this deed, just as he had received none for murdering his sister's lover in 1507.

Nearly sick with grief at the loss of this favourite, Julius left Ravenna immediately for Rimini, where more bad news was awaiting him. The schismatic cardinals, supported by the King of France and the Holy Roman Emperor, had decided to call an Ecumenical Council at Pisa in September, ostensibly for the reform of Church abuses, but in effect with the aim of deposing the Pope. With a heavy heart, Julius left Rimini and began to make his way back down the peninsula towards Rome. On 5 June he was in Ancona and six days later he was again at Loreto. Racked with illness and defeated, he re-entered Rome on 26 June. The city was in turmoil as the feudal barons who opposed him incited the population to revolt. The papal and Venetian armies had been dispersed and the Papal States were at the mercy of their enemies, who were now in a strong enough position to dethrone Julius. Europe waited anxiously to see what would come to pass.

But the King of France, perhaps still wary of offending the majesty of the papal office in the eyes of his Catholic subjects, did not drive home his victory. He withdrew Trivulzio to Milan and began negotiations with Julius. The projected council of schismatic cardinals at Pisa was a failure before it had even begun. The cardinals were disunited and uncertain of their allegiance. Of their number, the Duke of Ferrara's brother, Cardinal Ippolito d'Este, hesitated and by the end of May, Cardinal Sigismondo Gonzaga had abandoned the schismatics and returned to Julius – a fact that could have some bearing on the Duchess of Amalfi's story.

During the six or seven months they had been living in Ancona, Antonio Bologna had been trying to obtain permission to remain in the city, while the Cardinal of Aragon had been putting pressure on Cardinal Gonzaga to have him and his family expelled. Once Gonzaga had returned to Julius's camp at the end of May, Antonio must have known that his family's days in Ancona were numbered.[7]

He and Giovanna set about seeking another safe haven and Bandello says that Antonio obtained, via a friend, a safe conduct to Siena. Here again Bandello is not completely credible. If anyone had contacts in Siena, it was the Duchess of Amalfi. Her late husband's family came from Siena and they still had many close relatives there. The Lord of Siena at this time, Borghese Petrucci, was married to Vittoria Piccolomini, a cousin of Giovanna's first husband. How much Vittoria would have been able to help the fugitives is debatable, for she had been forced into marriage unwillingly after her father, Andrea, had quarrelled with the Petrucci. Her brother, Pier Francesco Piccolomini, eventually came to terms with Borghese Petrucci and by this time he was one of his staunchest supporters, so he would have been in the best position to obtain asylum in Siena for Antonio and Giovanna. But Vittoria's other brother was Giovanni Piccolomini, Cardinal of Siena, and both he and Borghese's brother, Cardinal Alfonso Petrucci, were close companions of the Cardinal of Aragon in Rome. This boded ill and the situation in Siena was not a promising one for the fugitives.

Antonio knew that their expulsion from Ancona was imminent, and that when it became final, the Cardinal of Aragon's men would be lying in wait for them along their escape route. Therefore, as soon as permission arrived to take refuge in Siena, he sent his three children on ahead with some servants. He and Giovanna remained in Ancona to wind up their affairs, so that as soon as the expulsion order was issued, rather than wait the given fifteen days for it to become binding, they could leave immediately and travel rapidly to Siena on horseback before the Cardinal's men realised that they had gone.[8] Bandello is accurate in giving them six or seven months in Ancona, from November 1510 to May 1511, for they probably left towards the end of May, after the legate of Ancona had abandoned the schismatics. They would certainly have departed before the Pope arrived on 5 June on his way back to Rome, for fear of encountering Luigi. If Luigi did accompany the Pope to Ancona, he found that his prey had escaped; the lovebirds had flown.

The duration of Antonio and Giovanna's stay in Siena, and the whereabouts of their lodgings in the city, are uncertain. In documents contained in the *Consorteria Piccolomini* in the State Archives in Siena, there is mention in 1577 of a *palazzo* in Siena known as the Palace of the Duchess of Amalfi, but this may refer to the *palazzo* of Silvia Piccolomini (Andrea Piccolomini's granddaughter), who married her cousin Inigo Piccolomini, Duke of Amalfi (Giovanna's grandson), thus reuniting the two branches of the family in the mid-sixteenth century. Antonio and Giovanna may even have stayed in the traditional Piccolomini fief of Pienza, which was within the boundaries of Sienese territory.[9]

It is certain that as soon as Luigi had traced his sister and her husband to Siena, he began putting pressure on the government there to have them expelled. The Petrucci family, who governed the city, did not enjoy an honourable reputation. When Pope Pius III (Francesco Piccolomini) died so quickly after his election, it was rumoured that he had been helped on his way by a dose of poison sent by the then ruler of Siena, Pandolfo Petrucci, who feared that the new Pope would oppose his lordship over the city.[10] A reputation for poisoning seemed to run in the family, for when Pandolfo's sons, Borghese and Cardinal Alfonso Petrucci, later came into conflict with Pope Leo X in 1516, Cardinal Petrucci organised an ill-fated plot to try to poison him. The scheme brought down many cardinals in its wake and Luigi d'Aragona narrowly missed being caught up in its consequences.

These then were the Petrucci upon whose limited mercy Antonio and Giovanna had fallen. Once Luigi had begun to exert diplomatic pressure on Borghese and Cardinal Petrucci, and possibly also on Cardinal Piccolomini, there would have been little that Vittoria or Pier Francesco Piccolomini could have done to save the situation for their kinswoman. Antonio was again expelled and his wife and children went with him. There appears to be no record in the Sienese archives of an expulsion order for Antonio Bologna signed by Borghese Petrucci; it may have been lost or never have been issued. But if Antonio tried to pre-empt the Cardinal again, this time Luigi was prepared for his sudden moves.

The flight from Siena was more hurried and less well coordinated than the one from Ancona. Luigi had had time to organise his spies and set a squadron of his men at the ready to follow Bologna as soon as he left Sienese territory. Antonio and Giovanna had decided to try for the Republic of Venice. The Doges of Venice liked to boast that the Republic was one of the freest lands in Italy, because it had neither gates nor walls to enclose it. Even so, it seems to have been a foolish decision, for it would have taken them straight into the lion's mouth – the theatre of war in the Papal States, where there was a good chance of encountering Cardinal Luigi and his men. It is strange that they did not head in the opposite direction, towards French-held Milan.

In the absence of adequate records, one way of measuring how long Giovanna and Antonio spent in Siena is to examine the political situation which may have influenced their decision as to when to leave, and for where.

In August 1511 Pope Julius was again seriously ill in Rome; so much so that the cardinals met to make arrangements for his funeral and the city was thrown into turmoil. It was a delicate situation for both the Pope's supporters and opponents, but, according to Sanudo, Cardinal Luigi d'Aragona was absent from the city in August: a dispatch from Rome mentions that he returned to his Roman *palazzo* on 2 September (from where it is not said).[11] This leads to the possibility that Luigi recaptured his sister during this month and that she and Bologna had spent only a few weeks in Siena. But why would she have fled in the direction which would take her towards rather than away from her brother?

According to Bandello, Antonio Bologna spent just over a year in Milan, from the late summer of 1512 to October 1513. If he and Giovanna had left Siena during the summer of 1511, this would leave a year in Antonio's peregrinations unaccounted for, though it would not be impossible for him to have wandered from place to place until he finally found asylum in Milan. Perhaps Antonio and Giovanna had been informed that the Pope had returned to Rome with his entourage and was gravely ill there, which led them to presume that Cardinal Luigi would be too preoccupied by this crisis to dedicate his attention to their moves. By the end of August, however, Julius had again miraculously recovered and was back to his old bellicose ways, as determined as ever to drive the French out of Italy and bring Ferrara into submission.

From September 1511 to September 1512, momentous political events took place in Italy and Pope Julius, after severe setbacks, began finally to gain the upper hand in the conflict. The schismatic Ecumenical Council, which finally met in November 1511 at Pisa, turned out to be poorly attended and was a fiasco. Julius excommunicated those schismatic cardinals who did attend and deprived them of their benefices. Luigi d'Aragona, who had staunchly supported the Pope throughout this period, was handsomely rewarded for his loyalty with new benefices.[12] He already possessed several and during the course of his life his excessive accumulation made him one of the chief transgressors in this misconduct. His primary aim in this was to reach the goal set out for him by his grandfather King Ferrante: to obtain the papal throne for the House of Aragon. It is a truism that money brings power; the strategic distribution of patronage was an essential tactical counter in the complex network of Vatican politics.

It seems unlikely that Giovanna and Antonio would have left Siena during the winter of 1512, as armies were on the move again up and down Italy. While the Venetians tackled the French in Brescia and Milan, the Viceroy of Naples, Raimondo Cardona, marched north with a combined Spanish/

Neapolitan army and laid siege to Bologna. The French had one trump card to play: their brilliant young commander, Gaston de Foix, nephew of King Louis XII. With a series of shrewd tactical moves and forced marches, he ran circles round the Spanish, Venetian and papal forces, and managed to relieve Bologna. A rapid victory was essential to the French in order to depose Julius and place a francophile schismatic, Cardinal Sanseverino, in charge of the Papal States. Once these were under French influence, Spain could be expelled from Naples and the whole of Italy would be subject to French hegemony.

Time was on the side of Julius and his allies and Cardona did his best to avoid being drawn into battle with Gaston de Foix, but when the latter moved towards Ravenna, Cardona was forced to intervene and prevent his taking the city because it contained all the supply stores for the papal armies. Thus it was that, on Easter Sunday, 11 April 1512, along the tiny River Ronco, about two miles outside Ravenna, the armies of de Foix and Cardona faced each other and fought the bloodiest battle that had ever taken place on Italian soil. Cardona was outnumbered: the French had approximately 25,000 to his 20,000 men. Fighting beside the French, the Duke of Ferrara's powerful artillery wrought havoc among the squadrons of Julius's Holy League, literally blowing the Spanish soldiers to pieces. At the end of the eight-hour conflict 10,000 mutilated bodies were left on the battlefield; a third of them were French. The French had won but some thought it a pyrrhic victory because their leader, Gaston de Foix, perished during the battle. Ravenna was sacked and most of the other towns of Romagna fell to the French. The schismatic Cardinal Sanseverino took over the leadership of the French army and began marching south along the Via Emilia towards Rome. His aim now was to depose Pope Julius.

But French determination soon faltered as the members of the Holy League began to react to the disaster of Ravenna: Henry VIII brought English troops to bear on France; the Swiss mobilised and the Emperor Maximilian was temporarily induced to sign a truce with Venice and abandon his French alliance. With a masterly stroke, Julius dispersed support for the schismatic Council of Pisa by calling a council of his own for the reform of the Church. Because of the hostility of the Pisans, the schismatics had been forced to retire to Milan, where they received a similarly hostile reception. The pendulum, which had swung towards the French after their victory at Ravenna, now moved inexorably back again towards Julius, and the French found themselves more and more isolated and unable to follow up their gains.

Although the name of Luigi d'Aragona is not mentioned in the chronicles (he was not among the many illustrious noblemen killed, wounded, or taken prisoner by the French at Ravenna), he almost certainly participated in the battle, as did Carlo d'Aragona's young nephew, the Marquis of Pescara (Francesco Ferrante D'Avalos). But Carlo himself was not present because he died about three weeks before the battle took place – a fact which seems to have been ignored by Bandello and other contemporary writers when they attribute the tragic end of Antonio Bologna to the Aragon 'brothers'.

A brief entry in the diary of the contemporary chronicler, Passaro, reads:

> On Monday the 21 March 1512, at four in the night [i.e., one o'clock in the morning], the lord Don Carlo d'Aragona died and was buried in the church of Monteoliveto in Naples.[13]

There is no mention of the cause of his death.

Unless the Duchess moved from Siena before Carlo's death in March 1512, he cannot be blamed for her end or that of her children. The responsibility must fall solely and squarely on Cardinal Luigi's shoulders. The mad, murderous Ferdinand of Webster's play was a figment of the playwright's imagination. It is tempting to imagine that Webster had access to secret Spanish tracts that revealed the real end of the Duchess: perhaps she did leave Siena during that summer of 1511, was captured and taken back to Naples, and, when she refused to cooperate or renounce her marriage to Bologna, was killed in a fit of rage by Carlo, who then took his own life, in remorse. But there are no extant historical sources to corroborate this hypothesis or even to suggest it.

A measure of Carlo's lack of grandeur and standing as a personage is the fact that his demise passed unnoticed, apart from the entry in the journal of the Neapolitan Passaro. His death did not become generally known in Italy and Bandello, the Corona manuscripts and Filonico do not specify that at the denouement of the tragedy, one of the brothers was already dead.

'*Ego sum pastor bonus*' – 'For I am the good shepherd' was the passage from the Gospel Luigi d'Aragona recited to the Lateran Council called by Pope Julius in Rome in May 1512.[14] This shepherd, however, was probably preparing to gather in the straying members of his flock in a less than Christian manner. Believing that Luigi would be unable to extricate himself from the Council in Rome, it is likely that this was the moment chosen by Giovanna and Antonio to move from Siena. If they had intended to reach Venice, it would certainly have been difficult and dangerous for them to enter the Romagna before this time. But by May 1512, the French forces were already retiring towards Milan.

This time the children were not sent on ahead but travelled with their parents, either because in Venice there was no one who could have taken them in or because this departure was hastier than the last, as Antonio struggled to forestall the Cardinal. Let us assume that they set off for Venice in the late spring of 1512, when Cardinal Luigi was beside the Pope at the Lateran Council. According to Bandello, the journey was slow and laborious, with the two younger children riding in a litter, and the elder one on his own horse. Since Federico was at most about five years old, the latter does not sound altogether credible.

They made their way along the dusty, white roads of the rolling Chianti hills down into the Valdarno, then over the higher and more rugged Tusco-Emilian Apennine mountains to reach the coastal plain of Romagna, where they hoped to find a boat to take them to Venice. When they arrived in the vicinity of Forlì, not far from Ravenna, they realised that a band of horsemen was following them, in the distance. Giovanna and Antonio knew immediately who the pursuers were. Informed of their itinerary by a spy, the Cardinal had unleashed a band of henchmen to overtake them. There was no escape, for though Antonio, Giovanna and Federico were riding speedy mounts, the two smaller children in the litter held them back. At first they decided to head for a nearby village in order to hide there, but the horsemen were gaining on them too rapidly and Giovanna realised they had to separate if Antonio were to save himself. She was convinced, as he was, that Luigi would not harm her, and probably not harm the children either, since they were of the same royal, Aragon blood of which he was so proud.

She pleaded with Antonio to spur on his horse and leave them to their fate. He hesitated, unwilling to abandon his wife and children, but he knew she was right. It would be suicidal to stay. She pressed a bagful of gold ducats into his hands and, weeping, begged him to waste no more time but to go; God willing, her brother[15] one day would be reconciled and they could be reunited. They kissed and embraced for the last time and Antonio, bidding the grooms to follow, left the Duchess with her children, her maid and the other attendants. Bandello says that Federico, seeing his father ride away, suddenly spurred on his own horse and rode off to join him, and that Giovanna let him go. If nothing else, his presence would have been a comfort to Antonio during their separation. It seems more likely that Federico was mounted behind Antonio or one of the grooms and it was for this reason he followed his father.

Perhaps to shake the Cardinal's men from their trail, instead of continuing towards Venice, Antonio, his son and their four servants headed for Milan. When the horsemen caught up with Giovanna and her party, to allay her fears their leader assured her that they meant her no harm. They had been sent, he said, by her brother[16] to conduct her back home to the Kingdom of Naples where, the Cardinal commanded, she should resume the duties of governing her son, the Duke, and his estates, that she had so irresponsibly abandoned, instead of wandering hither and thither about Italy with a man like Antonio Bologna, who would merely exploit her for his own gain and, when he was tired of her, leave her destitute. She was told not to fret and to follow the men calmly and quietly, for no harm would come to her or her children.

Reassured, the Duchess allowed herself to be led back to the Kingdom of Naples, where the trail fades away into mystery. It was a long, sad journey, and although Giovanna fully expected to take up her position again as Duchess of Amalfi, she must have felt a certain anxiety for the fate of her children by Bologna, and for her faithful maid. But when they arrived at Amalfi, she was not taken to her usual apartments; instead, she was imprisoned with her two children and Lucina in the castle keep, while the rest of her party were allowed to go free. In prison she awaited news of the Cardinal's intentions, never imagining that he had coldly decided that the smear on the honour of the House of Aragon, which her marriage to Bologna represented, could only be wiped clean by the deaths of Bologna's family, of which she was now a part. Late one night, one of the Cardinal's henchmen arrived from Rome with orders to kill Giovanna, the children and her maid. They were strangled to death and their bodies secretly and hurriedly buried in the gardens of the castle.[17]

This is the version of Giovanna's disappearance given by Bandello and the Corona manuscripts. Bandello does not specify in which castle Giovanna was imprisoned, but merely says it was a castle belonging to her son the Duke, while the old Corona manuscript specifies Amalfi. Giovanna could have been taken to Celano, or Capestrano, or Scafati, but according

The Torre dello Ziro: according to popular legend, Giovanna died here.

to local folklore, her prison was the Torre dello Ziro on the cliff above the town of Amalfi. At the time it was a watchtower, part of the extensive fortifications of Scala Castle. Its name derives from its cylindrical shape which resembles a *ziro*, an Arab vessel for storing grain or oil.

Scala Castle was the main fortification of the Duchy of Amalfi and it was here that Giovanna's son Duke Alfonso lived when residing in the Duchy. It is also probable that Thomas Hoby visited the Piccolomini family here in 1550. The castle walls stretched from Pontone at the head of the valley behind Amalfi, along a steep craggy limestone spur, as far as the Torre dello Ziro on the cliffs overlooking the sea. The entrance to the tower was half-way up the wall and was reached by a wooden stepladder which, once removed, would have rendered escape impossible. However, it seems unlikely that Giovanna and her children would have been imprisoned in this watchtower at the castle's extremity and more probable that, as Bandello says, they were placed in the keep in the main body of the castle. Perhaps the legend of Giovanna's prison became linked with the tower because it had been renovated by her father-in-law, Duke Antonio, and was thus linked with the Piccolomini name. But wherever the prison was situated, Giovanna, her two younger children and her maid died there, reputedly murdered.

It is difficult to believe that Giovanna was escorted straight back to Amalfi without some sort of direct contact with her brother to clarify matters. He was no doubt extremely angry with her, for her deception had made him into a laughing stock and he would certainly have wanted to punish her in some way. But Luigi was an astute politician. He had nothing to gain and much to lose by assassinating his sister – first and foremost his influence over the important, strategic Duchy of Amalfi. He was still nurturing the desire to re-establish his dynasty in Naples, for which all points of influence in the Kingdom were crucial. If the young Duke were to fall completely under the sway of his Piccolomini relations, the Duchy would not necessarily remain sympathetic to Luigi's cause.

There can be no doubt that Luigi intended to eliminate Bologna. His betrayal and defiance of the Cardinal's authority were unpardonable. Nor would the Duchess's maid escape punishment for having aided and abetted her mistress's clandestine relationship and flight. But as for Giovanna herself and her children, who bore the royal blood of Aragon and could be used as valuable pawns in the dynastic marriage game, there was every reason to keep them alive. So what happened?

It is extremely unlikely that Luigi deliberately ordered Giovanna's murder, or that he degenerated into a frenzy of rage comparable to that of Webster's Aragon brothers. Such behaviour does not tally with the cool, wily politician that we know Luigi to have been. But it is not impossible that, in a fit of exasperated anger at Giovanna's obstinate refusal to obey his bidding, this veteran of many bloody military campaigns may have inflicted some physical harm on her in a face to face encounter.

A mysterious entry in Sanudo's diary indicates that such an encounter may have occurred. At the end of August 1512, Luigi suddenly left Rome for Naples. The report received by Sanudo reads:

> From Rome, I saw a particular letter, on 28 [August] about how the Florentine Cardinal Soderino with six cardinals went to the pope to seek aid for Florence against the Medici without obtaining anything: the pope continues his policy against Spain because he wishes to expel her from Italy and make the Cardinal of Aragon King of Naples, and this Cardinal went to Naples because of his nephew the Duke of Ferrara, without any objection from the pope. . . .[18]

Sanudo is mistaken when he speaks of the Duke of Ferrara as Luigi's nephew; the Duke was Luigi's cousin, his only nephew of ducal rank being the Duke of Amalfi. Perhaps the emissary had heard that the Cardinal of Aragon had suddenly departed for Naples to deal with the affairs of 'his nephew the Duke' and erroneously presumed 'the Duke' in question to be the Duke of Ferrara, for at this time Luigi was negotiating a reconciliation between the Pope and the ex-communicated Duke of Ferrara.

Luigi's sudden visit to Naples at the end of August 1512 'to deal with affairs of his nephew the Duke' may have occurred in conjunction with his sister being brought back there, or perhaps even with her death. If Giovanna was still alive, it is probable that he did have some personal, animated discussion with her over the matter of her marriage. But any thought of a reconciliation between Luigi and Antonio Bologna was now finally excluded by Pope Julius's decision to place Luigi on the throne of Naples (as referred to in the above report by Sanudo). The Cardinal would certainly have had greater plans for his sister than marriage to a mere major-domo and there was no question of her being permitted to renounce her birthright. It was inalienable.

One can only speculate as to the cause of the Duchess's death. She may simply have abandoned herself to a melancholic decline when she realised that Luigi wished to marry her elsewhere and never intended to allow her to be reunited with Antonio. Once the intense passion, whose expression had carried her to such extreme gestures, was thwarted, it consumed itself by eroding her desire to live. Or perhaps her end was less dramatic and she merely fell prey to illness. If she had spent any length of time at Scafati, instead of Amalfi, during the summer months, it could have prejudiced her health. Fatal malarial fevers were endemic in Italy and Scafati Castle was situated in an increasingly malarial area, thanks to the building of the Piccolomini water mills there.

As for the destiny of Giovanna's two youngest children, it is possible that the Cardinal took them from her to use them as counters to barter her submission to his will. If she were already so emotionally tried by the separation from her husband and the execution of her beloved maid, this new torment would have been intolerable when combined with the terrible burden of guilt that she now bore. Her wilful defiance of convention had brought misery to all those she loved most dearly. If only she had been able to maintain the veil of deception, Lucina, Antonio and the children would all have been kept safe.

Did Luigi really murder her children? It seems unlikely that he was, as Painter puts it, bent on 'rooting out the whole name and race of Bologna' in a bloody purification of the tainting of his family honour. The baby born at Ancona could easily have died of natural causes, since infant mortality rates were high at the time. Eleonora may have survived, if faith can be put in the Filonico manuscript, which has Eleonora growing up and marrying.

Certainly Giovanna's elder son by Bologna did not fall victim to his uncle's vendetta: Federico was permitted to return to his father's family in Naples, where he grew up peacefully and died of illness in adolescence.[19] But he was still alive when Luigi d'Aragona died in 1519 and appears to have been mentioned in his will. Luigi left all his private possessions to be divided between his nephews, the sons of his three sisters: Caterina's son, Enrico Orsini, Count of Nola; Ippolita's son, Enrico Pandone, Count of Venafro; and Giovanna's sons, Alfonso Piccolomini, Duke of Amalfi and Federico d'Aragona (Antonio Bologna's son).[20] Was the mention of Federico in Luigi's will an act of penitence for the evil he had perpetrated? Or had the Cardinal in reality no direct responsibility for the deaths of Giovanna, her baby son and small daughter?

The later Filonico and Corona manuscripts explicitly accuse the Cardinal of having his sister and her children murdered. But when Bandello first wrote the story in 1514, the Cardinal was still alive and extremely powerful and, for fear of incurring his wrath and a vendetta, he does not dare to accuse him personally, but merely says that he heard from Cesare Fieramosca, a Neapolitan soldier, that the children, together with the maid, had been 'strangled' and 'died miserably'. (Filonico, who is less reliable, has them being poisoned in Ancona).

That they died, or at least the Duchess died, sometime in 1512 or 1513 is almost certain. After this date there is a gap in the annual nomination of the vice-dukes of Amalfi. The nominations were made by Giovanna as regent and, during the course of 1512, the vice-duke for the following year was nominated, presumably by the imprisoned Duchess. After that there is a gap until 1516, when the young Duke's uncle, Francesco Piccolomini, Bishop of Bisignano, stepped in as a lieutenant-general to take the reins of government in hand. After 1516, the Duke reached his maturity and the nominations recommenced regularly again. With the demise of the Duchess, and her elder son still in his minority, there must have been a period of administrative confusion, as there had been in 1499, after the death of Giovanna's first husband, Duke Alfonso.[21]

Whenever Giovanna died, it is likely that Luigi would have tried to keep the fact a secret for as long as possible so that he would not lose the bait to draw Antonio Bologna back into his grasp. While Antonio was in Milan, he continued to receive assurances from the Cardinal, after Giovanna's death, that he would soon be reunited with her. From the blanket of secrecy, however, rumours spread about the brutal nature of the deaths of

Giovanna and her innocent children at the hands of her brother. The Spanish Viceroy of Naples and his government would certainly have actively encouraged such gossip, for it blackened the reputation of Luigi d'Aragona and discouraged support for his claim to the throne of Naples.

As a consequence of this combination of circumstances, the true end of the Duchess of Amalfi is shrouded in a winding-sheet of secret plans and manipulated hearsay. It is not known whether she suffered the mental and physical torments spawned by John Webster's dramatic imagination. For posterity, her death, as portrayed by Webster, has overshadowed her life. In the real historical drama, it is the paradox and complexity of her life that is the real focus of interest. She was a woman 'beyond her time', at loggerheads with the society of her day; a figure with whom many could, and still can, identify.

CHAPTER 13

Bologna's Exile

ANTONIO	What think you of my hope of reconcilement To the Arragonian bretheren?
DELIO	I misdoubt it; For though they have sent their letters of safe-conduct For your repair to Milan, they appear But nets to entrap you.

John Webster, *The Duchess of Malfi*, V.i.1–5

Antonio took refuge in Milan with his eldest son Federico and waited hopefully for news of Giovanna and his other two children. He probably arrived around the beginning of September 1512, since Bandello says he spent just over a year there, and remained until October 1513. These dates would tally with his separation from the Duchess in late August of 1512, and with Luigi d'Aragona's sudden visit to Naples in that period.

By the autumn of 1512, the retreating French had been driven from the city of Milan, leaving only a garrison to hold the castle citadel. This was placed under siege by troops fighting on behalf of Il Moro's son, Massimiliano Sforza, who had regained his father's title of Duke of Milan. On 29 December 1512, Antonio may have watched the spectacular parade as Sforza made his triumphal entry into the city of his birth, flanked by the Spanish Viceroy of Naples, Raimondo Cardona. The Neapolitan soldiers who accompanied Cardona were to convey news to Antonio of his family in Naples.

The return of the Sforzas brought a renewed pleasure-seeking atmosphere to Milan. It had been the seat of one of the most brilliant courts of Europe until it was shattered and its members dispersed by the storm of the French invasion. Writers, mime-artists, musicians and painters (pre-eminent among whom had been the great Leonardo da Vinci) were drawn like a magnet towards the munificence of that ill-fated Maecenas of the *Cinquecento*, Ludovico il Moro. With the return of Il Moro's son, there was an attempt to recreate the splendid licentious times of his father.

In January 1513 came another triumphant arrival, that of Antonio's former employer, Isabella d'Este, Marchioness of Mantua, who had come to Milan to visit her nephew, the new Duke. Was Antonio relieved or alarmed at her arrival? After his disgrace at the Gonzaga court of Mantua, he may not have dared to approach her, but if he had been working secretly for her, then he might already have contacted her to obtain his safe conduct to Milan, through her nephew.

The Milanese were certainly cheered to see Isabella and her bevy of beautiful, elegant ladies-in-waiting, for it really seemed as though the old glorious, if spendthrift, times were returning. But Isabella had come to Milan not merely to resurrect the magnificent carnival festivities of the time of Il Moro; she had come to weave her diplomatic threads. First, she wanted to ensure that her rather ineffectual nephew was firmly under her influence; and, secondly, she wanted to neutralise Pope Julius II's policy against her brother's Duchy of Ferrara.

Julius was still determined to confiscate Ferrara, but the Spanish forces under the command of the Viceroy of Naples, Cardona, with which he hoped to realise his ambition, were distracted by Isabella and her ladies at the carnival in Milan. Cardona turned a deaf ear when Julius ordered him to march immediately against Ferrara, for he was far too busy indulging his passion for Isabella's most attractive, maid-of-honour, the seventeen-year-old Eleonora Brogna de' Lardis, familiarly known as La Brognina. At the conclusion of one festive evening, Cardona presented La Brognina with a casket of jewels and two lengths of the finest velvet, one crimson and one black, the crimson to celebrate the joy of a kiss received, the black to signify mourning for a kiss refused.[1] Antonio Bologna looked on from afar at these new love affairs, which were taken up as current gossip, while his own, now history, was forgotten by all except the Cardinal of Aragon.

The Cardinal's ambition to sit on the throne of Naples was effectively nipped in the bud, though not definitively shelved, with the untimely death of Pope Julius II, which also cut short the carnival festivities in Milan. The news arrived on 22 February. It was received by Isabella d'Este with a good deal of relief, for it promised to release her brothers in Ferrara from the immediate threat of papal annexation, which had been due to take place that very week, while she was still desperately trying to delay Cardona.

The last six months of Julius's life had been ones of unquiet triumph. He achieved his aim of expelling the French, but, in so doing, tipped the balance of power towards Spain and left the whole of Italy open to the danger of becoming a Spanish province, like Naples. The threat perturbed him, the more so because the heir of the Holy Roman Emperor, Maximilian, Charles, Duke of Burgundy (son of Juana d'Aragona and Philip of Burgundy) was also the heir of Ferdinand of Spain; thus it would be impossible to use the Holy Roman Empire as a counterbalance to the power of Spain. For this reason his thoughts had turned to Naples and to his ever-faithful collaborator, Luigi d'Aragona, and he let it be known that he aimed to place Luigi on the Neapolitan throne. But Julius never fully recovered from his illness during the summer of 1511 and his death prevented him from taking effective steps to implement his plans.

Julius's bellicose character earned him numerous enemies at home and abroad and there were many who breathed a sigh of relief at his passing – first and foremost the King of France and the Este family of Ferrara. But the population of Rome paid homage and tribute to this Pope who had striven to render both Italy and the Catholic Church great and independent. His methods may have been debatable, but his grand vision and determination were clear.

During his papacy, Rome saw a glorious gathering of some of the greatest artists Italy had ever produced – Raphael and Michelangelo were the giants among them. Both artists worked tirelessly for Julius, pushed inexorably along by his indomitable spirit. Julius met his character match with the strong-minded Michelangelo and their fierce arguments over the decoration of the ceiling and walls of the Sistine Chapel and other commissions left contemporaries dumbfounded. But Julius recognised and respected greatness and he had a profound respect for Michelangelo's artistic prowess. Julius might have been unfortunate in his choice of leaders, but he lacked for nothing in his aesthetic taste.

His relationship with Raphael was less tempestuous, but equally fruitful. Raphael's frescoes on the walls of the Vatican apartments are considered masterpieces of Italian Renaissance art. Both Raphael and Michelangelo eventually worked on Julius's greatest and most lasting project, the rebuilding of St Peter's Basilica in Rome. A true son of the Renaissance, Julius had aimed at reviving the ancient glory of Rome as the fulcrum of western civilisation; St Peter's was the symbol of this glory and Julius's legacy.

The papal election temporarily distracted the Cardinal of Aragon from dealing with the problem of Antonio Bologna in Milan. In the opening scene of John Webster's play, set in 1504, Antonio tells Delio that the Cardinal of Aragon is 'a melancholy churchman', and that 'He should have been Pope; but instead of coming to it by the primitive decency of the church, he did bestow bribes so largely and so impudently, as if he would have carried it away without heaven's knowledge.'[2] This appraisal of him seems fairly accurate, but it is at this point in the story, however, not in 1504, that Luigi 'should have been pope'.

When the cardinals gathered for the conclave, Luigi, now extremely rich and powerful, was at the forefront of the manoeuvres. He was already a veteran of two conclaves, as was his rival Giovanni de' Medici, and both were well versed in the subtleties of the procedure. But Luigi was immediately outmanoeuvred by Bibbiena and de' Medici, who managed to get the new conclave to subscribe to Julius II's anti-simoniacal Bull regarding papal elections, which effectively froze the resources of all the richer cardinals. So even though Luigi had accrued immense riches, which rivalled those of Giovanni, he was unable to buy enough support for his own candidacy. Moreover, his youth was against him; he was too young and healthy. It was rare for young popes to be elected by the College of Cardinals, for there was the risk that they would be politically dominant for too long and accrue to themselves and their supporters excessive wealth and power.

However, the young cardinals at this conclave had decided to remain united and elect one of their number.[3] Luigi d'Aragona was forced to renounce his ambitions and lend his support instead to Giovanni de' Medici. It is interesting to note that during Giovanna's absence from her position as regent of the Duchy, de' Medici had obtained the bishopric of Amalfi. The choice of the young cardinals fell on de' Medici mainly because he did not appear to be in the best of health, despite his young age (he was thirty-seven). He was suffering from an anal fistula and had to be carried into the conclave on a stretcher, accompanied by his secretary, the wily Bibbiena. The fistula had been deliberately left untreated and gave off such a stench that the older cardinals believed Giovanni's health was much more gravely compromised than it in fact was. Naturally, Bibbiena helped to nurture this opinion. The ruse succeeded and eventually Giovanni procured the votes of the older cardinals. Around midday on 9 March 1513, Cardinal Alessandro Farnese announced to the people of Rome that a new pope had been elected and that he had adopted the name Leo X (Plate 10).

On 11 March the Venetian ambassador to Rome, Lipomano, reported that the new Pope had gone to St Peter's with the College of Cardinals and, as the younger ones, led by Marco Cornaro, entered, they were all grinning with satisfaction because they had had their way. Giovanni de' Medici knelt before the high altar. Alessandro Farnese took his mitre and Luigi d'Aragona removed his damask beret. Then, after making his oration, he stood up, placed the mitre on his head, and the cardinals filed before him one by one to kiss his feet. When the new Pope was eventually crowned on 19 March, his papal crown was placed on his head by the same two cardinals. It was symbolic of the primary position they intended to occupy in the new papacy.

During the initial period of Leo's papacy, Luigi d'Aragona was constantly at his side and by October 1513 Rome and Naples were buzzing with rumours regarding the Cardinal of Aragon and the throne of Naples. On 22 October the Venetian ambassador in Naples reported that the city was awaiting 10,000 troops that were to be sent from Sicily, because news had reached the ears of Ferdinand the Catholic that Luigi d'Aragona and the Pope's younger brother, Giuliano de' Medici, were planning to take the Kingdom of Naples from him.[4]

Giuliano de' Medici was the same age as Luigi's sister Giovanna. He was a handsome, cultured man, and unmarried. A masterly stroke for Luigi would have been to bind his family to that of the Pope by a marriage between the two. There is no historical record to confirm this idea, but Lope de Vega, in his version of the Duchess's story, introduces into the plot a Medici suitor sent by her brother (though he calls him Ottavio, not Giuliano). If Giovanna were still alive at the time of the papal election, it is certainly more feasible that Luigi would have had a project of this kind in mind, given his close links with Giuliano de' Medici, rather than a connection with the declining Malatesta family, which Webster suggests in his play. In reality, Giovanna's refusal to countenance such a match may have brought about her death.

In the course of time, however, it became obvious that Pope Leo had no serious intentions of putting Luigi d'Aragona on the throne of Naples. He was happy for rumours to run and frighten Ferdinand the Catholic, but as

15 Portrait formerly known as 'Giovanna d'Aragona', but now believed to represent Isabel de Requesens, Vicereine of Naples. Attributed to Giulio Romano, pupil of Raphael (*Musée du Louvre, Paris*).

16 King Alfonso I of Aragon, Giovanna's great-grandfather. Sketch by Pisanello (*Musée du Louvre, Paris*).

17 King Ferrante I of Naples, Giovanna's grandfather.

18 Two of Giovanna's uncles: Alfonso, Duke of Calabria, King Alfonso II of Naples 1494–5;

19 Don Federico d'Aragona, King Federico III of Naples 1497–1501. Life-size terracotta figures by Guido Mazzoni, 1492, from the church of Sant' Anna dei Lombardi (Monteoliveto), Naples.

20 The Piccolomini castle at Capestrano.

21 View over the Tirino valley from a window of the castle.

22 Castelnuovo, residence of the Aragon Kings of Naples. The white marble triumphal arch of Alfonso I stands between the two central towers.

23 Left, foreground: Ludovico Sforza, Il Moro, Duke of Milan, with his elder son Ercole Massimiliano; right foreground, his wife, Beatrice d'Este, granddaughter of King Ferrante I of Naples, with their younger son Francesco (Pinacoteca di Brera, Milan © *Ministero per I Beni e le Attività Culturali*).

24 *Below, left:* Baldassare Castiglione, author of *The Courtier*, an acquaintance of Giovanna's elder brother. Portrait by Raphael (*Musée du Louvre, Paris*).

25 *Below:* Cesare Borgia, illegitimate son of Pope Alexander VI. Portrait by Altobello Melone (© *Alinari*).

26 King Charles VIII of France. Crowned King of Naples in 1495, he was ousted a few months later by Giovanna's cousin, King Ferrante II of Aragon (© *Alinari*).

27 King Ferdinand II of Aragon, better known as Ferdinand the Catholic. Portrait thought to be by Michael Sittow (*Kunsthistoriches Museum, Vienna*).

28 Fresco of the *Coronation of Pope Pius III*, by Pinturicchio, 1504. The child on a man's shoulders in the bottom right-hand corner could be the young Duke of Amalfi (born March 1499), while his mother stands in the back row, nearer to the Pope, beneath the coat of arms of her husband's family (*Biblioteca Piccolomini in the Cathedral of Siena, Opera della Metropolitana of Siena, 795/01. Photograph: Fabio Lensini*).

29 Isabella d'Este, Marchioness of Mantua, Giovanna's cousin. Drawing by Leonardo da Vinci (*Musée du Louvre, Paris*).

30 Isabella d'Aragona, Duchess of Milan and Bari, Giovanna's cousin. Portrait by Giovanni Antonio Boltraffico, pupil of Leonardo da Vinci (*property of © the Ambrosian Library. All rights reserved. Reproduction forbidden*).

31 Federico da Bozzolo, probably the anonymous 'Lombard Lord' who organised Antonio Bologna's murder in Milan in October 1513. Federico Gonzaga of Bozzolo was married to the daughter of Giovanna's elder sister, Caterina. Portrait by Sebastiano del Piombo (*photograph © Board of Trustees, National Gallery of Art, Washington*).

32 The tomb which Cardinal Luigi d'Aragona shares with two Orsini cardinals, in the church of Santa Maria sopra la Minerva, Rome.

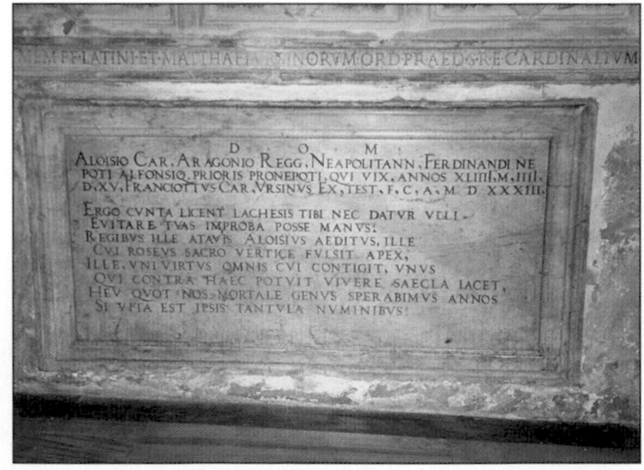

33 The marble plaque commemorating Cardinal Luigi d'Aragona.

far as France and Spain and the Empire were concerned, he was determined to follow a policy different in practice, if similar in aim, to that of his predecessor. Leo, rather than attempting to expel foreign influence, intended to keep it tamed by a game of diplomatic 'ping-pong', playing off one country against the other without ever siding conclusively with either of them, or allowing any one to obtain a position of supremacy in the Italian peninsula. When it became obvious that Leo would not adopt Julius II's plans regarding Naples, Luigi d'Aragona began to withdraw his wholehearted support from the Pope, and contemporaneously his political influence declined. However, in October 1513, the Cardinal of Aragon was still enjoying the peak of his power and it is at this time that the final act of the Duchess of Amalfi's tragedy came to pass.

By the time of the Pope's death, Antonio Bologna was running seriously short of funds in Milan. His assets in Naples had been frozen by order of the Cardinal of Aragon and the bag of gold ducats that Giovanna had given him was rapidly diminishing. Silvio Savelli,[5] one of the leaders of the Sforza troops, took pity on him and offered him hospitality. This was the Silvio who corresponds to the character of that name in Webster's play. He was a *condottiere* who came from one of the most powerful noble families in Rome and who had been engaged by Sforza to re-establish his dynasty in Milan. The French had still not been expelled from the citadel of the castle, the siege of which Savelli participated in between March and August 1513.[6]

In August, the French released from the citadel some of the prisoners they had taken at the battle of Ravenna. One of these, who had been badly injured during the battle and obliged to pay a substantial ransom for his release, was Francesco Acquaviva, Marquis of Bitonto, a nephew of the Duchess of Amalfi.[7] Shortly after Acquaviva's release, Silvio Savelli moved to Crema to direct the military operations there. Antonio Bologna was thus left without a patron, so he turned to this nephew of his wife for hospitality. It was in Acquaviva's company that the writer Matteo Bandello first saw Antonio.

Bandello had been quick to make contact with the *lieta brigata* (merry band) who hoped to recreate the hedonistic times of Il Moro. He lived in the Dominican monastery of Santa Maria delle Grazie in Milan, where he consumed his frugal meals in the refectory, gazing at the fine, but peeling, brushwork of Leonardo da Vinci's fresco of the *Last Supper*. Staring down at him in the guise of Judas was the face of his late uncle, Vincenzo.

The refectory of the monastery of Santa Maria delle Grazie, Milan. Matteo Bandello was living in the monastery when he met Antonio Bologna in 1513. On the far wall is Leonardo da Vinci's *Last Supper* (*photograph courtesy of Laboratorio Fotografico, Pinacoteca di Brera, Milan*).

Vincenzo Bandello had been prior of the monastery of Santa Maria delle Grazie when Leonardo was working on his *cenacolo* between 1497 and 1498, and his importunity had so exasperated Leonardo that he had avenged himself by giving Judas Vincenzo's features.

The re-emergence of ostentation was certainly not at odds with Bandello's worldly tastes. Once he had consumed his frugal repast at the monastery, he would take himself off to supplement the austerity of monastic catering at some Lucullan banquet in one of the elegant patrician salons of the city. He spent most of his time socialising and, like a honey bee dipping from flower to flower, he moved from one *palazzo* to another for receptions, parties, balls, games and masques. In this way he established contacts with all the most important Milanese families, but the centre of his social network was the court of Alessandro Bentivoglio, near the Porta Commense. It was Bentivoglio's wife, Ippolita Sforza, who became Bandello's chief artistic patron in Milan and who first encouraged him to write his *Novelle*. She was a highly educated woman who composed verse both in Italian and Latin, and Bandello spent much time in her company.

The development of the printing press and consequent wider diffusion of books had stimulated the development of witty erudite conversation and the flowering of intellectual salons, or *salotti*, which were often held under the auspices of wealthy noblewomen like Ippolita Sforza. As an accomplished courtier, Antonio Bologna was welcomed at these social gatherings in Milan, where he contributed the wisdom imbibed from his illustrious grandfather, Il Panormita, together with his own poetry, music and entertaining tales of happenings at the court of Naples. He drifted listlessly from one gathering to another, biding his time, waiting and hoping for news of his wife and family.

At one such gathering, at the *salotto* of Camilla Scarampa,[8] Bandello first saw Antonio Bologna, in the company of Acquaviva. After one of Camilla's ladies had played and sung, Antonio offered to tell a story that he once heard at the court of Naples. It was about a woman called Bindoccia who shamelessly made a fool of her jealous, aged husband, Angravalle, during the time of King Alfonso I. Bandello copied down the story and then dedicated it to Antonio's host, Francesco Acquaviva.[9]

Acquaviva did not stay long in Milan after his release and when he left to return home to the Kingdom of Naples, Antonio Bologna was taken in by Acquaviva's brother-in-law, Alfonso Visconti, Count of Saliceto, a francophile opponent of the Sforzas. Visconti, like Acquaviva, was married to one of the Gonzagas of Bozzolo.[10] It is significant that the man who finally assassinated Antonio Bologna also came from Bozzolo. In Webster's drama, the murderer Bosola is transformed into a complex character who plays an important part in the evolution of the drama. In the real story he was merely a ruthless hired assassin, but one who had mysterious connections with those who purported to be Antonio Bologna's protectors in Milan.

Antonio appears to have felt fairly reassured in this period. He had exchanged written communication with the Cardinal, who led him to believe that some form of accommodation could be reached and that his wife and children would eventually be returned to him. Luigi was using old King Ferrante's tactic – make your enemy think you have forgiven him, then pounce on him when he is no longer prepared for the attack. But Antonio was living in a fool's paradise, and when soldiers from the Kingdom of Naples, who had come to Milan with the Viceroy's forces, tried to tell Bologna that his wife and children were dead and that his own life was in danger if he remained in Milan, he categorically refused to believe them. It was one of these soldiers, a captain in the troops of Prospero Colonna, called Cesare Fieramosca, who first spoke of Bologna's plight to Matteo Bandello. Since at this point Bandello actively enters the story, he uses the pseudonym 'Delio' for himself in his novella and we can begin to have a little more faith in the truth of his account.

Fieramosca had been recruited by Cardinal Luigi d'Aragona to assassinate Antonio Bologna in Milan. He told Bandello, however, that he considered himself an honourable soldier, not a butcher who could be called upon to do someone else's dirty work. So, instead of murdering Bologna, whom he had known in Naples, and quite liked, he had warned him of the danger. He also told him it was certain that his wife and children and the maid had been strangled and their bodies secretly buried. It should be noted, however, that Fieramosca had not been present at the Duchess's death and since it had been veiled in mystery, his information was based on hearsay, so we cannot accept his testimony (from which Bandello's was derived) without reservation. Antonio rejected the possibility that Giovanna was dead, but he must surely have begun to suspect that something tragic had come to pass.

Soon after Fieramosca had warned Bologna, Bandello (Delio) visited the *palazzo* of his patron, Ippolita Sforza Bentivoglio, and found Bologna there, playing the lute and singing one of his own compositions in *terza rima*, which bewailed his recent misfortunes. There is no version of this composition given in Bandello's *Novelle*, but William Painter, in his *Palace of Pleasure*, includes a song at this point in the story. Of no great literary merit, it was a translation of the song included in Belleforest's French version of Bandello's novella and was doubtless one of the Frenchman's debatable embellishments to the story.[11]

Though he had not spoken to him before, Bandello had seen Antonio on frequent occasions and felt a certain sympathy and pity for this young man, who was more or less his own age (Bologna was thirty and Bandello twenty-nine). As Antonio finished playing and set down his lute, Bandello, much moved by his baleful lament, felt bound to call him aside and try to help him. He explained the futility of Bologna's hopes of embracing his wife and children again, and assured him it was certain that they were dead. Then he tried to warn him of the dire danger in which he was placing himself by remaining in Milan, for there were people who had already been hired to kill him.

Antonio thanked Bandello for the warning, but replied: 'You are mistaken. I have letters from my family in Naples assuring me that my property will soon be restored to me, and from Rome I have assurances that the illustrious reverend Monsignor is no longer angry with me, and neither is his brother and without doubt I will have my wife returned to me.'[12]

(Of course as we have seen, Carlo could not be angry because he was dead; a fact of which Bandello and perhaps also Antonio were unaware.) Bandello, knowing Bologna was being deliberately deceived, told him what he thought, then took his leave.

Those who sought to have Bologna murdered (Bandello uses this circumlocution so as not to implicate and offend the powerful Cardinal of Aragon directly), seeing that the captain at arms from Naples had revealed himself disinclined for the task, turned instead to a Lombard lord, inciting him to have Bologna assassinated as soon as possible. Bandello does not specify which Lombard lord, but it could have been Federico Gonzaga, Lord of Bozzolo (Plate 31), brother of the Gonzaga sisters who had given Antonio Bologna hospitality in Milan. Federico had links with the Cardinal of Aragon and the Duchess of Amalfi, for he married their niece Giovanna Orsini, daughter of their sister Caterina. If Antonio was the same Bologna who had fallen foul of Francesco Gonzaga, Marquis of Mantua in 1504, did the Marquis now take advantage of the situation to settle the old score and, at the instigation of the Cardinal of Aragon, encourage his kinsman of Bozzolo to organise Bologna's murder?

Up to this point Bandello recounted the whole story to his great friend Lucio Scipione Attellano, declaring that he intended to derive a novella from it, for he was certain that sooner or later Bologna would end up being killed. In fact, Bandello and Attellano were almost eyewitnesses when this did eventually come to pass. One day in early October 1513 (probably 6 October), as they were walking together towards the principal monastery in the city, the Benedictine Monastero Maggiore, Antonio Bologna passed them, riding in the opposite direction on a fine *giannetto*.* He was on his way to hear mass at the church of San Francesco. Two servants preceded him, one was carrying a lance, the other a prayer book. Bandello, noticing the dismayed expression of bewilderment on Bologna's face, remarked to his friend: 'Ah here's poor Bologna.' And Attellano replied: 'By God, he would do better to carry another lance instead of that prayer book, with the risk that he is taking!'

Bandello and his companion had barely reached the church of San Giacomo when they heard a great fracas behind them. They hastily retraced their steps and found that before Bologna arrived at San Francesco, he had been assailed by a Lombard captain called Daniele da Bozzolo and three of his well-armed henchmen. They had dragged Antonio from his horse and, passing him rapidly from one to the other, mortally stabbed him before anyone could come to his aid.

Bozzolo and his men were allowed to leave the city unmolested. This may have been permitted because they had been sent by someone who enjoyed the highest esteem of the young Duke of Milan, such as his cousin, Cardinal Luigi d'Aragona, or perhaps the threads of the mystery are more complexly

*A *giannetto* or *ginnetto* is a jennet, a small agile Spanish breed of horse.

interwoven with the Gonzaga family. It is impossible to say. We must accept Bandello's version as the nearest to the truth, bearing in mind, however, that he was in close relations with the Gonzagas, and the year after he wrote the Duchess's story, that is in 1515, he transferred himself to the Gonzaga court of Mantua. This would hardly have been possible if he had circulated a novella which accused them of inciting a cold-blooded murder.

Bandello's account concludes with the unpursued flight of Daniele da Bozzolo and his men from Milan, but the Corona manuscripts in the Biblioteca Nazionale of Naples (published in Naples from 1525 onwards) add one more piece of information. Antonio's body was carried back to the house of his host, Alfonso Visconti, who organised his funeral. Once this was completed, Antonio's son was accompanied to Naples by his father's servants and handed over to the care of the Bologna family there. John Webster's play significantly ends with Delio bringing in Bologna's surviving son, as a symbol of renewal. This is not mentioned in Webster's main sources (Painter, Belleforest and Bandello) and may be just another dramatic ploy such as that of the Duchess being a twin, but it may also indicate that Webster had access to other sources, perhaps a translation of a Corona manuscript.

The Milanese *necrologio* from 1450 to 1550 corroborates Bandello's chronology of the events in Milan. There is an entry which reads:

> Die Jovis sexto mensis Octobris 1513 Antonius de Bononia
> de Neapoli annorum XXX ex vulneribus.[13]
> (On Thursday the sixth day of the month of October 1513 Antonio da Bologna of Naples, thirty years, from wounds.)

This confirms the cause and time of Antonio's death in Milan. As for the intrigues behind it, we only have Bandello's word, and that, as has been shown, is not always reliable. Why had Bologna looked so distraught when Bandello had seen him riding through the streets of Milan virtually unprotected? Had he finally received irrefutable information from his family in Naples that confirmed Giovanna was dead? Did his own life, without the woman he loved, suddenly hold little value? Did he seek his own death as an end to his tribulation, or was he simply a reckless and presumptuous fool?

The Duchess's brothers considered Antonio a social climber who aimed to rebuild his family's decaying finances with a handsome, royal dowry.

Porta Ticinese, Milan, 29 December 1512. The keys of the city are presented to Massimiliano Sforza, son of Ludovico il Moro, as he begins his triumphal entry, accompanied by the Viceroy of Naples, Raimondo de Cardona (*Civica Raccolta delle Stampe Bertarelli, Milan*).

Perhaps they knew him to be a convicted embezzler and plotter unworthy of trust, but the general opinion, as expressed by Bandello and Lucrezia Borgia, was that he was a noble, talented, likeable, young man. He was passionate and charming and had inherited a good dose of sensuality from his grandfather, Il Panormita. But he allowed his passion to override both his own good sense and the decorum of his time, when he fell uncontrollably in love with a woman far beyond his station. In this he was sincere and well aware of the consequences of his actions. If his motives had been base, he could have withdrawn from the affair in time to save himself and had no further contact with Giovanna or her family. That he continued to negotiate with her brother to the very last is proof of his sincerity.

The real Antonio was far more complex than Webster's bland portrayal. Noble yet devious, sensual yet sincere, talented and ambitious, foolhardy but courageous and steadfast, Antonio Bologna was all of these and, like Giovanna, he was full of contradictions. Their love affair was a tragic anachronism and 'time' did not 'easily scatter the tempest'[14] it caused.

CHAPTER 14

The End of the Cardinal

CARDINAL O Justice!
I suffer now for what hath former bin:
Sorrow is the eldest child of sin.

John Webster, *The Duchess of Malfi*, V.v.52–4

During the years that followed Giovanna's 'disappearance' and her husband's murder, her brother the Cardinal did not seem to be racked by a sense of remorse. On the contrary, he continued to live his brilliant life in Rome. Occasionally he occupied himself with the affairs of his nieces and nephews, chiefly negotiating, or approving, suitable matches for them. In 1517 Giovanna's son, Alfonso, Duke of Amalfi, married Carlo's niece, Costanza D'Avalos.[1] Although Alfonso named his first son Antonio, it is unlikely that this was a declaration of sympathy for his stepfather; it was more likely in memory of his grandfather Antonio Piccolomini, for none of his daughters were given his mother's name of Giovanna. It does not necessarily follow that Alfonso would have condoned his mother's behaviour; she had, after all, abandoned him and, by the canons of the time, brought the name and honour of his family into disrepute.

It is unlikely, in any event, that Alfonso Piccolomini's uncle, the Cardinal of Aragon, attended his wedding on the island of Ischia. Quite independent of any personal family rancour, the reason for Luigi's absence was political. Since the Cardinal's rumoured plotting against the Spanish throne of Naples in 1513, he was no longer a persona grata in the land of his birth. Ferdinand the Catholic had forbidden him to enter the Kingdom and this policy was continued by his successor, his grandson Charles V.

In the early period of Leo's pontificate, Luigi d'Aragona continued to augment his wealth by building up his collection of benefices, until his

Palazzo San Clemente, Via della Conciliazione, near St Peter's Square, Rome; the home of Cardinal Luigi d'Aragona from 1513 until his death in 1519.

annual income eventually reached the substantial sum of 24,000 ducats.[2] In May 1513, perhaps with financial gains from the conclave, he bought himself a fine new palace in Rome. It had been designed by Baccio Pontelli for Domenico della Rovere, Cardinal of San Clemente, in the early 1480s and was known as Palazzo San Clemente. Subsequently Pope Julius's favourite, Cardinal Alidosi, occupied it, but after his murder it passed to Gianfrancesco della Rovere, from whom Luigi acquired it.

Luigi's cousin Alfonso d'Este was one of his first guests at the new palace. He paid him a visit not long after the coronation of the new Pope, Leo X. Since Leo had temporarily reversed Julius II's hostility towards Ferrara, Alfonso was now able to visit Rome freely. A letter to Isabella d'Este from her envoy in Rome, describes her brother's visit and mentions how much Monsignor d'Aragona enjoyed gazing from the windows of his new residence over the bustling Piazza Scossacavalli. At the time, Scossacavalli was the second largest piazza in Rome after St Peter's Square, to which it was adjacent. There would certainly have been a continual bustle of traffic to and from the building site of the new St Peter's Basilica.[3]

In October of the following year, Isabella herself visited Rome as Luigi's guest. Contemporary reports say she and her maids-in-waiting risked being submerged by the quantities of sugar confetti and sweetmeats offered to them at the splendid banquets he gave in their honour. Luigi escorted her from Rome as far as the border between the Papal States and the Kingdom of Naples, but there he was obliged to turn back, since he was forbidden entry.

The splendour of his life and the patronage at his disposal almost rivalled those of the Pope himself. The receptions at Palazzo San Clemente were in no way inferior to papal gatherings and on one occasion Luigi even lent some of his magnificent silver and gold plate to decorate the tables at a banquet Leo gave at the Campidoglio to honour his brother Giuliano and his nephew Lorenzo de' Medici. Luigi was naturally invited to all the grand social occasions in Rome. He was present at the stupendous banquet costing 1,700 ducats offered by the wealthy banker, Agostino Chigi at his *palazzo* (now known as The Farnesina), where the guests were entertained by the comic writer, actor and singer, Domenico Campana, better known as Strascino. Campana may have been related to Luigi's mistress, Giulia Campana, and perhaps it was from this side of the family that their daughter Tullia inherited her literary talent, as well as from her Guardati great-grandmother. Did Luigi arrive at the banquet with Giulia, or had their relationship dwindled by then? There is no mention of her, but Luigi was present at dinners given by his fellow cardinals where courtesans presided and entertained the guests, so presumably Giulia Campana, or a successor, continued to be part of Luigi's entourage.[4]

Together with the other pleasure-seeking younger cardinals, Luigi soon became the butt of satire in Rome – what Webster calls 'Pasquil's paper-bullets'.[5] In a small square just off Piazza Navona is still to be found the famous statue known as Pasquino. Erected in 1501, it was actually a fragment of a Roman marble group representing Menelaus with the body of Patroclus, which may once have decorated the Stadium of Domitian. It became the custom for the citizens of Rome to attach witty or caustic comments on topical events to the pedestal of this statue and the credit for initiating this method of public satire was attributed to a tailor called Pasquino, who lived in the vicinity. The comments thus became known as *pasquinate* (pasquinades). In one pasquinade, called the *Testamento dell' elefante* (composed probably between 1516 and 1517), the various parts of an elephant's body are divided up between the cardinals of Rome and the elephant's teeth are left to Luigi d'Aragona so that he can shave his beard 'which grows malignantly for many reasons' (*la quale nasce con malignità per molte cause*). And in another satire, an insolent sonnet entitled *In Leonem et cardinales*, composed probably in early 1517, the verse dedicated to Luigi reads:

> . . . the occult or rather manifest
> great love between cardinals
> is the bitter penitence of Aragona . . .

The young cardinals were listed according to the chief virtue that they lacked – 'modesty' for Sigismondo Gonzaga, Cardinal of Mantua, and 'contrition' for Luigi's friend Marco Cornaro, but 'great love between cardinals' for Luigi himself. This sarcasm was probably alluding to Luigi's increasing disaffection with the Pope and his closest advisers. But what were the 'malignancy' and the 'bitter penitence' of Luigi's life? Could they refer to the widely rumoured fact that he had caused the death of his sister and her family, just a few years earlier?[6]

For the first two years or so of Leo's pontificate, Luigi d'Aragona was one of his chief collaborators. Both men shared a passion for the chase and Luigi was director of the Pope's hunting expeditions to the castle at Magliana in May and October of 1513, when Leo was accompanied by the group of young cardinals to whom he owed his election.[7] But as time went by, and it became more and more obvious that Leo intended to do nothing about devolving the throne of Naples to Luigi, so their relationship cooled; and as Luigi's political influence with the Pope diminished, so his resentment increased. His last important political position was, very briefly, that of papal legate for the Marches in 1514. He accompanied Leo to negotiate with Francis I at Bologna in 1515, but after this he was given no further political office and failed to obtain from Leo the post of *camerlengo papale* (Lord Chamberlain of the Vatican court).

By 1517, when *In Leonem et cardinales* was written, the distance between the Pope and the Cardinal of Aragon had become obvious to observers. The Venetian ambassador to Rome notes that the Pope was withholding 4,000 ducats and the abbey of Chiaravalle, promised during the conclave to the Cardinal of Aragon, and that Leo did not behave well towards this Cardinal, who had always held an influential position at his court and to whom His Holiness owed, in part, his papal throne.[8]

Leo's policies created friction in other quarters, too, and culminated in a plot to assassinate him, which came to light during the first months of 1517. The prime mover in the plot was Cardinal Alfonso Petrucci, the man who had urged his brother Borghese Petrucci to expel Antonio Bologna from Siena in 1512. It was now the turn of Borghese himself to be banished from the city, and Pope Leo condoned his expulsion. Cardinal Alfonso Petrucci swore to avenge his brother's fall and employed the services of a doctor to poison the medication of the fistula from which the Pope still suffered. Towards the end of April an incriminating letter was intercepted that led to the imprisonment and interrogation of Petrucci's secretary in Rome. Petrucci himself had prudently kept away from the city. Recalled by Leo to the Vatican to discuss the question of Siena, he returned on 18 May, after he had been assured safe conduct. This he was given, but only as far as the papal antechamber, where he was arrested with his friend, Cardinal Bandinello Sauli, and thrown into one of the deepest dungeons of Castel Sant' Angelo, known as the 'Marrocco'.[9]

On 29 May, to the astonishment of everyone (including the papal master of ceremonies, Paride de Grassi, who had to spy through the keyhole of the Pope's chamber to discover what was happening), one of the most powerful and respected of the older cardinals, Riario, was called for an audience with the Pope, and he too was arrested.

Before all this came to pass, as soon as the conspiracy was discovered, Luigi d'Aragona hurriedly left Rome. His departure, according to Sanudo, was against the Pope's will.[10] On 23 April, the secretary of Lorenzo de' Medici, Duke of Urbino, informed a colleague in Rome that Luigi was in Florence and was making his way to Ferrara. From there he intended to travel to Flanders to pay his respects to the new King of Spain, Charles of Burgundy. Luigi had declared that he hoped to obtain the liberation of his cousin, Ferdinand, Duke of Calabria (son of King Federico), who was still a prisoner in Spain. If the King departed early from Flanders and it proved impossible to reach him, he would divide his time between Ferrara and Mantua, then rest a while in Milan and Genoa and, 'when the moment is right, he will return to Rome'.[11]

The moment was obviously not right for him to be in Rome! His sudden departure had been no trifling contingency. He was judiciously putting enough miles between himself and the Pope to ensure that he would not be caught in a snare. The German historian Ludwig von Pastor found no evidence in the secret Vatican archives to indicate that Luigi made his

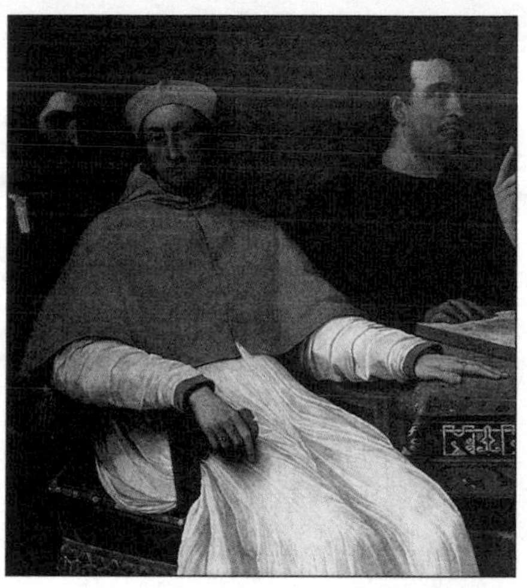

Bandinello Sauli, who was implicated in the plot to assassinate Pope Leo X in 1517. Portrait by Sebastiano del Piombo, *c.* 1516 (*photograph © Board of Trustees, National Gallery of Art, Washington, DC, Samual H. Kress Collection*).

journey to Flanders as an official papal legate, but neither did he manage to find any evidence to link him with the assassination plot.[12]

In the climate of distrust which ensued, other cardinals fell under suspicion. Riario had refused to admit his guilt until he was transferred to the discomfort of a cell in Castel Sant' Angelo. There he confessed that he was to have been the new candidate for the papal throne and he named two other cardinals, Soderini and Castellesi, as parties to the conspiracy. (Pope Alexander VI had dined with Castellesi the night his fatal illness began.) These two cardinals fled Rome. After a long and tempestuous consistory on 22 June, Petrucci, Sauli and Riario were found guilty. Petrucci was deprived of his cardinal's hat and all his benefices and handed over to a secular court, where he was condemned to death. The 27-year-old former cardinal was then strangled in the dungeons of Castel Sant' Angelo. The injustice against the Pope (and perhaps also that against Antonio Bologna and the Duchess of Malfi) was thus redressed.

The case against the other implicated cardinals – Sauli, Riario, Soderini and Castellesi – was that they had been informed of Petrucci's plot, but had done nothing to warn the Pope; they were thus accessories to the fact. Leo was especially wounded by the betrayal of Sauli, whom he had generously favoured. But Sauli was a vain, ambitious young man with, as one pasquinade put it, a brain that limped as much as his foot (one of his legs was shorter than the other). Sauli has been suggested as the possible subject of Raphael's portrait of the unidentified cardinal (Plate 5). There is a certain physical similarity between this portrait and a portrait of Sauli by

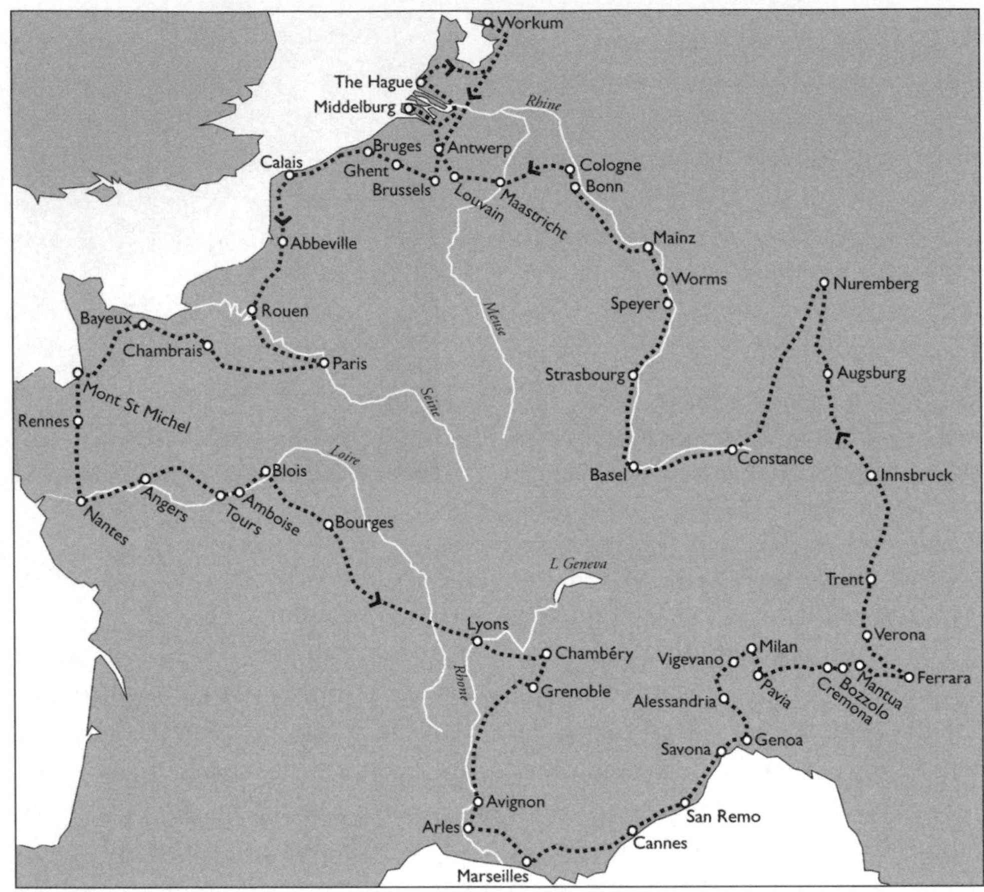

Map of the Cardinal's travels 1517–18

Sebastiano del Piombo,[13] but Raphael's cardinal has harder, more angular features, and the expression, definitely more intelligent, has the hauteur of one born to high social rank. Sauli certainly demonstrated little intelligence in allowing himself to be so openly implicated in Petrucci's hot-headed conspiracy. It is thought his motive stemmed from his anger that the Pope had not given him the newly vacated bishopric of Marseilles; it went instead to the Pope's cousin, Cardinal Giulio de' Medici.

Sauli and Riario got away with a heavy fine and the curtailing of their patronage.[14] The ageing Riario, humiliated, impoverished and powerless, lived until 1521, when he passed away in exile in Naples, where Soderini too had taken refuge. Castellesi fled to Venice and did not return to Rome until after Leo X's death in 1521, when he was called to the conclave. He did not reach his destination, however, for he died on the way – poisoned, it was said, by a servant in the pay of Cardinal Giulio de' Medici, who had never put aside his resentment towards any of the cardinals suspected of being party to the conspiracy against his family.[15]

As the names of other cardinals who might have been acquainted with Petrucci's plot were revealed, those of Luigi d'Aragona and his friend Marco Cornaro were mentioned, and although no concrete evidence was ever discovered, the mantle of suspicion which hovered about them was never quite removed. Giulio de' Medici must have realised that, with his fine network of spies, it was unlikely that Luigi d'Aragona had been unaware of the plot, and his sudden departure from Rome as soon as it was discovered had to be more than mere coincidence.

The journey made by the Cardinal of Aragon between May 1517 and January 1518 deserves a volume all to itself; a few paragraphs here cannot render it justice. A detailed description of the itinerary has been passed down to us in the journal, kept throughout, by Luigi's personal chaplain, Antonio de Beatis. It constitutes a sort of vade mecum to Renaissance Europe and is replete with infinite details of everyday life at that time. The original version is preserved in the Biblioteca Nazionale in Naples, in pristine condition, as if it had been written a mere hundred years ago instead of nearly five times that, and the occasional red-ink doodles in the margins act as century-spanning links to its good-humoured author.[16]

Throughout his travels Luigi only wore his cardinal's robes on gala occasions at the courts of the Spanish and French Kings. Normally, he and his companions wore the same livery of pink silk with bands of black velvet, while the servants' livery was plain pink silk. The Cardinal, says Beatis, was always generous in paying for the company's board and lodging, and the whole journey cost Luigi about 15,000 ducats (well over half his annual income). Generosity is a virtue often attributed to Luigi in contemporary texts, but if we bear in mind his behaviour towards his sister and her family, perhaps this generosity should be interpreted in a narrow material sense. It was a generosity that often exceeded his means and was aimed primarily at bolstering his political and social prestige. Like many of his fellow cardinals, Luigi died in debt.[17]

Very little transpires from the narrative to suggest an ulterior motive for the journey. Beatis begins his prologue by explaining that his master, having decided, in all appearance, to visit the new King of Spain, and being already familiar with most of Italy, Iberia and parts of France, took advantage of this opportunity to visit and 'make himself known' (*demostrarse*) to the more northerly countries of Europe. He undertook the journey primarily for his own enjoyment and instruction, and Beatis makes little reference to possible political motivations. The chaplain was either not informed of these, or told to remain silent. But the mere fact of Luigi making himself known to the courts of Europe could have had political undertones. Certainly the English court feared this.

Luigi had intended to cross the Channel to England to visit the court of his kinswoman, Queen Catherine of Aragon, and her husband, King Henry VIII. But while he was staying as a guest of the English governor at Calais, Richard Wyngfield, he was informed of a severe outbreak of the sweating sickness in London and decided to relinquish this plan and remain in France. Behind this deceptively simple occurrence was a frenzied exchange of espionage intelligence as Henry's Chancellor, Cardinal Wolsey, attempted to decipher the true aims of Luigi's planned visit to England. Wolsey suspected that Luigi was seeking benefices from the King or support for his cause in Naples. He decided it was more prudent to keep him at bay, since it was not certain in what capacity he came, nor what his relations with the Holy See were.[18]

Certainly Luigi's primary aim (as the letter from Florence cited above confirms) was to meet the new King of Spain, who was waiting in Flanders for a ship to take him to his new Kingdom. At Speyer at the end of June, Luigi passed over the possibility of a meeting with the Emperor Maximilian at Augsburg in order to reach Flanders before the King of Spain departed. Ferdinand the Catholic had died on 23 January 1516 and been succeeded nominally by his eldest daughter, Juana d'Aragona. She, having been declared insane, was set aside in favour of her seventeen-year-old son, Charles of Burgundy (later the Emperor Charles V). Luigi managed to reach him at Middelburg on the Zeeland peninsula on 12 July 1517, just a few days before Charles was due to sail. Beatis only describes the ceremonial of the meeting, not what was discussed. A dispatch sent to Henry VIII in England gives a vivid description of Luigi's ostentatious arrival at King Charles's court. Accompanied by forty horsemen, a rich cloak draped about his shoulders and his sword strapped to his side, he approached proudly on horseback, flamboyantly putting his horse through its paces. Henry VIII's agent in Flanders, Spinelly, commented disparagingly to Cardinal Wolsey: 'your grace may conjecture what manner of man he is'

– and so may we. Spinelly's letter concludes shrewdly: 'The said Cardinal's profession is rather of a temporal lord, than spiritual.'[19]

Beatis's descriptions of the important royal personages he met are often candidly amusing. He finds the young Spanish King's habit of leaving his mouth hanging open, with his lower lip drooping, extremely unmajestic, but adds by way of compensation that Cardinal Luigi says he rides very well. When the Cardinal and his company arrived at the court of the French King, Beatis allowed his habitual discretion to slip for a moment when he reported the Cardinal's comment that: 'King Francis I's legs were out of proportion and too long and spindly for his large body.' Then he hastily adds, to stem any offence, that 'in spite of his exceptionally large nose, the King's face was pleasant and he was excellent company'. His description of Francis's Queen, Claude, is less complimentary – she is as small, ugly and as physically deformed as her father, King Charles VIII, but by way of compensation she is very virtuous! The same cannot be said for the libertine King Francis, who, Beatis euphemistically says, is 'lascivious and willingly enters the gardens of others to drink different waters'.

But of the whole journey, the highpoint for the historian, is the visit which the Cardinal paid to Leonardo da Vinci at the castle of Cloux, near Amboise, on 10 October 1517. Leonardo was by now over seventy and suffering from paralysis of the right hand which Beatis says will preclude any further good work from the maestro. He was doubtless unaware that Leonardo was ambidextrous. Leonardo showed Luigi three of his paintings, one of which was probably the *Mona Lisa*, and explained some of his scientific tracts. Although Beatis makes no mention of it, he may even have presented the Cardinal with one of his manuscripts, for a tract by Leonardo is mentioned in an inventory of the Duke of Amalfi in 1566, and it may have come into the Duke's hands via his great-uncle, the Cardinal of Aragon.

Apart from the vivid descriptions of important personages, Beatis gives us an accurate portrait of the different places through which he passed, noting with scientific accuracy the variations in architecture, vegetation, crops, people's dress and diet. He gives us intimate details, such as the changes in the types of bed, from the wool or straw-stuffed mattresses of Italy to the thick, feather quilts of Germany, which were 'oiled' to protect them from vermin. Conditions of hygiene at the inns where the party stayed were a natural concern. The streets and houses of Flanders were judged to be the cleanest. Cleanliness was so prized here that there were even cloths provided to clean your shoes when you entered a house. France was at the other extreme. Paris had muddy streets and in the inns there was no provision for relieving oneself during the night. In Germany there had been tin cans, in Flanders clean brass night-vases, in France nothing. Beatis and his companions found themselves obliged to urinate in the fireplace. One wonders how women managed when the fires were lit!

Women seemed to be one of Beatis's main preoccupations. After he has described the general aspect of a place and whether or not the streets and buildings are attractive and well kept, he immediately launches into an assessment of the beauty of the local women and their style of dress. The women of Flanders were more beautiful than the German women, had better teeth and sweeter breath, and he was very taken with the French women's habit of kissing visitors on both cheeks as a form of courtesy. There is no gossip about the Cardinal as far as women are concerned, except indirectly: at a banquet held for him at Avignon (in November 1517) 'many beautiful women were present and after dinner there was dancing until midnight with great licence and lascivious pleasures'. What these pleasures were, and who participated in them, is left to the reader's speculation.

It is doubtful, however, that the Cardinal took part in the dancing, as he was suffering badly from gout. This was then a common illness in Europe, even with relatively young people (Luigi was now forty-three), but it especially afflicted the wealthier classes because their diet was rich in alcohol and red meat and poor in fibre. A severe attack of gout in both feet immobilised Luigi at the French court for two weeks in August 1517, and in order to continue his journey, he had to purchase a litter. Then, when the party returned to Ferrara the following January, he was laid low again, this time for three weeks.

It may be that Luigi had executed some commissions in Germany on behalf of his Este cousins of Ferrara. His itinerary makes a distinct deviation from the direct route to Flanders, first to visit the powerful and rich German banker, Jacob Fugger, at Augsburg, then to Nuremberg, which was famous for its ironworks and armaments workshops. Beatis says vaguely that Luigi spent an enormous sum there on 'iron and brassware'. Were these arms? If so for whom? Himself? The Este family? According to Beatis, Cardinal Ippolito d'Este had recently visited the same city. Was a loan negotiated with Fugger for Luigi's acquisitions? Antonio de Beatis, if he was informed, knew better than to disclose the facts.

Neither does Beatis mention signs of the religious tension developing in Germany in that seminal year of 1517. On 31 October, the eve of All Saints' Day, Martin Luther affixed his 95 theses to the door of the church at Wittenberg and laid the foundations of a schism that was destined to permanently split the Church. But late in that same October, the Cardinal of Aragon was still wending his way leisurely through the south of France. On 28 October, he was handling the Holy Shroud of Christ at Chambéry, while Luther was busy compiling his theses protesting against the immorality and corruption of the Church.

Before returning to Ferrara, Luigi and his party passed through Milan in order to see Leonardo's *Last Supper* in Santa Maria delle Grazie. Beatis remarks that the fresco was already in a bad condition and peeling from the wall. This monastery, it will be remembered, had been the home of Matteo Bandello, but after Milan had again fallen into French hands, following the battle of Melegnano in September 1515, he had removed himself to the Gonzaga courts of Mantua.

When the Cardinal and his party went on to visit first his niece, Giovanna Orsini, and her husband, Federico Gonzaga, at Bozzolo and then Isabella d'Este at Mantua, Beatis does not mention meeting Bandello. After his criticism of Luigi d'Aragona in the novella he had circulated about the Duchess of Amalfi, Bandello probably found it wiser to keep a low profile during the Cardinal's visit.

The Cardinal finally returned to Rome on 16 March 1518. Just two weeks after his return, Cardinal Bandinello Sauli fell ill and died suddenly. As usual, poison was suspected. The reverberations of the plot to kill the Pope were still echoing in the Vatican City. If Luigi felt any of the 'bitter penitence' attributed to him in the *pasquinate*, there was little evidence of it during the pleasures of his long tour. Although, throughout his travels, he had made a point of handling the precious and sacred relics preserved in various churches, he seems to have been motivated more by scientific curiosity than by Christian repentance and hope for the miraculous forgiveness of his sins. His comments read more like those of an expert antiquarian than a faithful Catholic. At Burges he sceptically pronounced that a gold and chalcedony chalice was mere crystal, and at Chambéry, where he was able to handle the Holy Shroud, he was perplexed because he could not define the type of material, which was neither wool nor silk.

Luigi's real penance began soon after his return to Rome. That his health was failing is evident from an exchange of letters with the poet Jacopo

Sannazaro. The rich banqueting he had indulged in throughout his journey had obviously aggravated his gout and he now hoped to detoxify his system at the volcanic mineral spa of Pozzuoli, near Naples. But the Viceroy, Raimondo Cardona, on behalf of King Charles of Spain, refused him permission to enter the Kingdom. Had the ambassadors from Naples, whom Luigi had joined at Middelburg, put the new King Charles on his guard against the machinations of this survivor of the fallen dynasty?

Sannazaro, sympathising with the Cardinal, says: 'Where then is the greatness and the power of these grand monarchs, who with a single nod would bring down the Turks and the whole world with them, if they are afraid of a single unarmed person who wishes to come and cure his health?'[20] Where indeed? But Viceroy Cardona's suspicions had more foundation than the biased Sannazaro liked to admit.

Despite his failing health, Luigi flung himself back enthusiastically into the social life of Rome and to observers it seemed that any former breach with Pope Leo had been healed. On the evening of his return, the Pope offered a grand banquet in his honour at the Vatican Palace. This may have been a gesture of reconciliation, or proof of Luigi's extraneousness to the assassination plot. In either case, the path had doubtless been smoothed before Luigi's return to Rome and the conversation that evening revolved around such light-weight matters as the progress being made at the Brussels factory visited by Luigi in July, which was making the new arrases for the Sistine Chapel from cartoons by Raphael.

Raphael had fulfilled numerous commissions for Pope Leo during Luigi's absence, so many that he had perforce been obliged to delegate much work to his pupils. But with the wealth earned from these commissions he was able to move into a splendid new house in Piazza Scossacavalli, just opposite Luigi d'Aragona's Palazzo San Clemente. Raphael had become such an important artistic figure that his works were used as political tools in international negotiations. When Francis I reconquered the Duchy of Milan, Pope Leo sent the shrewd Cardinal Bernardo da Bibbiena as papal legate to France to try to obtain a new alliance with the French King. Francis was an avid art collector and to curry his favour, Bibbiena decided to present him with three paintings by Raphael.

Bibbiena had long been one of Raphael's chief patrons in Rome. He had even browbeaten the artist into marrying his niece – though the marriage was never consummated (some said because Raphael was too busy with his mistresses; others that he was aiming for a cardinal's hat). Despite his enormous number of commissions, Raphael was so closely linked to Bibbiena that he could not refuse his request when he ordered the portrait of a beautiful woman, a large Holy Family and a Saint Michael. All three were delivered to Francis I in December of 1518. A month later Cardinal Luigi d'Aragona was dead.

Although the panic of the assassination plot had subsided by the end of 1518, other grave problems afflicted the papacy. The war waged in Urbino against Francesco Maria della Rovere in order to carve out a state for the Medici family, had plunged the papal finances into a disastrous state and the confiscations and fines imposed on cardinals involved in the assassination plot of 1517 had given only a short-lived respite. The Cardinal of Aragon's patrimony was an appetising morsel that his demise would have brought within the Pope's grasp.

Luigi had ostensibly been cleared of complicity in the assassination plot, but some believed that the Pope and his closest advisers, such as his cousin Cardinal Giulio de' Medici (later Pope Clement VII), still harboured suspicions. It was for this reason that when Luigi died on 21 January 1519, those closest to him suspected foul play and demanded an autopsy. The cause of death is not given in contemporary documents; they indicate merely that the death had been extremely painful and relatively swift and had suddenly overtaken the Cardinal at eleven o'clock at night. Its very rapidity led to suspicions of poison and, to silence the accusatory murmurings, the Pope was obliged to consent to an autopsy. The surgeons who performed the investigation declared that there was no sign of poison and that all the principal organs were intact; whether they were accurate and impartial in their verdict remains to be seen.[21]

The effigy on Luigi's tomb in the church of the Minerva in Rome shows the strained features of a man who had suffered a painful death. If Luigi d'Aragona had been responsible for the murders laid at his door, perhaps the agony of his death went some way to expiating his sins. His death cannot, however, have been so unexpected as contemporary sources would suggest. His health had been failing for some time (he suffered from both gout and syphilis) and he must have been ill enough to fear that his end was nigh, for three days before he died he had seen fit to dictate his will.[22]

The arrangements for the funeral of the Cardinal of Aragon also gave rise to much controversy in the College of Cardinals. Although Luigi had expressed the desire for little pomp at the ceremony, the new limit imposed by the Lateran Council that the expenses for cardinals' funerals were not to exceed the sum of 1,500 florins, meant that the obsequies were to be far too humble for a personage of royal rank and great standing. Luigi's close friend and companion in arms of many military expeditions, Marco Cornaro, wanted Luigi's 300-strong household to escort the nocturnal funeral cortège in a torchlit procession, and requested a special dispensation to enable him to organise this fitting ceremony. The Pope adamantly refused on the grounds that it would set an undesirable precedent and did not conform to the testamentary wishes of the deceased.

The funeral service took place on 25 January, at the Dominican church of Santa Maria sopra la Minerva in Rome, where Luigi had requested that his body be interred in the chapel dedicated to St Thomas Aquinas, if it could not be laid to rest beside his royal ancestors in Naples. Not even after death was Luigi permitted to return to his homeland, and it was necessary to disturb the sepulchre of the artist Fra Beato Angelico to make room for the Cardinal of Aragon on the left-hand side of the chapel in the Minerva.

Cardinal Cornaro composed and read the funeral oration at the commemorative service. He gave a brief summary of Luigi's royal origins, his career and accomplishments. He mentioned especially the contacts Luigi had had with the monarchs of Europe in his role as an able diplomat, and his crucial part in Pope Julius II's campaign against Bologna in 1511 to secure the Papal Marches. Luigi had lived with dignity and splendour and the only reproof that could be taken into consideration was his excessive love of hunting.[23] While Cornaro lamented the misfortunes which had befallen Luigi's family, he made no reference to the mysterious disappearance of Luigi's sister, Giovanna d'Aragona, Duchess of Amalfi. This, like the circumstances of Luigi's own sudden demise, was left to the same speculation as the disappearances of their father, Enrico d'Aragona, and their maternal grandfather, Antonio Centelles, many years earlier. Mysterious deaths dogged their family history.

In the epitaph, which was tardily affixed to Luigi's tomb in 1533, there is no Christian prayer or plea for forgiveness of sins, merely a poem full of classical allusions, which appears to regret most of all that he was not allowed a longer time on this earth to enjoy the pleasures of his promising, hedonistic life. Its hyperbole made the French historian of the *Minerva*,

Brother Berthier,[24] cringe, but it would probably have brought a smirk to the face of the cynical Cardinal of Aragon had he been alive to read it:

So everything is permitted to you, oh Lachesis,
And no one can avoid your iniquitous, powerful hands?
That descendant of kings, Luigi,
On whose consecrated head saw the splendour of the sacred scarlet beret,
He who was blessed by every virtue,
And could have lived for centuries,
Now lies here,
Oh what hope is there for us mere mortals against these events
If life is so brief for such superior beings.[25]

Both from Cornaro's amicable, if at times exaggerated, eulogy, and from de Beatis's nostalgic reminiscences of his master, emerges a man capable of inspiring affection, as well as fear and respect, in those around him. Luigi was perhaps a little eccentric; the Venetian ambassador to Rome once defined him as 'bizaro molto' (very strange or bizarre);[26] but was he really the monster portrayed in so many literary accounts? His anxiety for the welfare of his sister in the hands of a convicted plotter and embezzler (if her lover was the Bologna of the Gonzaga court) was justifiable according to the social canons of the time, as was his wish to vindicate his family's honour, which his sister had impugned. He may have been unjustifiably denigrated by posterity on the basis of fallacious gossip; nevertheless, the suspicion remains that his actions were primarily motivated by selfish ambition and thirst for power.

In the light of Bandello's testimony, it seems almost certain that Luigi was the instigator of Antonio Bologna's murder in Milan, and it is also probable that he had Giovanna's maid executed for her part in the deception which had caused him so much embarrassment. In an age hardened to brutality, these murders were almost accepted as righteous retribution. But the more terrible crime of ordering the murder of his sister and her two young children shocked even Luigi's contemporaries. And yet, bearing in mind his political acumen and the disadvantages such an act would have brought him, apart from any emotional considerations, the accusation seems an improbable one and here we must give him the benefit of the doubt. It will never be known for certain whether he was really guilty of this, the most heinous crime of which he lies accused.

CHAPTER 15

Epilogue: The Portraits

DUCHESS Necessity makes me suffer constantly.
And custom makes it easy. Who do I look like now?
CARIOLA Like to your picture in the gallery,
A deal of life in show, but none in practice;
Or rather like some reverend monument
Whose ruins are even pitied.

John Webster, *The Duchess of Malfi*, IV.ii.31–4

Was there a picture of the Duchess of Amalfi in her own picture gallery? Having told her story and that of her brother the Cardinal, the possible existence of their portraits, mentioned in the preface, can now be dealt with. How far is it possible that they were both portrayed by Raphael or another contemporary artist, and was either of the paintings entitled 'A Portrait of Giovanna d'Aragona', a portrait of the Duchess of Amalfi?

No connection has ever been made between the effigy on the tomb where Luigi d'Aragona's body lies and the Raphael portrait of an unknown cardinal in the Prado because it has always been assumed that the effigy was of someone else (Plates 4 and 5). The mysteries surrounding the Cardinal do not end with his death; even his tomb is cause for speculation. It lies hidden in a dark corner, on the right-hand side of the vestibule of the rear entrance to the church of Santa Maria sopra la Minerva in Rome. On the other side of the vestibule wall is the much grander tomb of his great rival, Pope Leo X, Giovanni de' Medici. Luigi is obliged to share his modest resting-place with two Orsini cardinals, to whom there is a dedication in Latin carved in the stone sarcophagus (Plates 32 and 33). On top of the sarcophagus is a high, sculpted, draped bier bearing a full-length effigy of a cardinal in his robes. It has always been presumed that this effigy portrays one of the Orsinis and that the plaque dedicated to Luigi d'Aragona, beneath the sarcophagus, almost at floor level, is the only indication that his remains are interred there. The plaque reads:

DOM ALOISIO CAR. ARAGONIA REGG. NEAPOLITANN FERDINANDI NEPOTI ALFONSIQ, PRIORIS PRONEPOTI, QVI VIX, ANNOS XLIIII,M,IIII,DXV, FRANCIOTTUS CAR, URSINUS EX, TEST, F,C,A,M DXXXIII.
(Maximum Lord Cardinal Luigi d'Aragona, grandson of Ferrante King of Naples, great-grandson of the first Alfonso, who [Luigi] lived 44 years, 4 months and 15 days, according to his will Cardinal Franciotto Orsini had this made in the year of Christ 1533.)

Together with Cardinal Marco Cornaro, Franciotto Orsini was one of the two executors of Luigi's will. In 1533, Orsini, who had taken Luigi's title of Cardinal of Santa Maria in Cosmedin,[1] placed the marble tablet commemorating Luigi d'Aragona on the left wall of the chapel of Saint Thomas Aquinas in the Minerva. (It was subsequently moved to its present position on the right.) Why had fourteen years elapsed between Luigi's death in 1519 and the placing of the inscription in 1533 on the completed tomb?

According to Vasari, the Florentine sculptor Jacopo Sansovino was commissioned to make the funeral monument of Cardinal Luigi d'Aragona. He had already begun working the marble for the decorations and made many models for the figures, when suddenly Rome was thrown into havoc by the six-day sack at the hands of the soldiers of Charles V in May 1527. It was one of the most calamitous events in the modern history of the city. Sansovino was forced to flee to Venice and from there he travelled to France to enter the service of Francis I.[2] It is doubtful that he ever returned to Rome to complete the commission.

Franciotto Orsini was taken hostage during the sack of Rome and doubtless had to pay a conspicuous ransom before regaining his freedom. This would account, perhaps, for his delay in implementing Luigi's testamentary instructions. It is possible that some of the work begun by Sansovino survived the upheaval of the sack and was included in the dignified monument to Cardinal Luigi d'Aragona erected on the left-hand side of the chapel in the Minerva. In the jubilee year of 1600, the chapel was transformed into a rear entrance for the church. But even before this transformation took place, the remains of Luigi d'Aragona had already been disturbed and transferred to the facing right-hand wall. In 1565, when the chapel was sold to Giovanni Battista Vittorii and structural maintenance work had to be carried out, his bones, together with those of the two Orsini cardinals, Matteo and Latino Malabranca, were exhumed and placed temporarily in the sacristy. They were then replaced in the chapel, all together, in the right-hand wall.[3]

Does the effigy on the Orsini sarcophagus represent one of the Orsini cardinals or Luigi d'Aragona? It is improbable that it is a likeness of Matteo Orsini, for he had died at Avignon in 1341, and only some years later were his bones brought to the church of the Minerva in Rome. Latino Malabranca Orsini had died in Perugia in 1294, but his remains had already been united with those of Matteo Orsini long before their temporary transfer to the sacristy in 1565. It seems most likely that when the remains of the three cardinals were placed together in the right-hand wall of the chapel, the funerary monument of the Orsinis and that of the Cardinal of Aragon were united too; the stone bier and effigy of the latter being placed on top of the Orsini sarcophagus. It could, therefore, be possible that the effigy, which so much resembles Raphael's mysterious cardinal, is actually that of Cardinal Luigi d'Aragona.

Further proof of the identity of the effigy can be sought by comparing the distinctive aquiline nose in portraits of King Ferrante I and his father King Alfonso I, with the profile of the effigy's face. Since Marin Sanudo, who met Luigi d'Aragona during his trip to Venice in January 1507, affirmed that he resembled his grandfather King Ferrante, it seems that Luigi had inherited the distinctive 'Aragon nose' of his ancestors, and it is clearly portrayed on the face of the effigy. It would be useful, for further comparison, if there were other known portraits of the Cardinal of Aragon. One possibly exists in the fresco of *The Coronation of Charlemagne by Pope Leo III* (painted about 1516/17) in the Raphael Stanzas of the Vatican Palace. It was meant to celebrate the concordat of 1515 between Francis I and Pope Leo X, portrayed respectively as Charlemagne and Leo III. It was a crucial point in Luigi's political career, for his influence with the Pope had begun to decline. In the right-hand corner, on the back row of prelates, there is a cardinal turning his head sideways in a scowl; this could be the person portrayed in the effigy.

The Raphael portrait in the Prado has been dated to 1510/11, when Luigi d'Aragona was at the peak of his political career. There were only about half a dozen young cardinals in 1511. Luigi's cousin Ippolito d'Este can be ruled out, for although he too could have inherited the Aragon nose, his family was at odds with the papacy at this time and it is unlikely that Raphael would have risked incurring the displeasure of Pope Julius II by taking on a commission from the Estes. Those cardinals already identifiably portrayed by Raphael, such as Alessandro Farnese and Giovanni de' Medici, can be ruled out too, as can those who were too young, like Alfonso Petrucci and Bandinello Sauli. The subject of the portrait appears to be in his mid-thirties: Luigi d'Aragona at the time was thirty-six.

The face of Raphael's portrait seems to fit Luigi's character well, too. Raphael gives a masterfully subtle psychological analysis of his subject, just as he did in his portrait of the cantankerous Julius II, painted at about the same time. The cardinal's bearing has the proud self-assurance of one born to high social rank; the sharp eyes and sensuous, devious twist to the mouth give the impression of a man of wit and intelligence; and yet, his shadowy sardonic smile is tinged with melancholy. It is the sort of smile one would expect from the Cardinal of Aragon had he been able to read the composition in Latin verse that Cardinal Orsini inscribed on his memorial plaque. All things considered, Luigi d'Aragona is the most likely candidate for the subject of Raphael's portrait.

If it can be presumed that the Cardinal of Aragon was portrayed by Raphael, does it follow that his sister, Giovanna d'Aragona, Duchess of Amalfi, may also have been one of his subjects? There are paintings illustrating the creation of such a work (Prosper-Paul Allais's *Raphael faisant le portrait de la princesse d'Aragon* of 1856) and poems to celebrate the same (Karl August Böttiger [1760–1835] *Raffael: Johanna von Aragon*), but today there is no longer a portrait of Giovanna d'Aragona in the Louvre. The painting I saw is still there, but it now has a new name. Vasari referred to the painting as being of the 'Viceregina di Napoli' (wife of the Viceroy of Naples) and for centuries this had been considered one of his many mistakes. Now, however, it has been decided that the portrait, which for four hundred years has been called 'Portrait of Giovanna d'Aragona', was in fact that of another woman, Isabella de Requesens, wife of the Viceroy of Naples, Raimondo de Cardona. Since 1998, the name of the painting has been officially changed to *Portrait of Doña Isabel de Requesens i Enríquez de Cardona-Anglesola* (Plate 15).

The name of Giovanna d'Aragona is thought to have become mistakenly connected with the portrait in France during the sixteenth and seventeenth centuries. It was first associated with the fourteenth-century Queen of Naples, Giovanna I of Anjou,[4] then the error was compounded by changing the surname from Anjou to Aragon.[5] In 1803 Giovanna d'Aragona, Princess Colonna, cousin of the Duchess of Amalfi, was proposed as the subject.[6] She was the daughter of Ferrante d'Aragona, Count of Arena, the youngest illegitimate son of King Ferrante I of Naples, who betrayed his father during the Great Barons' Revolt of 1485–7. She too has now been ruled out.[7]

The Louvre painting is the work Cardinal Bibbiena commissioned from Raphael to present to Francis I in 1518. Bibbiena reputedly ordered Raphael to travel to Naples to portray the subject from life. Why, and who was she? There are two candidates other than the Duchess of Amalfi: Isabella de Requesens, the fifteen-year-old wife of the Viceroy of Naples, Raimondo de Cardona, and his seventeen-year-old mistress, Eleonora Brogna de' Lardis, known as La Brognina.

Cardona, it will be remembered, had been trying to seduce La Brognina during the carnival festivities in Milan in 1513, during the period of Antonio Bologna's exile there. La Brognina fled to a convent near Mantua, determined to take the veil rather than a lover, but Cardona offered her a not insignificant dowry of 2,000 gold scudi, if she would accept his court. La Brognina disappeared again. Finally, she re-emerged in the vicinity of Cardona's military camp at Lendinara. Some time later, in a comfortable villa at Goito, she was delivered of Cardona's twin sons, who were born, unusually, a month apart from one another. Cardinal Bernardo da Bibbiena was their godfather. Unfortunately, duty recalled Cardona almost immediately to Naples and to his wife, Isabella de Requesens. But for La Brognina the adventures had not yet ended.[8]

In 1515, the King of France, Francis I, invaded Italy and reconquered the Duchy of Milan from the Sforzas at the battle of Melegnano. According to contemporary sources, Francis had heard of the beauty of La Brognina and in the euphoria of conquest, he attempted to kidnap her in order to make her his mistress. Cardona, warned of what was happening, sent a troop of Spaniards to intercept the kidnappers and take the girl safely back to the state of Mantua. Francis may have been infatuated with La Brognina, but it seems more likely that he intended to use her as a pawn in his political manoeuvrings against Cardona.

According to a recent study, the sardonic Bibbiena decided to give Francis a portrait of Cardona's wife, since he had been unable to secure for himself Cardona's mistress.[9] So he ordered Raphael to travel to Naples to make a life drawing of the Vicereine. Raphael, however, was too busy with other commissions from the Pope to spare the time, so he sent one of his pupils to make the drawing of the subject for the cartoon of the painting. The pupil in question was, experts think, Giulio Pippi (known as Giulio Romano). Though it was given to Francis I on the understanding that it was a work by the master's own hand, by Raphael's own admission the pupil did most of the painting. Vasari affirms that Raphael only painted the face and the rest was completed by Giulio Romano. However, when the painting was X-rayed in 1982 there appeared to be another face beneath the visible one, or certainly some radical retouching.[10] It may have been the master correcting the imperfect work of his pupil, or perhaps, in his haste to complete the commission in time, Raphael adapted a pre-existing painting.

Almost everything points to the identity of the Louvre portrait as being Isabella de Requesens, yet there are some who believe it to be La Brognina. Is this possible? As La Brognina was also in Naples in 1518, with her children by Cardona, she could have sat for Giulio Romano. Cardona sent for her when the twins were about four years old and she was respectably married off to a member of his household. Certainly the pale complexion and small features of the girl in the Louvre painting seem more Nordic than Spanish, and the crimson velvet of the dress could be a reminder of Cardona's gift for a kiss received.

Several copies were made of the portrait, and at least one was ordered by the King of France in the early seventeenth century.[11] All of them resemble more or less the Louvre version, except for the copy in the Doria Pamphilj Gallery in Rome (Plate 1). No one has ever been able to suggest a reason for the face being changed in this version, or for the fact that its style resembles that of Leonardo da Vinci. The Louvre portrait, while beautifully executed, lacks the emotive intensity of other portraits from Raphael's workshop. The woman, who seems younger than her reputed twenty years, looks emptily into the distance, beyond the observer. Not so the face of the Doria Pamphilj 'copy'. The face is certainly an idealised one, but it expresses deep melancholy, and the *chiaroscuro* is so expertly painted that the expression changes when viewed from different angles, which makes it difficult to reproduce well. Why was the face changed in this copy, and to a Leonardesque model at that, and why should the face of the copy be more expressive than the original?

This is more easily explicable if we invert the premise and presume that the Doria Pamphilj portrait corresponds more closely to Raphael's original conception of the composition than the Louvre portrait. One of the most respected Italian art historians of the twentieth century, Venturi, declared that Giulio Romano's painting was copied from an original drawing by his master, which has since been lost.[12] If such a drawing had been made during the period in which Leonardo influenced Raphael's work (as exemplified by a Raphael sketch of 1506 in the Louvre), it could have had a Leonardesque face.

The Doria Pamphilj portrait is considered to be a copy of the Louvre portrait executed by members of Raphael's studio. If the Louvre version was adapted from a pre-existing painting, the underlying face revealed by the X-ray may be Leonardesque in style. If this is the case, the Doria Pamphilj portrait could have been copied from the original Louvre version before the face was changed. Or, alternatively, it was based on the original drawing rather than the version which was sent to Francis I.

Could the Duchess of Amalfi have been the subject of this original drawing? Raphael might have had contact with her while he was collaborating with Pinturicchio on the Piccolomini frescoes in Siena in 1503/4. A young woman, portrayed in the Piccolomini fresco of the coronation of Pope Pius III (Plates 6 and 28), could be the same person as the subject of the Doria Pamphilj portrait. She stands in the back row (that is, nearest to the Pope, which suggests a figure of some importance), directly beneath the coat of arms of the Todeschini Piccolomini d'Aragona family of the Dukes of Amalfi (Plate 14). The pose is similar to that of the Doria Pamphilj portrait. The woman's dark hair is worn parted in the middle, long and loose, and a further measure of her important standing is that her head remains uncovered in the Pope's presence. She is wearing a necklace, the heavy pendant of which falls inside the bodice of her dark green underdress. (Dark green was the colour of mourning widows in the Tuscany of the time.)[13] Over this she wears a regal, crimson Neapolitan-style *camorra* and on her shoulder is a fur stole. All these factors, it could be argued, were common characteristics of female dress of the time, but, if we examine the woman's features, they could plausibly be those of the woman in the Doria Pamphilj portrait.

Raphael and Giovanna d'Aragona might also have met later at a reception in Rome between 1508 and 1510, when the painter had transferred himself there and when she visited her brother Cardinal Luigi. Giovanna may have

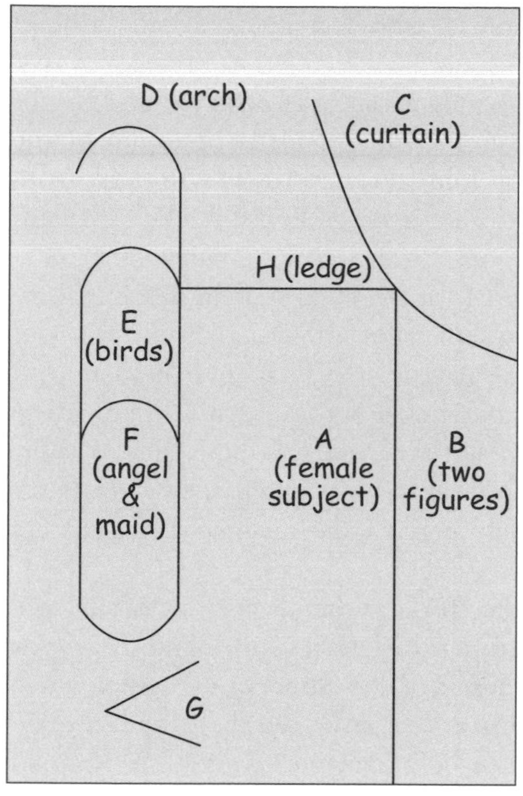

A – Female subject, facing towards B in picture 1 and away from B in picture 2.
B – Two figures. A cardinal (Oliviero Carafa, Cardinal of Naples) and Thomas Aquinas in picture 1, two lions in picture 2.
C – The curtain. In picture 1 it is slightly lifted (symbolising the Immaculate Conception?). In picture 2 it is knotted twice (symbolising two marriages?).
D – The arch is in the same position in both pictures.
E – In picture 1 there is a free-flying dove, symbol of divine love. In 2 the birds are imprisoned in cages.
F – In picture 1 there is an angel of mercy. In 2 there is a maid touching the cage bars.
G – The angle in picture 1 is a pediment, in 2 it is transformed into a musical instrument (probably a virginal) against which the subject leans.
H – In picture 1 the ledge is a shelf bearing books, probably the Bible and Aquinas's philosophical works (sources of wisdom). In 2 the ledge is reduced to an empty moulding (absence of wisdom?).

1: St Thomas Aquinas presents Cardinal Oliviero Carafa to the Virgin Mary. Painted 1488–92 by Filippino Lippi. church of Santa Maria sopra la Minerva, Rome (*photograph courtesy of the Soprintendenza per i Beni Artistici e Storici di Roma*).

2: Portrait known as 'Giovanna d'Aragona', from the workshop of Raphael. Date unknown (*Galleria Doria Pamphilj, Rome*).

been the mysterious masked noblewoman who accompanied Luigi around the stations of the cross in Rome in February of 1510.[14] The presence of two Raphael paintings in the Piccolomini family inventories could be evidence of a possible connection between Giovanna and the artist. A *tondo* of the Madonna and sleeping child with St John the Baptist was shipped from Talamone to Amalfi on behalf of Giovanna's son, Alfonso, Duke of Amalfi on 15 February 1542. This painting has since been lost, but another of a Madonna with her child reaching out to a sleeping St John, attributed to Raphael, was kept in the Piccolomini collection in Siena right up to about 1920, when it was sold abroad. Leonardesque elements of form and atmosphere pointed to a date of execution around 1508.[15] Since the inventories for Giovanna's period have not survived, it is impossible to assert whether or not one of these Raphael Madonnas was purchased by her, but it is a possibility not to be dismissed and could indicate some direct contact between the Duchess and the artist.

But it is when the symbolism of the Doria Pamphilj portrait is analysed that it seems to fit so perfectly the story of the Duchess of Amalfi. A key for this analysis is to be found in the church of the Minerva in Rome, where the Cardinal of Aragon lies buried. It has been affirmed that Raphael drew inspiration from a painting there when he portrayed Leo X,[16] so he could certainly have been inspired by a second work in the Minerva – that of the Madonna in the chapel of Cardinal Oliviero Carafa (Picture 1, page 201). The structure of the components of this painting by Filippino Lippi (painted between 1488 and 1492) and the portrait formerly known as 'Giovanna d'Aragona' are identical save for an alteration in the proportions (Plate 1 and Picture 2, page 201).

In the portrait, two stone lions replace the figures of St Thomas Aquinas and the Cardinal of Naples shown in Filippino Lippi's picture. Lions were a symbol of nobility or high birth, and with the Duchess of Amalfi in mind, they could be interpreted as symbols of two stonyhearted noble brothers who persecuted her; significantly, she has turned her back on them. The animal fur around her shoulders, as well as being a decorative element, could also be interpreted as the symbol of a creature being preyed upon.

The curtain in the Minerva painting is merely lifted, and perhaps represents the Virgin Mary's Immaculate Conception. In the portrait, the curtain is knotted twice and could represent the Duchess's two marriages.

The Angel of Mercy stepping forward towards the Madonna in Lippi's painting is replaced in the portrait by the maid on the balcony touching the cage bars. The maid was the Duchess of Amalfi's 'Angel of Mercy', without whose connivance she would never have been able to pursue her love affair with Antonio Bologna. It was the maid who opened the door of their 'caged love'.

The bird functions as a symbol of divine love and is free-flying in the Minerva painting, while in the corresponding area of the portrait the birds are imprisoned in cages. The cages could represent both the constraints which bound the Duchess's liberty of action in her love affair and the prison where she and the maid ended their days.

The subject in the portrait appears to be leaning against a musical instrument and Antonio Bologna was noted as a court musician. Behind the subject in both pictures is a horizontal ledge. In Lippi's version it is a shelf holding books, including probably the Bible, the ultimate source of wisdom; in the portrait the shelf is reduced to an empty moulding – could this represent wisdom set aside?

A last point to note is the necklace. The subject in the Louvre version wears no necklace, that in the Leipzig version wears a heavy gold chain, but the Doria Pamphilj subject wears what looks like a cameo, set with precious stones and suspended on a fine chain. Unfortunately, the records of inventories of the Piccolomini of Amalfi begin from the time of Giovanna's daughter-in-law, Costanza D'Avalos, but among the jewels in the possession of later duchesses is noted a precious cameo portraying the head of Alexander the Great.[17] Since family jewels were usually passed down and donated to the wife on her marriage, it is possible that this cameo could be the one represented in the Doria Pamphilj portrait. It would not have been portrayed in the Louvre version, for the subject did not possess this particular jewel.

In the Louvre portrait there also seems to be a male figure, just partially visible, skulking on the balcony behind the archway. This figure is absent from the Doria Pamphilj version, as is the stone bust of a cardinal over the door under the left-hand side of the arch. The bust is facing the two mysterious figures on the balcony. Could this represent the ruthless Cardinal of Aragon spying on the surreptitious activities of the maid and Antonio Bologna and refusing to allow his sister to make her exit from the royal House of Aragon? These latter elements may be absent from the Doria Pamphilj version because parts of the picture, such as the approximate rendering of the belt of the dress, would lead to the assumption that the portrait was never fully completed.

Thus interpreted, the iconography of the painting fits perfectly with the story of the Duchess of Amalfi. It also fits well with La Brognina's story: the lions could represent her twin sons, the two knots her two liaisons, the bust of the cardinal over the door, the children's godfather, Bibbiena himself. And the maid holding the cages? Just a decorative element in this case. But none of the symbolism seems to have any connection whatsoever with the uneventful life of the Vicereine of Naples, Isabella de Requesens.*

How and when the Doria Pamphilj version came to be painted is unknown, but it is thought that it may have come originally from the Este collection in Ferrara. The Duchess of Amalfi's cousin, Alfonso d'Este, Duke of Ferrara, had been in France in December 1518 and seen the portrait of the Vicereine of Naples when it was delivered to Francis I. He was so taken with it that he wrote to his ambassador in Rome, Costabili, ordering him to ask Raphael for the cartoon of the portrait. There were many subtle cross-currents at play here. The Duke of Ferrara was trying to obtain a painting by Raphael for his collection and had paid Raphael a substantial sum in advance. Raphael was submerged with work but sent him a sketch for the agreed work. Time dragged on without his being able to make a start on the painting for the Duke, who, in his impatience, had another painter compose an oil painting from Raphael's sketch. When news of this reached Raphael, he was furious, but unable to offend the powerful Duke openly, he reacted by keeping him waiting further. He refused to paint the agreed subject and suggested that the Duke choose another. The Duke was obliged to agree and sent a further 50 ducats in advance payment.

For three more years the Duke's agents in Rome pestered Raphael for the agreed painting.[18] To staunch this pestering, Raphael sent him the cartoon of the St Michael which he had painted for Francis I. The Duke was now afraid that Raphael was trying to wriggle out of the commission, so he ordered Costabili to ask Raphael for the cartoon of the Vicereine portrait too. It was duly delivered in February 1519. Had Alfonso heard in Paris that it was a portrait of 'la femme' (the same word for both wife and

* At the age of eight her father, Galeceran Bernat, died and left her heir to an enormous fortune. She was promptly married to Raimondo de Cardona, thirty years her senior, and they eventually had four children. Cardona died in 1522 and Isabella twelve years later. When Giulio Romano was sent to do the life drawing for the portrait in 1518, she was twenty years old.

woman in French) of the Viceroy and presumed her to be the wife not the mistress of Cardona? But if the portrait was not of the Vicereine of Naples, but of La Brognina, why did Raphael not correct the mistake during the exchange of letters? In another letter, a month later, Costabili assured the Duke that Raphael said he had not sent the cartoon of the Vicereine to pass it off as his own work; he freely admitted that it was by one of his pupils. However, if the Duke would like a version in oils, he would willingly do one for him.[19]

Did Raphael ever begin that version in oils of the portrait that he had promised, perhaps just the face, before he died in April the following year? There is also a possibility that the Duke of Ferrara had ordered the Raphael cartoon in his possession to be made up in oils by another artist and that the Leonardesque face was his caprice. The records are too incomplete to make a firm pronouncement.

But from the earliest mention of it in the records, the Doria Pamphilj portrait is connected with the name of Giovanna d'Aragona. In Scannelli's *Microcosmo* of 1657, it is listed as being part of the Aldobrandini collection and is called *A portrait from nature of Queen Giovanna in Naples*, as it had been defined in France a quarter of a century earlier. It may have entered the Aldobrandini collection when the Duchy of Ferrara suddenly reverted to the Church in 1597 and Pope Clement VIII (Ippolito Aldobrandini) took possession of most of the art collection of the Este family in Ferrara. The painting then passed, through a marriage settlement, between an Aldobrandini and a Doria into the Doria Pamphilj collection.[20]

The picture was listed in the Belli inventory of the Doria Pamphilj Gallery and, at the request of a certain Cardinal Pacca, the painting was examined and found to be 'a painting on wood representing Queen Joan, by Leonardo da Vinci'. This attribution has since been dismissed, but corroborates the finesse of the Leonardesque face.[21] It has subsequently been pronounced a contemporary copy from Raphael's workshop of the portrait in the Louvre, possibly executed by a Flemish painter who studied with Raphael. (Some have pointed out the distinct Flemish influence in the work of Giulio Romano, who is almost certainly the artist of the Louvre painting.) Which was the copy, and which the original, remains to be seen and the verdict, as with the Prado portrait, must naturally fall to the expert art historians.

As yet there is no definitive solution to the enigma. Arguments which connect Raphael to the Duchess of Amalfi may seem specious, but they are plausible. And whether or not the Doria Pamphilj painting is really a portrait of Giovanna d'Aragona, Duchess of Amalfi, her plight is portrayed in that equivocal, melancholic smile. Her ambiguity fascinated her contemporaries and still intrigues modern writers. The Italian literary critic Domenico Morellini placed her midway between Dante's adulterous Francesca, a victim of the overwhelming power of passionate love, and the idealised, pure spirit of Beatrice. The Duchess of Amalfi haunts the *Wasteland* of T.S. Eliot and the childhood of Harold Pinter. Most recently, Derek Mahon pays homage to her 'in our own violent time' as 'one who lights time past and time to come', not, as Webster's Cariola says, in 'the spirit of greatness or, of woman', but perhaps as a union of both.

APPENDIX

Synopsis of John Webster's The Duchess of Malfi

The play opens in Amalfi at the court of the widowed Duchess, early in 1504. The Cardinal and his younger brother (whom Webster calls Ferdinand, Duke of Calabria instead of Carlo, Marquis of Gerace, the Duchess's twin) are about to leave after the conclusion of a tournament. We are introduced to them in a conversation between a nobleman, Delio, and the Duchess's handsome young steward, Antonio Bologna, who has recently returned from France and entered her service.

Before they leave, the two brothers place a malcontent called Daniele de Bosola in the Duchess's household to spy on her and make sure that she does not take another husband. They have both political and financial reasons in opposing such a marriage. The Duchess, however, is already in love with Antonio Bologna. She secretly marries him and eventually has three children by him. Bosola informs her brothers, after discovering the birth of the first child, but he does not yet know the identity of the father. Some time passes and eventually Ferdinand visits his sister again, and with Bosola's help gains access to the Duchess's chamber. Unaware of his presence, she betrays herself by speaking of her husband.

To engineer Antonio's escape she invents a trumped-up charge and pretends to dismiss him. He flees to Ancona. At Bosola's suggestion, she joins him there by feigning a pilgrimage to nearby Loreto. But Bosola again betrays the Duchess to her brothers, who then banish their sister, Antonio and their children from Ancona. For safety they decide to split up. Antonio flees to Milan with their elder son, but the Duchess, the other two children and the maid Cariola, are captured and imprisoned by order of the Aragon brothers. The Duchess is subjected to psychological torture and persuaded that her husband and children are dead before she herself is strangled by Bosola's henchmen. The maid and two children are also strangled to death.

The brothers pretend that the Duchess is still alive and offer Antonio a reconciliation in order to trap him and have him murdered. While the wits of Ferdinand start to turn after his sister's death, her executioner Bosola begins to have a change of heart, too, and remorse for his deed nags at his conscience. He woos the Cardinal's mistress, Julia, and encourages her to extract a confession from the Cardinal. She does so, but is poisoned for her trouble.

Suspecting that now his own life is in danger Bosola stabs the person he assumes to be the Duke, but who is in fact Antonio, lured back to court in the hope of greeting his wife and children again. Bosola then stabs both the Cardinal and Ferdinand, but not before the now completely insane Ferdinand, during the confused scuffle, has delivered a fatal wound to both his brother and Bosola. Almost all the protagonists die violent deaths. One of the few survivors is Antonio's friend, Delio, who in the closing moments of the play, accompanies Antonio's elder son by the Duchess onto the stage and presents him as a symbol of hope and regeneration.

Acknowledgements

I should especially like to thank my agent Jonathan Williams for his advice and constant encouragement and Jaqueline Mitchell and Elizabeth Stone of Sutton Publishing for their guidance. Sincere thanks also go to Jacqueline Marshall and Maureen Ross for proofreading the manuscript; to Derek Mahon for allowing me to use part of his poem; to the British Library, Leeds University Library, the Biblioteche Nazionali in Naples, Salerno and Florence, the Library of Santa Maria sopra la Minerva in Rome, the Morgan Library in New York and the State Archive in Mantua, for the assistance of their helpful staff. A very special thanks to Signor Pasquale Natella of the Biblioteca in Salerno.

I also wish to express my gratitude to members of the Centro di Cultura e Storia Amalfitana for their support, to Sally Simpson, Dr Roberto de Cardona, Dr Bernard Légé, Professor Antonio Davide, Dr Elia Conti, Professor Andrea Proto, Sally Murray and Luigi Lucibello for their collaboration. And last but not least, I must thank my husband, Giuseppe Amendola, for all his help and forbearance.

TABLE 1: GIOVANNA D'ARAGONA DUCHESS OF AMALFI

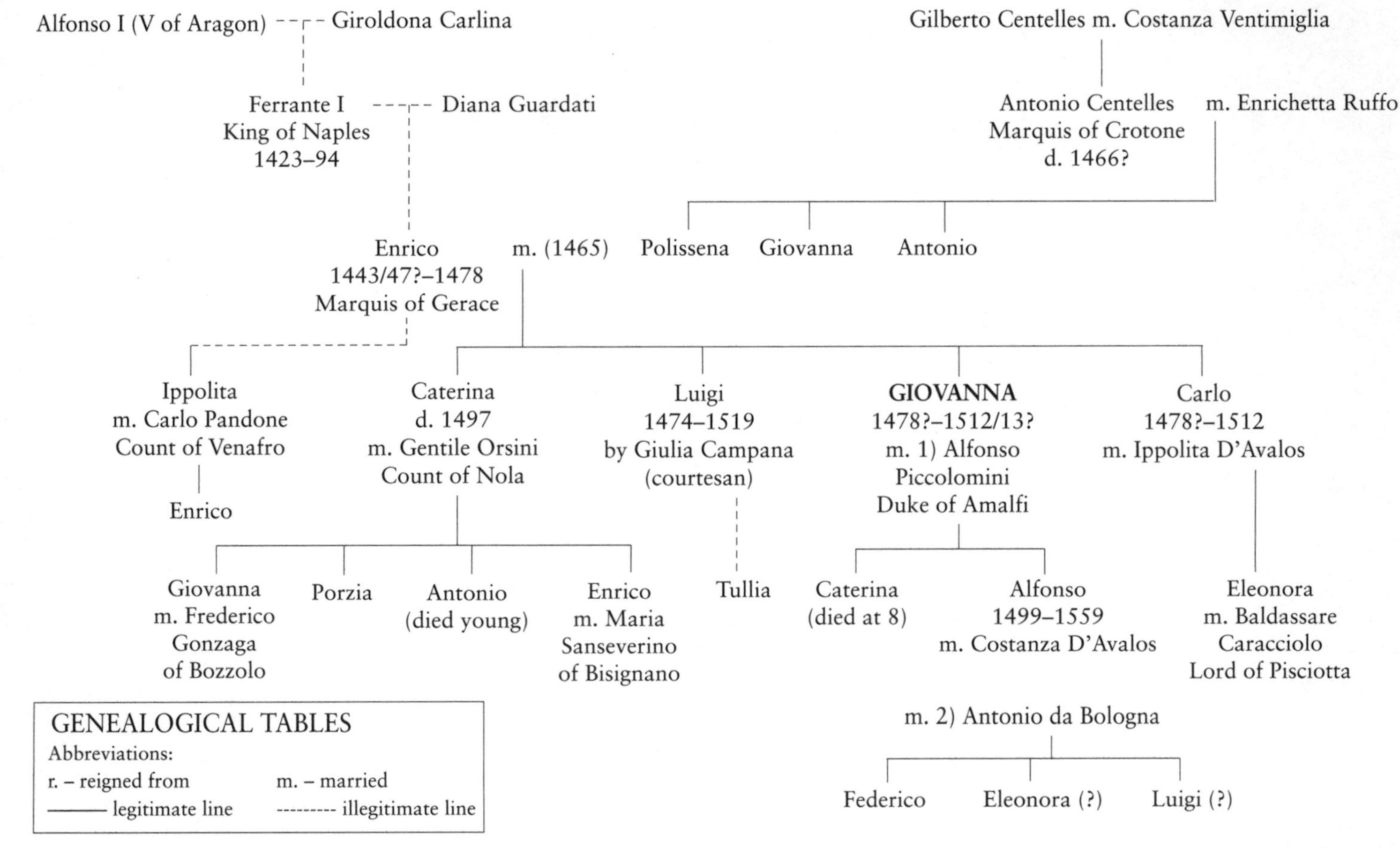

TABLE 2: THE SPANISH HOUSE OF ARAGON
The Trastamare Dynasty of Aragon

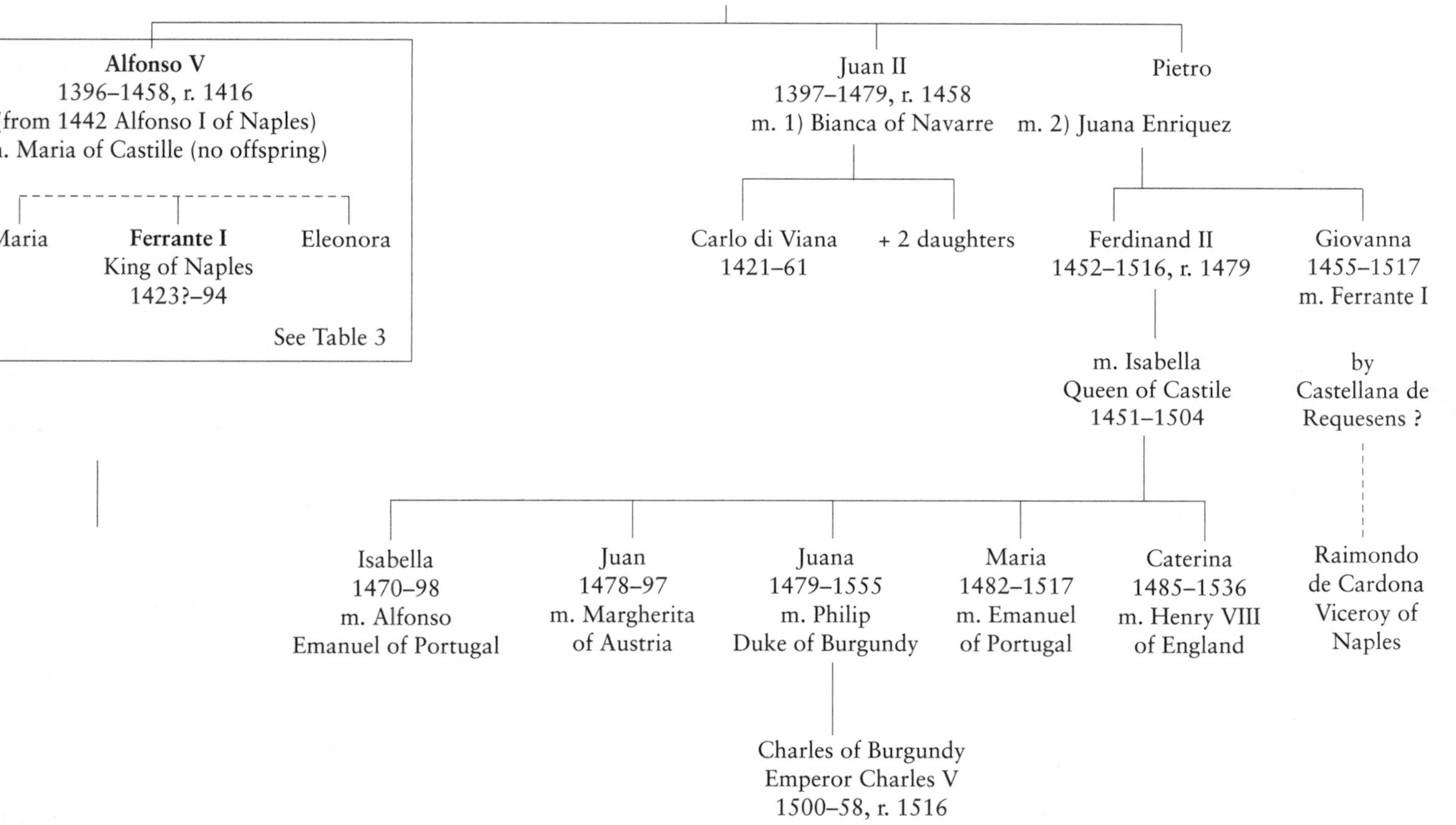

TABLE 3: THE NEAPOLITAN HOUSE OF ARAGON

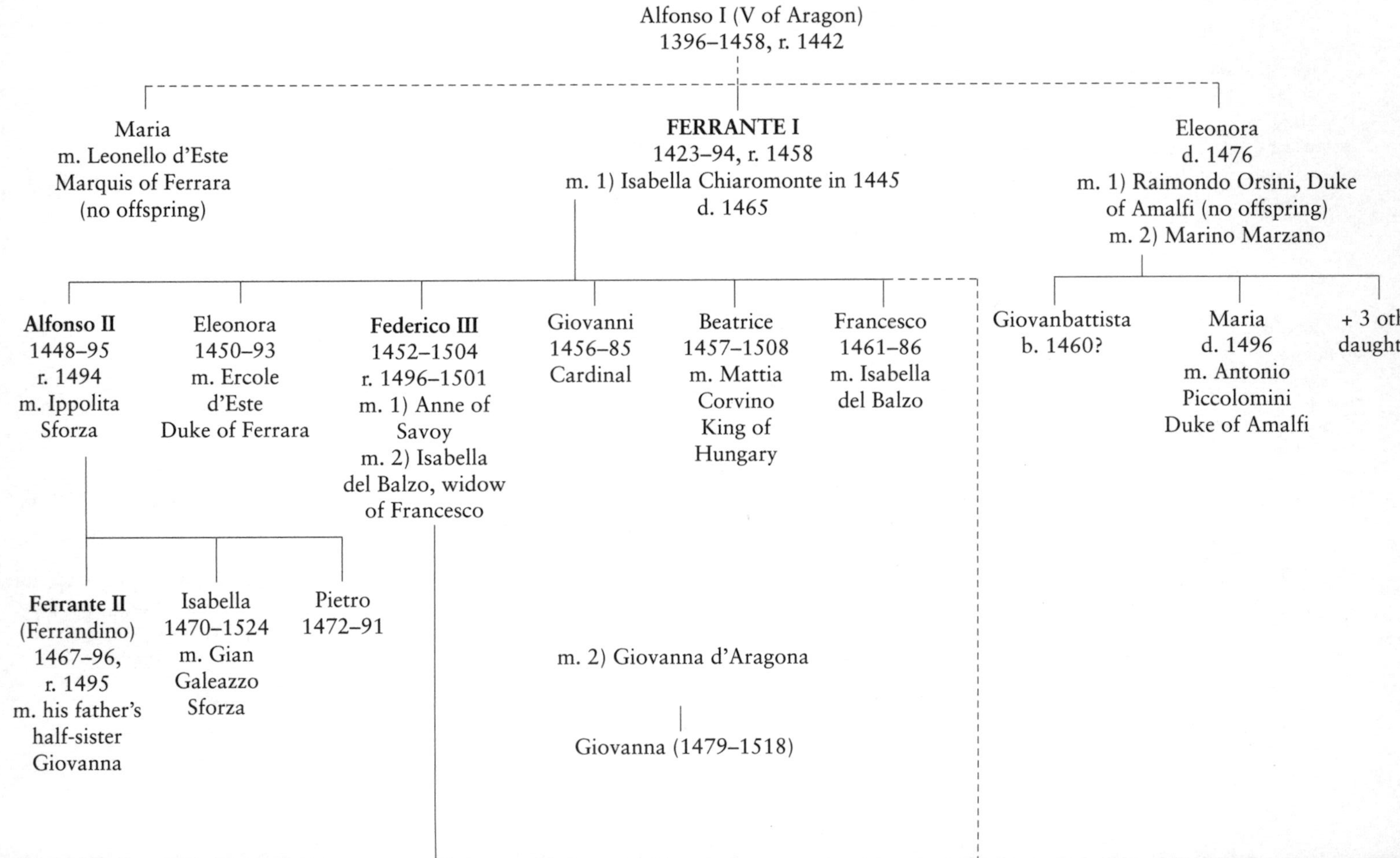

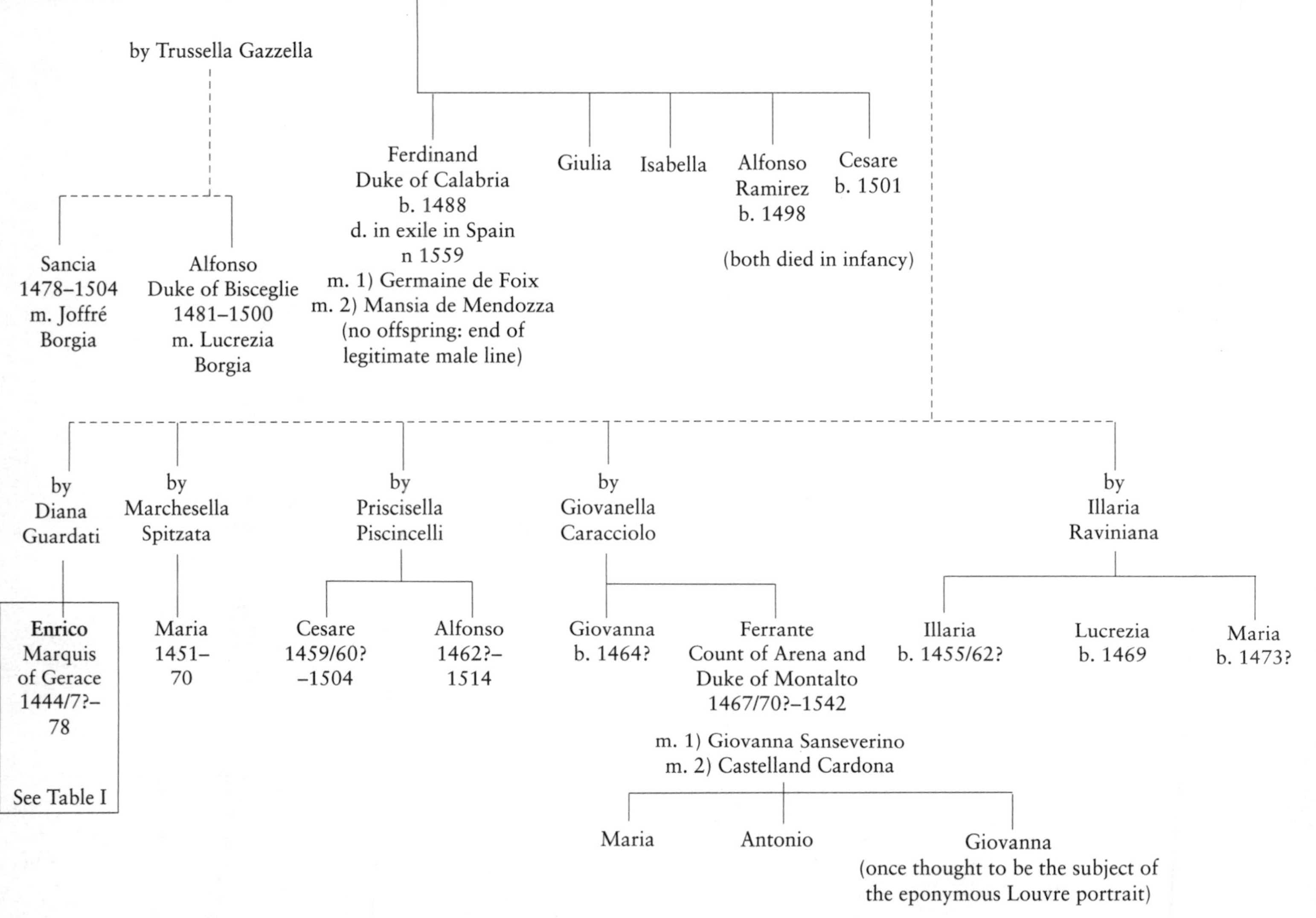
by Trussella Gazzella
Sancia 1478–1504 m. Joffré Borgia
Alfonso Duke of Bisceglie 1481–1500 m. Lucrezia Borgia
Ferdinand Duke of Calabria b. 1488 d. in exile in Spain n 1559 m. 1) Germaine de Foix m. 2) Mansia de Mendozza (no offspring: end of legitimate male line)
Giulia
Isabella
Alfonso Ramirez b. 1498
Cesare b. 1501
(both died in infancy)
by Diana Guardati
by Marchesella Spitzata
by Priscisella Piscincelli
by Giovanella Caracciolo
by Illaria Raviniana
Enrico Marquis of Gerace 1444/7?–78
See Table I
Maria 1451–70
Cesare 1459/60?–1504
Alfonso 1462?–1514
Giovanna b. 1464?
Ferrante Count of Arena and Duke of Montalto 1467/70?–1542
m. 1) Giovanna Sanseverino
m. 2) Castelland Cardona
Illaria b. 1455/62?
Lucrezia b. 1469
Maria b. 1473?
Maria
Antonio
Giovanna (once thought to be the subject of the eponymous Louvre portrait)

TABLE 4: THE PICCOLOMINI

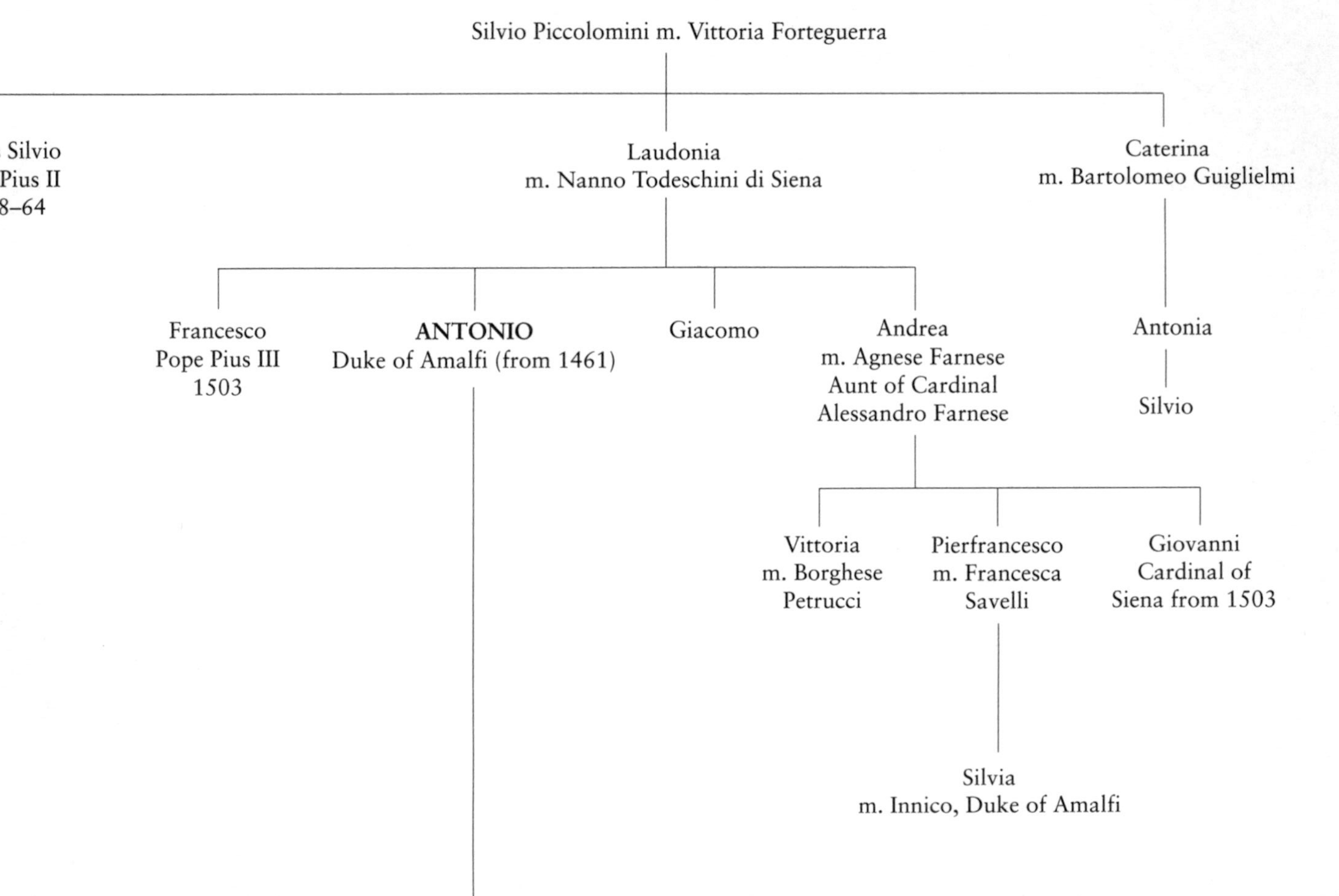

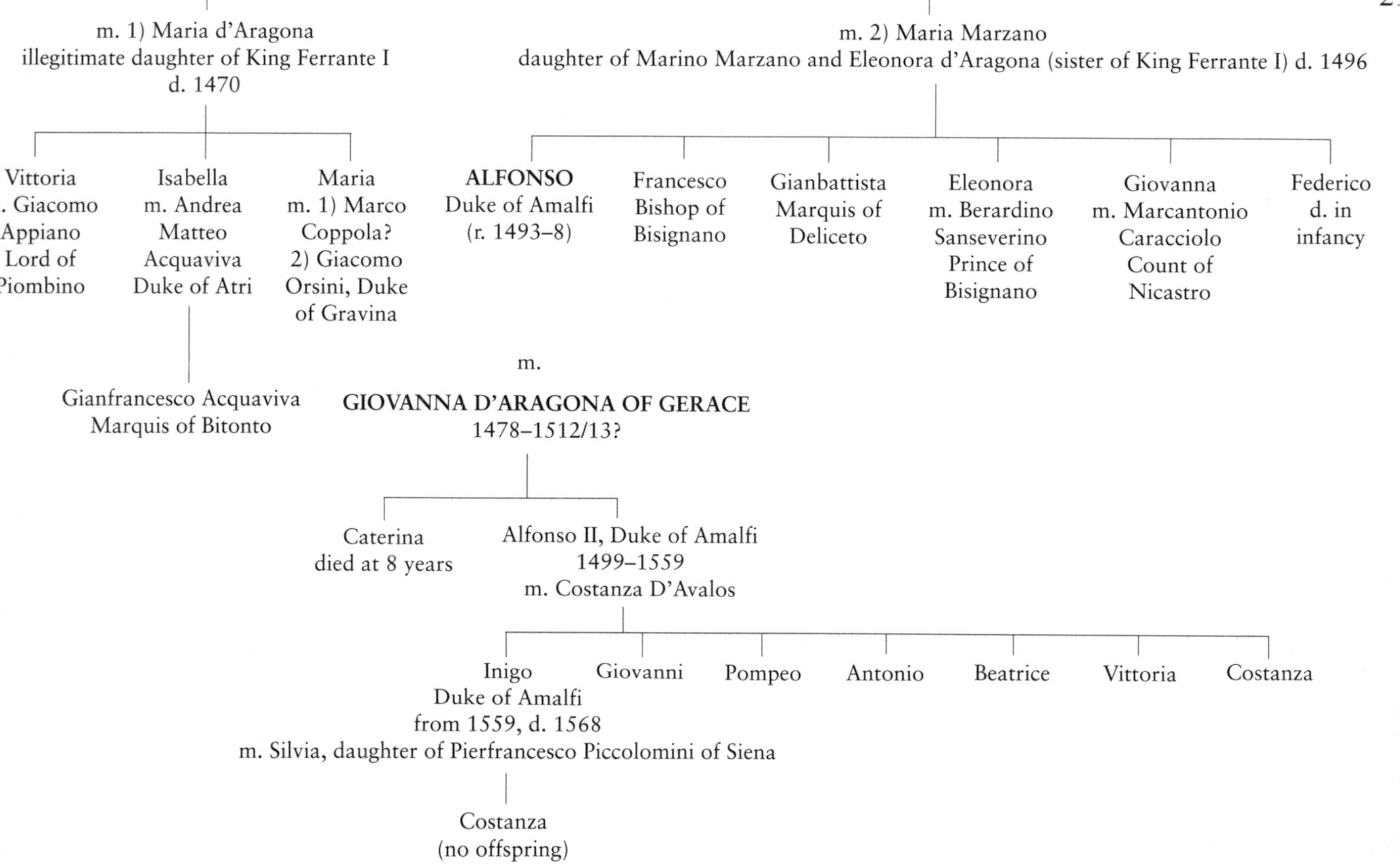
m. 1) Maria d'Aragona
illegitimate daughter of King Ferrante I
d. 1470
m. 2) Maria Marzano
daughter of Marino Marzano and Eleonora d'Aragona (sister of King Ferrante I) d. 1496
Vittoria
m. Giacomo
Appiano
Lord of
Piombino
Isabella
m. Andrea
Matteo
Acquaviva
Duke of Atri
Maria
m. 1) Marco
Coppola?
2) Giacomo
Orsini, Duke
of Gravina
ALFONSO
Duke of Amalfi
(r. 1493–8)
Francesco
Bishop of
Bisignano
Gianbattista
Marquis of
Deliceto
Eleonora
m. Berardino
Sanseverino
Prince of
Bisignano
Giovanna
m. Marcantonio
Caracciolo
Count of
Nicastro
Federico
d. in
infancy
Gianfrancesco Acquaviva
Marquis of Bitonto
m.
GIOVANNA D'ARAGONA OF GERACE
1478–1512/13?
Caterina
died at 8 years
Alfonso II, Duke of Amalfi
1499–1559
m. Costanza D'Avalos
Inigo
Duke of Amalfi
from 1559, d. 1568
m. Silvia, daughter of Pierfrancesco Piccolomini of Siena
Giovanni
Pompeo
Antonio
Beatrice
Vittoria
Costanza
Costanza
(no offspring)

TABLE 5: THE BECCADELLI DA BOLOGNA

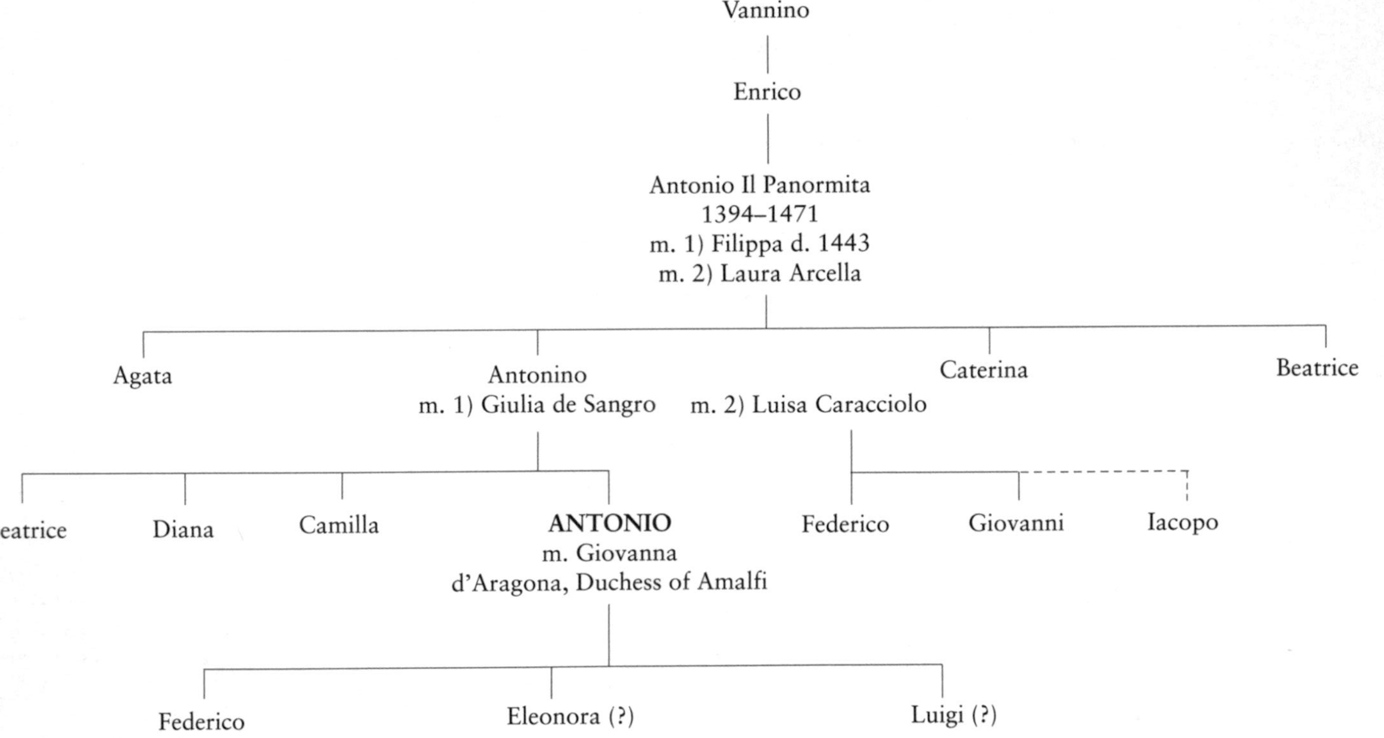

TABLE 6: THE GONZAGA OF MANTUA

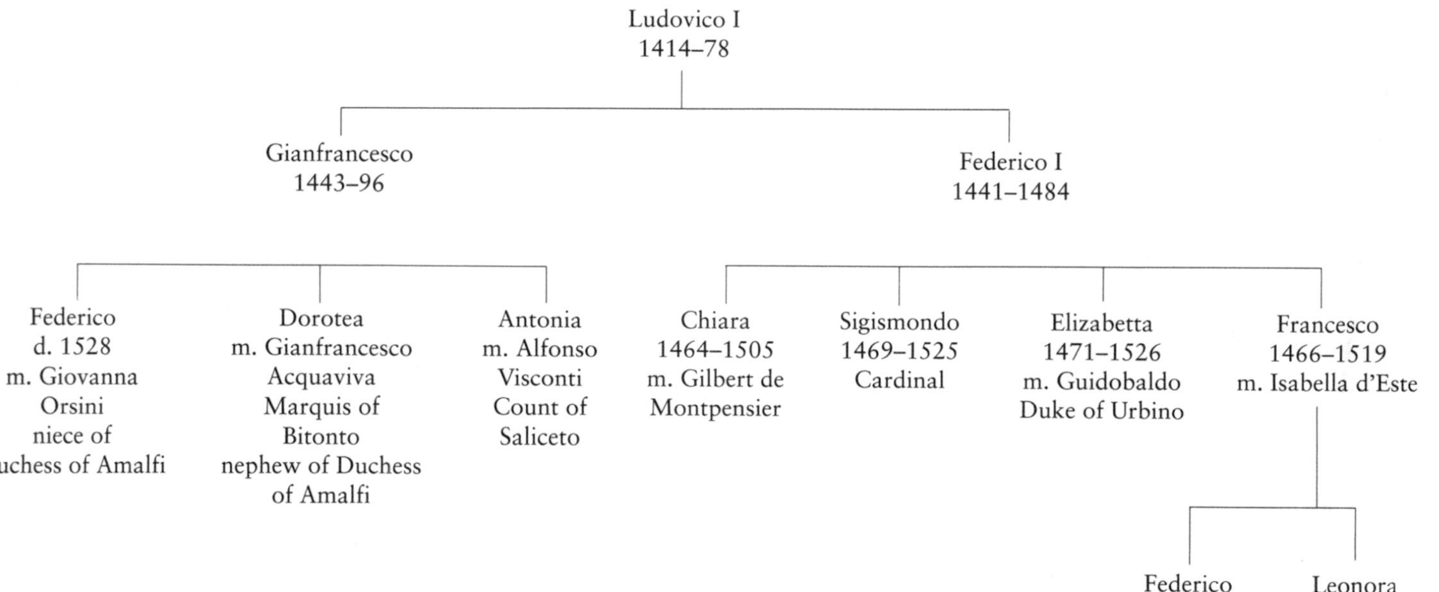

TABLE 7: THE ESTE OF FERRARA

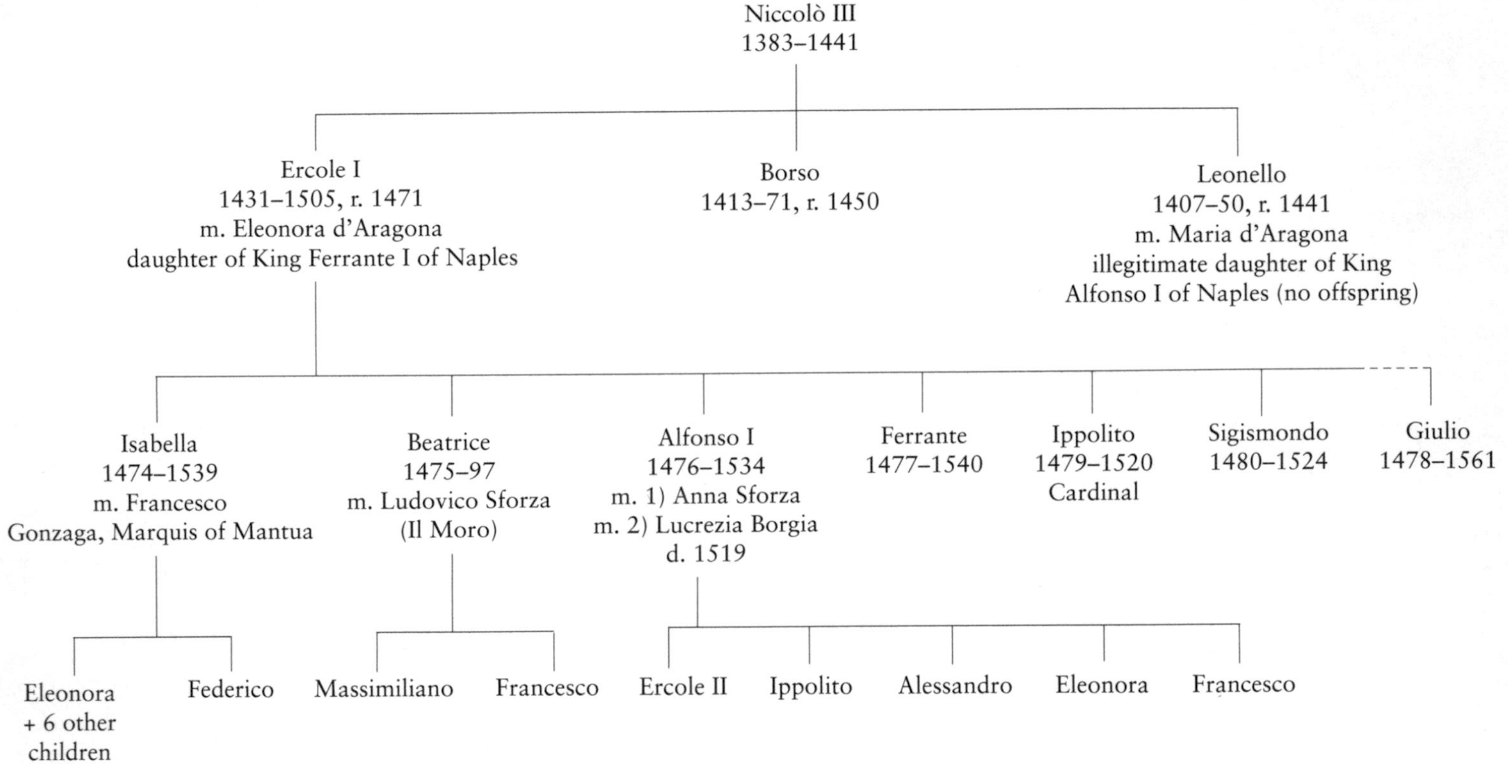

TABLE 8: THE SFORZA OF MILAN

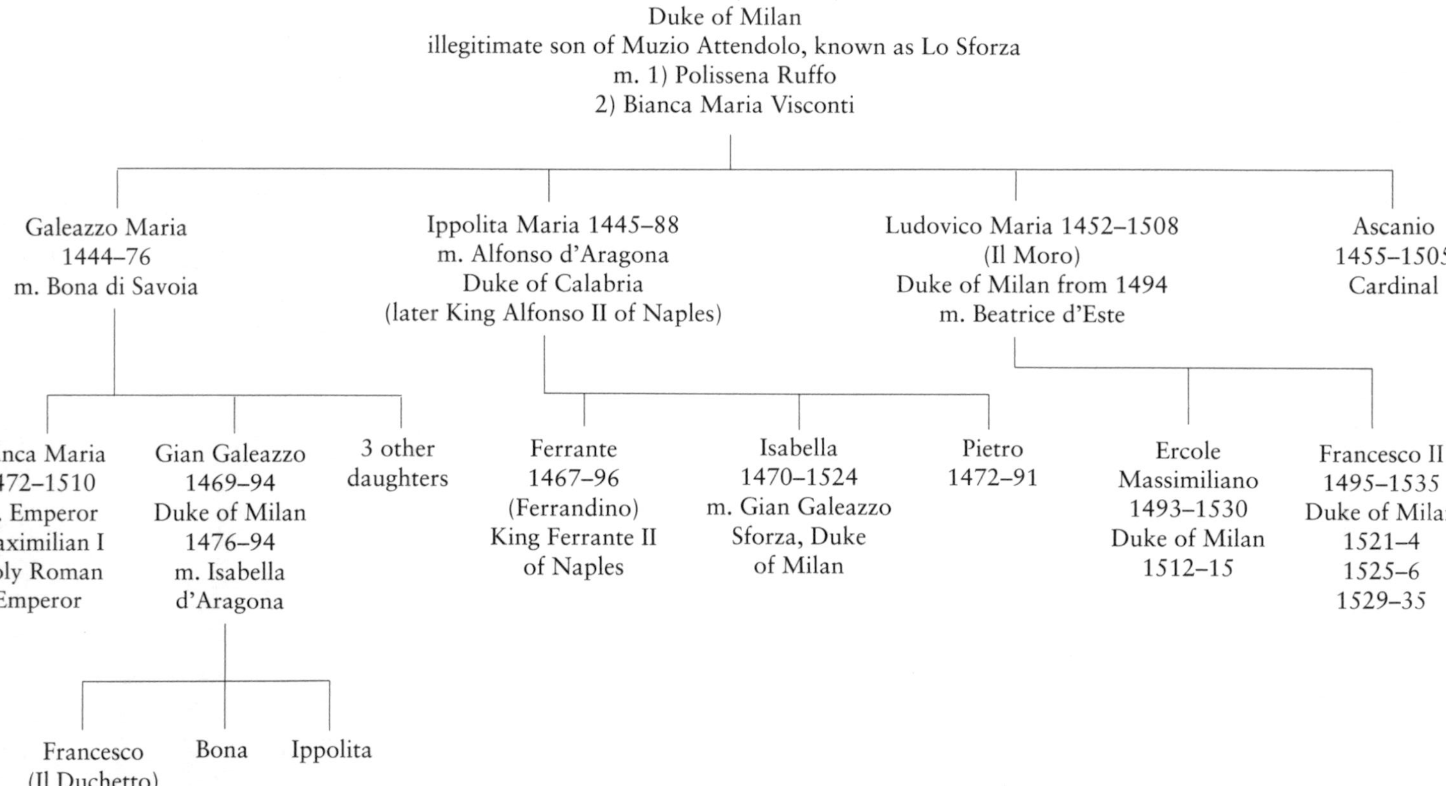

Notes

Abbreviations:
ASPN – Archivio storico per le province napoletane.
MSA – Mantuan State Archive.
NG – Notar Giacomo della Morte, *Cronica di Napoli.*
Leostello – Leostello da Volterra, Joam Piero, *Effemeridi delle cose fatte per il Duca di Calabria 1484–91.*
Codice Ferraiolo – MS 801, ff. 150, Pierpont Morgan Library, New York, reproduced by R. Filangieri in *Una cronaca napoletana figurata del Quattrocento*, Naples, 1956.

Chapter 1

1. Matteo Camera, *Memorie Storico-Diplomatiche dell' antica Città e Ducato di Amalfi*, Salerno, 1881, Vol. II, p. 80.
2. Diana may have been related to the writer Tommaso Guardati (Masuccio Salernitano), who was to fifteenth-century Italian literature what Giovanni Boccaccio had been to the fourteenth. Masuccio's family originated in Sorrento and he dedicated his *novelle XLV* to Enrico, though he makes no mention of their being related. Enrico must have been born some time between the Aragon conquest of Naples in 1442 and the birth of his half-brother Alfonso (Ferrante's eldest legitimate son by his first wife, Isabella di Chiaromonte) in November 1447.
3. *De Bello Napoletano*, Giovanni Pontano. The Centelles were of Spanish Catalonian origin, related to the Borgia and other conspicuous noble houses of feudal Iberia. Antonio's father, Gilberto, Aragonese military commander of Messina in Sicily, had married Costanza Ventimiglia, heiress to the vast county of Collesano, in Sicily.
4. Ernesto Pontieri, *Calabria a metà del secolo XV e le rivolte di Antonio Centelles*, F. Fiorentino, Naples, 1963.
5. A poem dedicated to Enrico (preserved in a manuscript at the Accademia de' Lincei in Rome under the incorrect title *Canzone in lode di D. Ferrante Re d'Aragona*, Misc. 51. A. 19. and discovered in 1888 by the Italian scholar Erasmo Percopo; ASPN, XIII, pp. 130–60) always mentions Caterina before Luigi and nine years had elapsed between Polissena's marriage and Luigi's birth (confirmed by his epitaph).

6. Idem., ASPN, XIII, pp. 153, 157–8, 160.
7. Notar Giacomo della Morte, *Cronica di Napoli*, Stamperia Reale, Naples, 1865, pp. 142–3. Perhaps Terranova di Sibari, not far from Cosenza, but more likely Taurianova (often called Terranova in documents of the period) not far from Gerace.
8. *c.* 1459/60–1504.
9. ASPN, VI, pp. 447–8.
10. 'gravida pir più dolo, & grossa prena, chi sta de iorno in iorno pir figliare', ASPN, XIII, pp. 150–1.
11. Webster puts the words 'She and I were twins' into a speech by the Duchess's brother 'Ferdinand'. There is no reference to this fact in any of the principal sources of the Duchess's story. See *The Duchess of Malfi*, IV.iii.262, in Revd Alexander Dyce, *The Works of John Webster*, George Routledge and Sons, London, 1858.
12. Camillo Porzio, *La Congiura dei Baroni*, Paolo Manuzio, Rome, 1565. Edizioni Osanna, Venosa, 1989, pp. 49, 104–5.
13. Made in 1492 by the Modenese sculptor Guido Mazzoni.
14. Nicola Barone, ASPN, XIV, *Notizie storiche raccolte dai registri Curiae della Cancelleria Aragonese*, p. 771, 7 June 1484 (f. 193), 10 June 1484 (f. 204).
15. Paul Kristeller, 'Studies in Renaissance Thought and Letters', Rome, pp. 401–10, in Carol Kidwell, *Sannazaro and Arcadia*, Duckworth, London, 1993, p. 57, and Massimo Rossi, *Napoli entro le mura*, Newton, Rome, 1995, p. 50.
16. Queen Giovanna II and René of Anjou.
17. Lorenzo Valla, Porcellio Pandone, Pier Candido Decembrio and Giannozzo Manetti, to name but a few. See J.H. Bentley, *Politics and Culture in Renaissance Naples*, Princeton University Press, 1987, pp. 51–62.
18. For example: Francesco Sforza in Milan and Borso d'Este in Ferrara.
19. K.J. Beloch, 'Bevölkerungsgescheschichte Italiens', Berlin, 1937, I, p. 172, in Giuseppe Coniglio, *I Viceré Spagnoli di Napoli*, F. Fiorentino, Naples, 1967, p. 46 and M. Rossi, ibid. p. 50. London during this period had between 60,000 and 75,000 inhabitants; Alison Wier, *The Wars of the Roses*, Jonathan Cape, London, 1995, p. 2.
20. Ernesto Celani, *Le Rime di Tullia D'Aragona*, Gaetano Romagnoli, Bologna, 1891, p. vi.
21. De Maio was a rhetorician and a leading figure of the Accademia Pontaniana, which had developed from the symposia of King Alfonso I.
22. Ferrante, Count of Arena in 1485. See chapter 3.
23. Riccardo Filangieri, *Il Castello Capuano*, Naples, (no date), p. 22.
24. Webster, *The Duchess of Malfi*, I.i.174–9.

Chapter 2

1. Giuliano Passaro, *Storie in forma di Giornali*, Vincenzo Maria Altobelli, Naples, 1785, p. 45, says he died 16 October from eating poisonous mushrooms.
2. Maria Piccolomini was Duke Antonio's daughter by his first wife who was King Ferrante's illegitimate daughter Maria d'Aragona. Alfonso Piccolomini was the eldest son of Antonio's second wife, Maria Marzano.

3. NG, p. 171.
4. Her mother Ippolita Maria Sforza was daughter of Francesco Sforza, Duke of Milan.
5. 19 September 1488, Leostello, p. 158.
6. 23 September 1488, Leostello, p. 158.
7. Death of Contessa di Pitigliano, 1 October 1488, Leostello, p. 162; Caterina's marriage, idem., p. 167.
8. Nicolò Caputo, *Descendenza della Real Casa d'Aragona nel Regno di Napoli*, Naples, 1667, pp. 72–3. For an idea of the value of ducats in the 1480s, 2,000 carts of grain were worth 12,000 ducats. Irma Schiapolli, *Napoli Aragonese: Traffici e Attività Marinare*, Giannini, Naples, 1972, pp. 195–6. A sixteenth-century Spanish ducat was worth (very approximately) about $150 in modern terms.
9. Maria d'Aragona died in 1470 and Antonio Piccolomini remarried shortly afterwards, so Alfonso was probably born in 1473 or thereabouts.
10. Leostello, p. 352. Also R. Filangieri, *Scene di vita in Castelnuovo*, Il Fuidoro, Naples, 1957, pp. 125–7.
11. Antonia Fraser, *The Six Wives of Henry VIII*, Mandarin, London, 1993, pp. 29–30.
12. *De Duobus Amantibus*.
13. Eneas Silvius Piccolomini, *In libros Antonii Panormitae poetae, de dictis et factis Alphonsi regis memora bilibus Commentarius*.
14. Pii Secundi Pont. Max. *Commentarii*, Frankfurt 1614. Tr. F.A. Gragg, Smith College, Northampton, Mass., 1937–57.
15. And a daughter Montanina.
16. C.M. Ady, *Pius II*, Methuen & Co. Ltd, London, 1913, p. 265.
17. Pius conceded to Antonio the fief of Scafati, which bordered on the confines of Amalfi, thus consolidating and extending his possessions. The concession was ratified by Ferrante in May 1465. *Fonti Aragonesi*, Vol. XII, ff. 231–2.
18. Camera, *Memorie Storico – Diplomatiche*, II, n. 1, p. 73.
19. Del Treppo and Leone, *Amalfi medioevale*, Giannino, Naples, 1977, pp. 291–304.
20. Hoby was born in Worcestershire in 1530, educated at Cambridge and Strasbourg, and toured Italy in 1549–50. He returned to England in 1550 and was presented at court. Between 1551 and 1553 he travelled to France and Belgium and again to Italy, accompanying his brother, English ambassador to the Holy Roman Emperor, on diplomatic missions. In 1566 Queen Elizabeth I nominated him ambassador to Paris, but he died there only a few months after his arrival. In 1561 his translation of Baldassare Castiglione's *Il Cortegiano* had been published in London under the title *The Courtier of Count Baldassar Castilio . . . done into English by Thomas Hoby*. Dieter Richter, 'Amalfi nel cinquecento vista da due viaggiatori del tempo', in *Rassegna di Storia e Cultura Amalfitana*, 12, anno VI, 1986, pp. 105–16.
21. Excerpt from 'The travels and life of Sir Thomas Hoby, Knight of Bisham Abbey, written by himself', 1547–64, Richter, ibid.
22. L. Pepe, *Memorie Storiche dell' antica valle di Pompei*, Valle di Pompei, 1887.
23. Subsequently known as the Madonna del Rosario. Unfortunately it was renovated during the baroque period and today there is no trace of the Piccolomini tombs.
24. L. Volpicella, *Regis Ferdinandi Primi Instructionum liber*, Naples, 1916, p. 403.
25. Camera, *Memorie Storico – Diplomatiche*, II, pp. 69–70.

Chapter 3

1. NG, p. 172.
2. Benedetto Croce, *I teatri di Napoli*, in ASPN 1889, Vol. XIV.
3. Pietro Nasi, 25 May 1491, in Ernesto Pontieri, *Ferrante d'Aragona re di Napoli*, Edizioni Scientifiche Italiane, 1968, p. 522.
4. Bishop Johannes Burkhardt wrote a chronicle of events in the Vatican from 1483 to 1506 (*Diarium sive Rerum Urbanarum Commentarii*). Born in Strasbourg about 1450 he moved to Rome in 1481 and subsequently became papal master of ceremonies.
5. Francesco Guicciardini, *Storia d'Italia*, Libro Primo. i–ii, p. 6, Oscar Classici Mondadori, Milan, 1975.
6. 4 October 1489, Leostello, p. 266.
7. Fonti aragonesi, Accademia Pontaniana, Vol. XIII, p. 237. Curie Summarie 1487–91.
8. Daughter of the Pope's daughter, Teodorina Cybo, and a noble merchant from Genoa, Gherardo Usodimare.
9. 3 June 1493, NG, p. 175; Passaro, p. 55.
10. F. Gregorovius, *Storia della città di Roma*, Sten, Turin, 1926, Book 13, ch. 4, pp. 26–7.
11. Gregorovius, ibid., p. 26.
12. *Dizionario Biografico degli Italiani*, Enciclopedia Italiana Treccani, 1961; G. De Caro on Luigi d'Aragona, pp. 698–700.
13. Geneviève Chastenet, *Lucrezia Borgia, la Perfida Innocente*, Oscar Storia Mondadori, Milan, 1996, p. 96.
14. Ludwig von Pastor, *Storia dei papi*, Desclee e C. Rome, 1905. Vol. III, Book II, ch. 1.
15. Gian Andrea Bocciacci, 4 May 1493; Chastenet, p. 351.
16. Letter dated June 1460 from Pius II to Rodrigo Borgia in Registro dei brevi dell' Archivio Segreto Vaticano; cited in Maria Bellonci, *Lucrezia Borgia*, Oscar Mondadori, Milan, 198, pp. 28–9, 570; Massimo Grillandi, *Lucrezia Borgia*, Rusconi, Milan, 1984, pp. 23–7; and also Chastenet, ibid., pp. 10–12, from Orestes Ferrera, *El papa Borgia*, Madrid, 1938.
17. Bellonci, *Lucrezia Borgia*, pp. 52–4; Grillandi, pp. 77–9.
18. Burkhardt, *Diarium*, Parisiis, 1883–5, tom. II, p. 443 and III, p. 167. Also Bellonci, *Lucrezia*, p. 234.
19. Caterina Santoro, *Gli Sforza*, T.E.A. Storica, Milan, 1994, p. 74.
20. Ludwig von Pastor, *History of the Popes*, Kegan Paul, London 1903, Vol. V, Book II, ch. 1, p. 409.
21. Juan was to marry Ferdinand's cousin Maria Enriquez and Joffre Sancia d'Aragona.
22. 'Lettre de Rome de Bartolomeo de Bracciano a Virginio Orsini (1489–94)', A. de Boüard in *Mélanges d'Archéologie et d'Histoire*, vol. XXXIII.
23. *Codice Ferraiolo*, pp. 91–7.
24. Francesco Petrarca, Canz. CXXVIII, in *Rime Trionfi e Poesie Latine*, R. Ricciardi, Milan, 1951, pp. 183–8.

Chapter 4

1. G. Grimaldi, *B. Dovizi alla corte di Alfonso II*, ASPN, XXI, p. 224.
2. NG, p. 181, and Passaro, *Storie in forma di Giornali*, p. 59; *Dizionario Biografico*,

p. 699. A protonotario is one of the seven primary notaries of the *Curia Romana* who registered the acts issued by the papal court.

3. *Codice Ferraiolo*, p. 92.
4. Carlo Pandone, Count of Venafro, considered himself greatly honoured by the marriage, even though Ippolita was illegitimate and came of two preceding illegitimate generations. Pandone was probably much older than his wife and after he died she enjoyed a merry widowhood and was mentioned in numerous scandals during the viceroy period. See Antonio Filonico Alicarnasseo, *Vite di XI Personaggi Illustri*, Biblioteca Nazionale di Napoli, MS XB67.
5. 8 December 1493, NG, p. 178.
6. Curiae II, 9, in A. Scandone, *Le Triste Reyne di Napoli di Napoli Giovanna III e Giovanna IV d'Aragona*, ASPN, LIII, p. 137.
7. *Codice Ferraiolo*, pp. 107–9.
8. Pastor, *Storia dei Papi*, Vol. III, Book II, ch. 5, p. 358. He was not as yet a fully recognised cardinal; his nomination was *in petto*, i.e. promised but not officially published (this happened in 1496 or 1497).
9. Massimo Felisatti, *Isabella d'Este*, Bompiani, Milan, 1982, p. 62.
10. In particular, his fierce repression of those who had participated in the *Grande Congiura* of 1485–7. According to Guicciardini, it was Alfonso who persuaded his father to have all the imprisoned nobles murdered. Francesco Guicciardini, *Storia d'Italia*, written 1537–40, edition Oscar Classici Monadori, Milan, 1975, p. 54.
11. Benedetto Croce, *Storie e Leggende Napoletane*, Adelphi, Milan, 1990, p. 164.
12. Passaro, *Storie in forma di Giornali*, p. 68, 12 February 1495, 'Pensate che non si può affaciare una mosca dallo Castiello.'
13. 6 May 1498, Volpicella, *Regis*, p. 240.
14. Marin Sanudo, *La Spedizione di Carlo VIII*, Fulin, Venice, 1883, p. 161.
15. Quotation from *La très curieuse et chevalaresque histoire de la conquête de Naples par Charles VIII publié par P.M. Gonon Lion 1842*, which is mainly a transcription of the contemporary chronicle *Vergier d'honneur*; cited by A. Colombo in *Il Palazzo e il giardino di Poggioreale*, ASPN, X, pp. 186–211.
16. Sanudo, *La Spedizione*, p. 261.

Chapter 5

1. Baldassarre Castiglione, *Il libro del cortegiano*, Mursia, Milan, 1972, I, xxvi, p. 61.
2. Croce, *Storie e Leggende Napoletane*, p. 160.
3. Croce, ibid, pp. 166–7. Chariteo appears in Sannazaro's *Arcadia* under the name Barcinio. He was from Barcelona. Ferrandino was making a pun on his name and the Latin for sword.
4. NG, p. 201.
5. NG, p. 203, and Marin Sanudo, *Diarii* (1496–1533), R. Fulin, Venice, 1884, Vol. I, p. 278.
6. Francesco Gonzaga, Marquis of Mantua, was married to Isabella d'Este, daughter of Duke Ercole d'Este and the Duchess of Amalfi's aunt, Eleonora d'Aragona.
7. Sanudo, *La Spedizione*, p. 573.

8. *Codice Ferraiolo*, p. 202.
9. 24 May 1496, NG, p. 203, and Passaro, *Storie in forma di Giornali*, p. 99.
10. Scipione Ammirato, *Famiglie Nobili Napoletane*, Florence MDLXXX, p. 272.
11. 7 August 1496, *Codice Ferraiolo*, p. 230.
12. Archivio di Stato di Napoli; Archivio privato dei Sanseverino di Bisignano, p. 15.
13. 'Gliuommero' means ball or tangle, as in agglomerate, from the Latin 'glomus glomeris', ball of thread. Kidwell, *Sannazaro and Arcadia*, p. 37, and Scandone, *Le Triste*, pp. 153–4.
14. Colombo, *Il Palazzo*, pp. 204–5.
15. Berardino's grandmother, Gozzolina Ruffo, and Giovanna's grandmother, Enrichetta Ruffo, were sisters. For Eleonora's wedding and dowry, Camera, *Memorie*, II, pp. 72–3.
16. This chapel was on the left side of the cathedral nave but was destroyed during baroque renovations. Camera, *Memorie*, II, p. 71 reports the inscription on Maria Marzano's tombstone, which has now disappeared.
17. Croce, *Storie e Leggende Napoletane*, p. 174.
18. Sanudo, *Diarii*, Vol. I, p. 720. Federico married Anna, daughter of Amedeo IX, Duke of Savoy and Isabella, sister of King Louis XI of France. Anna died after four years of marriage. They had one daughter, Carlotta, Princess of Taranto, born 1480. She was brought up at the court of the Queen of France, Anne of Brittany.
19. 22 October 1496, NG, pp. 210–11.
20. Sanudo, *Diarii*, Vol. I, p. 711, receives the news on 13 August 1497. A cross-reference with the *Codice Ferraiolo*, p. 244 places Caterina's death more precisely on 4 August 1497.
21. Married to Don Francesco, Ferrante I's youngest son in 1483. Francesco died in 1486. She gave birth to a posthumous son also named Francesco. After her father's defection during the Great Barons' Revolt, King Ferrante married her to his recently widowed older son, Don Federico, and her father's confiscated titles of Prince of Altamura and Duke of Andria passed to him. They had three sons and two daughters.
22. *Lo Balzino*, in eight cantos, by Ruggiero di Pacienza di Nardò. See Croce, *Storie*, pp. 181–208.
23. Anonymous manuscript in the Fondo Mansi preserved at Cava Abbey: 'Nel 1497 Alfonso duca di Amalfi sottoscriva in Celano una pergamena a certi creditori e la indirizzo al suo ragioniero a dogania . . . di Majori.'
24. *Notizie Storiche raccolte dai Registri Curiae della Cancelleria Aragonese*, Vol. 3°, f. 164t, Barone, ASPN, XIV, p. 467.
25. Annibale Piccioli, *Capestrano and the Val Tirino*, affirms that Alfonso was assassinated at Sulmona in 1498.
26. *Notizie*, Vol. 5, f. 188t, Barone ASPN, XIV, p. 470.
27. Scandone, *Le tristi reyne*, ASPN, LVI, pp. 165–71. Letters preserved in the Curia Summ. dated respectively 28 October and 13 December 1498, in Vol. 29, f. 30t., and 39; 24 November 1498 and 28 April 1499, in Vol. 28, f. 85.
28. Ludwig von Pastor, *Die Reise des Kard. Luigi d'Aragona*, Frieburg, 1905, pp. 1–3, and Volpicella, *Regis*, p. 255.
29. Don Juan died 1497, Isabella, Queen of Portugal 1498.
30. Charles's widow was Anne of Brittany, Cesare Borgia's wife Charlotte d'Albret.
31. Bellonci, *Lucrezia Borgia*, pp. 111–12.
32. Chastenet, *Lucrezia Borgia*, pp. 98–9; Grillandi, *Lucrezia Borgia*, pp. 112–14.

33. She signed a document there on 14 February 1500 making a donation of land to the Amalfitan convent of Santa Maria Dominarum. Camera, II, p. 80.
34. 4.Scandone, p. 165.
35. Caputo, *Descendenza della Real Casa d'Aragona*, p. 54.
36. Caputo, idem., p. 54 cites document *In Cancelleria nella Cassa segreta priuilegiorù 14. di Re Federico à car. 43. à ter.* 23 September 1499 Federico wrote to Inigo D'Avalos, Marquis del Vasto, Ippolita's remaining brother, inviting him to Naples to conclude the pact for his sister's marriage to Carlo, Barone, *Registri della Cancellaria Aragonesi*, ASPN, XIV, p. 708, f. 114.

Chapter 6

1. NG, p. 228.
2. Sanudo, *Diarii*, II, pp. 1202, 1268, and III, pp. 1182–3. Also Pietro Martire d'Anghieri to Cardinal Bernardino Caravajal from Granada on 15 November 1499 regarding Luigi's visit. Benedetto Croce, *La Corte delle Tristi Regine a Napoli*, ASPN, XIX, pp. 358–9, n. 3. Anghieri spent a considerable time at the Aragon court of Spain and was tutor to the future Queen of England, Catherine of Aragon.
3. Pastor, *Die Reise*, pp. 2–3.
4. André Chastel, *Luigi d'Aragona, Un cardinale del Rinascimento in viaggio per l'Europa*, Laterza, Bari, 1995, p. 129.
5. Biblioteca Storia e Patria, Naples, MS XXX,B,12.
6. Volpicella, *Regis*, p. 263.
7. Cesare was overheard by a servant of Lucrezia's husband. See Bellonci, *Lucrezia Borgia*, p. 194; Chastenet, *Lucrezia Borgia*, p. 149; Grillandi, *Lucrezia Borgia*, p. 176.
8. Alberto Berzeviczy, *Beatrice d'Aragona*, dall' Oglio, Milan, 1974.
9. Barone, ibid., p. 720, f. 204. t.
10. Kidwell, *Sannazaro and Arcadia*, n. 88, p. 225.
11. NG, p. 242.
12. Camera, *Memorie Storico – Diplomatiche*, II, p. 89.
13. Kidwell, *Sannazaro and Arcadia*, p. 87–9.
14. Webster, *The Duchess of Malfi*, I.i.1–4.
15. A letter from King Federico dated 19 January 1501 in Barone, ibid., p. 715, f. 69 proves Luigi was still in Spain then.
16. Sanudo, Guicciardini and others.
17. Pastor, *Storia dei Papi*, III, ch. 1, n.3, p. 530.
18. Pastor, *History of the Popes*, VI, Book II, ch. 1, p. 202.
19. Giorgio Vasari, in *Le vite dei più eccellenti pittori, scultori e architetti*, Florence 1550 (Newton, Rome, 1991), pp. 519–20; and Alessandro Cecchi, *The Piccolomini Library in the Cathedral of Siena*, Scala, Florence, 1982, p. 12.
20. Pastor, *Storia dei Papi*, III, ch. 1, p. 541.
21. Ferdinand, Duke of Calabria was imprisoned in the Rocca di Scattina in Spain until 1522 when Charles V appointed him Viceroy of Valencia and married him to the sterile, Germaine de Foix, widow of Ferdinand the Catholic. After her death, he married Mansia de Mendozza, second marchesa di Cenette, contessa del Cid and segnora of the

state of Zadrache. He died on 5 August 1559, without having had children by either wife: this was the end of the legitimate male line of Ferrante I.

22. Kidwell, *Sannazaro and Arcadia*, pp. 91–2 and nn. 1–14, p. 226.
23. On 18 May 1503 he borrowed 1,000 gold écus in Tours from Guillaume Briçonnet. Kidwell, *Sannazaro and Arcadia,* p. 101.
24. 2 November according to Passaro, *Storie in forma di Giornali*, p. 144; but NG, p. 273, says 15 September.
25. NG, p. 273. Passaro, idem., p. 144, says 9 November for Federico's death and 14 November for Cesare's. Unfortunately, in 1562 Protestants looted and destroyed Federico's tomb and scattered his bones. Today the chapel and monastery no longer exist.
26. NG, p. 274.
27. Federico's widow Isabella, her two younger sons, Alfonso and Cesare and two daughters were dismissed by Louis XII following the peace treaty with Ferdinand the Catholic. The sons died during the journey back to Italy. She died at Ferrara in straitened circumstances in 1533. After her death, her daughters went to live with their brother Ferdinand of Calabria in Valencia. Shortly after they both died.

Chapter 7

1. Belloncini, *Lucrezia Borgia*, pp. 390–2, 450; and Sanudo, *Diarii*, Vol. V, p. 1015. Sancia probably died in August 1504, when her nephew, Rodrigo (son of Lucrezia Borgia and Sancia's brother, Alfonso) was transferred from Sancia's household to that of Isabella, Duchess of Bari. See Chastenet, *Lucrezia Borgia*, p. 258.
2. Alessandro Cutolo, *Tra Vecchie Carte ed Amorose Storie*, Arturo Berisio, Naples, 1978, p. 36. This Corona manuscript, without a title was in the author's possession. Unfortunately, I have been unable to trace its whereabouts since Professor Cutolo's death.
3. Corona manuscript in Cutolo, *Tra Vecchie Carte*, p. 36.
4. Matteo Bandello, *La prima parte de Le Novelle*, n. xxvi, Edizioni dell' Orso, Alessandria, 1995, p. 250. 'Egli aveva servito il re Federico per maggiordomo molti anni.'
5. Filangieri, *Scene*, p. 141. In 1499 King Federico's major-domo was Berlingiero Carafa. Filangieri gives a comprehensive list of Federico's household and there is no mention of Antonio Bologna in any capacity whatsoever.
6. Nicola Della Monica, *Le grandi famiglie di Napoli*, Newton & Compton, Rome, 1998, p. 65.
7. F. Lucas, *The Duchess of Malfi*, Chatto & Windus, London, 1958, p. 18 cites a legend that the family of Il Panormita was descended from a seventh-century English ambassador to the Pope. The century may be incorrect (VII being interpreted for XII century), if the Beccadelli claimed to be descended from St Thomas à Becket, which V. Colangelo asserts in *Vita di Antonio Beccadelli soprannominato il Panormita* (Naples, 1920). A church dedicated to San Tommaso da Cantorbery in Naples had connections with the Beccadelli da Bologna family. See G.A. Galante, *Guida sacra della città di Napoli*, Stamperia del Fibreno, Naples, 1872. But Ammirato in *Famiglie Nobili Napoletane*, II, pp. 44–50, makes no mention of this connection and traces a possible connection of the Beccardelli of Bologna back to the fifth century.

8. In 1350 the Beccadelli obtained permission to return to Bologna. Some of the family remained in Sicily, while others returned. These latter preserved their surname of Beccadelli.
9. For Panormita's life and work see Bentley, *Politics and Culture*.
10. The Dutch art dealer Daniel Nys who acted as intermediary in the sale, wrote to Lord Dorchester in February 1629 that Vincenzo Gonzaga, Duke of Mantua, in order to pay his debts, was foolishly selling a large number of paintings of inestimable value for the paltry sum of 68,000 scudi. Castagna, R., *Mantova nella storia e nell' arte*, Scala, Florence, 1995, p. 28.
11. Bellonci, *Lucrezia Borgia*, pp. 269–70, and also Maria Bellonci, *Rinascimento Privato*, Oscar Mondadori, 1997.
12. Copialettere di Isabella d'Este, 9 August 1499, MSA, Archivio Gonzaga, (busta 2993, libro 10, c. 36r).
13. Tax exemption, 24 January 1500, MSA, Archivio Gonzaga, Decreti, Vol. 32, c. 148v. Letter from Isabella to her husband 23 July 1502, cited in A. Luzio and R. Renier *Mantova e Urbino*, Turin, 1893, p. 137; Felisatti, p. 134. and J. Cartwright, *Isabella d'Este*, J. Murray, London, 1903, Vol. I, pp. 236–7. Mention is also made of Antonio Bologna in other documents preserved at the MSA, e.g. a letter to him from Isabella d'Este, dated 17 October 1503 (busta 2994, libro 16, c. 55v.).
14. MSA, Archivio Gonzaga (busta 2459, c. 630).
15. MSA, Notary act, 1503 (Registrazioni notarili cc. 58r–v).
16. MSA, copialettere Francesco Gonzaga to Antonio Tebaldeo at the court of Lucrezia Borgia in Ferrara, 2 December 1504 (busta 2912, libro 184, cc. 69–70r) and 2 January 1504, ibid. (busta 2912, libro 184, cc. 94v–95r).
17. MSA, Letter (Autografi, busta 1, cc. 211–12). See also Grillandi, p. 299.
18. MSA Notary act 1505 (Registrazioni notarili c. 747r).

Chapter 8

1. Corona manuscript in Cutolo, *Tra Vecchie Carte*, pp. 35–6.
2. Bandello, *Novelle I*, xxvi, p. 251. Since Piccolomini family records have not survived for this period, we must assume that Bandello based these affirmations on fact.
3. Idem., pp. 250–1.
4. Idem., pp. 251–2.
5. Cutolo, *Tra Vecchie Carte*, pp. 37–8.
6. Gunnar Boklund, *The Duchess of Malfi. Sources, Themes, Characters*, Harvard University Press, 1962, p. 10. In Webster's play Lucina is given the name Cariola, which sounds well in English but in Italian unfortunately means 'wheelbarrow'.
7. Cutolo, *Tra Vecchie Carte*, p. 38.
8. 'Veleno a termine' was usually made from vinegar and a mixture of mysterious powders and substances obtained from infected, putrefied innards, which generated states of simultaneous inflammation and infection. See Grillandi, p. 62. Also known as *cantarella* or *acqua toffana*, their arsenic base produced intermittent gastro-intestinal or, more rarely, cerebral–spinal fever.

9. Auberii (Auvert), *Histoire Générale des Cardinaux*, Paris, MDCXLV, Part iii, p. 55. The date is right but the year, 1512, mistaken. The contemporary Sanudo (*Diarii*, XIII, p. 77) who was unlikely to mistake the year, gives the same date, 5 October, but in the year 1511, when he notes the death of Cardinal Borgia.
10. 7 October 1511, Passaro, *Storia in forma di Giornali*, p. 177. Also B. Croce and G. Ceci, *Lodi di dame napoletane del secolo decimo sesto*, Naples, 1894, p. 57.
11. Bandello, *Novelle I*, xxvi, p. 248.
12. Galleria Nazionale delle Marche, Urbino. Sanudo, *Diarii*, VII, p. 194; Enzo Gualazzi, *Vita di Raffaello*, Rusconi, Milan, 1984, pp. 149–54. Francesco Maria and his sister Maria were the children of Pope Julius II's brother, Giovanni della Rovere, and the Duke of Urbino's sister, Giovanna Feltria.
13. Bellonci, *Lucrezia Borgia*, pp. 145–7. Grillandi, pp. 130–3.
14. 'The duchess was delivered of a son, 'tween the hours twelve and one in the night:, Anno Dom: 1504, "–that's this year–" decimo nono Decembris . . .', Webster, *The Duchess of Malfi*, II.iii.56–9.
15. Some sources, e.g. Ammirato, give the child's name as Luigi, but it is generally presumed to be Federico, since Bandello and the Corona manuscript call him this.
16. Cutolo, *Tra Vecchie Carte*, p. 38.

Chapter 9

1. Celani, *Le Rime*, pp. i–xxi. Giulia Campana (?–1549) and her daughter, Tullia d'Aragona (1505?–56) were buried in the church traditionally patronised by the courtesans of Rome, Sant Agostino, near Piazza Navona. Documents in Siena regarding Tullia d'Aragona's act of marriage in 1543 give her as the daughter of Costanzo Palmieri d'Aragona. He corresponds to Webster's character, Castruchio – an amalgam of two figures in the real story: Palmieri and Cardinal Alfonso Petrucci (who had Antonio Bologna and the Duchess expelled from Siena in 1512). This combination arose from the transformation of Petrucci's name in Bandello's original version to Castruchio in François de Belleforest's French translation. The sound of this name had connotations with the word 'castrate' and was kept by Webster because it suited his portrayal of Julia's husband as an impotent cuckold.
2. M. Armellino, *Un censimento della città di Roma sotto il pontificato di Leone X tratto da un codice inedito dell' Archivio Vaticano*, Befani, Rome, 1887.
3. Bernardo was the father of the more famous Torquato Tasso, quoted anachronistically by Webster in *The Duchess of Malfi*, III.ii.178–80.
4. Pietro Aretino, *Ragionamento fra il Zoppino fatto frate e Ludovico puttaniere* (written before 1539), Cosmopoli, 1660, cited by Celani, p. xx. Aretino may also have been Webster's source for Giulia.
5. Letter from Battista Stabellino to Isabella d'Este, June 1537, in Luzio, *Rivista Mantovana*, I, p. 33 and Cartwright, *Isabella d'Este*, p. 348; Celani, pp. xlv–xlvi; Giambattista Giraldi (1504–73), known as 'Cinthio' or 'Cinzio', *Ecatòmmiti*, VII.
6. Bandello, 'La terza parte delle novelle'. In novella XLII he describes the home of the courtesan Imperia de Cugnatis, mistress of the rich banker, Agostino Chigi.
7. Celani, *Le Rime di Tullia d'Aragona*, p. xix.

8. Bentley, *Politics and Culture*, pp. 108–22.
9. Sanudo, *Diarii*, XXIV, p. 94.
10. Idem.
11. Castiglione, *Il libro del cortigiano*, II, lxxxvii, pp. 194–5.
12. Codice Vaticano 8106, foglio 40, bis 46. Orazione funebre.
13. Pastor, *History of the Popes*, VIII, ch. iv, pp. 144, 149; Pastor, *Die Reise*, pp. 3–5.
14. Bentley, *Politics and Culture*, p. 68.
15. Pastor, *History of the Popes*, VIII, ch. v, p. 218.
16. Pastor, *Die Reise*, pp. 10–11.
17. Kidwell, *Sannazaro and Arcadia*, p. 181. The records suggest that the *gesso* but not the medal itself, was made in Naples, so it may either have been lost or never actually made.
18. Vasari, *Le Vite*, Vita di Sebastiano Viniziano, pp. 886–7 (Sebastiano Luciani detto Veneziano or del Piombo 1485–1547).

Chapter 10

1. Sanudo, *Diarii*, VI, p. 530.
2. Giuseppe Coniglio, *I Viceré spagnoli di Napoli*, Fausto Fiorentino, Naples, 1967, pp. 7–8.
3. Edgarda Ferri, *Giovanna la Pazza*, Mondadori, Milan, 1996. Juana was the elder sister of Henry VIII's first wife, Catherine of Aragon. When Ferdinand died in 1516 Juana nominally succeeded him in Spain and Naples, but her eldest son, Charles (who later also succeeded to his grandfather Maximilian's title and became Emperor Charles V), took effective power. For a while official notary documents in Naples bore the names of Queen Giovanna and Emperor Carlo, but long before Juana's death in 1555 her name ceased to be used.
4. Coniglio, *I Viceré spagnoli di Napoli*, pp. 9–10 and NG, p. 277.
5. Ferri, *Giovanna la Pazza*, p. 185–6.
6. Idem., p. 150.
7. Filonico Alicarnasseo MS, pp. 50–2.
8. Sanudo, *Diarii*, VII, p. 96 and letter written by Jacopo d'Atri to Isabella d'Este from Naples; Cartwright, *Isabella d'Este*, Vol. II, p. 13.
9. Filonico Alicarnasseo MS, pp. 4–5. Camera, II, p. 98 (also unreliable) gives this Eleonora as daughter of Giovanna's brother-in-law, the Marquis of Deliceto.
10. Bandello, *Novelle*, I, p. 307.
11. No copies survive; there is only a report in Sanudo, *Diarii*, VII, p. 640.
12. Bishop of Bitetto to Ippolito's representative at his archbishopric of Capua. Archivio di Stato di Modena, Lett. dei vescovi esteri, Italia, Busta 3, in Berzeviczy, p. 297. Her death, NG, p. 310 and Passaro, *Storie in forma di Giornali*, p. 154.
13. The ruins of the convent of Saint Elena still lie alongside the flight of steps which leads from the valley of Amalfi up the mountainside towards the tiny village of Pontone, where the Piccolomini Castle of Scala and many other patrician residences were to be found during this period.
14. *filij nostri primogeniti charissimi*, Camera, II, pp. 79–80.
15. Camera, *Memorie Storico – Diplomatiche*, II, pp. 90–1.

16. Camera, ibid, II, p. 80.
17. The poem was probably written between the end of 1509 and the beginning of 1510, but was not published until 1527 in the *Cancionero general* (ff CLXXXII–III). MS in the Biblioteca Nazionale, Naples, segn. XLI. H. 34; Croce, *La Corte*, p. 363.
18. Vittoria Colonna is partnered by the Duchess of Amalfi's nephew Gianfrancesco Acquaviva, Marquis of Bitonto, while her betrothed, Francesco Ferrante D'Avalos, Marquis of Pescara, partners a Donna Porfida. Carlo d'Aragona is paired with a mysterious Donna Isabella from the Duchess of Milan's court, and Eleonora Piccolomini is partnered not by the Cardinal, her real lover, but by a certain Luys Dixar.
19. Ha bolado mi ventura
    tan alto que al fin la traxo
    congoxa e trabaxo abaxo.
    (My fortune has flown so high
    that it has diminished dismay and exertion.)
20. Caputo, *Descendenza della Real Casa d'Aragona*, p. 74.
21. Cutolo, *Tra Vecchie Carte*, p. 38.
22. Webster, *The Duchess of Malfi*, III.ii.178–80.

    DUCHESS . . . I must now accuse you
    Of such a feignèd crime, as Tasso calls
    Magnanima mensogna, a noble lie,
    'Cause it must shield our honours . . .

    The reference (anachronistic) is to Torquato Tasso's work *Gerusalemme liberata*, which was completed in 1575. The quotation is from Canto II, xxii, where in order to avoid the general persecution of the fellow members of her religion, Soprina admits to taking a statue of the Virgin Mary from a mosque. Compare also Horace's 'splendide mendax'.
23. Cutolo, *Tra Vecchie Carte*, p. 38.

Chapter 11

1. Bandello does not name which of the brothers he means when he says how quick one of them is with his fists, 'sapete com'un di loro sa menar le mani', but the Corona manuscripts name him as the Cardinal.
2. Webster, *The Duchess of Malfi*, III.ii.178–80.
3. Bandello I, xxvi; Filonico manuscript for Antonio Bologna's family tree. There is reserve as to Filonico's reliability.
4. Christine Shaw, *Julius II, the Warrior Pope*, Blackwell, Oxford, 1996, p. 187.
5. Shaw, ibid., p. 259.
6. *Codice Vaticano*, 8106, f. 43.
7. Pastor, *Storia dei Papi*, III, 5, p. 626.
8. Shaw, *Julius II, the Warrior Pope*, pp. 186–7.
9. Shaw, ibid., pp. 224–5.
10. Paride de Grassi, *Le due spedizioni militari di Giulio II*, p. 203, ed. Luigi Fratini, *Regia deputazione di Storia e Patria per le Province di Romagna: Documenti e Studi*, 1886.
11. Shaw, *Julius II, the Warrior Pope*, pp. 264–5.

12. Pastor, *History of the Popes*,VI, Book II, ch. v, pp. 339–40. Several versions of the portrait exist. There are two in Florence, one of which is thought to be a copy made by Raphael's pupil, Giulio Romano. But the original is considered to be in the National Gallery, London.
13. Shaw, *Julius II, the Warrior Pope*, pp. 260–9.
14. Camera, *Memorie Storico – Diplomatiche*, II, p. 100.
15. Bandello, *Novelle*, I, p. 254.
16. Coniglio, *I Viceré spagnidi di Napoli*, p. 17.
17. Bandello, *Novelle*, I, p. 254.
18. Camera, *Memorie Storico – Diplomatiche*, II, p. 229.
19. Webster, *The Duchess of Malfi*, III.ii.316.
20. Bandello, *Novelle*, I, p. 253.
21. Bandello, *Novelle*, I, p. 254. Bandello was not present at this event; he reconstructed it and the Duchess's speech is a mixture of fantasy and informed gossip.
22. NG, p. 331.

Chapter 12

1. Bandello, *Novelle*, I, p. 254; Ammirato, II, p. 50.
2. 'Vederò, si averò si grossi li coglioni, come ha il re di Franza!', Sanudo, *Diarii*, XI, p. 722.
3. 'E il papa non ha altro in boca che: Mirandola! Mirandola! E va parlando quasi cantando: Mirandola ! Mirandola! Qual fa rider tutti', Sanudo, *Diarii*, XI, p. 723.
4. Sanudo, *Diarii*, XI, p. 742.
5. Shaw, *Julius II, the Warrior Pope*, p. 270–1.
6. Pastor, *Storia dei papi*, III, 5, pp. 630–4.
7. Idem., p. 647.
8. Bandello, *Novelle*, I, p. 255.
9. For the Piccolomini family see Ady, *Pius II*; Camera II, pp. 96–8; and *Enciclopedia Storica Nobiliare Italiana*, Forni, Bologna, 1968–9, V, pp. 327–9.
10. Contemporary chronicle, Biblioteca Barberini, Rome. Cod. LIII, 12; Malvolti, *Istoria de' Sanesi*, VIII, 3, and Pastor, *Storia dei papi*, III, 1, p. 537.
11. Sanudo, *Diarii*, XII, p. 94.
12. Sanudo, *Diarii*, XI, p. 776 and Pastor, *Die Reise*, pp. 2–5.
13. 'Alli 21 di marzo 1512. de lunedi alle 4 hore di notte morio lo signore D. carlo di Ragona, & fo sotterato a monte Oliveto di Napoli', Passaro, *Storie in forma di Giornali*, p. 179.
14. Sanudo, *Diarii*, XIV, p. 229.
15. Bandello, *Novelle*, I, pp. 256–7, says 'brothers'.
16. Idem.
17. Bandello, *Novelle*, I, p. 256–7; Cutolo, p. 40.
18. Sanudo, *Diarii*, XV, p. 10.
19. Ammirato, *Famiglie Nobili Napoletane*, II, p. 50.
20. *Dizionario Biografico degli Italiani*, p. 700.
21. Camera, *Memorie Storic-Diplomatiche*, II, pp.71, 149–50. There was no vice-duke named in 1499 to succeed the one nominated by Alfonso Piccolomini before his death in

1498. No further nomination was made during the period of tumult and confusion when the French invaded and Federico lost his throne. The nominations resumed in 1501 for 1502.

Chapter 13

1. Cartwright, *Isabella d'Este*, Vol. II, p. 83; Bellonci, *Rinascimento*, p. 236.
2. Webster, *The Duchess of Malfi*, I.i.85–8.
3. The young cardinals were all deacons except for Bandinello Sauli (aged 32). They were: Giovanni de' Medici (37); Luigi d'Aragona (38); Marco Cornaro (30); Alessandro Farnese (40); Sigismondo Gonzaga (42) and Alfonso Petrucci (22). Ippolito d'Este (33) was absent from the conclave: since he was still flirting with the pro-French schismatics, he said he was indisposed. Sanudo, *Diarii*, XVI, pp. 31–3.
4. Report by the Venetian ambassador in Naples, Lionardo Anselmi, 22 October 1513, Sanudo, *Diarii*, XVII, p. 272.
5. Silvio Savelli, son of Pier Giovanni, was a captain in the service of Florence, the Emperor and the Sforza. His family was one of the oldest and important noble families of Rome and had provided a pope (Gregory II, 715–31), as early as the eighth century. Another two Savelli popes were Honorius II (1124–30) and Honorius IV (1285–9).
6. Sanudo, *Diarii*, XVI, pp. 37, 609, 653.
7. Francesco Acquaviva was the son of Andrea Matteo Acquaviva, Duke of Atri and Isabella Piccolomini, half-sister of Giovanna's first husband, Alfonso Piccolomini.
8. Camilla Scarampa (*c.* 1454–1517), was a highly cultured noblewoman and a gifted poet in vernacular Italian. She had been a lady-in-waiting to Beatrice d'Este.
9. Bandello, *Novelle*, I, v, p. 50.
10. There were three branches of the Gonzaga family, all descended from Ludovico Gonzaga (1412–78). The Gonzagas of Bozzolo were descended from Ludovico's third son, Gianfrancesco, who married Antonia del Balzo (elder sister of Queen Isabella del Balzo, widow of King Federico of Naples). Their daughters, Antonia and Dorotea, married, respectively, Alfonso Visconti and Francesco Acquaviva.
11. Belleforest, *Histoire Tragique*, XIX, p. 48.
12. Bandello, *Novelle*, I, xxvi, p. 257.
13. Domenico Morellini, *Matteo Bandello: novellatore lombardo*, E Quadrio, Sondrio, 1899, p. 58 and in Napoli Nobilissima XIV, p. 78.
14. Refering to the eventual discovery of the secret marriage, the Duchess tells Bologna: Yet, should they know it, time will easily/Scatter the tempest.

    Webster, *The Duchess of Malfi*, I.i.468.

Chapter 14

1. Daughter of Inigo D'Avalos, Marquis of Vasto.
2. Sanudo, *Diarii*, XXIV, p. 93.
3. Piazza Scossacavalli was absorbed into the wide Via della Conciliazione and no longer exists. Luigi's palace is still intact, though it has changed its name over the years, first to

Palazzo dei Penitenziari, then to Palazzo dei Cavalieri del Santo Sepolcro. In the 1490s many of the walls were frescoed and the coffered ceilings of the main rooms of the *piano nobile* decorated by Pinturicchio. *Studies in Roman Quattrocento Architecture*, ed., Institute of Art History of the University of Uppsala, Tipografia del Senato, Rome, 1958. Also Chastel, *Luigi d'Aragona*, p. 167.

4. For the Chigi banquet, see letter from Antonio de Beatis to Isabella d'Este, 1 May 1518 at MSA. For Luigi d'Aragona present at a dinner given by the Cardinal of Mantua, Sigismondo Gonzaga, which was presided over by a courtesan named l'Albina see A. Luzio, *Federico Gonzaga ostaggio alla corte di Giulio II*, in Archivio della R. Soc. Roma di Storia patria. IX, p. 550.
5. Webster, *The Duchess of Malfi*, III.i.49.
6. G.A. Cesareo, *Pasquino e Pasquinate nella Roma di Leone X*, Rome, 1938, pp. 72, 76, 94, 135.

   In Leonem et cardinales . . .
   . . . L'occulta over palese
   Tra cardinali gran benivolentia
   E di Aragona l'aspra penitenza . . .

7. Pastor, *History of the Popes*, VIII, iv, pp. 161–2 and appendix, p. 473.
8. Sanudo, *Diarii*, XXIV, p. 93.
9. Pastor, *Storia dei papi*, Leone X, Book I, ch. 4, p. 112.
10. Sanudo, *Diarii*, XXIV, p. 144.
11. Letter dated 23 April 1517 from Goro Gheri in Florence to Bernado Fiammingo in Rome; Chastel, *Luigi d'Aragona*, pp. 14–15.
12. Pastor, ibid.
13. *Cardinal Bandinello Sauli and Three Companions*, 1516. National Gallery of Art, Washington, DC, Samual H. Kress Collection.
14. Guicciardini, XIII, iii.
15. Pastor, *Storia dei papi*, Leone X, Libro I, ch. 4, p. 125.
16. Diary of Antonio de Beatis, Molfetta 31 August 1521. Biblioteca Nazionale Naples, MS X. F. 28 (also another version MS xiv. E. 35); Pastor, *Die Reise des Kard. Luigi d'Aragona*, and S. Volpicella, *Viaggio del Cardinal d'Aragona*, in ASPN, Vol. I, pp. 106–17.
17. Chastel, *Luigi d'Aragona*, p. 159.
18. Chastel, ibid., pp. 45–7.
19. Chastel, ibid., p. 158 and J.R. Hale, *The Travel Journal of Antonio De Beatis*, The Hakluyt Society, London, 1979, pp. 1–9.
20. The letters run from June 1517 to the Cardinal's death in 1519, after which the correspondence is continued by the Cardinal's secretary, Antonio Seripando. British Library, Add. MS 12,058, f. 65; also Nunziante, Emilio, *Un divorzio ai tempi di Leone X*, Loreto Pasqualucci, Rome, 1887.
21. For details of the death of Luigi d'Aragona, Auberii, Auvert, III, pp. 1–4. The surgeons found 'toutes le parties nobles s'étaint trouvées bien saines'.
22. *Dizionario biografico*, p. 700.
23. Orazione funebre, Codice Vaticano 8106, foglio 40, bis 46.
24. Fr. J.J. Berthier, *L'Église de la Minerve à Rome*, Cooperativa Tipografico Manuzio, Rome, 1910, p. 271.

25. ERGO CVNTA LICENT LACHESIS TIBI NEC DATUR VLLI
EVITARE TVAS IMPROBA POSSE MANUS?
REGIBUS ILLE ATAVIS ALOISIUS AEDITUS, ILLE
CVI ROSEVS SACRO VERTICE FULSIT APEX,
ILLE, UNI VIRTVS OMNIS CVI CONTIGIT, VNVS
QVI CONTRA HAEC POTVIT VIVERE SAECLA IACET,
HEV QVOT NOS MORTALE GENUS SPERABIMVS ANNOS
SI VITA EST IPSIS TANTVLA NVMINIBUS.

For REGIBUS . . . (A)EDITUS, compare Horace Carm. I, 1, v. I – Maecenas, atavis edite regibus. For LACHESIS . . . IMPROBA, reference to the god of destiny, Parca Lachesis, compare Ovid, *Tristia* 10, 45: 'O diram, Lachesim, quae tam grave sidus habenti; fila dedit vitae non brevi breviora meae!'

26. Sanudo, *Diarii*, XXIV, pp. 93–4.

Chapter 15

1. Franciotto Orsini was Leo X's cousin via Leo's mother, Clarice Orsini. Franciotto grew up and was educated at the court of Leo's father, Lorenzo il Magnifico. In 1517 he was a widower and Leo nominated him cardinal deacon of San Giorgio, for which he paid the Pope an exorbitant sum. On the death of Luigi d'Aragona he exchanged this for Luigi's title of Santa Maria in Cosmedin. He died aged sixty-one on 10 January 1534. Litta, P., *Famiglie Celebri Italiane*, n.n. Milan, 1835, Vol. 8, Tavola 9.
2. Vasari, *Le Vite*, p. 1306.
3. Berthier, pp. 254–7, 269–71 and G. Palmerio and G. Villetti, *Storia Edilizia di S. Maria sopra Minerva in Roma 1275–1870*, Viella, Rome, pp. 113–14.
4. Brantôme, *Recueil des dames galantes (1584–86)*. See Michael P. Fritz, *La vice-reine de Naples*, La Réunion des musées nationaux, Paris, 1997, p. 4.
5. Bagarris, 'La reyne Jane d'Aragon habillée en Bohémienne de Raphaël d'Urbin', in *Les plus rares peinture de Fontainebleau*, 1625, Fritz, n. 1, p. 56.
6. *Manuel du Muséum français*, Vol. IV, *École italienne, Oevre de Raphaël*, Paris, 1803; Fritz, n. 2, p. 56.
7. Ferrante of Arena married Castellana Cardona, sister of the Viceroy of Naples, and their daughter Giovanna, born on Ischia during the French occupation of 1501–4, eventually married Ascanio Colonna. Fritz, pp. 1–26.
8. Bellonci, *Rinascimento Privato*, pp. 236, 365–6.
9. Fritz, *La vice-reine de Naples*, pp. 8–11.
10. Fritz, ibid., p. 24.
11. Fritz, ibid., p. 53. Copies are to be found in the Berlin-Dahlem, Staatliche Museum and the Leipzig Museum of Fine Arts and another sixteenth-century copy by Nicolò dell' Abbate (1509–71) is preserved in a private collection in Milan.
12. '. . . certamente copiato da un disegno raffaellesco non può essere del Sanzio'; A. Venturi, *Storia dell' Arte Italiana*, Ulrico Hoepli, Milan 1926, Vol. IX; *La Pittura del Cinquecento*, Parte II, pp. 447–8.
13. Gualazzi, *Vita di Raffaello da Urbino*, p. 146.

14. Chastel, *Luigi d'Aragona*, pp. 170–1.
15. Carlo Pedretti, *Raphael – His Life and Work in the Splendours of the Italian Renaissance*, Giunti Barbèra, Florence, 1989, p. 92 and Gennaro Maria Monti, 'I Piccolomini d'Aragona Duchi di Amalfi, un quadro di Rafaello e la biblioteca di Papa Pio II.', in *Studi sulla Repubblica marinara di Amalfi*, Salerno, 1935, pp. 21–8.
16. Fritz, *La vice-reine de Naples*, pp. 16–17.
17. Monti, p. 29.
18. Andrea Bayer, 'Dosso Dossi, pittore di corte a Ferrara nel Rinascimento', Ferrara Arte, Ferrara, 1998, pp. 34–5.
19. Vincenzo Golzio, *Raffaello nei documenti nelle testimonianze dei contemporanei e nella letteratura del suo secolo*, Pontificia Insigne Accademia Artistica dei Virtuosi al Pantheon, Vatican City, 1936, pp. 74–7.
20. In 1638 Olimpia Aldobrandini (niece of Cardinal Pietro Aldobrandini), married Camillo Pamphilj, nephew of Pope Innocent X.
21. Angela Ottino della Chiesa, *The Complete Paintings of Leonardo da Vinci*, Weidenfeld & Nicolson, London, 1969, entries 1657 and 1819.

Select Bibliography

Notes on the Sources

It is not my intention here to enter into the complexities of identifying John Webster's diverse sources for his play *The Duchess of Malfi.* This has been exhaustively dealt with by Professor Gunnar Boklund and many other Webster scholars. My aim is only to identify the chain of principal historical sources of the real story, which eventually connected up with the literary versions.

The main primary sources from the Kingdom of Naples are the contemporary chronicles written by Passaro, Ferraiolo, Leostello and Notar Giacomo della Morte. There is direct reference to the Duchess only in the latter two, but references to members of her family in the others. Outside Naples, the diaries of the Venetian, Marin Sanudo are rich in historical background material and contain occasional references to the Duchess's relations, but only one to her personally. None of these sources is completely reliable and sometimes they present conflicting versions of facts and dates.

Official government documents from the Kingdom of Naples of the period should be more trustworthy, but those that survived the civil disorders of 1647 and 1701 were virtually all destroyed during the Second World War. Recourse must therefore be made to transcriptions in secondary sources in various pre-war volumes. Most of the Amalfitan documents regarding this period have been lost too. The Amalfitan historian Matteo Camera reproduced a few surviving ones, but, here again, the greater part of the sources he personally collected have been dispersed.

There are few epistolary exchanges to be exploited as sources for the Duchess's story. To fill in the details, I have necessarily had to hypothesise and refer to literary sources which are, by definition, unreliable. It is fortunate that the main literary source for the Duchess of Amalfi's story was written by an author who endeavoured, so he tells us, to write 'true histories' of events. Matteo Bandello tells the story to the best of his knowledge. While he can be considered fairly credible in his description of the events which took place in Milan, since he was present at the time, the rest of his writing was based on hearsay and gossip that he gathered from people who came from Naples.

Bandello's version of the Duchess's story was taken up and copied almost word for word in a collection of tales repeatedly published from the early sixteenth century onwards, under various titles but known collectively as the Corona manuscripts. The authors were reputed to be Silvio and Ascanio Corona, but these names have since been dismissed as pseudonyms. Who the real author was remains unknown, though some have suggested it was Costantino Castriota, who wrote under the pseudonym of Filonico Alicarnasseo. In his *Vita di XI personaggi illustri*, however, is a version of the Duchess's story which differs considerably from Bandello's and the Corona manuscripts. It was transcribed during the late sixteenth century by Monsignor Claudio Filomarino, who helpfully added marginal annotations and family trees regarding the personages mentioned.

Many versions of the Corona manuscripts were made. Copies are scattered in libraries throughout Italy and beyond, and numerous copies can still be found in private collections. It is possible that John Webster had access to one of these copies, or an English translation of one. His reference to the survival of Antonio Bologna's eldest son is a fact referred to solely in the Corona manuscripts, appearing neither in Bandello nor his translators.

After the fall of Milan to the French in 1515, Matteo Bandello removed to Mantua, where he spent five years at the courts of various branches of the Gonzaga family. He returned to Milan in 1520 and remained there until the renewed upheaval of the battle of Pavia and the subsequent sacking of the city, during which his father's house was burnt down and the precious manuscripts of his *Novelle* were lost.

He spent some years in aimless wandering before managing to obtain the post of secretary to the francophile *condottiere* Cesare Fregoso. After Fregoso's murder in 1541, Bandello remained with Fregoso's widow, Costanza Rangona, and followed her to France. Costanza's home there, the castle of Bazens near Agen, was always open to artists, poets and scholars and a frequent visitor, with other members of the French court, was King Francis I's sister, Queen Margaret of Navarre.

Bandello directed the education of Costanza's sons and in his leisure time continued to write. In 1550 he was nominated Bishop of Agen and shortly before this came to pass he miraculously managed to retrieve his manuscripts lost during the sack of Milan. This encouraged him to prepare his *Novelle* for publication. In 1554 the first three volumes were published by Busdrago of Lucca. The fourth and final volume was published posthumously, about ten years after his death. Bandello died in 1561 and was buried in the Church of the Jacobins at Agen. His last words spoken in public were reputedly '*Vivete lieti*!' (Live happily!), which summed up the greater part of his philosophy of life.

Among the literary coterie that Costanza Fregoso gathered around her at Bazens was a vain, self-satisfied youth named François de Belleforest, a protégé of her friend, Queen Margaret of Navarre. One of Belleforest's fellow students while studying at Bordeaux had been Michel Eyquem de Montaigne. He did not develop the wisdom of Montaigne but, like him, he too became a student at the great legal school of Toulouse. However, he soon tired of studying law and determined to devote himself to the more entertaining profession of poetry. He had a certain fluency of expression and might have made a tolerable verse-maker had he acquired enough self-criticism to be able to throw off his prolixity of style and his tiresome habit of moralising.

After coming into contact with Bandello's *Novelle* at the Countess Fregoso's court, Belleforest decided to translate them into French, augmenting the text where he saw fit – for he had no intention of translating them literally. So the *schietto* (open, frank) style of Bandello is lost in Belleforest's embellishments. He also omitted the interesting dedications with which Bandello introduced each novella. A first volume of eighteen tales adapted from Bandello's *Novelle* by P. Boistuau and Belleforest appeared in 1559, a second, containing another eighteen by Belleforest alone, appeared in 1565, and they were published in Paris under the title *Histoires Tragiques*. The story of *L'infortune marriage du seigneur Antonio Boloigne, avec la Duchesse de Malfi, & la mort piteuse de tous les deux* appeared as the *Histoire XIX* (that is the first story) of the second volume.

Two translations into English from Belleforest's French version of some of Bandello's *Novelle* appeared almost contemporaneously, in 1567. In one, the *Tragical Discourses* by Geffraie Fenton, the Duchess of Amalfi's story did not appear in the thirteen tales translated, but Fenton does act as a loose link between the Duchess and John Webster. In 1566 Fenton had arrived in Paris in the train of the new English ambassador, a lover of Italian culture and none other than the Thomas Hoby who had visited the Duchess of Amalfi's daughter-in-law at Amalfi in 1550. Hoby died in 1567, but Fenton continued to frequent the household of Hoby's learned widow for many years to come. During his sojourn in Paris, Fenton began his translations of some of Bandello's *Novelle* to while away the time. Twelve years later he went on to translate Guicciardini's *Storia d'Italia* (History of Italy), to which it is pretty certain John Webster made recourse.

Between 1566 and 1567 Belleforest's version of the Duchess of Amalfi's story, together with other tales lifted from Bandello, were published in English by William Painter under the title *The Palace of Pleasure*. (The Duchess's story was the twenty-third of volume two.) More or less a literal translation from the French, Painter's version of the story takes on the tone of prating Puritanism, although the author himself was certainly no paragon of virtue. He had had a varied career 'which ranged from the headmastership of Sevenoaks School to some highly successful embezzlement as clerk of Her Majesty's Ordnance. And so through the hands of a gentleman, a fool, and a knave [Bandello, Belleforest and Painter], the tale reached John Webster.' (Lucas, *The Duchess*, London, 1958.)

By 1570 Fenton's and Painter's Italian stories were being 'sold in every bookshop in London' and were in danger of alluring 'yong willes and wittes to wantonnes' (Roger Ascham, *The Scholemaster*, London, 1570). They achieved a great popularity in England in literary circles and with the literate public, but while Bandello had embodied a certain modernity in his open Renaissance attitudes, Belleforest and his translators were essentially medieval in their renderings of the Duchess's tragedy.

The story was taken up by a number of English writers during the Elizabethan period* and finally, in 1612, it came into the hands of John Webster. Only with Webster is the essential sympathy for the heroine, expressed by Bandello, brought to light again. Webster wrote his play about 1612. It was first performed in London by the King's men at their private theatre in Blackfriars and their public theatre, The Globe, between 1612 and 1614, but it was not published until 1623. Webster keeps the names of most of the people mentioned by Bandello, except for Cardinal Petrucci, who is transformed into the cuckolded Castruccio, using the name adopted by Belleforest to replace that of Cardinal Petrucci. Webster also adds other contemporaries, such as the Marquis of Pescara, who are mentioned elsewhere in Bandello (though not in the Duchess of Amalfi's story) and who were almost certainly derived from Fenton's translation of Guicciardini's *Storia d'Italia* (1579 and reprinted 1599).

Before Webster's drama, the Duchess of Amalfi's story was also used by the prolific Spanish playwright Lope de Vega, under the title *El mayordomo de la Duquesa de Amalfi*. This was written before 1609 and probably after 1603 when Bandello's *Novelle* were first published in

* George Whetstone, *An Heptameron of Ciuill Discourses* (1582); Robert Greene, *Gwydonius*; *the Carde of Fancie* (1584); Thomas Beard, *The Theatre of God's Judgement* (1597); Edward Grimeston's translation of Simon Goulet's version of the story in *Admirable and Memorable Histories* (1607).

Valladolid, Spain. However, Lope de Vega deviates notably from Bandello, changing the Duchess's name from Giovanna to Camilla and eliminating the Cardinal from the plot. The adoption of the name Eleonora for her daughter was either coincidence or suggests access to tracts from the Spanish Kingdom of Naples such as the manuscript of Filonico Alicarnasseo, where M. Filomarino gives this name for the Duchess of Amalfi's daughter. Lope de Vega's work was not published until 1618 and it is still a question of debate among English scholars as to how far it is possible that John Webster could have had access to it.

It is generally considered that Webster based his version on William Painter's *Palace of Pleasure*, but there are certain elements in Webster's work which closely correspond to the real events, such as his inclusion of the Cardinal's mistress Giulia and his mentioning that the Duchess was probably a twin. These facts are not mentioned in Painter, Belleforest, Bandello or the Corona manuscripts, which indicates possibly some further sources for Webster's play that still have not been fully identified.

While all the literary sources highlight and illustrate the issues involved, with the exception of Bandello, they contribute little to uncovering the real story of the Duchess of Amalfi. Perhaps the most complete combined historical and literary studies of recent times are those of Domenico Morellini, *Giovanna d'Aragona, Duchessa d'Amalfi* (1906), and Professor Boklund's *The Duchess of Malfi. Sources, Themes, Characters* (1962). But even these, historically speaking, contain some inaccuracies. This book has been an attempt to set the historical records straight and extrapolate the real course of events from that narrated in literary fiction.

Primary Sources

Filonico Alicarnasseo, Antonio, *Vite di XI Personaggi Illustri*, Biblioteca Nazionale di Napoli, MS XB67.

Codice napoletano del Ferraiolo, MS 801, ff. 150, preserved in the Pierpont Morgan Library, New York, reproduced by R. Filangieri in *Una cronaca napoletana figurata del Quattrocento*, Accademia Nazionale di Archeologia, Lettere e Belle Arti di Napoli, Naples, 1956.

Notar Giacomo, *Cronica di Napoli*, Stamperia Reale, Naples, 1865.

Leostello da Volterra, Joam Piero, 'Effimeridi delle cose fatte per il Duca di Calabria. 1484–91', in *Documenti per la Storia, le Arti e le Industrie delle provincie napoletane.* G Filangieri Di Satriano, Naples, 1883–91.

Passaro, Giuliano, *Storie in forma di Giornali*, Vincenzo Maria Altobelli, Naples, 1785.

Sanudo, Marin, *Diarii* (1496–1533), R. Fulin, Venice, 1884.

Secondary Sources

Ady, C.M, *Pius II*, Methuen & Co. Ltd, London, 1913.

Ammirato, Scipione, *Famiglie Nobili Napoletane*, Florence, 1580.

Armellino, M., *Un censimento della città di Roma sotto il pontificato di Leone X tratto da un codice inedito dell' Archivio Vaticano*, Befani, Rome, 1887.

Auberii, Auvert, *Histoire Générale des Cardinaux*, Paris, 1645.

Bandello, Matteo, *Le novelle*. Vols 1–3, Busdrago, Lucca, 1554. Orso, Alesandria, 1992.

Bellcforest, F. de, *Histoire Tragique*, Paris, 1565.

Bellonci, Maria, *Lucrezia Borgia*, Oscar Mondadori, Milan, 1989.

——, *Rinascimento Privato*, Oscar Mondadori, Milan, 1997.

Bentley, J.H., *Politics and Culture in Renaissance Naples*, Princeton University Press, 1987.

Berthier, Fr. J.J., *L'Église de la Minerve à Rome*, Rome, 1910.

Berzeviczy, Alberto, *Beatrice d'Aragona*, dall' Oglio, Milan, 1974.

Boklund, Gunnar, *The Duchess of Malfi. Sources, Themes, Characters*, Harvard University Press, 1962.

Camera, Matteo, *Memorie Storico-Diplomatiche dell' antica Città e Ducato di Amalfi*, Salerno, 1876 and 1881.

Caputo, Nicola, *Descendenza della Real Casa d'Aragona nel Regno di Napoli*, Naples, 1667.

Cartwright, Julia, *Isabella d'Este*, John Murray, London, 1903.

Castiglione, Baldassarre, *Il libro del cortegiano*, Mursia, Milan, 1972.

Celani, Ernesto, *Le Rime di Tullia D'Aragona*, Gaetano Romagnoli, Bologna, 1891.

Cesareo, G.A., *Pasquino e Pasquinate nella Roma di Leone X*, Rome, 1938.

Chastel, André, *Luigi d'Aragona, Un cardinale del Rinascimento in viaggio per l'Europa*, Laterza, Bari, 1995.

Chastenet, Geneviève, *Lucrezia Borgia, la Perfida Innocente*, Oscar Storia Mondadori, Milan, 1996.

Colangelo, V., *Vita di Antonio Beccadelli soprannominato il Panormita*, Naples, 1920.

Coniglio, G., *I Viceré spagnoli di Napoli*, Fausto Fiorentino, Naples, 1967.

Conti, Sigismondo de', *Le Storie dei suoi tempi dal 1485 al 1510*, Rome, 1883.

Croce, Benedetto, *Storie e Leggende Napoletane*, Adelphi, Milan, 1990.

Croce, B. and Ceci, G., *Lodi di dame napoletane del secolo decimo sesto*, Naples, 1894.

Cutolo, Alessandro, *Tra Vecchie Carte ed Amorose Storie*, Arturo Berisio, Naples, 1978.

Della Monica, Nicola, *Le grandi famiglie di Napoli*, Newton & Compton, Rome, 1998.

Del Treppo and Leone, *Amalfi medioevale*, Giannino, Naples, 1977.

Dizionario biografico degli Italiani, Istituto della Enciclopedia Italiana fondato da Giovanni Treccani, Rome, 1961.

Enciclopedia Biografica e Bibliografica Italiana, seria VII°, Istituto Editoriale Italiano, Milan, 1940.

Enciclopedia Storica Nobiliare Italiana, directed by V. Spreti, Forni, Bologna, 1968–9.

Felisatti, Massimo, *Isabella d'Este*, Bompiani, Milan, 1982.

Ferri, Edgarda, *Giovanna la Pazza*, Oscar Mondadori, Milan, 1996.

Filangieri, R., *Il Castello Capuano*, Naples (n.d.).

——, *Scene di vita in Castelnuovo*, Il Fuidoro, Naples, 1957.

Fritz, Michael P., *La vice-reine de Naples*, La Réunion des musées nationaux, Paris, 1997.

Galante, G.A., *Guida sacra della città di Napoli*, Stamperia del Fibreno, Naples, 1872.

Galasso, Giuseppe, *Storia d'Italia*, Vol. 15, tom. 1°, Il regno di Napoli. U.T.E.T., Turin, 1993.

Gleijeses, Vittorio, *La Storia di Napoli*, Società Editrice Napoletana, Naples, 1977.

Golzio, Vincenzo, *Raffaello nei documenti nelle testimonianze dei contemporanei e nella letteratura del suo secolo*, Pontificia Insigne Accademia Artistica dei Virtuosi al Pantheon, Vatican City, 1936.

Gregorovius, F., *Storia della città di Roma*, Sten, Turin, 1926.
Grillandi, Massimo, *Lucrezia Borgia*, Rusconi, Milan, 1984.
Gualazzi, Enzo, *Vita di Raffaello da Urbino*, Rusconi, Milan, 1984.
Guicciardini, F., *Storia d'Italia*, Oscar Classici Mondadori, Milan, 1975.
Hale, J.R., *The Travel Journal of Antonio De Beatis*, The Hakluyt Society, London, 1979.
Infessura, Stefano, *Diario della città di Roma*, ed. Tommasini, Rome, 1890.
Kidwell, Carol, *Sannazaro and Arcadia*, Duckworth, London, 1993.
Litta, Pompeo, *Famiglie Celebri Italiane*, Milan, 1835.
Lucas, F., *The Duchess of Malfi*, Chatto & Windus, London, 1958.
Morellini, Domenico, *Giovanna d'Aragona, Duchessa d'Amalfi*, Vignuzzi, Cesena, 1906.
——, *Matteo Bandello: novellatore lombardo*, Quadrio, Sondrio, 1899.
Nunziante, Emilio, *Un divorzio ai tempi di Leone X*, Loreto Pasqualucci, Rome, 1887.
Ottino della Chiesa, Angela, *The Complete Paintings of Leonardo da Vinci*, Weidenfeld & Nicolson, London, 1969.
Painter, William, *The Palace of Pleasure*, Jacobs, London, 1890.
Palmerio, G. and Villetti, G., *Storia Edilizia di S. Maria sopra Minerva in Roma 1275–1870*, Viella, Rome, (n.d.).
Pastor, Ludwig von, *Die Reise des Kard. Luigi d'Aragona*, Frieburg, 1905.
——, *History of the Popes*, Kegan Paul, London, 1903.
——, *Storia dei papi*, Desclee e C., Rome, 1905.
Pedretti, Carlo, *Raphael – His Life and Work in the Splendours of the Italian Renaissance*, Giunti Barbèra, Florence, 1989.
Pepe, L., *Memorie Storiche dell' antica valle di Pompei*, Valle di Pompei, 1887.
Piccioli, Annibale, *Capestrano and the Val Tirino. Guida storico-artististico a cura del Convento di S. Giovanni*, Capestrano (n.d.).
Pontieri, Ernesto, *Calabria a metà del secolo XV e le rivolte di Antonio Centelles*, F. Fiorentino, Naples, 1963.
——, *Ferrante d'Aragona re di Napoli*, Scientifiche Italiane, Naples, 1969.
Porzio Camillo, *La Congiura dei Baroni*, Paolo Manuzio, Rome, 1565. Edizioni Osanna, Venosa, 1989.
Santoro, Caterina, *Gli Sforza*, T.E.A. Storica, Milan, 1994.
Schiapolli, Irma, *Napoli Aragonese: Traffici e Attività Marinare*, Giannini, Naples, 1972.
Shaw, Christine, *Julius II, the Warrior Pope*, Blackwell, Oxford, 1996.
Studies in Roman Quattrocento Architecture, ed. the Institute of Art History of the University of Uppsala, Tipografia del Senato, Rome, 1958.
Vasari, Giorgio, *Le vite dei più eccellenti pittori, scultori e architetti*, Florence, 1550, Newton, Rome, 1991.
Vega, Lope de, *Obras*, Vol. XV, Madrid, 1913–31.
Venturi, A., *Storia dell' Arte Italiana*, Ulrico Hoepli, Milan, 1926.
Volpicella, L., *Regis Ferdinandi Primi Instructionum liber*, Naples, 1916.
——, *Federico d'Aragona e la fine del Regno di Napoli nel MDI*, R. Ricciardi, Naples, 1908.
Webster, John, 'The tragedy of the Duchess of Malfi', in *The Works of John Webster*, Alexander Dyce, George Routledge and Sons, London, 1858.

Index

Illustrations are in italics.

Abruzzo 27, 55, 59, 64, 72, 77
Accrociamuro, Ruggerone 65
Acquaviva, Gianfrancesco, Marquis of Bitonto 171, 173
Aldobrandini, family 205
Alidosi, Francesco, Cardinal of Pavia 139–40, 141, 142, 151, 152, 179
Amalfi xviii, xix 1, 2, 5, 14, 17, 21, 23, 24, 25, 26, 27, 28–30, 31, 32, 38, 43, 44, 47, 52, 58, 59, 63, 67–9, 72, 73, 74, 77, 84, 86, 88, 92, 93, 95, 106, 109, 112, 133, 134–5, 136, 144, 146, 147, 148, 149, 150, 154, 160–1, 162, 163, 164, 165, 169, 178, 187, 192, 194, 197, 200, 202, 203, 206, *Plates 2, 7*
Amboise, Charles d', seigneur de Chaumont 142, 143, 152
Amboise, Georges d', Cardinal of Rouen 88
Ancona 25, 138, 139, 140, 141, 146, 147, 153, 154, 155, 164
Anjou, House of 2, 10, 34, 198
Apulia, 64, 86
Aquinas, St Thomas 28, 192, 195, *201*, 202
Aragon, Catherine of, Queen of England 129, 186
Aragona, Alfonso d', Duke of Bisceglie 76, 81, 104
Aragona, Alfonso I d', King of Naples (Alfonso V of Aragon): conquest of Naples 9–10, 12, 26, 96, 97, 98, 118, 128, 173, 196, *Plate 16*
Aragona, Alfonso II d', King of Naples: Duke of Calabria 4, 5–6; war against Venice 8; lifestyle 14–15; barons' hostility 15–18, 19; transfers to Duchesca 21; Giovanna's wedding 22–4, 33; father's death 46–7; King *50*; coronation 48–51; war against Milan 52–3; French invasion 54–5; abdication 55; his death 56, 70, 99, 107, 128, *Plate 18*
Aragona, Beatrice d', Queen of Hungary 6, 82, 84, 131–3, 134
Aragona, Carlo d', Marquis of Gerace: xviii; visits Amalfi 1; birth 5; flight from plague 8–9; education 13, 15, 18; Giovanna's wedding 23; becomes Marquis 49; fighting for Ferrante II 64–5; absence from Federico's coronation 71; marriage 77; greets exiled Queen Beatrice 82; French hostage 84, 85, *92*; visit to Amalfi 134–5; lifestyle 135–6, 143; learns of Giovanna's marriage 149; his death 157, 174, 178, 207
Aragona, Carlotta d' 74, 75, 76
Aragona, Caterina d' 3, 18, 20, 38, 42, 43, 50–1, 71, 175
Aragona, Cesare d' 4, 73, 74, 75, 77, 91, (plate 00)
Aragona, Eleonora d', Duchess of Ferrara 8, 15, 44, 53, 133
Aragona, Eleonora d', Duchess of Amalfi, then Duchess of Sessa and Princess of Rossano 21
Aragona, Enrico d', Marquis of Gerace 2–5, 73, 149, 192
Aragona, Federico d', King of Naples: as Don Federico, 5–6, 7, 17–18, 33, 58, *64*; coronation 70–1; conflict with step-mother 73–5; attempt to placate Borgias 75–6; sends Luigi to Spain 78, 80; excommunication 81; letter to Giovanna 82–3; deprived of throne 83; truce with French 83–4; flight to Ischia and France 85; imprisonment of son, exile 90–1; his death 91, 95, 99, 105, 107, 121, 128, 135, *Plate 19*
Aragona, Ferdinand II d', King of Aragon and also of Naples, known as 'The Catholic' 14, 32, 45, 70, 74, 78, 80, 82,

83, 85, 86, 88, 90, 123, 126, 127, 128, 129, 130, 134, 135, 140, 143, 170, 178, 186, *Plate 27*

Aragona, Ferdinando d', Duke of Calabria 71, 74, 90, 133, 182

Aragona, Ferrante d', Count of Arena, Duke of Montalto 17, 84, 92, 198

Aragona, Ferrante I d', King of Naples: marriage and death of son Enrico 2–5; illegitimacy and accession 11; lifestyle 13–14; 2nd baronial revolt 17–19; 1st baronial revolt 21, 27; anxiety on death of Duke of Amalfi 30–1, 33; peace with papacy 34–5; affection for grandson Luigi 37; seeks to make Luigi cardinal 39, 45–6; renewed friction with papacy 44–5; his death & funeral 46–7; comparison with son Alfonso II 48, 51, 83, 89, 92, 97, 115, 121, 123, 128, 132, 156, 196, *Plate 17*

Aragona, Ferrante II d', King of Naples (Ferrandino): Prince of Capua 33, 35, 37, 38; King, accession 55–6; flees from French invasion 57–8; returns to Naples 61–2, 62; marriage 63, 66–7; expels French 65; his death 69, 70, 74, 99, 107, 128

Aragona, Giovanna d', Duchess of Amalfi: xvii–xxi; a twin xxii; family visits Amalfi 1–2; birth 2–5; flight from plague 8–9; return to Naples 12; education, lifestyle 13–15, 18–19; first marriage 21–5; becomes Duchess of Amalfi 30–1, 33; relationship with brother Luigi 36–7; Luigi's marriage 38–9, 42; moral climate 43–4; grandfather's death 46–7; coronation of Alfonso II 49–50; the French invasion 56, 65; King Ferrante's wedding 66–7; wedding of Eleonora Piccolomini 67–8; mother-in-law dies 68; death of sister Caterina 71; arrival of new queen, Isabella 71–2; death of daughter, new pregnancy 72–3; death of husband 72; widowhood, temporary loss of Duchy of Amalfi, birth of posthumous son 76–7; regains Duchy 77, 81; letter from King Federico 82–3; capitulation to the French 84; keeps control of Amalfi 86; visit to Rome (?) 88–9; return to Naples 93–4; Antonio Bologna engaged 93–5, 105, 100; arrival of Bologna 106; love, secret marriage 106–10; birth of first child by Bologna 113, 114, 116; arrival of new King and Queen 126–8; greets new Queen 129; visit of Cardinal Luigi to Naples 130; second child by Bologna 130–1; death of Queen Beatrice 133–4; visit of brothers and brothers-in-law to Amalfi 134, 135, 136–7; the Duchy 134–5; the '*Magnanima mensogna*' 137; Bologna's flight to Ancona 139; third child by Bologna 139, 141; escape 143–6; pilgrimage to Loreto 145–6; to Ancona 146–7; revelation of marriage 148; birth of third child by Bologna 150; expulsion of Antonio from Ancona 153–4; flight to Siena 154; flight towards Venice 155, 156, 158; interception 159; return to Amalfi 160; imprisonment 161; meeting with Luigi (?) 162; her death 163–5, 166, 169; a Medici suitor (?) 170, 174, 175, 176, 177, 178, 181, 183, 189, 192, 193; portrait 194, 197, 200, 202, 203, 206; 207–8, *Plates 1, 6, 15*

Aragona, Giovanna d', Princess Colonna 198

Aragona, Giovanna d', Queen Giovanna III of Naples 12, 18, 23, 33, 50, 52, 54, 55, 57, 58, 64, 65, 67, 69, 70, 72, 73, 74, 75, 77, 78, 129, 132, 135

Aragona, Giovanna d', Queen Giovanna IV of Naples 12, 23, 57, 58, 64, 65, 66, 67, 69, 72, 78, 83, 92, 126, 129, 132, 135

Aragona, Giovanni d', Cardinal 17, 45

Aragona, Ippolita d', Countess of Venafro 3, 22, 51, 63, 129

Aragona, Isabella d', Duchess of Milan and Bari 19, 20, 21, 44, 52, 53–4, 80–1, 82, 84, 94, 107, 132, *Plate 30*

Aragona, Juan d', King of Aragon 10, 12

Aragona, Juana d', La Loca, Duchess of Burgundy, nominal Queen of Castille, Aragon and Naples 126–7, 129, 168, 186

Aragona, Luigi d' Marquis of Gerace, later Cardinal: xviii, xix, xxii; visits Amalfi 1; birth 3, 5; becomes Marquis 7; flight from plague 9; life in Naples 15, 18; Giovanna's wedding 23; first diplomatic mission 35; tournament 35–6; administration of Gerace 37; marriage 37–9; nomination as cardinal 39, 45–6, 49; uncle's coronation 49, 51, 52; triumphal parade 53; fighting for

Ferrante II 57, 58, 62; contracts syphilis 58; return to Naples 66, 71; the King's minister 74; to Spain with old Queen 78; financial problems 79–80, 82; with exiled King in France 85; arrival in Rome for conclave 88, 90, 91, 92; engages Bologna 95, 105, 108, 113; lifestyle in Rome 114; mistress and putative daughter 114–18; companions 118–21; intellectual & aesthetic tastes 121–2; visits to Ferrara and Venice 123–4; participation in Pope's military campaign 124–5; carnival in Ferrara and Rome 125–6, 129; visit to Naples 130–1; meeting with Bandello 131, 132, 133; suspicions and visit to Amalfi 134; interrogation of Giovanna 137, 138, 139; fighting for Pope 139–40; siege of Bologna 141–2, 140, 141, 142, 143, 145, 146, 148; informed of Giovanna's marriage 149; marches with Pope to besiege Mirandola 150–1; attempt to have Bologna expelled from Ancona 152, 153; pressure on Petrucci of Siena 154, 155; new benefices, absence from Rome 156; battle of Ravenna 158; Lateran Council 158–9; Giovanna's capture and return to Amalfi 160; visit to Naples 162; Pope plans to make him king 162–3; guilt in death of sister and children (?) 163–5, 166; death of Pope 167; conclave 169–70; aspiration to throne of Naples 170–1; sends Fieramosca to murder Bologna 173–4, 175, 176; family rancour 178; new home in Rome 179–80; butt of satire 180–1; influence declines 181–2; departure from Rome following disovery of plot to assassinate Pope 182; European travels 185–9; return to Rome 190; his death 191; funeral 192; tomb 193, 194–6; portrait 196–7, 200, 203, 207–8, *Plates 4, 5, 32, 33*

Aragona, Maria d', Duchess of Amalfi 21, 22, 27, 28

Aragona, Pietro d' 6, 37

Aragona, Sancia d', Duchess of Squillace 19, 21, 22, 43, *50*, 51, 76, 81, 93–4, 110, 118

Aragona, Tullia d' 115–17

Attellano, Lucio Scipione 175

Aversa 83, 84

Baglioni, family of Perugia 124

Bandello, Matteo Maria *xxi*, xxi–ii, 36, 85, 90, 94, 95, 99, 109, 110, 111, 130, 131, 153, 154, 156, 157, 160, 164, 166, 171–2, 173, 174, 175, 176, 177, 189, 193

Bandello, Vincenzo 131, 171–2

Barletta, Disfida di 86

Baschi, Perron de' 38, 45,

Beatis, Antonio de 185, 187, 188, 189, 193

Bentivoglio, Alessandro 172

Bentivoglio, family 124, 143, 152

Bibbiena, Bernardo Dovizi da, Cardinal 48, *119*, 119–21, 169, 190, 198, 204

Blois 15, 90

Bologna, Antonino da 98, 99

Bologna, Antonio: xviii, xxi, xxii, 2, 25; possible first encounters with Giovanna 33, 67, 37; at the French court (?) 85, 90, 102; family 95–9; at the Gonzaga court, Mantua 99–105; enters the service of the Duchess of Amalfi 93–5, 106; love 106–8; secret marriage 108–10; birth of first child 113, 114; second child 129, 130, 134; courtly love 135–6; absence during visit of Giovanna's family to Amalfi 137; flight to Ancona 138–9, 141, 145; reception for Giovanna 146–7; revelation of marriage 148–9; third child 150, 152; expulsion from Ancona, flight to Siena 153–4; towards Venice 155, 156, 158; interception at Forlì 159; flight to Milan 160, 162, 163; in Milan 166–7, 169, 171; seen by Bandello 172, 173; move to Visconti household 173; warnings from Fieramosca and Bandello 174, 175; murder 175; funeral 176, 177, 183, 193, 198, 203, 207–8

Bologna, Antonio Beccadelli da, Il Panormita 26, 95–8, 172, 177

Bologna, city 23, 95, 96, 124, 125, 126, 139, 140–1, 142, 143, 145, 146, 149, 150, 152, 153, 157, 192

Bologna d'Aragona, Eleonora (?) 130–1, 139, 146, 148, 159, 160, 161, 163, 166

Bologna d'Aragona, Federico 113, 139, 146, 148, 150, 159, 160, 164, 176, 208

Bologna d'Aragona, Luigi (?) 150, 159, 160, 161, 163, 166

Bologna, Federico 99, 113, 139

Bologna, Giovanni 99, 139

Bologna, Jacopo 99, 139
Boltraffio, Giovanni Antonio 44, *Plate 30*
Bonito, Lucina 20, 109, 113, 138, 148, 160, 161, 163, 193, 203
Borgia, Alfonso, Pope Callixtus III 26, 40, 40–3
Borgia, Anna 119
Borgia, Cesare, Cardinal then Duke of Romagna and Valence 41–3, 70, 74, 75, 76, 81, 83, 85, 86, 87, 88, 90, 101, 102, 112, 124, *Plate 25*
Borgia, Joffre, Prince of Squillace 41, 45, *50*, 51, 76, 93
Borgia, Juan, Duke of Gandia 41, 45, 70, 76, 101
Borgia, Lucrezia 39, 41, 42, 45, 76, 104, 105, 112–13, 118, 125, 177
Borgia, Pedro Luis, Cardinal of Valencia 110–11, 119, 135
Borgia, Rodrigo, Pope Alexander VI 39, 40–3, *43*, 44, 45, 48, 49, 51, 55, 75, 76, 81, 82, 86, 87, 89, 112, 114, 115, 183
Bozzolo 173, 175, 189
Bozzolo, Daniele da 175, 176
Brogna de Lardis, Eleonora, La Brognina 167, 198–9, 204
Burkhardt, Johannes 34, 39, 41, 42, 51, 76, 87, 112, 141

Calabria: 4, 107; Webster's Duke Ferdinand of 16, 71, 207–8; for the real Dukes of *see* King Alfonso II d'Aragona, Ferrante and Ferdinand d'Aragona
Calderòn, Pedro (Perotto) 112
Cambrai, League of 60
Campana, Domenico, 'Strascico' 180
Campana, Giulia (Giulia Ferrarese) 114–15, 117–18, 180
Capestrano 27, 30, 73, 136, 137, 160
Capua 57, 70–1, 83, 84
Caracciolo, Berardino, Lord of Piciotta 136
Carafa, Oliviero, Cardinal 45, 140, *201*, 202
Cardona, Raimondo de, Viceroy of Naples 145, 156, 157, 165, 166, 167, 168, 173, 190, 197, 198, 199, 204, 205, *Plate 13*
Castelcapuano, Naples 6, 12, 14–15, 20, 33, 57, 58, 72, 76, 134, 136, *Plates 3, 7, 9*
Castellesi da Corneto, Adriano 87, 183, 184
Castelnuovo, Naples 3, 12, 18, 19, *22*, 35–6, 46, 47, 49–51, 56, 57, 63, *64*, 72, 76, *Plates 7, 8*
Castiglione, Baldassarre 112, 115, 119, 121, *Plate 24*
Castille, Queen Isabella of 32, 78, 126, 127
Castille, Queen Maria of 10
Celano 27, 30, *59*, *60*, 72, 160
Centelles, Antonio, Marquis of Crotone (the elder) 2–3, 15, 21, 27, 192
Centelles, Antonio, Marquis of Crotone (the younger) 5
Centelles, Polissena, Marchioness of Gerace, marriage, birth of children, death of husband 2–5; flight from plague 7–9, 20, 58
Cerignolo, battle of 86
Chambéry 189
Charles VIII, King of France 38, 45, 48, 53–5, 56, 58, 59–60, 68, 75, 128, 187, *Plate 26*
Charles, Duke of Burgundy, later Charles V, Holy Roman Emperor 168, 178, 186, 187, 189, 195
Chigi, Agostino 180
Colonna, Fabrizio 83, 86
Colonna, Prospero 81, 83, 86, 93, 94, 107, 173
Coppola, Francesco, Count of Sarno 17–19
Coppola, Marco 18–19
Cornaro, Marco, Cardinal 119, 121, 150, 151, 170, 181, 192, 193, 195
Corsignano, *see* Pienza
Costabili, Bernardo, Bishop of Adria, later Cardinal 204
Cybo Giambattista, Pope Innocent VIII 17, 32, 34, 38, 39–40, 44
Cybo Usodimare, Battistina 38–9, 42, 43
Cybo Usodimare, Peretta 34

D'Avalos, Alfonso, Marquis of Pescara 37, 38, 57, 62, 63, 77
D'Avalos, Costanza, Duchess of Amalfi 178, 203
D'Avalos, Francesco Ferrante, Marquis of Pescara 37, 158
D'Avalos, Ippolita, Marchioness of Gerace 77, 84, 135
De Foix, Gaston, Duke of Nemours 129, 157
De Foix, Germaine 129
De Grassi, Paride 141, 182
De Maio, Iuniano 13
Del Balzo, Isabella Queen of Naples, wife of King Federico 71–2, 84, 92

Del Pezzo, Pirro 143
Delio, pseudonym of Matteo Bandello and Webster's character xxi, 85, 169, 173, 176, 207, 208
Della Rovere, Francesco Maria, Duke of Urbino 112, 141, 151, 152–3
Della Rovere, Giuliano, Pope Julius II 45, 89, 90, 92, 121, 123, 124, 125, 126, 130, 132–3, 139–43, 145, 146, 150, 154, 155, 156, 157, 159, 162, 163, 167–9, 171, 179, 192, 197, *Plate 11*
Duchesca, Neapolitan palace of Alfonso of Calabria 21, 24, 58

Este, Alfonso d', Duke of Ferrara 92, 101, 104, 105, 123, 124, 125, 140, 152, 162–3, 167, 179, 204, 205
Este, Beatrice d', Duchess of Milan 44, 54, 100, *Plate 23*
Este, Ercole d', Duke of Ferrara 8, 53, 56
Este, Ferrante d' 56
Este, Ippolito d', Cardinal 45, 104, 105, 118, 125, 133, 153, 188, 197
Este, Isabella d', Marchioness of Mantua 91, 99–101, 102, 104, 116, 125, 141, 151, 152, 167, 179–80, 189, *Plate 29*

Farnese, Alessandro, Cardinal, later Pope Paul III 118, 170, 197
Farnese, Giulia 42, 115, 118
Ferrara xvi, 8, 15, 44, 45, 53, 55, 92, 101, 104, 114, 115, 116, 123, 124, 125, 126, 130, 140, 141, 142, 143, 150, 151, 152, 153, 156, 162, 163, 167, 168, 179, 182, 188, 189, 204, 205
Fieramosca, Cesare 164, 173, 174
Fieramosca, Ettore 86
Florence14, 32, 33, 35, 48, 54, 71, 115, 119, 162, 182, 186
Forlì 96, 159
France xviii, xx, 10, 35, 36, 38, 45, 48, 57, 60, 70, 78, 80, 82, 84, 85, 86, 88, 90, 91, 92, 94, 95, 101, 102, 105, 110, 123, 125, 126, 129, 130, 140, 142, 150, 153, 156, 157, 166, 168, 171, 186, 188, 189, 190, 195, 196, 197, 198, 199, 204, 205, 207
Francis I, King of France 181, 187, 190, 191, 195, 196, 198, 199, 200, 204
Frederick III, Emperor of Germany 26
Fugger, Jacob 188

Gaeta 10, 127
Gaetani, Onorato, Count of Traietta 19
Galilei, Galileo xxii
Gallipoli 8
Gareth, Benedetto, Il Chariteo 62, 66
Gerace *3*, 4, 7, 12, 13, 23, 35, 36, 37, 49, 58, 62, 86, 135, 207
Giraldi, Giambattista, Cinthio 117
Gonsalvo de Cordova 62, 66, 72, 83, 85, 86, 88, 90, 93, 94, 126, 127, 129–30, 143
Gonzaga, Antonia 173, 175
Gonzaga, Dorotea, Marchioness of Bitonto 173, 175
Gonzaga, Federico (son of Francesco), later Duke of Mantua 141
Gonzaga, Federico (son of Gianfrancesco), Lord of Bozzolo 175, 189, *Plate 31*
Gonzaga, Francesco, Marquis of Mantua 67, 99, *100*, 101, 102, 103, 104, 105, 125, 141, 175
Gonzaga, Sigismondo, Cardinal 118, 152, 153, 181
Granada 32, 33, 78, 79, 80; Secret Treaty of 80, 82
Guardati, Diana 2
Guicciardini, Francesco 35
Gutenberg, Johann xx

Henry VII, King of England 24, 129
Henry VIII, King of England 36, 157, 186
Hoby, Thomas 28–30, 161
Holy Roman Empire xx, 26, 80, 83, 96, 123, 126, 153, 157, 168, 186, 188, 189

Ischia 57–8, 84, 132, *132*, 178
Isvaglies, Pietro, Cardinal 142, 150, 151
Italy xviii, 7, 9, 10, 11, 17, 19, 33, 34, 35, 41, 45, 47, 53, 54, 60, 68, 75, 90, 92, 95, 96, 101, 121, 124, 131, 134, 140, 145, 155, 156, 157, 159, 160, 162, 163, 164, 168, 171, 186, 187, 198

Lateran, Church 89; Council 143, 158, 159, 192
Leonardo da Vinci xix, 44, 166–7, 171–2, 187, 189, 199, 200, 205
Leostello, Giampiero (Joam Piero) 22, 23
Lope de Vega 130
Loreto 138, 140, 141, 144, 145, 146, 149, 153

Louis XII, King of France 75, 78, 80, 82, 84, 85, 90, 91, 92, 101, 102, 123, 128, 129, 130, 140, 141, 142, 153, 157, 168
Luther, Martin 189

Macedonia, Beatrice 148
Machiavelli, Niccolò 35, 145
Mahon, Derek xvii–viii, 206
Mantua 24, 63, 67, 99, 100, 102, 103, 104, 105, 118, 141, 152, 167, 175, 176, 181, 182, 189, 198
Martiri d'Anghieri, Pietro 79, 122
Marzano, Maria, Duchess of Amalfi 21, 31, 58–9, 68–9
Marzano, Marino, Duke of Sessa and Prince of Rossano 21, 27
Maximilian I, Holy Roman Emperor 80, 82, 126, 153, 157, 168, 186
Medici, Giovanni, Pope Leo X 34, 117, 119, 121, 155, 169, 170, 171, 180, 181, 182, 183, 184, 185, 190, 191, 194, 196, 197, 202, *Plate 10*
Medici, Giuliano de', Duke of Nemours 170, 180
Medici, Giulio de', Cardinal, later Pope Clemente VII 184, 185, 191
Medici, Lorenzo de', Duke of Urbino 180, 182, 191
Medici, Lorenzo de', Lord of Florence, known as Il Magnifico 14, 32, 33–5, 47, 119, *Plate 12*
Medici, Piero de', Lord of Florence 34, 48, 54
Melegnano, battle of 189, 198
Messina, Sicily 56, 61
Michelangelo Buonarroti 152, 168
Middelburg 186, 190
Milan xviii, 44, 47, 52, 53, 60, 75, 80, 91, 96, 101, 102, 153, 155, 156, 166–7, 171, 175, 176, 182, 189, 190, 198
Milano, Giacomo 79, 80
Mirandola 150–1
Montefeltro, Guidobabldo, Duke of Urbino 112
Monteoliveto, church of Sant' Anna de' Lombardi, Naples 6, 68, 143–4
Morelli, Giovanni 4–5, 73

Naples: city of 2, 3, 4, 5, 6, 8, 9, 12, 15, 19, 20, 23, 24, 26, 28, 29, 33, 35, 46–7, 48, 49, 53, 54, 55, 58, 59, 61–2, 63, 64, 65, 66, 67, 68, 69, 71, 73, 78, 79, 80, 83–5, 86, 92, 93–4, 95, 96, 97, 98, 99, 105, 106, 111, 113, 127–8, 130, 131, 132–3, 137, 138, 139, 144–5, 149, 158, 162, 164, 170, 174, 176, 184, 198, 199; Kingdom of xviii, xx, 2, 7, 9–11, 15, 17, 21, 26, 27, 30, 31, 33–4, 35, 37, 38, 44–5, 47, 48, 49, 51–3, 58, 60, 70, 75, 78, 80 82, 85, 86–7, 90, 91, 96, 102, 110, 121, 122, 123, 126, 127, 130, 143, 156, 157, 160, 162, 163, 165, 167, 168, 170, 171, 173, 174, 178, 180, 181, 186, 190, 197
Nicastro 7, *8*, 7–8
Nola 19, 20, 71
Notar Giacomo della Morte 149

Orsini, Elena, Countess of Pitigliano 19–20
Orsini, Enrico, Count of Nola 164
Orsini, family xix, 19
Orsini, Franciotto, Cardinal 195, 197
Orsini, Gentile, Count of Nola 20, 71
Orsini, Giacomo, Duke of Gravina 19
Orsini, Giovanna 175, 189
Orsini, Latino Malabranca, Cardinal 196
Orsini, Lella 42
Orsini, Matteo, Cardinal 196
Orsini, Nicola, Count of Pitigliano 19, 38, 42
Ostia 121, 130

Painter, William xvii–xviii, 163, 174, 176
Palatine Chapel 22, 23, 24
Palmieri d'Aragona, Costanzo 115
Pandone, Enrico, Count of Venafro 164
Pantasilea 112
Pasquino 180, 183, 189
Pavia 54, 96
Petrarch, Francesco 47, 69,
Petrucci, Alfonso, Cardinal 152, 154, 155, 182, 183, 184, 197
Petrucci, Antonello 17–19
Petrucci, Borghese, Lord of Siena 153, 154, 155, 182
Petrucci, Pandolfo, Lord of Siena 155
Philip, Duke of Burgundy 126–7, 129, 168
Piccolomini, Andrea Todeschini 27, 31, 89, 154
Piccolomini, Antonio Todeschini, Ist Duke of Amalfi 18, 21, 24, 27, 28, 30–2, 38, 73, 161, 178

Piccolomini, Alfonso Todeschini I, 2nd Duke of Amalfi: 18; marriage to Giovanna d'Aragona 21–4, 27, 38, 47, 49, 52, *56*, *57*, *59*, 63, 63, 64–5, 71, 72–3, 108, 164
Piccolomini, Alfonso Todeschini II, 3rd Duke of Amalfi 1, 88–9, 143, 144, 146, 147, 149, 150, 160, 161, 162, 164, 178, 202
Piccolomini, Caterina Todeschini 26, 50, 130
Piccolomini, Eleonora Todeschini, Princess of Bisignano 22–3, *56*, *59*, 66, 110–11, 113, 116, 135, 136, 144
Piccolomini, Eneas Silvio, Pope Pius II 24, *24*, 25, 26–7, 30, 40, 41, 96
Piccolomini, Francesco Todeschini, Bishop of Bisignano 1, 134, 164
Piccolomini, Francesco Todeschini, Pope Pius III 27, 31, 88–9, 155, 200, *Plate 28*
Piccolomini, Giacomo Todeschini 27, 31
Piccolomini, Giambattista Todeschini, Marquis of Deliceto 1, 71, 134
Piccolomini, Giovanni Todeschini, Cardinal of Siena 154
Piccolomini, Inigo Todeschini, Marquis of Capestrano, then Duke of Amalfi 28–30, 154, 187
Piccolomini, Laudonia Todeschini 26
Piccolomini, Maria Todeschini, Duchess of Gravina 18
Piccolomini, Pier Francesco Todeschini 154
Piccolomini, Silvia Todeschini 154
Piccolomini, Vittoria Todeschini 153, 154
Pienza (Corsignano) *25*, 26, 30, 154
Pinter, Harold 206
Pisa 153, 156, 157
Poderico, Paolo Antonio 130
Pontano, Giovanni 34, 35, 48, *55*, 98
Popes: Alexander VI (*see* Borgia, Rodrigo); Callixtus III (*see* Borgia, Alfonso); Clement VII (*see* Medici, Giulio de'); Innocent VIII (*see* Cybo, Giambattista); Julius II (*see* Della Rovere, Giuliano); Leo X (*see* Medici, Giovanni de'); Paul III (*see* Farnese, Alessandro); Pius II (*see* Piccolomini, Eneas Silvio); Pius III (*see* Piccolomini, Francesco)
Porzio, Camillo 6
Pucci, Francesco 46, 121
Ragusa 38, 149
Raphael Sanzio: xviii, xix, 112, 117, 119, 143, 168, 184, 190, 191; portraits xviii–xix, 194, 196–7, 198, 199, 200, *201*, 202, 204, 205, *Plates 1, 5, 10, 11, 15, 23*
Ravenna: 140, 151, 152, 153; battle of 157, 171
Requesens i Enrìquez de Cardona-Anglesola, Isabella de, Vicereine of Naples 197, 198, 199, 204, 205, *Plate 15*
Riario, Raffaele, Cardinal 182, 183, 184
Rimini 140, 153
Romano, Gian Cristoforo *100*, 122, 130
Romano, Giulio (Pippi) 199, 200, 205
Rome 17, 27, 35, 37–9, 45, 83, 85, 87, 89, 114–15, 120, 124, 126, 153, 155, 156, 159, 168, 170, 174, 179–80, 182, 189–90, 202, 204
Romagna 86, 112, 124, 159

Salerno 17, *55*, *65*, 70, 72, 144
San Domenico Maggiore, church and Dominican monastery, Naples 24, 28, 47, 69, 98, 131
San Sebastiano, convent Naples and Amalfi 144, 145, 148
Sannazaro, Iacopo 9, 33, 58, 66, 78, 122, 189–90
Sanseverino, Antonello, Prince of Salerno 17, 53, 65, 70, 72, 144
Sanseverino, Berardino, Prince of Bisignano 53, 65, 67–8, 70–1, 110–11, 144
Sanseverino, Federico, Cardinal 157
Sansovino, Jacopo 195
Sant' Elena, convent Amalfi 133–4
Santa Maria delle Grazie, Dominican monastery, Milan 171–2, 189
Santa Maria sopra la Minerva, church and Dominican monastery Rome xix, 191, 192, 193, 194, 195, 196, 201
Sauli, Bandinello, Cardinal 152, 182, 183, *183*, 184, 189, 197
Savelli, Silvio 171
Savona 130
Savonarola, Girolamo 55
Scafati 27, 30, *56*, 65, 84
Scala 161
Scarampa, Camilla 173
Seggi: 97, 127; Seggio del Nido (or Nilo) 97, 98, *98*
Sforza, Ascanio, Cardinal 44, 88
Sforza, Ercole Massimiliano, Duke of Milan 166, 167, 175, *Plate 23*

Sforza, Francesco, Il Duchetto 54, 80
Sforza, Francesco, Duke of Milan *Plate 23*
Sforza, Gian Galeazzo, Duke of Milan 19, 20, 43, 44, 45, 52, 54
Sforza, Giovanni 39, 42, 45
Sforza Bentivoglio, Ippolita 172, 174
Sforza, Ippolita Maria, Duchess of Calabria 13, 18
Sforza, Ludovico Maria (Il Moro), Duke of Milan 44, 47, 52, 53, 54, 60, 75, 80, 88, 166, 167, *Plate 23*
Sicily 10, 55, 58, 83
Siena 26, 96, 115, 153, 154, 155, 156, 158, 159, 182
Sigismund, Holy Roman Emperor 96
Soderini, Francesco, Cardinal 162, 183, 184
Somma 66, 67
Spain xviii, xx, 10, 12, 14, 32–3, 40, 44–5, 74, 75, 77, 78, 79, 80, 83, 85, 86, 88, 90, 91, 102, 122, 126, 129, 130, 133, 140, 157, 162, 168, 171, 182, 186, 190
Speroni, Speron de 115
Spinelly, Thomas 186, 187
Squillace, Principality of, Calabria 2
Sulmona 65, 73

Taranto 84, 90
Tasso, Bernardo 115
Terranova, Calabria 4
Todeschini, Nanni 27
Tolosa, Paolo 127, 143–4, 145, 148
Torre dello Ziro xviii, 161
Trissino, Giangiorgio 122
Trivulzio, Giangiacomo 57, 80, 152, 153

Urbino xvi, 102, 112, 141, 182, 191

Valla, Lorenzo 118
Varavalle, Jacopo de 73
Vasari, Giorgio 88, 122, 195, 197, 199
Vatican 26, 34, 38, 40, 45, 76, 81, 86, 88, 95, 140, 142, 156, 168, 181, 182, 189, 190, 196
Venafro 63, 71, 129, 164
Venice 7–8, 15, 115, 123, 124, 125, 126, 142, 149, 150, 151, 155, 156, 159, 184, 196
Vercelli, Edict of 56, 59
Visconti, family: 96; Filippo Maria, Duke of Milan 96; Alfonso, Count of Saliceto 173

Webster, John xvii, xviii, xix, xxi–ii, 1, 2, 16, 17, 32, 37, 48, 61, 71, 78, 85, 93, 95, 106, 113, 114, 123, 135, 137, 138, 139, 145, 146, 150, 158, 162, 165, 166, 169, 170, 171, 173, 176, 177, 178, 180, 194, 206, 207
Wolsey, Cardinal Thomas 186
Wyngfield, Richard 186